REGIONAL RISK AND SECURITY IN JAPAN

Japan's unusual position in the realm of international politics encapsulates a three-fold juxtaposition: both in and out of Asia, both occupied by and a close ally of the United States, and both a key trade partner and a strategic rival of China. Whilst international relations theory offers a number of ways to analyse these relations, this book instead utilizes the concept of risk to provide an innovative perspective on Japan's relations with China, North Korea and the US.

The book elucidates how risk, potential harm and actual harm are faced disproportionately by certain groups in society. This is demonstrated by providing an empirically rich analysis of the domestic implications of security relations with China, North Korea and the United States through the presence of US troops in Okinawa. Beginning with a theoretical discussion of risk, the book goes on to demonstrate how the concept of risk adds value to the study of international relations in three senses. First, the concept helps to break down the boundaries between the international and domestic. Second, the focus on risk and the everyday directs us to ask basic questions about the costs and benefits of a security policy meant to secure the national population. Third, what implications do these two points have for governance? The question is one of governance as Japan's externally oriented security policy produces domestic insecurity shared disproportionately, not equally, as this volume makes clear.

Developing the theory of risk as a tool for understanding international relations, this book will be of great interest to students and scholars of Asian politics, Japanese politics, international relations and security studies, as well as to policymakers and practitioners working in the field.

Glenn D. Hook is Toshiba International Foundation Anniversary Research Professor, School of East Asian Studies at the University of Sheffield, UK and director of the National Institute of Japanese Studies, part of the White Rose East Asia

Centre, a collaboration between Sheffield and the University of Leeds, UK. His recent books include *Japan's International Relations: Politics, Economics and Security* (co-author, Routledge, 2012, third edition).

Ra Mason is a lecturer in Asia-Pacific Studies at the University of Central Lancashire, UK, special research fellow with the Japan Society for the Promotion of Science at the University of the Ryukyus (2014–15), Japan, and an honorary fellow of the White Rose East Asia Centre, University of Sheffield, UK. His recent publications include *Japan's Relations with North Korea and the Recalibration of Risk* (Routledge, 2014).

Paul O'Shea is an assistant professor of Asian Studies at Aarhus University, Denmark and an honorary fellow of the White Rose East Asia Centre, University of Sheffield, UK. He has recently co-edited a volume entitled *Risk State: Japan's Foreign Policy in an Era of Uncertainty* (2015).

Sheffield Centre for Japanese Studies / Routledge Series
Celebrating 50 Years of Japanese Studies at The University of Sheffield, 1963–2013

Series Editor: Glenn D. Hook
Professor of Japanese Studies, University of Sheffield

This series, published by Routledge in association with the Centre for Japanese Studies at the University of Sheffield, both makes available original research on a wide range of subjects dealing with Japan and provides introductory overviews of key topics in Japanese Studies.

1. **The Internationalization of Japan**
   Edited by Glenn D. Hook and Michael Weiner

2. **Race and Migration in Imperial Japan**
   Michael Weiner

3. **Japan and the Pacific Free Trade Area**
   Pekka Korhonen

4. **Greater China and Japan**
   Prospects for an economic partnership?
   Robert Taylor

5. **The Steel Industry in Japan**
   A comparison with the UK
   Hasegawa Harukiyo

6. **Race, Resistance and the Ainu of Japan**
   Richard Siddle

7. **Japan's Minorities**
   The illusion of homogeneity
   Edited by Michael Weiner

8. **Japanese Business Management**
   Restructuring for low growth and globalization
   Edited by Hasegawa Harukiyo and Glenn D. Hook

9. **Japan and Asia Pacific Integration**
   Pacific romances 1968–1996
   Pekka Korhonen

10. **Japan's Economic Power and Security**
    Japan and North Korea
    Christopher W. Hughes

11. **Japan's Contested Constitution**
    Documents and analysis
    Glenn D. Hook and Gavan McCormack

12. **Japan's International Relations**
    Politics, economics and security
    Glenn D. Hook, Julie Gilson, Christopher W. Hughes and Hugo Dobson

13. **Japanese Education Reform**
    Nakasone's legacy
    Christopher P. Hood

14. **The Political Economy of Japanese Globalisation**
    Glenn D. Hook and Hasegawa Harukiyo

15. **Japan and Okinawa**
    Structure and subjectivity
    Edited by Glenn D. Hook and Richard Siddle

16. **Japan and Britain in the Contemporary World**
    Responses to common issues
    Edited by Hugo Dobson and Glenn D. Hook

17. **Japan and United Nations Peacekeeping**
    New pressures, new responses
    Hugo Dobson

18. **Japanese Capitalism and Modernity in a Global Era**
    Re-fabricating lifetime employment relations
    Peter C. D. Matanle

19. **Nikkeiren and Japanese Capitalism**
    John Crump

20. **Production Networks in Asia and Europe**
    Skill formation and technology transfer in the automobile industry
    Edited by Rogier Busser and Yuri Sadoi

21. **Japan and the G7/8**
    1975–2002
    Hugo Dobson

22. **The Political Economy of Reproduction in Japan**
    Between nation-state and everyday life
    Takeda Hiroko

23. **Grassroots Pacifism in Post-War Japan**
    The rebirth of a nation
    Mari Yamamoto

24. **Interfirm Networks in the Japanese Electronics Industry**
    Ralph Paprzycki

25. **Globalisation and Women in the Japanese Workforce**
    Beverley Bishop

26. **Contested Governance in Japan**
    Sites and issues
    Edited by Glenn D. Hook

27. **Japan's International Relations**
    Politics, economics and security
    Second edition
    Glenn D. Hook, Julie Gilson, Christopher W. Hughes and Hugo Dobson

28. **Japan's Changing Role in Humanitarian Crises**
    Yukiko Nishikawa

29. **Japan's Subnational Governments in International Affairs**
    Purnendra Jain

30. **Japan and East Asian Monetary Regionalism**
    Towards a proactive leadership role?
    Shigeko Hayashi

31. **Japan's Relations with China**
    Facing a rising power
    Lam Peng-Er

32. **Representing the Other in Modern Japanese Literature**
    A critical approach
    Edited by Rachael Hutchinson and Mark Williams

33. **Myth, Protest and Struggle in Okinawa**
    Miyume Tanji

34. **Nationalisms in Japan**
    Edited by Naoko Shimazu

35. **Japan's Security Policy and the ASEAN Regional Forum**
    The search for multilateral security in the Asia-Pacific
    Takeshi Yuzawa

36. **Global Governance and Japan**
    The institutional architecture
    Edited by Glenn D. Hook and Hugo Dobson

37. **Japan's Middle East Security Policy**
    Theory and cases
    Yukiko Miyagi

38. **Japan's Minorities**
    The illusion of homogeneity
    Second edition
    Edited by Michael Weiner

39. **Japan and Britain at War and Peace**
    Edited by Nobuko Kosuge and Hugo Dobson

40. **Japan's National Identity and Foreign Policy**
    Russia as Japan's 'other'
    Alexander Bukh

41. **Japanese Cinema and Otherness**
    Nationalism, multiculturalism and the problem of Japanesenesss
    Mika Ko

42. **Asian Regionalism and Japan**
    The politics of membership in regional diplomatic, financial and trade groups
    Shintaro Hamanaka

43. **Decoding Boundaries in Contemporary Japan**
    The Koizumi administration and beyond
    Edited by Glenn D. Hook

44. **Japan's International Relations**
    Politics, economy and security
    Third edition
    Glenn D. Hook, Julie Gilson, Christopher W. Hughes and Hugo Dobson

45. **Japan's Security Identity**
    From a peace-state to an international-state
    Bhubhindar Singh

46. **Nationalism and Power Politics in Japan's Relations with China**
    A neoclassical realist interpretation
    Lai Yew Meng

47. **Risk and Securitization in Japan**
    1945–60
    Piers Williamson

48. **Japan's Relations with North Korea and the Recalibration of Risk**
    Ra Mason

49. **The Politics of War Memory in Japan**
    Progressive civil society groups and contestation of memory of the Asia-Pacific War
    Kamila Szczepanska

50. **Governing Insecurity in Japan**
    The domestic discourse and policy response
    Edited by Wilhelm Vosse, Reinhard Drifte and Verena Blechinger-Talcott

51. **Regional Risk and Security in Japan**
    Wither the everyday
    Glenn D. Hook, Ra Mason and Paul O'Shea

REGIONAL RISK AND SECURITY IN JAPAN

Whither the everyday

Glenn D. Hook, Ra Mason and Paul O'Shea

LONDON AND NEW YORK

First published 2015
by Routledge
2 Park Square, Milton Park, Abingdon, Oxon OX14 4RN

and by Routledge
711 Third Avenue, New York, NY 10017

Routledge is an imprint of the Taylor & Francis Group, an informa business

© 2015 Glenn D. Hook, Ra Mason and Paul O'Shea

The right of Glenn D. Hook, Ra Mason and Paul O'Shea to be identified as authors of this work has been asserted by them in accordance with sections 77 and 78 of the Copyright, Designs and Patents Act 1988.

All rights reserved. No part of this book may be reprinted or reproduced or utilised in any form or by any electronic, mechanical, or other means, now known or hereafter invented, including photocopying and recording, or in any information storage or retrieval system, without permission in writing from the publishers.

Trademark notice: Product or corporate names may be trademarks or registered trademarks, and are used only for identification and explanation without intent to infringe.

British Library Cataloguing in Publication Data
A catalogue record for this book is available from the British Library

Library of Congress Cataloging in Publication Data
A catalog record for this book has been requested

ISBN: 978-1-138-82353-2 (hbk)
ISBN: 978-1-138-82389-1 (pbk)
ISBN: 978-1-315-74200-7 (ebk)

Typeset in Times New Roman
by Apex CoVantage, LLC

CONTENTS

List of figures   *xi*
Preface   *xii*
Acknowledgements   *xiv*
Note on translations, Romanization   *xv*
Abbreviations   *xvi*
Glossary   *xviii*

Introduction: risk in Japan's regional relations   1

PART I
The 'China threat' and Sino-Japanese relations   **19**

1   Food security, safety and bioterrorism   26

2   Transboundary pollution   42

3   East China Sea dispute   57

4   Immigration and the demographic crisis   72

PART II
Deconstructing the framing of North Korea   **89**

5   Missile testing   97

6 Abductions by North Korea	112
7 Nuclear testing	127
8 Drugs and money	142

PART III
Internalizing the US–Japan alliance in Okinawa   **159**

9 Military accidents	168
10 Military incidents	183
11 Environmental degradation	197
12 Noise pollution	212
Conclusion: risking the everyday	227

Index   *233*

FIGURES

0.1	Risk as an embedded process	14
1.0.1	Affinity/no affinity with China	20
2.1	Technical and grant aid to China	51
3.1	Number of articles with 'Senkaku' in the title	59

PREFACE

The title of this book, *Regional Risk and Security in Japan: whither the everyday*, encapsulates our interest in how Japanese national security policy regarding the region, narrowly defined as the People's Republic of China (hereafter China), the Democratic People's Republic of Korea (hereafter North Korea) and the United States gives rise to risk, potential harm and actual harm in domestic society. The book employs the concept of the 'security of the everyday' in order to expose how an externally oriented security policy can blow back as harm for the domestic population, for a security policy aimed at keeping the state and nation secure against external threats and risks simultaneously erodes security at home. But not for all. Rather, the book elucidates how risk, potential harm and actual harm are faced disproportionately by certain groups in society. The point is made by providing an empirically rich analysis of the domestic implications of Japan's security relations with China, North Korea and the United States through the presence of US troops in Okinawa.

The book starts with a theoretical and conceptual discussion of risk. It aims to build on the limited amount of work using risk in international relations. The concept of risk adds value to the study of international relations in three senses. First, the concept helps to break down the boundaries between the international and domestic, elucidating how a security policy targeting external enemies can have wider implications, including the security of the everyday for the domestic population. Second, the focus on risk and the everyday directs us to ask basic questions about the costs and benefits of a security policy meant to secure the national population. Which groups in society bear the costs of that policy? Third, what implications do these two points have for governance? The question is one of governance as Japan's externally oriented security policy produces domestic insecurity shared disproportionately, not equally, as this volume makes clear.

The three main parts of the book shed light on these questions by tracing the risk, potential harm and actual harm produced as a result of the government's security policy. The whole book was conceived and written as a collaborative endeavour, although each of us took primary responsibility for separate parts of the book. Part I focuses on China (Paul O'Shea), Part II on North Korea (Ra Mason) and Part III on the US presence in Okinawa (Glenn D. Hook). All three parts of the book offer concrete, empirical evidence of how the recalibration of risk as a result of national security policy is manifested as harm. Although the focus of the case studies differs, taking account of the divergent nature of the security relationship between Japan and China, North Korea and the United States, they all consider the domestic implications of Japanese security policy. What unites the three parts of the book is a common focus on elucidating the link between risk and harm in the complex interaction between the state, market and society in the governance of the population.

The main conclusion drawn from this work is that, by deploying risk as a heuristic device, we have been able to reveal in empirically rich detail how a national security policy for the nation as a whole gives rise to a range of harms for a minority of the population. This disproportionality in the way the exposure to harm is distributed is quintessentially a question of governance and democracy in Japan. From that perspective, how risks are deployed in order to legitimize and maintain specific mechanisms of governance and forms of democracy remains a topic for future study.

ACKNOWLEDGEMENTS

This book was made possible by a grant from the Toshiba International Foundation (TIFO), for which we are very grateful. TIFO's support enabled the authors to conduct overseas fieldwork as well as to hold a number of meetings at the University of Sheffield to discuss in detail the structure and content of the book. The outcome is a collaborative work. All of the chapters have been revised numerous times, taking account of each other's feedback as well as the input of colleagues. We would like to thank in particular Routledge's three anonymous referees and the audience at the European Association for Japanese Studies at Ljubljana, Slovenia, August 2014, for their contribution to this process.

NOTE ON TRANSLATIONS, ROMANIZATION

Translations

Unless otherwise noted, quotations from Japanese sources have been translated by the authors.

Romanization

Apart from commonly used proper nouns such as 'Tokyo,' or when an author publishes using a different transcription (e.g. Sato rather than Satō; Ohnishi rather than Ōnishi), Japanese has been transcribed into Roman script based on the Modified Hepburn system.

ABBREVIATIONS

AJW	Asia Japan Watch
BMD	Ballistic Missile Defence
CCP	Chinese Communist Party
CNN	Cable News Network
DNA	deoxyribonucleic acid
DPJ	Democratic Party of Japan
DPRK	Democratic People's Republic of Korea
EANET	Acid Deposition Monitoring Network in East Asia
EEZ	Exclusive Economic Zone
ERD	Elimination of Racial Discrimination
EU	European Union
G8	Group of Eight
GDP	Gross Domestic Product
GNP	Gross National Product
IPSS	National Institute of Population and Social Security Research
JCG	Japan Coast Guard
JCP	Communist Party of Japan
JETRO	Japan External Trade Organization
JITCO	Japan International Training Cooperation Organization
JSDF	Japan Self-Defense Forces
LDP	Liberal Democratic Party
LSD	lysergic acid diethylamide
LTP	Long-range Trans-border Air Pollutants in Northeast Asia
MAFF	Ministry of Agriculture, Forestry and Fisheries
METI	Ministry of Economy, Trade and Industry
MHLW	Ministry of Health, Labour and Welfare
MHW	Ministry of Health and Welfare (now MHLW, see above)

MITI	Ministry of International Trade and Industry (now METI, see above)
MOD	Ministry of Defense
MOE	Ministry of the Environment
MOF	Ministry of Finance
MOFA	Ministry of Foreign Affairs
MOJ	Ministry of Justice
MSDF	Maritime Self-Defense Force
NARKN	National Association for the Rescue of Japanese Kidnapped by North Korea
NDPG	National Defense Programme Guidelines (or Guidelines)
NGO	non-governmental organization
NHK	Nippon Hōsō Kyokai (the national broadcaster)
NPA	National Police Agency
NPT	Nuclear Non-Proliferation Treaty
ODA	Official Development Assistance
PCB	polychlorinated biphenyls
PM	particle matter
PRC	People's Republic of China
ROK	Republic of Korea
SACO	Special Action Committee on Okinawa
SCAP	Supreme Commander for Allied Powers
SDF	Self-Defense Forces
SOFA	Status of Forces Agreement
SPT	Six Party Talks
UK	United Kingdom
UN	United Nations
UNC	United Nations Command
UNCLOS	United Nations Convention on the Law of the Sea
US	United States
WHO	World Health Organization
WMD	Weapons of Mass Destruction

GLOSSARY

Beiatsu   US pressure (on Japan)
Beigunkōseiin   US service personnel, US civilian contractors and their families
Bōryokudan   criminal gang
Chōsensōren   General Association of Korean Residents in Japan
Dai ippo   the first step
gaijin hanzai   foreigner crime
gyōza   dumplings
hōkatsuteki   comprehensive
jūminhyō   residency registration
kazokukai   family committee (family of abductees)
Keidanren   Japan Business Federation
kokusan   domestic product
kōsa   yellow dust
koseki   family register
Nikkei   descendants of Japanese emigrants
Sukūkai   National Association for the Rescue of Japanese Abducted by North Korea (NARKN)
yakuza   organized crime syndicate
Zainichi   residents
zaitokukai   *Zainichi Tokken o Yurusanai Shimin no Kai* (Citizens against the Special Privileges of the *Zainichi*)

INTRODUCTION
RISK IN JAPAN'S REGIONAL RELATIONS

1 Context

Japan's international position epitomizes a three-fold juxtaposition: a key trade partner and a strategic rival of China; simultaneously in and out of Asia, as exemplified by its relations with both North and South Korea; historically occupied by and now a close ally of the United States. Historically, Chinese culture provided the bedrock for the cultural development of Japan in the seventh to tenth centuries, with the wholesale importation of Chinese writing, religion(s) and philosophy. Japan's defeat of China in the First Sino-Japanese War at the end of the nineteenth century, and its subsequent invasion and occupation of the mainland from the 1930s until defeat in 1945, led to a reversal of roles: from 'little brother' to imperial occupier. Indeed, the combination of the emotional impact of this role reversal together with the often cruel and violent nature of the occupation has left an indelible scar on Chinese national consciousness. Similarly, the colonization of the Korean peninsula from the early twentieth century to 1945 continues to define Japan's relations with the two Koreas, the Democratic People's Republic of Korea (DPRK) in the North and the Republic of Korea (ROK) in the South. The bipolar postwar system served to exacerbate the divide between Japan and the DPRK but it also turned its wartime adversary, the US, into the defeated country's number one ally. Since the US occupation from 1945 to 1952, Japan has remained the United States' key regional partner, its 'unsinkable aircraft carrier' off the East Asian coast (Nakasone 1983). Approximately 50,000 US troops are currently deployed in the country, of which 50 per cent are stationed on military bases in the tiny southern prefecture of Okinawa. The advent of the twenty-first century, the 'Asian Century,' promised an improvement in ties between Japan and the rest of East Asia as the regional economies became ever more deeply intertwined. Instead, structural and historical legacies persist as an invisible barrier running from the Sea of Japan south to the East China Sea, constraining Japan's relations with its nearest neighbours.

Meanwhile, dramatic changes are afoot in East Asia. Japan's economy, once fuelled by access to US markets, remains unable to reproduce anything like the growth of the earlier postwar period, and was surpassed by China in gross terms in 2010. Further, the People's Republic has replaced the US as Japan's number one trade partner, and may soon even overtake the American superpower as the world's largest economy. The rise of China economically and militarily has served to reinvigorate Japan's alliance with the United States as, after a brief dalliance with a more Asia-centric approach during the Democratic Party of Japan (DPJ) administration of Hatoyama Yukio in 2009 (Hughes 2010), Japan has now returned to its earlier policy of taking shelter under the US umbrella whilst hedging against China. The People's Republic is not the only reason Japan is concerned about the neighbourhood, though. Japan-DPRK relations remain mired in the Cold War. Despite sixty years of co-existence and the numerous attempts mounted, the two states have yet to normalize relations. A number of core issues, not least of which are the North's missile tests and the abduction of Japanese citizens in the 1970s, have dominated recent bilateral negotiations and prevented any substantive developments, although the second Abe Shinzō administration made tentative steps in improving relations during the latter part of 2014.

International relations (IR) offers a number of ways to analyse Japan's regional relations. This book seeks to contribute to the field by utilizing the concept of *risk* as an innovative perspective on the country's relations with China, the DPRK and the US. In each set of bilateral relations Japan must deal with a number of issues that are constituted as external risks posed to the security of the state and people. A number of these risks are manifested as harm to the domestic population. Illustrative is the harm caused by the territorial dispute in the East China Sea over the Senkaku/Diaoyu Islands. The dispute, already having derailed bilateral relations with China, harbours the potential to spill over into armed conflict, as well as influence areas such as the interpretation and dissemination of risks associated with areas as distinct and diverse as imported Chinese food, transboundary pollution and Chinese immigration in Japan. As far as the Korean peninsula is concerned, the missile and nuclear tests conducted by the DPRK have not only presented the ostensible issue of Japan's (in)sufficient geo-military defence capabilities, but have also exacerbated anti–North Korean sentiment associated with abductions and other state-sponsored criminal activity across all sectors of Japanese society. The resulting political environment has for many years immobilized actors seeking to engage Pyongyang constructively and even now constrains the government's ability to promote regional integration more proactively. Finally, the dispute over relocating a US base on Okinawa has caused local, national and bilateral conflicts, as well as contributed to the resignation of the DPJ's Hatoyama Yukio, the first non-Liberal Democratic Party (LDP) majority prime minister since Japan Socialist Party prime minister, Murayama Tomiichi, in the mid-1990s. The manner in which these risks are constructed, calibrated and responded to by a range of actors at the national and subnational levels plays a determinative role in the security of the everyday for the population of Japan, whether Okinawans, Chinese immigrants or the *Zainichi* Korean community. This book's engagement with the security of the 'everyday' challenges the statist focus of most studies of security and instead addresses critically how state security policies focused on risks arising from outside of the state can at the same time impact on the security of the everyday for the domestic population.[1]

Before proceeding to the three substantial parts of this book to investigate these relationships further, however, our first task is to explicate how risk as an approach adds value to the study of IR and its interactive relationship with everyday lives in Japan. In essence, the approach offers a heuristic device to explore how the external risk posed by other states is dynamically linked to the exposure to risk and harm manifested in the domestic population. This results from the security policy adopted by the government in responding to the perceived risk posed by the external environment.

2 Risk and harm

The central aim of this volume, then, is to elucidate how risks that are constructed and deployed in the domain of international relations pose risks, potential harm and harm to human security at the sub-state level – i.e. the security of the everyday. Specifically, we explore the everyday impact upon security for those living in Japan who face the backfire and boomerang (side) effects of the risks being taken by the Japanese state in response to China, North Korea and in relation to the security treaty with the US.

2.1 Origins of the risk state

Risk is a thoroughly modern idea – the concept, if not the word, dates back only a few hundred years. In *academic studies*, the use of risk as an analytical concept dates back only a few decades. It was popularized in the social sciences by the work of Ulrich Beck (1992). In the field of IR, whilst the number of studies deploying risk is increasing, a coherent and structured approach has yet to crystallize. If risk is to generate impact on the discipline, however, a certain level of theory-building, refinement and focus is required. This is one of the subsidiary goals of this volume. In this section we define our approach to risk in Japan's international relations in contrast to various leading theories and conceptualizations of risk in the extant literature.

Risk as a sociological concept came to prominence in the guise of Ulrich Beck's theory of 'risk society' (1992). Basically, Beck tried to construct (in the finest German tradition) a grand theory of modern society in response to postmodernist critics who saw the changes of the second half of the twentieth century as fundamentally transforming society. Rather than a transition from modern to postmodern, Beck posited a transition from industrial to risk society. Unlike the postmodernists, though, he is not hostile to the Enlightenment; rather he shares with Anthony Giddens (1991) an attachment to the concept of reflexive modernity, the idea that individuals are freer than ever before, and this freedom allows the space for reflexivity (10). This risk society is characterized by the almost exponential increase in risks to everyday life, and these risks are produced by the very industrialization at the foundation of modern society's affluence. A nuclear accident is the realization of a classic Beckian risk – an unpredictable, potentially global, catastrophic risk posed even to the citizens of countries not using nuclear power (35). These kinds of risks prompt individual actors in society to question the government, along with the specialist scientists whose judgement hitherto had been considered sound. Thus the irony of modern society, in Giddens's words, is 'that modernity reduces the overall riskiness of certain areas and modes of life, yet at the same time introduces new risk parameters largely or completely unknown to previous eras' (Giddens 1991: 4). The approach adopted here moves away from this basic concept, however, by viewing the risk society as the manifestation of everyday insecurity, rooted in the state's deployment of risk politically (Coker 2009). For example, Japan's development of military technologies such as Ballistic Missile Defence (BMD) and the Japan Coast Guard (JCG) weaponry is ostensibly to combat the risk of a potential attack of some sort by the People's Republic of China (PRC) or DPRK. Yet, such developments are contingent upon the proliferation, embedding and influence of a particular risk narrative that portrays Japanese militarization as necessary for state security, but at the same time exposes a minority of the domestic population at greater risk as a result of their associations with these rival external states. This leads the risks to be recalibrated and these minority actors to be recast as part of the risks themselves.

In this sense, our approach moves beyond both Beck's and Giddens's all-encompassing explanation of the risk society, as well as the state-led securitization of risks introduced by Buzan *et al.* (1997), Aradau, Lobo-Guerrero and Van Munster (2008) and others. Instead, it examines the governance of risk from the perspective of the domestic harms generated by state behaviour in response to internationally identified risks. Indeed, we see our approach to risk as contrasting with but most comparable to those sourcing their inspiration from the Copenhagen School's development of risk management, that is, as a means to control agenda setting and legitimize state policy (see Rasmussen 2006; Hameiri and Kühn 2011). As Rasmussen states:

> Risk is a scenario followed by a policy proposal for how to prevent this scenario from becoming real. When policy makers approach 'security questions' in terms of risk, they no longer seek to address specific and calculable threats like the Red Army during the Cold War. Instead they focus on trends that give a future significance to present challenges. In such a world policy makers can no longer promise perfect security – all they can do is avoid, preempt, or manage risk. . . . Increasingly governments fail to believe in the

possibility of achieving more perfect security because new risks will arise as a 'boomerang effect.'

(2010: 1)

Yet, the boomerang effects underscored by Rasmussen still refer to the reflexive effects upon the state. In contrast, the approach adopted in this book identifies the linkage between the international and domestic spheres, with an especial focus on the domestic impact of the risks manifested in international relations. Put simply, our focal point is the process by which risks are distributed across these spheres and people's everyday security suffers harm as a result.

2.2 Risk governance

Whereas risk society is primarily concerned with risk assessment and management as carried out by experts, our approach instead explores 'what implication risk has for the political process of state governing' (Hook and Takeda 2007: 96; also see Hook 2012). This 'governance' or 'governmentality' approach understands risk 'as a complex category made up of many ways of governing problems, rather than as a unitary or monolithic technology' (O'Malley 2004: 7; Dean 2009). The approach draws extensively on the concept of governmentality, which stems from the work of Michel Foucault and is commonly understood as meaning 'governmental rationality,' although this is not necessarily what Foucault himself intended (Gordon *et al.* 1991). Governmentality is concerned with how the state governs its subjects through various technologies and rationalities. What Foucault's analysis demonstrates is how the state eventually produces a subject 'governing the self,' that is, the subject internalizes the established code of conduct and acts accordingly. So the state no longer needs to apply itself directly to the task of governing the subject (Peters 2007). Here we view risk not only as 'a technique of governing in the same way as in the governmentality literature' (Hook 2010: 140–1), but demonstrate concretely how the international governance of risk is oft-times manifested as unequal harm to the everyday security of a minority of the population.

The key point is that risks are 'real,' but inevitably in part subjective. In that sense, risks are always constructed. This is why we locate this book as a constructivist work: the quantification and objectification of risk take place and are contested within an intersubjective sphere (Wendt 1999). By drawing on a governmentality approach we are able to explain how risks are constructed and (re)calibrated based on a given, subjectively contested framing. The framing of a specific risk is dependent upon the particular discourse within which it is embedded, as discussed further below. In terms of how this volume contributes to the broader discussion of how risks and security are understood, we underscore how the nature of the risks being embedded in discourse cannot be ignored. As clarified later in this section, the reason can be found in how risks, such as those posed by China and North Korea, as well as those contingent upon the US-Japan security alliance, are deployed by the state at the international level. How these risks are constructed, framed and recalibrated can result in harm being inflicted upon specific groups within the population. In order to address the mechanisms by which this process transpires, we therefore focus on discourse, which expresses linguistically how risks are constructed, framed and recalibrated on different levels. These risks are ultimately utilized in determining policies which have an impact not only on interstate relations, but on the everyday security of the population as a function of the particular discourse on risk deployed.

In the chapters that follow, this is shown to have complex and highly damaging effects upon domestic sub-groups, depending upon the nature of the discourse on security risks in the region. In this sense, the dominant discourse on a particular risk becomes a narrative discourse. How risk is narrated helps to shape the state-led responses to risk, as well as to structure how the resulting harms are distributed. In light of this basic process, the book focuses on case studies of how this dominant narrative is constructed and how the risks are recalibrated in response to China's rise, North Korean brinkmanship and the US military outposts in Okinawa. In each case, the form in which risks are shifted from state responsibility and action into tangible harms that threaten the security of the everyday for individual citizens is of central concern.

This line of argument helps to explain how the security of the state and the security of the people are linked, yet also illustrates the extent to which their linkage is often under-analysed in the extant literature. We take up this lacuna by recasting the idea of security risks into risks to the everyday (Bajc and de Lint 2011). The aim of such an approach is to address the misconceived gap between security policy and the domestic consequences of the policy pursued. This is based on a dual premise: (1) typically, risks are selectively mediated in terms of (in)accurately portraying the probability of suffering harm and inhere a strong reaffirmation/confirmation bias, whereby risks are highlighted on the rare occasions their consequence is manifested as harm; (2) risk narratives are (often fallaciously) produced, gain their own momentum (Taleb 2007: 62) and are mediated between and amongst various state, societal and market actors. The implications of these points for the approach we adopt in our case studies can be found in the shared aim of not only elucidating the risks embedded in discourse, but of also exploring how the recalibration of these risks by state, market and societal actors produces new risks. The final purpose of our approach is to reveal in concrete detail how the materialization of these old and new risks as harm is distributed unequally among the population, on the one hand, and to consider the implications of such disproportionality for governance, on the other.

A concrete illustration of this process is evident in how the response to the risks posed by China and North Korea engenders the risk as well as harm of the abuse of the human rights of children, as in the case of ethnically Chinese and Korean school children in Japan being attacked by nationalists as a result of the framings of those two countries and the associated recalibration of risks. Similarly, in the case of the deployment of US troops in Okinawa, we find the risk as well as harm arising from the abuse of the human rights of the local population, as in the case of an Okinawan woman being sexually assaulted by US military personnel. These cases can be juxtaposed with the probability of being endangered by a Chinese invasion via the Senkaku Islands or a DPRK missile launch on Japan, or the increased probability of either due to US troop redeployments from Okinawa, thus highlighting the gap between the empirical and conceptual.

2.3 Risk, IR and the security of the everyday

Whilst excellent IR scholarship employing the various interpretations and understandings of risk has been published, as seen below, a risk approach has yet to sink firm roots in IR or political science more generally and is almost totally lacking as far as the international relations of East Asia are concerned (for an exception, see Maslow *et al.* 2015). A number of lacuna in the leading approaches to IR – led by realists, liberals and constructivists and institutional inertia as well as the absence of any other convincing approach – opens the way for a risk approach to try to better explain phenomena such as the localized, everyday impacts of policy decisions resulting from a state's international relations. As outlined in the above discussion of its subjectivity, risk at all levels is in some ways elusive by nature. This is because the concept of risk is open to reinterpretation and hence recalibration. What, then, is the concept of risk, when employed as a heuristic device to bridge the analytical dichotomy between the security of the state and the security of the people as represented by the security of the everyday?

A condensed review of the limited IR literature which is informed by the concept of risk brings to light the problems associated with it. For instance, even before Beck's popularization of risk as an analytical tool, Barry Buzan tackled a number of related issues from an IR perspective in *People, States and Fear: The National Security Problem in International Relations* (1983).[2] This was achieved through an exposition of 'securitization,' a concept which is used to explore the more individual and sociologically based factors which influence how risks are framed in relation to constructed threats. Buzan's work offers a ground-breaking analysis of how security in international relations intersects the state, market and society. Nevertheless, his focus on the construction of potential threats means that, despite references to risk, the use of risk as a political tool, and its knock-on effects on the population, remains under-developed, not least in terms of how risk recalibration can give rise to harm to the security of the everyday. Although less focused on security than many traditional IR studies, Beck himself took up the study of risk in international relations in a later work, *Power in the Global Age* (2005). His core thesis is based upon the premise that the greatest risks posed to humankind in socio-political terms are manifested in nationalism. His antidote to nationalism is global 'cosmopolitanization,' which he distinguishes from Americanization, globalization, neo-liberalism and multiculturalism (Beck 2006). In order to combat risks identified with a nationalistic analytical framework, however, Beck uses the seemingly contradictory examples of various nation-state and state alliances (Germany, France, European Union, etc.) in order to illustrate how wider institutional change could be realized. In contrast, the analyses carried out in this book depart from these theoretical and conceptual understandings of risk in IR and instead deploy risk as a heuristic device to illuminate how the recalibration of risk is manifested as harm to the security of the everyday.

Indeed, aside from the special issues of the journals *International Relations* (Hameiri and Kühn 2011) and *Security Dialogue* (Aradau, Lobo-Guerrero and Van Munster 2008), the provocative article in *Global Society*, 'Trust us and be scared: the changing nature of contemporary risk' (Handmer and James 2007) must be highlighted as one of the most valuable contributions to scholarship on risk. As far as IR is concerned, their most significant claim is that external (international and transnational) risks are effectively being produced and maintained by states as a mechanism for perpetuating a societal sense of fear and vulnerability. What this means concretely is that citizens become susceptible to the state's hijacking of a given foreign policy agenda, even without the ability to effectively counter the incumbent risk (e.g. global terrorism). This observation underscores the political function of risk recalibration as we here witness a stark departure from the previous *modus operandi*, whereby risks posed to the state were identified and action taken against them, justified on the grounds of being able to ameliorate a specific state-security risk dynamic.

Nevertheless, all of the above works point to the lack of a consistent operationalization of the concept of risk in IR. What is required from our perspective is twofold: first, a way to bring together analytically the consequences of internationally based security policies for the security of the everyday; and second, the ambition to provide such an analytical framework. This book thus seeks to be bold: it argues that, without the ambition to create such a consistent and operational approach, without an approach offering the tools for other scholars to adopt and refine, the potential of risk as a heuristic device to open up new perspectives in the study of international relations will remain unfulfilled. Viewing risk as a social construction, we remain fully aware of the dynamic contestation between and among various actors across potentially limitless sites of action, but still strive to realize this ambition with the aim of adding value to the study of risk in a range of IR settings. In this sense, our conception of risk, advanced for other scholars to not only draw upon, but to criticize, refine and develop, falls under the constructivist umbrella. Having said that, the approach adopted does allow for and is indeed conceived of as a way to push forward concrete empirical analysis of how state-level policies give rise to sub-state risks, potential harm and actual harm to the security of the everyday. The key to unlocking the opportunities provided by such a conceptual framework can be found in combining an understanding of how risk is constructed with *sensitivity* to the power relations at the crux of the unequal distribution of risk in domestic society. Specifically, this focuses on an analysis of the mediation and recalibration of the external risks that give rise to additional risks for the domestic population, as well as the potential and actual harm to the security of the everyday, all tied dynamically to the functioning of

Japan's interstate relations. As this book will argue in detail later, this harm is suffered disproportionately by a minority of the domestic population.

In terms of how tangible actors in the state, market and society construct, frame and recalibrate risk in the process leading up to or challenging a heightened potential for harm, our work can be understood as an attempt to examine the intersubjective 'reality' of risk. Risk is only limited by the human capacity to define something as risky: in theory, just about anything can be constructed as a risk by the actors holding the power to construct it. For example, whilst cigarettes are universally considered a health risk in Western countries, this was hardly the case even in the last century. The power of the tobacco companies was deployed in the state, market and society complex in order to constrain or indeed prevent the construction of the risk of smoking to health. Even when the link between the risk of smoking and the harm to health was established through the countervailing challenges mounted by a range of other actors, including the medical profession, the fight back by the tobacco giants succeeded for decades in recalibrating downwards the risk of harm to health from smoking. Thus, the 'what' question about risk cannot be addressed adequately without the subsequent questions: why, who, and, ultimately, how? The 'why' question requires analysis which is dependent upon and inseparable from the 'who' question: in order to understand why the risk was constructed and instrumentalized in such a manner, the state, market or societal actors with the power to construct, frame and recalibrate risk must become the focus of analysis. Just as an objective risk is an oxymoron, no risk is ever uncontested. For every risk is constructed in a contested process, with actors seeking to construct, frame and recalibrate risk in discourse and society. Any analysis of risk thus requires us to ask the eternal question, *cui bono*? The investigation thus turns to 'how' that is accomplished and its tangible implications.

2.4 Recalibrating risks

So we have seen how the constructivist approach adopted by this book views the concept of risk as a technique of governance. We have also seen how this technique is contested between and amongst the actors involved, specifically in terms of how the risk is constructed, framed and (re)calibrated. There is one final key part to this puzzle. We paid attention above to how, in the risk society literature, the focus is placed on the actual risk itself, neglecting the way in which risk is deployed by the state. However, we cannot deny that risks have some form of existence, even if that existence is a subjective construct. Similarly, the response to the risk has tangible consequences for those self-same actors who are involved in the power struggle to construct it. Britain's now famous Nutt case is illustrative here: Professor Nutt, at the time the chair of the United Kingdom (UK) government's Advisory Council on the Misuse of Drugs, compared the harm of the drug ecstasy with horse riding, demonstrating statistically how horse riding was likely to cause far more harm per exposure than taking ecstasy (one serious adverse event every 350 exposures compared to one every 10,000 exposures, [Nutt 2009]). Nutt asked 'why society tolerates – indeed encourages – certain forms of potentially harmful behaviour but not others, such as drug use' (Nutt 2009: 4). The professor eventually lost his job for asking such questions, but his fundamental point remains. Indeed, his intervention caused tangible harmful repercussions (he was relieved of his post), further highlighting the intensity with which actors, including the state, seek to defend and reinforce particular recalibrations of risk. This suggests that, as the recalibration of risk is quintessentially political, actors will seek to recalibrate risk, or resist such recalibration, more in line with their own social identity and political objectives than the associated empirical probabilities of harm.[3]

What is especially telling for our discussion here is the manner in which the response to the constructed risk differs, on the one hand, and serves to exacerbate the existing harms and produce new ones, on the other. Despite its high-risk, horse riding can be easily enjoyed within the boundaries of the existing law. It is much celebrated as a traditional activity and socially accepted not only in the UK, but in many other countries around the world. Equestrian events such as show-jumping are included as Olympic sports. Still, the risk of potential and actual harm is acknowledged both at the height of the Olympics as well as the local gymkhana. In competitions, the wearing of a helmet is usually mandatory; a regulatory system of specific international standards for the production of these helmets is in place – events have ambulances on standby for both rider and horse, and so on. In short, the potential harm is acknowledged and mitigated by the state's regulatory response to the risk.

In contrast, ecstasy, whilst less of a risk than horse riding in terms of the probability of harm, remains illegal. As an illegal drug, the black market sets the price in a non-legal regulatory environment created through criminal market activities. This lack of legal regulation can result in the drive for profit, leading drug dealers to mix recreational drugs with other more dangerous chemicals. Ecstasy's illegal status forces the user to take the drug clandestinely, which in turn can compound the potential of the risk leading to harm. This harm can be manifested as death or serious injury to the drug user due not only to the drug, *per se*, but also because of the drug taker's fear of seeking help should anything go wrong: taking ecstasy is, after all, an illegal activity. The recent newspaper headlines about Isobel Reilly, a girl who died from an ecstasy overdose after requesting her friends not to ring an ambulance, is a case in point (*The Guardian*, 1 August 2010). This is not to dwell on how injury and death could have been prevented were medical staff on hand at illegal raves; still, the contrast with the presence of horse ambulances at equestrian events is stark. At the least, the juxtaposition of dropping ecstasy and horse riding highlights how these activities are quite different depending upon their framing.

The reader may by now be pondering: well, yes, this is all fascinating stuff, but what exactly do the trials and tribulations of drug users and horse riders have to do with risk, East Asian IR and the security of the everyday in Japan? Two points are here germane. First, the contrast between the two illuminates how the response to the construction of risk sourced from ecstasy can produce harm. Second, it shows how the response to the risk construction sourced from horse riding mitigates harm. Similarly, the patterns of risk mediation, recalibration and resulting harm can be observed in a range of interstate risks faced by Japan. From victims of child rape by US servicemen in Okinawa to persecuted resident Koreans and stigmatized Chinese foreign students, the mediation and recalibration of the external risks perceived by Japanese policymakers and security managers have engendered harm to the security of the everyday in Japan. Yet, the marines stationed on Okinawa, whose ranks cause the majority of criminal activity by US military personnel, are an offensive, war-fighting force, not designed or equipped to deal with what Japanese policymakers and security managers articulate as the risks to Japanese security from China or the DPRK. The US presence on the islands aims to deter the risk being manifested as harm to the national community and polity, but the harm inflicted on the security of the everyday as a result of the US–Japan alliance is born disproportionately by Okinawans. Similarly, no North Korean missile or nuclear device has ever struck or landed on Japan, and no DPRK policymakers have expressed the intention to deploy nuclear weapons against Japan. Yet, the introduction of BMD technology and the increase in military spending on the JCG is embedded in a Japanese discourse of countering those risks. Finally, China has at least not openly suggested that the build-up of its military hardware is designed to challenge its regional rivals, let alone instructed its foreign students to infiltrate Japan for anything other than a better education or work. Yet, particularly after the formation of the second Abe Shinzō administration, policymakers and security managers increasingly focus on how to counter the risks and threats identified with a 'rising China.'

In short, it is not enough for us simply to study the process of risk construction, mediation and recalibration. We must trace the potential and actual harm, too, as this harm is produced precisely as a result of the risk calibration process itself: the harm of falling off a horse or having a fatal reaction to ecstasy; or of being abused for being an ethnic Korean or Chinese. Additionally, we must take into consideration the harm produced by the response to the risk, as illustrated by the girl who refused to allow her friends to ring an ambulance; or, the Korean school children in Kobe bruised following being stoned by right-wing Japanese. Finally, such potential harm and actual harm need to be set in the context of the construction and recalibration of risk by policymakers, as illustrated by the building of a new US base in Henoko or the deployment of PAC3 missiles across the country to secure Japan against the risk of a pre-emptive strike by Pyongyang.

Returning briefly to the broader perspective, the invasion of Iraq in 2003 offers an opportunity to highlight how the risk approach adopted in this book can help to shed a different light on the implications of the way Britain came to play a role in the war. The ostensible reason for the invasion was the removal of weapons of mass destruction (WMD), including the potential to build nuclear weapons, as their construction was claimed to be possible within a year or two. The government of Prime Minister Tony Blair even published a now-famous dossier, which 'sexed up' claims of Iraq being able to attack British forces with chemical weapons within 'forty-five minutes.' Most of the claims were based on little or no evidence, as known in Downing Street at the time (Rawnsley 2010). Across the Atlantic, the administration of President George W. Bush was able to conflate the terrorist threat post-9/11 with the regime of Saddam Hussein, which proved to be unsubstantiated. This was clear to many observers prior to the invasion: the Ba'ath party's ideological roots are secular and socialist, far from the Islamists who made up the ranks of terrorist networks such as Al Qaeda. Despite things being 'sexed up' and Downing Street's awareness of their unsubstantiated nature, Iraq was constructed as a risk to the United Kingdom. The subsequent war, according to Prime Minister Tony Blair, was not about regime change, but about 'weapons of mass destruction.'

So, in this case, state policymakers and security managers were able to construct Iraq as a risk to the citizenry, although later evidence revealed the risk to have been exaggerated, at the least. The media's hand was in the construction of this risk, too, as several of Britain's main news outlets came out in support of the invasion. For instance, all of the Newscorp media outlets, which include *The Sun, The Daily Telegraph* and *The Times*, printed headlines backing the invasion. Newscorp owner Rupert Murdoch himself spoke in favour of the invasion, too, describing Tony Blair as 'brave' (*The Guardian*, 11 February 2003). Speculation on the reasons for the invasion divides opinion to this day; however, WMD was a diversion at best. So the risk that was calibrated high, was then rather low. Whether Iraq posed a direct threat to British forces or citizens can be debated, but the regime certainly posed a threat to some of its citizens. What about the harm, then? The number of lives lost as a result of the invasion and subsequent occupation and uprising is generally considered to be in excess of 190,000, with up to 140,000 of them civilians (Iraq Body Count 2014). In 2005, London was the site of a terrorist attack in which fifty-six people died. The UK, and London in particular, remains a high-profile terrorist target. Yet the point of the war was, ostensibly, to reduce the risk to both British forces and the British public. Instead, the prosecution of British policy in the Middle East seems instead to have increased the risk of death or injury through terrorist attacks on British citizens globally, or at least does not seem to have reduced it. A secondary point of the war, according to the former prime minister, was to end Hussein's 'evil' regime, to protect Iraqi citizens from their own government. Yet, we have seen how, as a result of the way risk was recalibrated, the cost in terms of harm was borne by large numbers of the Iraqi population, too, as illustrated by the civilian deaths resulting from the invasion.

3 Approach

The above discussion of risk has underscored some of the major concerns at the heart of the approach to risk adopted in this book. Applying a fully operationalized concept of risk to an analysis of our three areas of concern enables us to highlight the processes within which certain areas of bilateral relations have been constructed and recalibrated as either a risk or a non-risk. The three parts of the book explore in detail a number of issues in Japan's bilateral relations with China, North Korea and the US in terms of how risks are recalibrated as well as how policymakers and other actors from the state, market and society play a role in risk-mitigating activities. Such risks are often characterized in a dramatically different way to comparable risks constructed from sources identified within Japan's own ethnic or societal structures, as in the case of the risk of eating certain Japanese foods, being the victim of crimes committed by Japanese criminals or facing repressive law enforcement procedures at the hands of the National Police Agency in outlying regions of Japan such as Okinawa Prefecture.

In order to be clear about the significance of the risk construction, mediation and recalibration process guiding the analysis in the subsequent three parts of this book, prior understanding and consideration of two key points is essential. The first is to untangle the complex relationship between risk and threat; that is, we need to distinguish between – but avoid decoupling – the two concepts. This is in order to eschew the common misunderstanding that, in developing our argument about risk, we are actually talking purely of a fluctuating level of potential harm created by an external actor, event or object, as illustrated by a North Korean missile, riots in China or an American marine rapist on Okinawa. In essence, *threat* refers to these kinds of concrete external sources of harmful agency, action or attribute. But, crucially, a threat, *per se*, can be the source for but not the object of volition: unlike a risk, that is, a threat cannot be 'taken.' Risk, in this sense, is a process of decision-making. More precisely, a risk is the result of internalizing threats and deciding on the course of action (or non-action) to be taken in response. In short, risks are responses to uncertainties and opportunities, and include active as well as passive elements – i.e. risks can amount to active choices as well as the isolated potential of harm that is manifested in threats (Luhmann 1996: 6).

The distinction, therefore, between risk and threat reveals how dynamic environments, such as in international relations and in domestic society, are evaluated and acted upon through processes of decision-making related to risks. This is what we refer to as the mediation of risk. These risks are usually distinguishable from the isolated perception and calculation of threats. Put simply, not only can risks be posed and incurred but also selected and taken. Threats in international relations are seen to be mainly limited to external sources of potential harm.

This leads to the second area of significance for our understanding of the explanatory power of risk in international relations. It is the mechanism by which risks are constructed, framed and recalibrated and then deployed by political actors in arenas of competing political agendas. Ultimately, these mechanisms involve the process of agenda-setting, which leads to the legitimization and implementation of specific policy trajectories in the governance of the population. Put simply, we need to know which actors determine how one set of risks is prioritized ahead of or in place of another and how such prioritization is linked to governance. We witness such a process in the police crackdown on 'Chinese criminal gangs' in Japan, unilateral sanctions imposed against Pyongyang and the continued or increased deployment of US military personnel and equipment in Okinawa. Figure 0.1

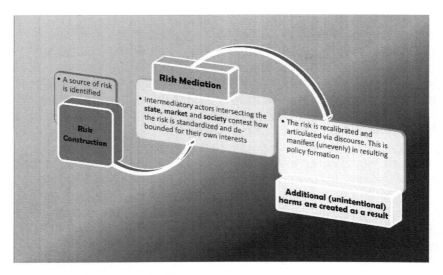

FIGURE 0.1   Risk as an embedded process
Source: Authors

captures the essential elements of this mechanism, demonstrating how risk plays a crucial role in decision-making across a wide range of arenas.

Within the process represented in Figure 0.1, a dialectic contestation ensues over the construction of risk as well as its recalibration via mediation. Actors from different arenas compete to frame, legitimize and embed issues as representing specific categories of risks, which are deployed to further interests, national or otherwise. A more nuanced understanding of these contested processes opens up a pathway to discover how a policy trajectory results from the influence exercised by the different actors involved. For example, those who suffer from US aircraft noise pollution in Okinawa struggle to frame this risk as such in the national security discourse. Their ability to recalibrate the noise as a risk to health rather than as akin to the 'chirping of birds,' as one Tokyo politician referred to aircraft noise, effectively marginalizes the Okinawan voice vis-à-vis the national policymakers and security managers, who instead prioritize security risks to Japan as a whole and highlight the benefits of the alliance with the US.

What is novel about the approach adopted in this book is that, on top of identifying such risks and the manner of their construction, framing and recalibration, we address a more complex issue: the potential harm and actual harm produced by the risk mediation and recalibration process itself. The discussion above has demonstrated how risk is a human, subjective and highly contingent concept, such that the harm produced by a given risk construction, and the harm of the response to the risk as recalibrated, diverge. By tracing the construction, mediation and recalibration of risk in the case of a number of key issues in relation to China, North Korea and the US, through the postwar and post–Cold War periods, we are able to pinpoint the power struggle over risk. Though not always made explicit, the following three empirical parts of the book include answers to the following questions:

- Who is empowered to make and calibrate the decisions regarding risk?
- What is to be identified as a risk, and how risky is it?
- Why is risk constructed in the way it is – *cui bono*?
- How is risk recalibration implemented?
- What is the potential harm and actual harm of the risk, and of the response to it?

The book focuses on the case studies of Japan's bilateral relations, with China, the DPRK and the US respectively. Each part highlights certain risks in Japan's bilateral relations, such as the territorial dispute with China, the DRPK missile tests and US military accidents in Okinawa. In each case, the combination of chapters interweaves the risk approach with empirically rich data in order to elucidate how the perception of specific risks, *per se*, is constructed, mediated and recalibrated to achieve political ends. Each part then investigates the implications of how these risks are manifested in Japan's regional relations. In so doing, these combined three parts of the book trace the narrative of risk in each case, from the realm of interstate security through to the potential harms and actual harms to the security of the everyday in Japan. This is explained in terms of how the harm caused by the response to the recalibration of risk is manifested. Finally, whilst the book deals separately with Japan's relations with China, the DPRK and the US, the three are deeply interlinked and interdependent, as seen in the process of risks being manifested as harm to sub-state actors. In this sense, the risks dealt with separately in the three parts of the book are defined in relation to one another. Thus, the conclusion to the book draws out the similarities and differences in risk, potential harm and actual harm and the response to them across these three parts of the book. The chapter underscores the implications of our findings for risk in East Asian international relations, the impact of risk upon the security of the everyday and the implications for Japanese governance and democracy.

From this brief sketch, then, we can see how a risk-harm analysis enables us not only to understand the power relations involved in the construction of risk (Mason 2014), but also how we can bolster this analysis by examining the potential harm and harm, perceived and materialized, from the risk and responses to it. This understanding is of central importance to any meaningful, critical examination of the security of the everyday in Japan. The triumvirate of interdependent case studies to follow starts with the application of this approach to Japan's relations with China.

Notes

1 For other work inspired by an interest in the security of the 'everyday,' see Lister and Jarvis (2013); Jarvis and Lister (2013); and Bubandt (2005).

2 See also Buzan *et al., Security a New Framework for Analysis* (1997).
3 The continuing conflict over drug use in the United Kingdom came to light again in the interpretation given to a Home Office report by the Conservative Party and the party's coalition partner, the Liberal Democrats. The Liberal Democrat minister, Norman Baker, said the report showed that 'banging people up and increasing sentences does not stop drug use,' and 'lazy assumptions in the rightwing press [indicate] that if you have harsher penalties it will reduce drug use, but there is no evidence for that at all.' In contrast, the prime minister's office stated: 'The report provides no support whatsoever for the Lib Dem's policy of decriminalisation. In fact, it clearly states that it would be inappropriate to draw those kind of conclusions.' See *The Guardian*, 30 October 2014.

References

Aradau, Claudia, Luis Lobo-Guerrero and Rens Van Munster, (2008) "Security, technologies of risk, and the political," *Security Dialogue* (Special Issue), 39, 2–3: 147–357.

Bajc, Vida and Willem de Lint (eds) (2011) *Security and Everyday Life*, New York and London: Routledge.

Beck, Ulrich (1992) *Risk Society: Towards a New Modernity*, London: Sage. First published in 1986 as *Risikogesselschaft Auf dem Weg in eine andere Moderne*, Frankfurt aum Main: Suhrkamp Verlag.

—— (2005) *Power in the Global Age: A New Global Political Economy*, Cambridge: Polity Press.

—— (2006) *The Cosmopolitan Vision*, Cambridge: Polity Press.

Bubandt, Nils (2005) "Vernacular security: the politics of feeling safe in global, national and local worlds," *Security Dialogue*, 36, 3: 275–96.

Buzan, Barry (1983) *People States and Fear: The National Security Problem in International Relations*, London: Pearson Longman.

Buzan, Barry, Ole Waever and Jaap de Wilde (1997) *Security: A New Framework for Analysis*, Boulder, CO: Lynne Rienner Publishers.

Coker, Christopher (2009) *War in an Age of Risk*, Cambridge: Polity Press.

Dean, Mitchel (2009) *Governmentality: Power and Rule in Modern Society*, New York: Sage.

Giddens, Anthony (1991) *Modernity and Self-identity: Self and Society in the Late Modern Age*, Stanford: Stanford University Press.

Gordon, Colin, Graham Burchell, Peter Miller and Michel Foucault (1991) *The Foucault Effect: Studies in Governmentality*, Chicago: University of Chicago Press.

Hameiri, Shahar and Florian P. Kühn (2011) "Risk, risk management and international relations," *International Relations* (Special Issue), 25, 3: 275–397.

Handmer, John and Paul James (2007) "Trust us and be scared: the changing nature of contemporary risk," *Global Society*, 21, 1: 120–30.

Hook, Glenn D. (2010) "Risk and security in Japan: from the international to the societal," *Japan Forum*, 22, 1–2: 139–48.

—— (2012) "Recalibrating risk and governing the Japanese population: crossing borders and the role of the state," *Critical Asian Studies*, 44, 2: 309–27.

Hook, Glenn D. and Hiroko Takeda (2007) "'Self-responsibility' and the nature of the postwar Japanese state: risk through the looking glass," *Journal of Japanese Studies*, 33, 1: 93–123.

Hughes, Christopher W. (2010) "The Democratic Party of Japan's new (but failing) grand security strategy: from 'reluctant realism' to 'resentful realism'?" *Journal of Japanese Studies*, 38, 1: 109–40.

Iraq Body Count (2014) Iraq Body Count. Available online at: https://www.iraqbodycount.org/. Accessed 7 July 2014.

Jarvis, Lee and Michael Lister (2013) "Vernacular securities and their study: a qualitative analysis and research agenda," *International Relations*, 27, 2: 158–179.

Lister, Michael and Lee Jarvis (2013) "Vernacular securities and everyday life," *E-International Relations*. Available online at: http://www.e-ir.info/2013/06/19/vernacular-securities-and-everyday-life/. Accessed 8 July 2014.

Luhmann, Niklas (1996) "Modern society shocked by its risks," *Social Sciences Research Paper* (Occasional Paper) 17, Hong Kong: University of Hong Kong Social Sciences Research Centre.

Maslow, Sebastian, Ra Mason and Paul O'Shea (eds) (2015) *Risk State: Japan's Foreign Policy Processes in an Era of Uncertainty*, Farnham: Ashgate.

Mason, Ra (2014) *Japan's Relations with North Korea and the Recalibration of Risk*, Abingdon, Oxon: Routledge.

Nakasone, Yasuhiro (1983) Press Statement, Head of State Summit Meeting, Washington. Available online at: http://www3.grips.ac.jp/~kitaoka/2011winter/2011gng10refrev1.pdf. Accessed 2 November 2014.

Nutt, David (2009) "Estimating drug harms: a risky business?" Centre for Crime and Justice Studies. Available online at: http://www.crimeandjustice.org.uk/sites/crimeandjustice.org.uk/files/Estimating%20drug%20harms.pdf. Accessed 3 August 2013.

O'Malley, Pat (2004) *Risk, Uncertainty and Government*, New York: Glasshouse.

Peters, Michael A. and Tina Besle (eds) (2007) *Why Foucault?: New Directions in Educational Research*, New York: Peter Lang Publishing.

Rasmussen, Mikkel V. (2006) *The Risk Society at War: Terror, Technology and Strategy in the Twenty First Century*, Cambridge: Cambridge University Press.

Rasmussen, Mikkel V. (2010) "Risk and security," in Robert A. Denemark (ed) *The International Studies Encyclopedia*, New York: Wiley and Blackwell.

Rawnsley, Andrew (2010) *The End of the Party: The Rise and Fall of New Labour*, London: Penguin.

Taleb, Nassim N. (2007) *The Black Swan*, London: Penguin.

Wendt, Alexander (1999) *Social Theory of International Politics*, Cambridge: Cambridge University Press.

PART I
The 'China threat' and Sino-Japanese relations

1 Introduction

This part of the book analyses how China has come to be perceived as a source of a variety of risks to Japan, both external and internal. It examines in particular the development of the 'China threat' concept in Japan and how this 'threat' has percolated throughout Japanese society because of the construction of food, environmental, territorial and crime risks. This introduction first sets out the context for the subsequent chapters by exploring the broader context of Sino-Japanese relations before turning to the development of the China threat and its implications for Sino-Japanese relations. The following chapters examine the construction and recalibration of the aforementioned risks as well as the potential and actual harm of these risks themselves as well as the response to them.

2 Context

The Sino-Japanese relationship is frequently characterized as involving 'hot economics' and 'cold politics.' Economically, the two states are in a pattern of interdependence which, although asymmetrical, has created a situation where each economy's existence depends on the other. Where once China depended on Japan as a key trade partner and supplier of much-needed investment and capital goods, as well as a market for made in Japan goods, the tables have turned recently as China has become the workshop of the world, diversifying and expanding trade across the globe. Meanwhile, the Chinese Communist Party (CCP) has turned to history to provide part of the legitimization for its authoritarian rule through a narrative casting the party as the defenders of China and the victors of the Second Sino-Japanese War (1937–45). Despite effective normalization of Sino-Japanese relations in 1972 (and formal normalization with the signing of the peace treaty in 1978), the CCP has actively encouraged anti-Japanese sentiment, through the patriotic education programmes, and this sentiment has been mobilized by the central government in recent years, most notably in 2005, 2010 and 2012. In each case, events surrounding the disputed Senkaku/Diaoyu Islands and maritime zone in the East China Sea were either a contributory or primary causal factor. The rise of China as the region's number one economy and potential leader has further facilitated greater assertiveness in this respect.

The antipathy is mutual: in Japan, sentiment towards China has hardened since the late 1990s over a range of issues, perhaps most clearly as a result of the territorial dispute (Cabinet Office Opinion Polls 2013). China's phenomenal rate of economic development and growth, coupled with its dramatic increase in military expenditure has, in some quarters, led to the characterization of China as a threat to Japan, as outlined below. This has been reflected in the redeployment of Self-Defense Force (SDF) troops from the north (facing the Soviet Union) of the country in Hokkaido to the southwest (facing China) in Okinawa. The old policy of commercial liberalism, i.e. that promoting trade and prioritizing good relations with China would lead to a kind of liberal peace in East Asia, has been replaced by a much more cautious, sometimes overtly assertive, policy of trade combined with containment (Mochizuki 2007). This shift mirrors the downward trajectory of bilateral relations since the 1990s, particularly following China's firing of live ammunition into the Straits of Taiwan and launching of missiles near Okinawa's Yonaguni Island. The heightened tension in the territorial dispute is both a cause and a result of this downturn. The dispute, which has plagued relations in recent years, is charged with historical associations to Japan's imperial expansion, on the one hand, and the perception of China as an aggressive, assertive state – a risk to Japan – on the other. Thus, managing the Sino-Japanese relationship

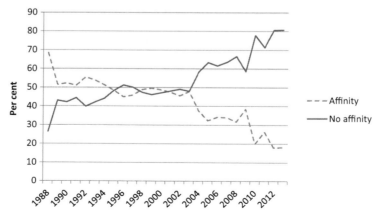

FIGURE 1.0.1 Affinity/no affinity with China
Source: Cabinet Office Opinion Polls (2013)

remains one of the greatest challenges facing Japan, and, unquestionably, the most challenging issue at the heart of the bilateral relationship is the territorial dispute.

3 The 'China threat' narrative

Realist accounts of China's rise invariably perceive it as an immediate threat to regional security, and a long-term threat to the United States (US). Since the end of the Cold War one of the 'first objectives' of US policy has been, in the words of the highly influential neoconservative thinker and policymaker Paul Wolfowitz, 'to prevent the re-emergence of a new rival' (*New York Times*, 8 March 1992). Neoconservatism may be discredited, but the implicit association of the word 'threat' with the word 'China' pervades not only the popular but also the academic discourse. This is likely a function of the US-centric nature of much realist scholarship and the theoretical predestination which is an article of faith in much realist literature. The most obvious example of the latter comes in the form of power transition theory, a theory which posits that when a rising power reaches parity with a dominant power, if that rising power is dissatisfied with the system, war is the likely result (Organski 1968). Similarly, offensive realist theory is premised on the twin assumptions that the strongest states always compete for regional hegemony and that the ultimate goal of strong states is to dominate the entire interstate system (Mearsheimer 2001). The result is seen to be that, should China's rise continue, conflict with its powerful neighbours, and indeed with the US, is *inevitable*.[1] The theory is said to be underpinned by an objective and value-free science, a 'tragedy' which sadly cannot be avoided, in Mearsheimer's famous rendition (2001).

This kind of inevitability, 'scientific' realism, has taken hold in Japan, too. The China threat is well established in domestic discourse, and enjoys varying degrees of support in all the major parties as well as in the Ministry of Defense (MOD) and in parts of the Ministry of Foreign Affairs (MOFA). Indeed, probably the DPJ's most popular personality, Maehara Seiji, was one of the first mainstream politicians to publicly announce that he considered China, with its strong economic performance and increased military spending, to be a threat as far back as 2005 (Maehara 2005). Similar statements were made by then foreign minister Asō Tarō later that same year, though even Prime Minister Koizumi Junichirō disavowed the notion, insisting that China was not a 'threat' to, but rather a 'chance' for, Japan (Przystup 2005).[2] Until taking power the DPJ was considered to be less hawkish than the LDP, but with the decline in influence of Ozawa Ichirō and Hatoyama Yukio, and Maehara's own 'rise' in the political world, the two became bedfellows as far as security policy is concerned. Their closeness is illustrated by the controversial 2010 National Defense Programme Guidelines (NDPG), the first to be published under a non-LDP government, which specified China as a threat, as have all subsequent MOD white papers. The 2010 collision incident involving a Chinese trawler and two JCG patrol vessels in the waters around the Senkaku

Islands, in which China flexed its political and economic muscle to force Japan to back down (from a crisis the DPJ itself had instigated), undoubtedly contributed to this perception, as have subsequent events in the dispute. This is further illustrated by prominent right-wing politician Ishihara Shintarō, expressing his worries that, if Japan fails to physically occupy the islands, Japan itself might 'end up as a second Tibet' (*The Japan Times*, 27 November 2012). Similarly, the head of the MOD-affiliated Research Institute for Peace, Nishihara Masashi, calls for a tough stance against Chinese expansionism, and warns that Chinese control of the disputed islands would 'pose a serious security threat to the region' (Nishihara 2012). Whilst the veracity of such a statement is questionable,[3] it is indicative of how the island issue is now widely perceived in Japan, perhaps best summed up in the old far-right warning that a Chinese occupation of the islands would be the first step in an eventual Chinese invasion of Okinawa and eventually the main islands.

This is not to say that China, demonized by militarist US and Japanese analysts, is a benign state. Numerous authors have identified a strong realist streak in Chinese foreign policymaking (e.g. Johnston 1995; Lynch 2009). Nor is it a simple case of US ideas sailing across the Pacific and dropping anchor in the minds of Japanese politicians and policymakers: anti-Chinese sentiment has a long and sombre history in Japan. Still, the US influence is unmistakeable: China hawks such as Maehara have close ties with US security policymakers and security managers as have members of the present Abe Shinzō administration (Jerdén 2013). Moreover, these policymakers have long deployed *Beiatsu* (US pressure) on Japan to take a tougher stance towards China. The highly negative US response to Hatoyama's idea of an East Asian community is indicative of the long-standing US fear that China might pull Japan away from the US and into its own orbit (O'Shea 2014). Whilst such an eventuality seems unlikely with the return to LDP governance, *Beiatsu* is now focused on pressuring Japan to take stronger measures against the aforementioned China threat to the disputed islands: Kevin Maher, former head of the Office of Japan Affairs in the US State Department, has gone on record as calling for the Japanese government to 'be decisive and realistic about the threat from China,' the response to which requires an increase in military spending *and* the development of military bases on the islands nearest to the Senkakus (*Japan Times*, 16 December 2012). This kind of pressure often involves the implication that, if Japan does not accede to such demands, US support may not be forthcoming in Japan's time of need – in this case, Maher stated that spending increases 'send a very important signal to Washington that Japan is serious about meeting its own defence responsibility under the security alliance with the United States.'

Since 2010 the idea that China represents a threat to Japan, most immediately in the disputed waters and islands of the East China Sea, has gained currency to the extent that it is now conventional wisdom. Japan maintains a strict, non-negotiable 'no dispute exists' policy on the dispute; and the debate, such as exists, is on the appropriate level of response to Chinese provocations and the means of defending the islands. However, this threat-based approach focuses solely on defending the islands without addressing broader issues: (1) why are the islands claimed?; (2) why does Japan have outstanding territorial disputes with all of its neighbours?; and (3) what alternative policies might better serve Japan in the long-run? These questions are unasked, as the national interest is taken as read. Shifting the focus from a threat-based to a risk-based approach to Sino-Japanese relations, and specifically to the dispute, suggests alternative interpretations, and does so without ignoring the reality of Chinese territorial ambitions or military assertiveness. Instead of studying the China threat, as is dominant in the IR literature, the approach taken here instead assesses the recalibration of risk produced by the China threat in the areas of food, environmental, territorial and immigration risks.

4 Structure of Part I

This part of the book details how the narrative of China as a threat to Japan has manifested itself, as seen in the perception of China as a source of a wide variety risks. More specifically, it examines how the 'China threat' has percolated throughout Japanese society because of the construction of food, environmental, territorial and immigration risks. Whilst the 1990s were generally a time of positive Sino-Japanese relations, as China has grown in economic and military strength so too has the idea of China as a source of risks to Japan. This has led to a recalibration of risks across a wide spectrum of issues including risks associated with food from contaminated Chinese imports (Chapter 1), the environment, as in the case of Chinese transboundary air pollution (Chapter 2), the maritime and territorial dispute in the East China Sea (Chapter 3) and Chinese immigrants in Japan (Chapter 4). Each chapter considers these risks in terms of the actors responsible for their recalibration. These actors vary across the spectrum of risks, as illustrated by the central government promoting the recalibration of the territorial risk, whereas the recalibration of the food risk has been largely in the hands of the market and society (specifically the media). Even where the actors differ, the root causes remain the same: both the recalibration of and response to risk in each chapter are in part a function of the portrayal of China as a threat to Japan, and together the four chapters demonstrate how the risks to the security of the everyday in Japan are linked on multiple levels with the bilateral and the international.

With the recalibration of risk comes the potential for harm, and each chapter highlights potential as well as actual harms that are considered risky to the Japanese state, society or market. For example, the risk of imported Chinese food is based on the potential harm caused by contamination, deliberate or otherwise, of the imported food, despite the relatively low level of harm caused by Chinese food when compared to the actual harm caused by certain Japanese food risks such as raw beef liver. Similarly, there is a widespread perception in Japan that the number of crimes committed per capita by Chinese immigrants compared to Japanese nationals is substantially higher. Here the market, in the form of media outlets, interacts with society to perpetuate and expand this perception by a disproportionate coverage of Chinese immigrant crime. As argued in the introduction of this book, potential harm is only one side of the coin – the response to risk also produces actual harm which affects a range of actors, from the marginal (Chinese immigrants in Japan) to the mainstream (Japanese businesses trading with China).

The first part of this book proceeds as follows:

Chapter 1 on food risks examines how state, society and market actors combined to transform the consumption of Chinese food into a risky activity. The chapter compares the risk construction and recalibration as well as the actual harm caused across a number of food scares in Japan, including contaminated Chinese *gyōza*, raw beef liver and cesium-tainted beef from Fukushima. It demonstrates how the deterioration in bilateral relations and the narrative of China as a source of risks has exerted a powerful influence in risk recalibration with regard to seemingly unrelated issues, and illustrates how the relationship between risk and harm can be tenuous.

Chapter 2 considers environmental risk, specifically the risks posed by transboundary pollution originating from China and the impact of such pollution on Japan. As with most countries, Japan's industrial and economic development resulted in large-scale environmental destruction, exemplified by the Minamata disaster most obviously exemplifies. After years of neglect, the Chinese government is beginning to tackle the environmental crises now faced, some of which have had repercussions for Japan, particularly the annual 'yellow dust' storms as well as acid rain. Although the Japanese state has for many years supported China's attempts to tackle these environmental problems, with the growing sense of China as a source of other risks, this support has gradually been phased out. This has taken place at the same time as the media emphasize the environmental risks posed by China.

Chapter 3 details the territorial dispute, elucidating how Japan's recalibration of risk is intrinsically connected to the China threat, along with China's own behaviour in the dispute. The construction and recalibration of risk have contributed to an inflexible response in the form of the 'no dispute exists' policy. Designed to mitigate the potential harm of losing administration of the islands, the policy has in turn led to actual harm to Japanese business interests in China as well as causing damage to Sino-Japanese relations overall.

Chapter 4 takes up the risks and harms associated with Chinese immigrants in Japan. Although the level of crime by ethnic Chinese is marginally higher than that of Japanese nationals, this fact has been developed as a serious risk by sensationalist media outlets to boost sales and by anti-immigration and anti-China politicians. The recalibration of risk has contributed to existing anti-Chinese sentiment and resulted in harm to Chinese immigrants. It also produces potential harm to Japan as a whole in light of the rapidly aging population and the incompatibility of providing care for the aged without some form of immigration reform.

Notes

1 Indeed Mearsheimer, the father of 'offensive realism,' explicitly stated as much in an article entitled 'The rise of China will not be peaceful at all' (2005).
2 Chinese officials responded by pointing out that, at the time, Japanese official military spending was almost twice that of Chinese official military spending (*Japan Times*, 23 December 2005).
3 The islands are tiny and rugged, thus unable to support any serious military base, and are located in the middle of the East China Sea, rather than as part of the wall of islands which control entry to the Pacific Ocean (O'Shea forthcoming).

References

Cabinet Office, Government of Japan (2013) "Gaikō ni kansuru yoron chōsa, zu 14 chūgoku ni taisuru shinkinkan." Available online at: http://www8.cao.go.jp/survey/h24/h24-gaiko/zh/z06.html. Accessed 10 October 2014.
Jerdén, Björn (2013) "The Asia-Pacific epistemic community: decoding U.S. staying power in East Asia," paper presented at the 2013 ISA Annual Convention, San Francisco, 3–6 April.
Johnston, Alastair Iain (1995) *Cultural Realism: Strategic Culture and Grand Strategy in Chinese History*, Princeton, NJ: Princeton University Press.
Lynch, Daniel (2009) "Chinese thinking on the future of international relations: realism as the Ti, rationalism as the Yong?" *The China Quarterly*, 197: 1–21.
Maehara, Seiji (2005) "The national image and foreign policy vision aimed for by the DPJ," speech given at Center for Strategic and International Studies, Washington. Available online at: http://www.dpj.or.jp/english/news/051215/01.html. Accessed 29 November 2013.
Mearsheimer, John J. (2001) *The Tragedy of Great Power Politics*, New York: Norton.
—— (2005) "The rise of China will not be peaceful at all," *The Australian*. November 18. Available online at: http://mearsheimer.uchicago.edu/pdfs/P0014.pdf. Accessed 2 December 2013.
Mochizuki, Mike M. (2007) "Japan's shifting strategy toward the rise of China," *The Journal Strategic Studies*, 30, 4–5: 739–76.
Nishihara, Masashi (2012) "Japan should stand firm on the Senkaku Islands dispute," *AIJSS-Commentary No. 164*, 6 November.
Organski, A.F.K. (1968) *World Politics*, New York: Alfred A. Knopf.
O'Shea, Paul (2014) "Overestimating the 'power shift': the role of the United States in the failure of the Democratic Party of Japan's 'Asia pivot,'" *Asian Perspective*, 38, 3: 435–59.
—— (forthcoming) "How economic, strategic, and domestic factors shape patterns of conflict and cooperation in the East China Sea dispute," *Asian Survey*.
Przystup, James J. (2005) "Japan-China relations: Yasukuni stops everything," *Comparative Connections*, Available online at: http://csis.org/files/media/csis/pubs/0504qjapan_china.pdf. Accessed 29 November 2013.

1
FOOD SECURITY, SAFETY AND BIOTERRORISM

1 Introduction

Food is the 'political topic par excellence' (Lien 2004: 1). Traditional politicizations of food have tended to dominate the study of the politics of food, given that food runs the gamut from international trade disputes to food security and access. In recent years, however, 'a notion of risk has been introduced' (Lien 2004: 2). Food contamination, genetic modification and environmental issues – to name but a few – have changed the way in which actors in all spheres, from the central government down to the consumer in the supermarket, think and act in relation to food. The 'risk society' approach outlined in the introduction to this book speaks to some of these fears and is well suited to the focus on food risks produced by modernity, such as the unknowable risks represented by genetically modified foods or environmental issues caused by intensive food production. However, as we have argued, such an approach is less suited to the study of the role the state plays in constructing, framing and recalibrating risks and how these risks once constructed are developed in interactions with the societal and market spheres. This approach is especially relevant when it comes to the politicization of risks associated with food contamination, and even more so when the source of the contamination is another state.

This is precisely what occurred in Japan in 2008. A worker in Heibei, China, frustrated with poor working conditions, deliberately injected harmful pesticides into a number of bags of frozen *gyōza* (dumplings) in an attempt to hit back at his employer. Some of the contaminated *gyōza* were exported to Japan where ten people fell ill, of which one lost consciousness. All of the victims made complete recoveries.[1] The incident was the subject of saturation media coverage, much of it sensationalist, and sparked a national debate on Japan's food security and its dependence on Chinese food imports. Three years later five people died, and many more fell critically ill, after eating contaminated raw beef at various branches of a chain restaurant. It transpired that, after an investigation, the chain and its meat supplier had ignored state health and safety regulations for at least two years. This incident also garnered attention, but hardly commensurate with the coverage of the preceding *gyōza* incident. This chapter analyses these two cases, combining an approach deploying the construction, framing and recalibration of risk with an elucidation of the nature of food security and food terrorism, along with the development of China as a source of multiple risks to Japan. Its aim is to provide an understanding of the differences in the construction of and response to the risks of the consumption of imported Chinese food and Japanese raw beef respectively.

The chapter proceeds as follows. The first section details the concepts of food security and food terrorism in relation to risk. The chapter next provides an outline of Sino-Japanese relations at the time the *gyōza* incident took place, assessing the state of affairs not only at the level of bilateral exchanges but also domestic public opinion. This combination of the international and the domestic provides the context for the subsequent discussion of Japan's culinary nationalism in the context of its low rate of food self-sufficiency and dependence on Chinese imports. Japan itself has a long history of food scandals; however, these conditions together with China's recent issues with food safety have created an image of China as a source of 'double' food risks to Japan. The chapter then outlines the events surrounding the *gyōza* poisoning incident in 2008 as well as detailing the response at the levels of state, market and society. In order to provide a comparative perspective on our analysis of the *gyōza* case, the next section outlines the raw beef contamination incident, again analysing the response at the three levels of state, market and society. The penultimate section compares these two cases, after which we conclude by considering the development of food terrorism in Japan and placing these cases in the broader theoretical context of risk.

2 Food security and food terrorism

Whilst the term 'food security' became part of common usage only in the latter half of the twentieth century, concerns regarding the security of food have been the subject of scholarly work for centuries. As early as the eighteenth century Robert Malthus famously wrote that, while the population grows exponentially, food supply only increases arithmetically, meaning that populations would be kept in check by hunger, disease and war (Malthus 1798). Although agriculture, medicine and international relations have developed since Malthus's time, the importance for a state of securing adequate food supplies for its population remains a key concern globally. However, the nature of the issues facing states, and thus the nature of food security, varies dramatically depending on the situation of a given state. The World Health Organization's (WHO) definition of the term is based on three pillars: food availability, food access and food use, the former two being relatively straightforward, whilst the latter refers to knowledge of nutrition and sanitation (WHO 2013). What is clear, nevertheless, is the salience of global differences: food security means something very different in sub-Saharan Africa to what it does in East Asia, and Japan's food security issues are quantitatively and qualitatively different from those affecting states such as Somalia, Ethiopia and Sudan. As outlined below, the key concern of the Japanese government is neither availability, access nor use, but rather self-sufficiency. Similarly, whilst Japan shares with virtually all states unresolved questions regarding food distribution, the focus here is not on those who go hungry in Japan – though of course they do exist – but rather on the response to the risks associated with the consumption of particular kinds of food. More useful for our purposes, then, is the approach taken by Just *et al.* (2009), who discuss the nature of threats to food security. They identify two sources of threats: '(a) threats that are naturally occurring due to incidental or neglectful contamination in the normal processing and production of food, and (b) those occurring due to intentional human interference such as terrorist action' (93).

As far as the latter is concerned, a global consensus has developed recently that all 'intentional human interference' leading to contamination, politically motivated or not, can be considered as 'food terrorism' (Mohtadi and Murshid 2009). Indeed, the WHO defines food terrorism in broad terms: 'an act or threat of deliberate contamination of food for human consumption with biological, chemical and physical agents or radionuclear materials for the purpose of causing injury or death to civilian populations and/or disrupting social, economic or political stability' (WHO 2008). Research shows that food terrorism is a comparatively rare occurrence, 'naturally occurring' threats being orders of magnitude more likely than the latter 'deliberate contamination.' Yet, as Mohtadi and Murshid (2009) point out, this gap between likelihood and risk perception is often ignored because of the confusion between *vulnerability* and *risk*. Simply put, the food chain may appear vulnerable to a terrorist attack but this does not mean that such an attack is likely. Rather, as we have just noted, inadvertent contamination is far more likely at some point in the chain of production. The situation is further complicated by the fact that the 'impact of a food scare depends on whether the people believe the threat was naturally occurring or whether it was a result of bioterrorism [food terrorism]' (Just *et al.* 2009: 102). This effect can be further exacerbated by stigma and the behaviour of social groups. Schulze and Wansink's (2012) review of the recent literature on food risks in *Psychology and Behavioural Economics* shows that if a product is stigmatised, and a 'significant number of consumers agree on this behaviour, a social norm may evolve to avoid the act, product or commodity . . . [and] widespread avoidance may develop' (680).

3 Sino-Japanese relations and Japanese food (in)security

Although the *gyōza* poisoning incident dominated the headlines and threatened to damage perennially fraught Sino-Japanese relations, 2007 and 2008 were relatively peaceful years for the bilateral relationship. During the Koizumi Junichirō administration relations had sunk to a level not seen in the post–Cold War era, as anti-Japanese sentiment in China manifested itself in the form of massive street demonstrations, most notably in 2005. However, the first Abe Shinzō administration (2006–7) surprised many observers: the prime minister was well known for his conservative nationalist streak and for his open desire to reform education as well as the constitution in order to make Japan a 'beautiful country' once again (Abe 2006) – yet once in power Abe refrained from making public visits to the controversial Yasukuni shrine and prioritized Sino-Japanese relations. High-level bilateral exchanges were resumed after a five-year hiatus. Indeed, Abe went so far as to make Beijing the destination for his first overseas trip as prime minister. Although the Abe administration lasted exactly one year, this approach was maintained by his successor, Fukuda Yasuo, who was even more pragmatic. In autumn of 2007, for instance, he met Chinese president Hu Jintao in Beijing and the two agreed that the Chinese leader would visit Japan the following spring. Meanwhile, negotiations were underway to strike a deal on the joint development of the East China Sea undersea oil and gas deposits, culminating in the consensus agreement signed in 2008 (see Chapter 3).

However, while high-level bilateral ties recovered, the societal impact of the previous years continued to linger on, as seen in the mounting public pressure for the government to take a tougher line on the East China Sea maritime and territorial dispute, and the negative public sentiments towards China remained despite the upswing in political relations. The annual cabinet office opinion polls indicate that, from 2003 onwards, feelings of affinity towards China among Japanese citizens fell sharply (see Figure 1.0.1). In 2007, only 34 per cent of respondents felt affinity towards China, falling to 31.8 per cent in 2008.[2] Similarly, the number of respondents who believed that the Sino-Japanese relationship was in good shape sank to as low as 23.7 per cent in 2008 – prior to 2003 this number had never dropped below 39.4 per cent, whilst since 2003 this figure has never been equalled (Cabinet Office, Government of Japan 2013). In the introduction to this part of the book, we discussed the emergence of the 'China threat' theory – a narrative framework in which China's economic growth, military modernization, territorial claims and authoritarian status are perceived as 'threatening' not only to Japan but to regional security and stability. By the late 2000s the China threat theory had firmly established itself in the societal sphere, driven in part by substantial media coverage of the territorial issue and the expression of anti-Japanese sentiment in China. However, as also argued in the introduction to this part of the book, the narrative of China as a threat was not confined to traditional security fields. The 'threat' to Japan's food security was prominent and, as we shall now see, China was and remains a source of multiple food risks.

Japan's dependence on imports has increased steadily since the 1970s, but food insecurity is far from a new phenomenon. Securing food supplies was one of many considerations involved in the Japanese imperial expansion, and it was during this period that many hitherto 'foreign' foods, including *gyōza* and the Korean style barbecue, which was the source of the contamination in 2011, became both popular and Japanized to the extent that they are now considered 'Japanese' rather than 'foreign' foods (Barclay and Epstein 2013). In the postwar period, government subsidies and import tariffs have promoted domestic agriculture, but these measures have failed to stem the tide of import dependency. In 1970, for instance, food self-sufficiency was approximately 60 per cent, whilst today it has fallen below 40 per cent on a per calorie basis (Friman *et al.* 2011). As with the broader patterns of Japanese trade, the nature of food reliance is changing. Much as the US was once Japan's number one trade partner, only to be overtaken by China, so too has China become a major source of fresh and frozen vegetables as well as processed food. As it stands, Japan's continental neighbour accounts for almost half of the total volume of frozen vegetable imports, whilst Japan consumes seven times more frozen vegetables than it produces (Japan External Trade Organization 2011). Similarly, over half of the total volume of imported fresh vegetables consumed in Japan comes from China. Since 2000 a number of food scandals have contributed to an image of Chinese food as a source of risk to Japan. These include the well-publicized domestic food contamination cases in China as well as cases where excess pesticides were found on imported Chinese food in Japan. Also, Japanese companies, attempting to capitalize on the perception of Japanese food as healthy and safe (see below), were found to be relabelling food sourced in China as Japanese, as illustrated by a number of companies selling Chinese eel as Japanese, enabling them to double the sales price (Hall 2010).

Imports of tainted Chinese food play into Japan's culinary nationalism, in which Japanese food (*kokusan*) is elevated above foreign food in terms of quality, health and safety (Takeda 2008, Sakamoto and Allen 2011).[3] These notions pervade Japanese discourse on food, and are behind the Japanese government's 2005 *Shokuiku* (food education) campaign. The stated primary aim of the campaign was to promote healthy eating habits, but the campaign was also political in nature: it advocated a return to traditional Japanese foods such as rice and miso, thus reducing Japan's dependency on food imports (Assmann 2011). Various studies and opinion polls have shown that imported food (irrespective of origin) is considered to be less safe than *kokusan*, and indeed the aforementioned re-labelling scandals exemplify the way in which it is highly valued in comparison to imported food (Barclay and Epstein 2013; Hall 2010). This elevation of *kokusan* works at all levels – state, market and society. The consumer preference for *kokusan* is reinforced not only by marketing campaigns, but also by government programmes such as *Shokuiku* and Food Action Nippon (Walravens 2013). For example, Hall's study of MAFF's (Japan's Ministry of Agriculture, Forestry and Fisheries) promotion of food traceability notes the emphasis on domestic traceability and an almost complete absence of import traceability. As Hall points out, the stated goals of the traceability systems focus on food safety and provenance, yet given that the majority of food consumed in Japan is imported, the lack of any serious import traceability systems is striking and sets Japan apart from the rest of the industrialized world. This is all the more surprising given the high levels of distrust aroused by imports as against *kokusan* products. The implication is that MAFF is less interested in making food in general safer and instead is focused on promoting and protecting Japanese agriculture.

Although Japan's attitude toward Chinese and other foreign foods can be seen as partly a function of the numerous scandals, this does not tell the full story. Japan has hardly been immune to food contamination incidents. To the contrary, the postwar era in Japan saw a litany of such scandals, resulting from both 'incidental or neglectful contamination' and 'intentional human interference' (Just et al. 2009). As for the former, Japan has been home to some of the world's deadliest food contamination incidents, perhaps most famously the Minamata poisoning of 1953 in which high concentrations of mercury were released into Minamata Bay by a chemical factory in Kumamoto Prefecture. In order to evade detection the factory then pumped its wastewater directly into a nearby river, further escalating the outbreak of what would come to be known as Minamata disease, whilst simultaneously seeking to discredit the researchers who had identified the source of the outbreak (see Chapter 2). This prolonged the contamination for over a decade and resulted in outbreaks of the eponymous Minamata disease as late as the 1970s. Another outbreak took place in Niigata Prefecture in 1965, again caused by mercury discharge, and again industry hindered the process of identification and treatment: current estimates of both outbreaks indicate 2,002 dead out of 2,995 total victims (*Japan Times*, 21 February 2006). Other scandals include the Morinaga milk incident in 1955, when 138 babies were killed as a result of arsenic contamination of milk, and the Kanemi rice oil incident in 1968, which led to 1,900 recognized cases of poisoning (Jussaume et al. 2000). More recently, the Snow brand milk incident in 2000 poisoned 14,780 people because of a bacterial contamination in processed milk which was covered up by company officials. The most recent serious case of contamination, the contaminated beef incident, led to five deaths and is outlined in detail later in the chapter. As we have seen, 'intentional human interference' occurs far less frequently than the accidental type, though Japan again experienced both types of incidents. Between 1964 and 1966 a doctor named Suzuki Mitsuru deliberated poisoned patients' food, leading to an outbreak of typhoid which affected approximately 200 people, leaving four dead (Gurr and Cole 2005). During the 1980s Japan was gripped by the actions of 'the Man with the 21 Faces,' who terrorized Japanese food companies in what has come to be known as the Glico-Morinaga affair (Ivy 1996). The criminal group engaged in various actions against these companies including the kidnapping of the Glico president, but most relevant for our purposes was the threat and eventual actual poisoning of Glico products, the recall of which cost Glico millions. More recently, in 1998 Hayashi Masumi was found guilty of deliberately poisoning a pot of curry at a summer festival in Wakayama Prefecture. Two children and two adults were killed and dozens of others were hospitalized.

Despite these and other examples too numerous to outline here, the narrative of the inherent superiority of *kokusan* operates not only within each of the state, market and societal spheres, but also across the political spectrum. Conservative nationalism emphasizes the consumption of Japanese food as a requirement of being Japanese: preserving traditions, supporting Japanese agriculture, improving food security. Local environmental activists also cite their preference for Japanese food, using the same health/safety/quality conditions outlined thus far. Tsurumi cites examples of these activists contrasting 'eating a rice ball containing plum pickles in the fresh air' to 'living in dirty air polluted by factories and eating beef steak' (cited in Takeda 2008: 21). Here Japanese food represents a clean, healthy, safe life, whereas imported food is associated with dirt and pollution.

Such conceptions may be jarring for some Western readers, socialized within their own culinary nationalisms. Indeed, the authors of this book hail from countries where steak is associated with cattle grazing in lush green pastures, an image wrapped up in notions of nature and tradition which are themselves reproduced in interactions between the state, market and society. Indeed, the inhabitants of the British Isles might find the idea of rice wrapped in seaweed encompassing a bright pink pickled fruit rather unappetizing or worse, illustrating how food nationalism is not limited to Japan. The point here is not to enter into a nationalistic debate on the superiority of particular cuisines but rather to emphasize the contingent nature of the construction of food in general and Japanese food in particular (Cwiertka 2006). We can conclude, then, that Japanese food is (broadly) constructed as healthy, safe and delicious, whilst by implication foreign food is unhealthy, unsafe and perhaps even unpleasant to the taste. This ties into the China threat narrative, which portrays China as a source of double food risks: the risks associated with the consumption of Chinese food, together with the implications of the dependency on Chinese food imports for Japan's food (in)security (Friman *et al.* 2011). It is in this context that the response to the poisoned *gyōza* case, to which we now turn, must be understood.

3.1 Gyōza poisoning incident

As we saw in the introduction to this chapter, the *gyōza* poisoning incident first hit the headlines on 31 January 2008, when it emerged that after eating imported frozen *gyōza*, a number of Japanese citizens had fallen ill, many of whom were hospitalized. Although no fatalities occurred, one girl lost consciousness but later recovered. The offending *gyōza*, imported and distributed by JT Foods Co., were recalled because of traces of a pesticide banned in Japan. The recall was insufficient to prevent an outbreak of mass hysteria, as thousands reported symptoms of food poisoning after eating uncontaminated *gyōza* and other uncontaminated foods imported from China, fuelling media coverage and turning the issue into a major national news story. In the end only ten people were confirmed as being poisoned but intense media coverage continued, especially after suspicious holes were found in one of the bags containing the *gyōza*. Given the number of recent food scandals in China, Beijing's initial response – that the *gyōza* could not have been contaminated in China – failed to convince the Japanese media and public.

Confirmation that the *gyōza* were deliberately poisoned did not come until 2010 when it was announced that the culprit, a worker at a processing plant in Heibei province, had been arrested. The motivation was not anti-Japanese sentiment but rather dissatisfaction with recent changes in working conditions. Indeed, it transpired that some Chinese consumers had also been poisoned by the food.[4] At the time of the incident in 2008 none of this was known, but that did not prevent the media speculation that engulfed Japan in February 2008. Even before the holes were discovered the issue received blanket coverage in the mainstream press (see below). The discovery of the holes served only to fuel the fire: online nationalism surged as netizens from both sides accused the other of conspiracies. Japanese netizens began to refer to Chinese 'food terrorism' (*Yomiuri Shimbun*, 5 February 2008), as did the *Sankei Shimbun* (14 March 2008) and the Japanese weekly magazines; the *Yomiuri Weekly* went as far as to suggest that the *gyōza* could be potential 'weapons of mass slaughter,' whilst the *Shūkan Playboy* warned of 'indiscriminate food terrorism' (*Sankei Shimbun*, 14 March 2008; *Tokyo Shimbun*, 16 February 2008). Despite the absence of any proven links between the phantom symptoms and the *gyōza* contamination, the weeklies also erroneously confirmed the mass outbreak of poisoning (Rosenberger 2009). Indeed, even three months later, then Tokyo governor Ishihara Shintarō published an article in the *Sankei Shimbun* repeating the now debunked assertion that the poisoning was widespread and went as far as to compare it to the 9/11 terrorist attack on the US and the 2005 London bombings (*Sankei Shimbun*, 5 May 2008). Even the moderate *Asahi Shimbun* was highly critical of the Chinese response, describing it as 'extremely obstinate' and the incident as a 'symbolic problem' (4 May 2008).

The solution for Japanese consumers was exactly what might have been expected in light of the discussion earlier in this chapter: the dichotomy of Japanese/foreign food and the exacerbated consumer response to a food terrorist threat, combined with the stigmatization of *all* imported Chinese food and the development of a norm that Chinese food should be avoided, led to the collapse in sales of imported Chinese food (Japan External Trade Organization 2011). A Kyodo survey showed that 75.9 per cent of respondents stated that they would no longer eat Chinese imported food – an impossible claim in light of Japan's dependency on Chinese imports (Kyodo, 10 February 2008). Whilst the societal and market (media) spheres responded to the *gyōza* poisoning with mass hysteria and mass coverage, the state response was surprisingly muted, adopting a cautious, low-key wait-and-see approach. This approach, although perhaps prudent based on the actual extent of the harm caused by the poisoned *gyōza*, was incongruous with the public mood, and the Fukuda administration was criticized in the media for not speaking out on the issue and for prioritizing Sino-Japanese relations over the health and welfare of Japanese citizens (Rosenberger 2009). Although Fukuda did not seek to exploit the issue for diplomatic or domestic political gain, neither were there carefully choreographed scenes of the prime minister or cabinet members eating Chinese *gyōza* for the cameras. This may sound absurd, but should be considered in light of the aftermath of the nuclear meltdown at Fukushima Daiichi plant, when Prime Minister Kan Naoto and his cabinet colleagues publicly consumed fresh Fukushima vegetables, and then invited South Korean president Lee Myung Bak and Chinese president Hu Jintao to do the same during their visit to Japan – even the Japanese emperor was included (*Asahi Shimbun*, 21 May 2011). It is worth noting that this public display took place *before* it was discovered that cesium-tainted Fukushima beef had been sold and consumed unknowingly in various prefectures across the country, and that certain tea producers were required to issue recalls after testing indicated unsafe levels of cesium contamination.

So what explains the different responses to the incident in the state, market and societal spheres? In essence, once a narrative frame is established, actors will make connections between events regardless, even in the absence of empirical connections between the dominant frame and the unfolding events. As we have seen, the China threat theory was by now well established in Japan. The *gyōza* poisoning took place two years after Koizumi stepped down and Sino-Japanese political relations began to thaw, and only three years after the massive anti-Japanese protests of 2005 – as noted earlier, the period from 2002 to 2006 fundamentally altered Japanese perceptions of their nearest neighbours (Johnston 2007). Even though the change in leadership led to significant improvement in political relations, the aforementioned cabinet opinion polls suggest that public sentiment had changed little. Indeed, the fact was that, whilst the Fukuda administration was noted for its attempts to improve Sino-Japanese relations (like Abe, Fukuda, too, refrained from visiting Yasukuni), as outlined in the introduction to this part of the book, previous administrations and other politicians had displayed a very different attitude. In essence, the state had already played a major role in recalibrating China as a source of risks to Japan's security, both in the traditional and non-traditional sense of risks to the security of the everyday. Prominent among these risks was the (double) risk to Japan's food security, as outlined above. It was into this narrative frame that the *gyōza* poisoning was subsumed, even though the intentions behind the poisoning had nothing to do with Japan or Sino-Japanese relations; nor was the act even directed at Japan, but rather the whole incident was caused by workers' rights issues in China.

3.2 Raw beef

In order to put the *gyōza* incident into perspective, we turn now to the most deadly case of food contamination in Japan since the 1990s: the 2011 case of tainted raw beef. Every year in Japan dozens if not hundreds of people are hospitalized with food poisoning as a consequence of consuming raw beef, especially raw beef liver, which was until recently a popular dish served most commonly at *yakiniku* (Korean barbecue) restaurants. In 1996 eight people died after eating raw beef liver and other foods tainted with *E. coli* O-157, after which the Ministry of Health, Labour and Welfare (MHLW) imposed a number of standards to govern the consumption of liver, including the requirement that meat intended for raw consumption must be handled and processed at temperatures at or below 10 degrees Celsius. Yet, with no legislative backing, no punishment, and therefore no effective enforcement, these regulatory standards were largely ignored by the industry (see below), and in the period from 1998 to 2010 there were 116 reported cases of *E. coli* caused by the consumption of raw beef liver alone (*Yomiuri Shimbun*, 5 May 2011, 16 December 2011). Thus, the deaths of five people from food poisoning after eating raw beef were not unprecedented.⁵ The same *E. coli* outbreak affected over 180 people, with many being hospitalized in critical condition (MHLW 2011b). The cause of the outbreak was contaminated beef served in the Korean dish *Yukhoe* (known in Japanese as *Yukke* and made up of seasoned raw beef topped with a raw egg) at various branches of the chain Yakiniku-zakaya Ebisu. The restaurant's parent company, Food Forus, and the Tokyo-based wholesaler, Yamatoya, both laid the blame at each other's door after it emerged that basic health and safety procedures had not been carried out. It transpired that both sides were guilty of violating health laws, as the Yamatoya had mislabelled the meat, whilst the restaurant chain had stopped testing its raw beef in 2009 and had failed to trim the raw beef to remove the exposed parts, that is, those most likely to host surface bacteria (*Yomiuri Shimbun*, 4 May 2011, 11 May 2011).

As the MHLW investigation proceeded, it was broadened out to survey the entire *yakiniku* industry. It was found that 50 per cent of the restaurants in Japan serving raw meat failed government sanitation standards. Those that failed were instructed to suspend the handling of raw meat, but the MHLW was unable to confirm whether these instructions had been carried out because of the aforementioned lack of an enforcement mechanism (*Yomiuri Shimbun*, 16 June 2011). In the wake of the incident, the MHLW announced plans to toughen the rules governing the handling and preparation of raw beef, and in October 2011 these standards – including requirements to heat the meat and trim it at the processing stage – were introduced. Violation was punishable by fines, suspension of business and imprisonment. The immediate response from the industry and some consumers was that the standards were too strict and that people would be unable to eat raw beef because of the increased costs involved in the new regulatory regime (*Yomiuri Shimbun*, 3 October 2011). After the MHLW found *E. coli* O-157 in raw beef livers tested in autumn of 2011, a plan to completely ban the dish was announced and eventually implemented in the summer of 2012. The reaction to this move was also mixed, and an online Yahoo! poll showed that a large majority of respondents were against the ban (Yahoo News Japan 2011).⁶ The MHLW received thousands of complaints from people stating their desire to eat raw beef liver regardless of the risk: the consumer should make the decision based on 'self-responsibility.'⁷ The meat industry issued a statement arguing that culinary culture should be preserved and warning that this ban represented the thin end of the wedge – if the government was to ban beef liver, next would be raw egg, and even sashimi (All Japan Meat Industry Co-operative 2012). It is worth noting once more that the 'culinary culture' to which the industry statement referred was introduced after World War II, and indeed prior to the Meiji Restoration (1868) the consumption of meat in Japan was banned for a thousand years, with very few exceptions (Cwiertka 2006).

Let us now take up the question of the actual harm caused by these two incidents, and compare the harm to the response to the risks posed. In 2008, although the poisoned *gyōza* was responsible for making approximately ten people ill, one seriously so, no lasting effects occurred. Still, the outbreak was followed by mass public hysteria and saturation news coverage, and the question is – why? A straightforward answer would be that the case was seen as a deliberate act perpetrated by China with the intention of causing harm to the security of the everyday rather than as ordinary food poisoning. We have seen that if the cause of an incident is food terrorism, rather than inadvertent contamination, the consumer impact will be greater, and this certainly helps to explain the significant drop in the sales of food imported from China (see below). However, it is important to note that for the first two days of the media coverage the Japanese authorities were quoted as stating explicitly that there was no evidence of tampering with the *gyōza* packaging. Moreover, the outbreak was so small that it would not have merited any national media coverage and would likely have been confined to the local media in Chiba Prefecture, where the most serious case of food poisoning occurred – if it even got that far. Over one thousand outbreaks and 20,000 cases of food-borne disease have been reported annually in Japan since 1996 (Hara-Kudo *et al.* 2013). Despite this, the relatively small outbreak of food poisoning was national news, and was printed on the front page of both the *Asahi Shimbun* and the *Yomiuri Shimbun*. Clearly, when the holes in the packaging were discovered, the nature of the issue was fundamentally altered; nonetheless, the case was front-page news even when it was simply one comparatively minor outbreak of unexplained food poisoning. The suggestion that it was the unexplained nature of the food poisoning that roused suspicion can also be dismissed, as every year Japan sees over one hundred cases of *unidentified* food poisoning associated with the consumption of raw fish alone (Kawai *et al.* 2012). Rather, it would appear that the source of the harm – *gyōza* from China – was the crucial factor at work here.

The raw beef contamination comparison is illustrative, highlighting how the harm manifest from the risk led to serious consequences. Five people died and dozens were hospitalized, many in critical condition, as a direct result of negligence by both the restaurant chain and the meat supplier. Moreover, raw meat had been responsible for deaths and serious illness before, so much so that the MHLW had imposed regulatory standards which the industry chose to ignore. From this, the state's decision to regulate the industry and impose mandatory standards might have seemed to be an expected and popular outcome, together the outright ban of the most dangerous form of raw beef – the liver. Yet as we have seen, the market and societal response was quite the opposite. Indeed, on 31 June 2012, the day before the ban went into effect, *yakiniku* restaurants across the country were packed as Japan said 'sayonara' to raw beef liver (*Yomiuri Shimbun*, 1 July 2012). The consumption of raw beef liver, and raw beef in general, was portrayed as part of Japan's traditional food culture, and whilst there was an awareness of the risks involved in the restricted foods, the consensus across the market and societal spheres (i.e. media, public opinion and industry) seemed to be that individuals should take on 'self-responsibility' to mediate the risks to their own everyday security. Yet, the response to the *gyōza* incident showed no such consideration of individual risk; rather, the public response was to avoid Chinese food whilst there were even calls in the media for a ban on food imports from

China (Rosenberger 2009). Sales of frozen Chinese food in Japan crashed after the incident and remained down until 2010, when price increases on domestic vegetables led to a recovery (Japan External Trade Organization 2011). The extent of media coverage, too, is telling: in the two biggest selling dailies, the *Yomiuri Shimbun* and the *Asahi Shimbun*, the *gyōza* incident was given far more extensive coverage than the raw beef contamination. In the one-month period after the news of each outbreak first broke, the two newspapers published 1,564 articles on the *gyōza* incident compared to 304 on the raw beef contamination.[8] We have already seen the sensationalist nature of this coverage, but it is well worth repeating that all this took place essentially because of poor working conditions which led a worker in distant Heibei, China, to engage in a criminal act to exact revenge on his employer, which led to ten documented cases of illness and no fatalities.

4 Conclusion

Food, as Lien stated, is a political topic which is infused with risk. This chapter has shown that food risk is not simply associated with modernity, but rather that food risks and the response to them are constructed, framed and recalibrated by complex interactions between various state, market and societal actors. It also demonstrated how the response to a food risk depends as much if not more on the nature of the risk itself than on the actual likelihood of harm to the security of the everyday. Research suggests that deliberate contamination has a greater impact on consumers than does inadvertent contamination, which helps in part to explain the response to the *gyōza* incident. Yet, this response to the *gyōza* incident was not limited to changes in patterns of consumption – a change which did not last long in any case – and began before the intentional aspect was revealed, leading to an outbreak of mass hysteria and phantom symptoms at the societal level. This chapter suggests that the response was thus a function not only of the nature of the incident – food terrorism – but also the state of bilateral relations and perceptions of China as a source of risks to everyday security in Japan. We saw how the response to the *gyōza* incident can be understood through the narrative framing of the incident – which again was related to working conditions in Heibei – and was subsumed into the dominant pre-existing framework of the China threat narrative. The confirmation bias outlined in the introduction to this book is illustrated here, too. The confirmation bias refers to the tendency to favour information confirming existing beliefs and prejudices; the idea of China as a source of food terrorism was suddenly bandied about not only online but also in the media. The result, as we saw, was that one news outlet referred to the *gyōza* as potential weapons of mass slaughter, whilst Ishihara compared the incident to the 11 September terrorist attacks and the 2005 London bombings. And, technically, this was indeed a case of food terrorism as defined by WHO. It may not have been successful; indeed it was not even aimed at Japan, but by definition it was food terrorism with potentially profound implications for the security of the everyday in Japan.

In September 2008 the *Weekly Economist (Shūkan Ekonomisto)*, a sober business magazine covering international economic trends from a Japanese perspective, published an article by Yaguchi Yoshio, a respected researcher and author on agricultural affairs, in which he described the act as food terrorism (Yaguchi 2008). What is perhaps most interesting about this article is not the fact that he used the term 'food terrorism,' but the context in which he did so. Yaguchi stated that this was the first such incident in his memory, and for the record he was born in 1952. Yet, as we have seen, Japan in the mid-1980s was gripped by the actions of the 'Man with the 21 Faces,' who terrorized Japanese food companies in the previously mentioned Glico-Morinaga affair. And as recently as 1998 the Wakayama poisonings, a lethal act of food terrorism, killed four people. Both of these incidents of food terrorism are very well known in Japan, and Yaguchi ought to be familiar with them. Moreover, the association of China with food risks belies the reality of Japan's food contamination scandals, which run throughout the postwar period and continue to this day, as with the raw beef incident, suggesting how the regulation and governance of food consumption is an issue with a long and unhappy history.

The response to the risk of food terrorism is not dissimilar to Japan's broader response to terrorism. The 11 September attacks on New York led to major overhauls in Japan's security policy, including the controversial overseas deployment of the SDF, but also led to the compulsory fingerprinting and photographing of all aliens entering Japan at air and seaports. The 'extensive immigration examination procedure' was explicitly prescribed 'for the purpose of preventing terrorists from entering this country' (Ministry of Justice statement, cited in *Japan Times*, 30 August 2010). Japan has suffered from terrorists acts before; in fact, the 1995 Tokyo subway gas attack is one of only two terrorist attacks in human history that have inflicted over 5,000 casualties, the other being 11 September. Yet, terrorism in Japan, from the Tokyo subway attacks to the Matsumoto incident (perpetrated by the same group) and the activities of the Japanese Red Army – a communist terror group active in the 1970s and 1980s – as with the fatal cases of food terrorism in Japan, has been domestic in origin. Thus the terrorism response, as with the food response, preferred to overlook or downplay the domestic source of risk whilst simultaneously focusing on the risk from overseas. If we return to the horse riding/ecstasy example from the introduction to this book, we can see further parallels. Raw beef is now considered 'traditional,' 'natural' and rooted in Japanese culture. It is socially acceptable and the risks should be taken by the individual, based on 'self-responsibility,' but minimized as much as possible by the regulations governing the food's preparation. Horse riding in the United Kingdom is culturally rooted, too: it is 'traditional,' and the risks are acknowledged and mitigated by various regulations and procedures. Whilst ecstasy is hardly the same as imported Chinese food, the construction of and response to the risks are not incomparable: ecstasy is an illegal drug and those who consume it are considered to have done so at their own risk, and must take moral responsibility. Those who consume Chinese food instead of Japanese *kokusan* must also take some moral responsibility (Rosenberger 2009) because Japanese food is known by everyone to be safer and healthier, and its consumption supports the nation, in terms of food self-sufficiency and preserving agricultural traditions. In this way, consumption of *kokusan* and avoidance of imported food is understood to contribute to the security of the everyday for Japanese consumers.

Notes

1 A number of people also fell ill in China, although this was not disclosed at the time.
2 Prior to 2003 this figure had hovered between 45 per cent and 55 per cent for over a decade. Also, the question is posed as a dichotomy, meaning that in 2007 63.5 per cent stated that they did not feel affinity towards China, and in 2008 this reached 66.6 per cent – today the figure stands at 80.7 per cent (Cabinet Office, Government of Japan 2013).
3 Culinary nationalism as a phenomenon is hardly unique to Japan, but the Japanese brand of culinary nationalism has its own characteristics; see Cwiertka (2006) for a comprehensive history.
4 The worker was arrested in 2010 and in January 2014 was sentenced to life in prison (Reuters, 20 January 2014).
5 Some sources cite the number as four; however, the MHLW's own findings indicate the number as five (MHLW 2011a).
6 Of the 49,257 who responded, 32,216 or 65.4 per cent were against the ban.
7 For a detailed study of the changing relationship between the individual, risk and self-responsibility in Japan, see Hook and Takeda (2007).
8 Based on searches of using the Nikkei database, using the following search terms and periods: *gyōza*, 30th January–29 February 2008; *yukke*, 30 April–30 May 2011.

References

Abe, Shinzō (2006) *Utsukushii Kuni e*, Tokyo: Bungeishunju.
All Japan Meat Industry Co-Operative (2012) "Gyūnamareba- no kisei ni hantai suru yōbōsho no teishutsu to shomeikatsudo no onegai," 10 May. Available online at: http://www.ajmic.or.jp/kumiai/topics.html?tpics_cd=92#p3. Accessed 26 November 2013.
Assmann, Stephanie (2011) "Food education in Japan: a review of the online representation of the *shokuiku* campaign," *Asian Politics and Policy*, 3, 1: 149–58.
Barclay, Kate and Charlotte Epstein (2013) "Securing fish for the nation: food security and governmentality in Japan," *Asian Studies Review*, 37, 2: 215–33.
Cabinet Office, Government of Japan (2013) "Gaikō ni kansuru yoron chōsa, zu 14 chūgoku ni taisuru shinkinkan." Available online at: http://www8.cao.go.jp/survey/h24/h24-gaiko/zh/z06.html. Accessed 10 October 2014.
Cwiertka, K. J. (2006) *Modern Japanese Cuisine: Food, Power and National Identity*, London: Reaktion Books.
Friman, Richard H., Derek Hall and David Leheny (2011) "Guns, butter, and more guns: Japanese security through March 11th," paper prepared for the "PK Fest," Cornell University, October 14–15. Available online at: http://pacs.einaudi.cornell.edu/system/files/Friman-Hall-Leheny-PKFest2011.pdf. Accessed 10 November 2014.
Gurr, Nadine and Benjamin Cole (2005) *The New Face of Terrorism: Threats from Weapons of Mass Destruction*, London: I. B. Taurus.

Hall, Derek (2010) "Food with a visible face: traceability and the public promotion of private governance in the Japanese food system," *Geoforum*, 41, 5: 826–35.

Hara-Kudo, Yukiko, H. Konuma, Y. Kamata, M. Miyahara, K. Takatori, Y. Onoue, . . . T. Ohnishi (2013) "Prevalence of the main food-borne pathogens in retail food under the national food surveillance system in Japan," *Food Additives and Contaminants: Part A*, 30, 8: 1450–58.

Hook, Glenn and Hiroko Takeda (2007) "'Self-responsibility' and the nature of the postwar Japanese state: risk through the looking glass," *The Journal of Japanese Studies*, 33, 1: 93–123.

Ivy, Marilyn (1996) "Tracking the mystery man with the 21 faces," *Critical Inquiry*, 23, 1: 11–36.

Japan External Trade Organization (JETRO) (2011) "Guidebook for export to Japan (food articles) 2011 <Vegetables, fruits, and processed products>," JETRO Development Cooperation Division, Trade and Economic Cooperation Department. Available online at: http://www.jetro.go.jp/en/reports/market/pdf/guidebook_food_vegetables_fruits_processed_products.pdf. Accessed 25 November 2013.

Johnston, Eric (2007) "Japan under siege: Japanese media perceptions of China and the two Koreassix decades after World War II," in Michael Heazle and Nick Knight (eds) *China-Japan Relations in the Twenty-First Century: Creating a Future Past?*, Cheltenham: Edward Elgar, pp. 111–24.

Jussaume, Raymond A., Shūji Hisano and Yoshimitsu Taniguchi (2000) "Food safety in modern Japan," *Contemporary Japan*, 12: 211–28.

Just, David R., Brian Wansink and Calum G. Turvey (2009) "Biosecurity, terrorism, and food consumption behaviour: using experimental psychology to analyse choices involving fear," *Journal of Agricultural and Resource Economics*, 34, 1: 91–108.

Kawai, Takao, T. Sekizuka, Y. Yahata, M. Kuroda, Y. Kumeda, Y. Iijima, . . . T. Ohnishi T. (2012) "Identification of kudoa septempunctata as the causative agent of novel food poisoning outbreaks in Japan by consumption of paralichthys olivaceus in raw fish," *Clinical Infectious Diseases*, 54, 8: 1046–52.

Lien, Marianne (2004) "The politics of food: an introduction," in Marianne Lien and Brigitte Nerlich (eds) *The Politics of Food*, Oxford: Berg, pp. 1–18.

Malthus, Robert Thomas (1798) "An essay on the principle of population." Available online at: http://www.econlib.org/library/Malthus/malPop.html. Accessed 2 December 2013.

MHLW (2011a) "Inshoku Che-nten no Chōkanshukktsuseidaichōkin no Hassei nitsuite Dai 15 HO," Available online at: http://www.mhlw.go.jp/stf/shingi/2r98520000025ttw-att/2r98520000025tz2.pdf. Accessed 25 November 2013.

——— (2011b) "Inshoku Che-nten no Chōkanshukktsuseidaichōkin no Hassei nitsuite Shiryō 2–1," Available online at: http://www.mhlw.go.jp/stf/houdou/2r9852000001dpi2-att/2r9852000001dpm2.pdf. Accessed 23 November 2013.

Mohtadi, Hamid and Antu Panini Murshid (2009) "Risk analysis of chemical, biological, or radionuclear threats: implications for food security," *Risk Analysis*, 29, 9: 1317–35.

Rosenberger, Nancy (2009) "Global food terror in Japan: risk perception in media, nation, and women," *Ecology of Nutrition and Food*, 48, 4: 237–62.

Sakamoto, Rumi and Matthew Allen (2011) "There's something fishy about that sushi: how Japan interprets the global sushi boom," *Japan Forum*, 23, 1: 99–121.

Schulze, William D. and Brian Wansink (2012) "Toxics, Toyotas, and terrorism: the behavioral economics of fear and stigma," *Risk Analysis*, 32, 4: 678–94.

Takeda, Hiroko (2008) "Delicious food in a beautiful country: nationhood and nationalism in discourses on food in contemporary Japan," *Studies in Ethnicity and Nationalism*, 8, 1: 5–30.

Walravens, Tine (2013) "Japan facing a rising China: implications on the dynamics of identity formation. Food safety as a framework," *Acta Asiatica Varsoviensia*, 26: 115–35.

WHO (2008) "Terrorist threats to food: Guidance for establishing and strengthening prevention and response systems," WHO website. Available online at: http://www.who.int/foodsafety/publications/general/en/terrorist.pdf. Accessed 23 November 2013.

WHO (2013) "Food security," WHO website. Available online at: http://www.who.int/trade/glossary/story028/en/. Accessed 20 November 2013.

Yaguchi, Yoshio (2008) "Fukanzen na Nihon no shokuryō kyōkyū taisei," *Shūkan Ekonomisto* 23 September.

Yahoo News Japan (2011) "Gyū no namareba- no teikyō wo hōritsu de kinchi suru koto ni sansei? Hantai?," 16 November. Available online at: http://polls.dailynews.yahoo.co.jp/domestic/6852/result. Accessed 20 November 2013.

2
TRANSBOUNDARY POLLUTION

1 Introduction

The industrialization of East Asia has exerted profound effects on the environment of East Asia and the everyday security of the Japanese population. In the 1960s and 1970s Japan held the dubious honour of being dubbed the world's most polluted country (Broadbent 1999), but today it is images of Beijing's lethal smog that are broadcast across the world. Climate change is a global risk related to the proportion of carbon dioxide and other greenhouse gases in the earth's atmosphere. Clearly then, climate change does not respect international boundaries and must be dealt with at the interstate level as an issue of global governance. Since the 1970s and 1980s a scientific consensus has developed around the idea that other environmental issues, specifically air and water pollution, are similarly borderless and have an environmental impact on regions hundreds or even thousands of kilometres away. Awareness of this transboundary pollution has led to major international agreements in Europe and North America, significantly mitigating its impact. Despite its recent and ongoing pollution crises, East Asia is famous for its low level of regional integration and the absence of strong multilateral institutions, and perhaps unsurprisingly such binding environmental agreements are absent.

This chapter assesses the environmental risk to Japan of transboundary pollution originating in China. Clearly, given the nature of this book, this is not a scientific assessment based on a risk management framework. Rather, the chapter focuses on the relationship between Japan's own pollution experience, its perception of the risk from China, and its response to this risk. Moreover, although there are concerns regarding the East China Sea and transboundary water pollution, the chapter focuses on transboundary air pollution, as it is this risk which has captured the attention of the Japanese media and government, as well as Japanese citizens themselves, concerned about the security of the everyday. Furthermore, whilst climate change and air pollution are linked, climate change is an issue of global governance and regulation, whereas air pollution is regional and thus is more directly a bilateral issue of regulation and governance between Japan and China (although Taiwan, South Korea and Mongolia are also involved, as is discussed later). As noted, Japan was once the 'world's most polluted state.' Today, Japan is a world leader in green technology. Thus, one might assume that given Japan's recent history and experience with severe and lethal pollution levels, it would be well placed to provide support and assistance to China in dealing with its current environmental crisis. It is true that much of Japan's Official Development Assistance (ODA) to China has involved green technology transfer and pollution mitigation programmes. Yet, as China's environmental crisis worsens, and as China-sourced transboundary pollution is perceived to put the security of the everyday at risk, Japan's environmental aid to China has declined. Whilst this at first may appear paradoxical, this chapter argues that the development of the 'China threat' narrative framework has played an important role in Japan's environmental policy vis-à-vis China.[1] In other words, despite increased risk perception as well as actual harm to Japan's environment, rather than serious efforts to mitigate this harm, the response has instead been to incorporate it into the China threat narrative framework, further demonizing China.

The rest of the chapter proceeds as follows: the next two sections outline Japan's recent history of environmental problems, providing the context for Japan's approach to environmental risks and the emergence of Japan as an environmental activist state. The subsequent section outlines the current air pollution crisis in China and the possible impact this may have on Japan. The chapter then turns to Japan's response, using media and government sources to describe and analyse the inverse relationship between the increasing risk recalibration with the decline in Japan's provision of environmental assistance, before drawing these threads together to highlight the discrepancy between Japan's own recent history as well as the current pollution problem, the demonization of Chinese pollution and the reduction in environmental assistance to China.

2 Pollution in Japan

Today, Japan is a leader in green technology and an environmental activist state (though it remains one of the world's biggest CO_2 emitters in both gross and per capita terms). It was not always thus. In the 1960s and 1970s, Japan was a 'toxic archipelago' (Walker 2010). From Hokkaido in the north to Okinawa in the south (see Chapter 12 for the role of US bases in polluting Okinawa), Japan's land, air and water were heavily polluted, resulting in countless premature deaths. In ways that bear striking resemblance to urban China today, Japan's major cities were frequently engulfed in smog and the industrial discharge of mercury, cadmium and other pollutants seeped into the food chain, killing and disfiguring infants and adults alike. The complete history of Japan's pollution crisis is far too big a topic to cover here. However, in order to provide background on the situation facing Japan during the postwar industrialization era, this section briefly outlines the 'big four' pollution diseases (affecting Minamata, Niigata, Yokkaichi and Toyama) before discussing Japan's acid rain deposition problems, and finally, outlining how Japan got itself out of its pollution crisis.

The first of the big four pollution diseases hit Toyama Prefecture in the Jinzū river basin, when the Mitsui Mining and Smelting Company began intensive production at the upstream Kamioka mine. Cadmium and other heavy metals seeped directly into the river, which was widely used for irrigation, drinking, washing and cooking (Toyama Prefectural Itai-Itai Museum 2014). The river slowly died and in 1912 the first victims of a new disease, *Itai Itai* (literally 'it hurts'), were recorded. Although not officially confirmed until the 1960s, the disease was a result of the accumulation of cadmium in the body, causing extreme levels of pain and often ending in a slow, painful death. Although the disease was identified by a general practitioner as early as 1961, the Ministry for Health and Welfare (MHW, now MHLW) did not formally begin researching the issue until 1967. We have already seen in Chapter 1 how residents of Minamata suffered from mercury poisoning after consuming fish and shellfish from Minamata Bay in Kyushu in the south of Japan. Because of collusion by the government and the polluting company, Chisso Corporation, the Minamata outbreak continued for years after the disease had been identified. A similar outbreak took place in Niigata, although the Niigata case ended in a (relatively) speedy court case. Estimates of the combined total of deaths from both incidents run into the thousands, whilst research suggests that 'as many as two million people might have ingested enough mercury to bring on milder symptoms, such as headaches, loss of hearing, and an inability to distinguish hot from cold' (McCurry 2006).

The last of the big four relates not to heavy metal poisoning but air pollution. In 1959 a major petroleum refinery was opened in Yokkaichi, Mie Prefecture, in central Japan. Within two years of opening, authorities noted a sharp increase in respiratory illnesses such as asthma and bronchitis. In 1963 a second complex was completed in northern Yokkaichi (Wilkening 2004: 124). In 1964 the first death was recorded when Furukawa Yoshio, who suffered from asthma, died following a three-day smog. Images of residents wearing face masks became a symbol of the extent of the crisis (mirroring modern-day China), and the death toll rose, especially amongst children and the elderly. Although the MHW attempted to mitigate the crisis through a number of recommendations to reduce the sulphuric emissions, most of these were vetoed or watered down by the Ministry of International Trade and Industry (MITI, now METI) – the plant was a government pet project, part of Prime Minister Hayato Ikeda's economic development and 'income-doubling plan.' Finally in 1973, again years after the cause of the pollution was first identified, local citizens successfully took the polluting company to court, after which desulphurization technology was used to reduce the sulphuric output from 100,000 tonnes to 17,000 in 1975 (Wilkening 2004: 126). As one Tokyo professor put it, during Japan's postwar period of rapid industrialization and economic growth, for many citizens Gross National Product (GNP) came to mean not gross national product but gross national pollution (*The Harvard Crimson* 1971).

2.1 Acid rain in Japan

Acid deposition is a generic term used to describe precipitation and other forms of deposition of acidic compounds. This can be wet deposition, usually described using the generic term 'acid rain,' although this also encompasses snow, mist, dew, and so on. The deposition can also be dry, when acidic atmospheric gases, such as sulphur dioxide, settle on the ground in the form of gas or salt. Acid deposition in Western states has caused severe damage to forests in both continental Europe and Scandinavia, and resulted in large-scale lake death in both Europe and North America. Moreover, given the absence of industry in those regions badly hit by acidification, it was apparent at an early stage that acid deposition is a transboundary phenomenon. Japan's acid rain problem has been less severe than that of Europe or North America. There are a variety of possible reasons for this, including the shorter time span of industrialization in East Asia, the nature of Japanese soils, and the relative absence of lakes (lake death being one of the more striking consequences of severe acid rain, especially in Canada and the Nordic countries). Nevertheless, acid deposition in Japan has a one hundred year history, coinciding with the prewar industrialization phase (Wilkening 2004).

In the postwar industrialization period acid rain damage was again evident, though it paled in comparison to the effects of the big four pollution cases. The best-known case of acid deposition took place in the mid-1970s, and has come to be known as the 'moist air pollution problem' (Wilkening 2004). For three years in a row thousands of people living on the Kanto plain north of Tokyo sought medical treatment after summer mists' drizzle triggered eye, throat, nose and skin irritation, as well as damage to crops. Studies showed that the precipitation was unusually acidic, the lowest Ph measurement being just 2.85. However, the 'moist air pollution' stopped as abruptly as it started – likely a result of the anti–air pollution measures which the 'Pollution Diet' initiated in the late 1960s and 1970s. This does not mean that acid rain has simply gone away, though. Rather, as we will see in the next section, acid rain has become a major part of the Sino-Japanese transboundary air pollution problem.

3 Japan goes green

Until the 1970s, Japan was amongst the most polluted states on earth. Since then Japan has developed a reputation as a green-technology leader and environmental activist state (Miyazaki 2015). This was not a top-down process. Local opposition led to activist groups which, although ignored by the central government in collusion with big business, won a number of key legal cases against the polluting industries. Similarly, municipal governments enacted anti-pollution laws far more advanced than anything at the state level, where the MITI and the MHW were at odds: the MITI prioritizing growth at all costs, whilst the MHW sought to increase pollution control with tighter regulations on industry (Broadbent 1999). The MITI was able to either overrule the MHW, or at least water down its proposals, for much of the 1960s – effectively implementing a system of governance where the harm from pollution was regulated in a way to lead to the victimization of a minority of the population. However, by 1970 the issue of pollution had come to a head, and opposition politicians were defeating LDP candidates at the local level across Japan (Broadbent 1999: 120). The sense of crisis within the LDP trigged the 'Pollution Diet' of 1970. The fourteen bills which constituted the core of the 'Pollution Diet' legislation contributed to a rapid improvement in the regulation and governance of the environment, such that pollution diseases on the scale of the big four have not been witnessed again.

Still, the central government soon carefully readjusted some of the regulatory measures to minimize the impact on big business, and, as in the case of food safety regulation (Chapter 1), enforcement of the existing regulations has been lax (Rosenbluth and Thies 1999). Put simply, state and market actors continued to perceive the risk to economic growth as more consequential than the actual harm to the security of the everyday for a minority of the population due to environmental pollution. Furthermore, one of the solutions made explicitly available to business by the central government was pollution export – sending the most polluting industry abroad to states with lax regulations and no history of organized civil society opposition to pollution (Hall 2009). More recently, Japan has become a major exporter of hazardous waste. It has long opposed the Basel Ban, an international treaty prohibiting the export of hazardous waste; meanwhile China has been the primary dumping ground for this electronic waste (Hall 2009). As the next section shows, China has taken up the mantle of Asia's worst polluter, largely as a result of its export-based economy – a large proportion of the exports going to Japan, as well as to the US and the European Union (EU). Together with those exports, China also emits transboundary pollution heading Japan's way.

4 China's current pollution crisis

It is no exaggeration to say that China's domestic pollution problem is on a scale never before witnessed in human history. In the previous section we saw how Japan was, and in some ways to this day still is, plagued by domestically produced pollution, resulting in thousands of deaths and injuries over the past century. Europe and North America, the two other main centres of industrialization in the twentieth century, have faced issues similar to Japan, from tainted water supplies poisoning the food chain to air pollution producing London's infamous 'pea-soup fog' and Los Angeles's ever-present car-induced haze. Although the situation has greatly improved, air pollution still results in thousands of premature deaths per year in both regions – in the United Kingdom alone the effect on mortality is a loss of approximately 340,000 life-years, equivalent to 29,000 deaths (Committee on the Medical Effects of Air Pollutants 2010). Indeed, as recently as spring 2014 much of western Europe lay under a cloud of thick smog, leading to a spike in respiratory illness (Lewis 2014). Still, the situation in Japan, North America and Europe has improved dramatically in recent decades. This is partly because of the regulation of pollution through legislation, as the governments responded to demands for a cleaner environment, recognizing the risk to the security of the everyday for the population. This is only part of the story. Manufacturing in these regions has decreased dramatically, much of it relocating to China, the new 'workshop of the world.' The result has also been the relocation of pollution to China. For example, a recent study found that a large percentage of China's air pollution is a direct result of manufacturing products for the US market, including as much as 36 per cent of total sulphur dioxide and 22 per cent of carbon monoxide emissions (Lin et al. 2013). Whilst China bears the brunt of manufacturing pollution, the Chinese value added for many of the products is tiny. Apple's iPhone and iPad are both assembled in China under the auspices of a Taiwanese company, Foxconn, with China's primary benefit being in the form of labourers' wages, which account for only 2 per cent of the overall value of each unit (Kraemer et al. 2011). Put bluntly, much of the pollution in China is either directly or indirectly a result of consumption in the rest of the industrialized world, including Japan, suggesting clearly how the security of the everyday in terms of pollution is transboundary in nature, too.

The Chinese Communist Party's (CCP) emphasis on economic growth to the detriment of the environment has further contributed to the destruction of the local environment. On the one hand, state policy has lifted millions out of poverty. On the other hand, though, hundreds of thousands die premature deaths as a result of the harm inflicted through widespread, often catastrophic, pollution. Just as Japan's industrialization led to major outbreaks of pollution-related diseases such as Minamata and *Itai Itai*, China has witnessed severe contamination of its water and soil. Water in many Chinese cities is undrinkable, and severe water shortages in northern China have led to the drilling of wells deeper and deeper, reaching a geological stratum rich in arsenic and causing an epidemic of arsenic poisoning (Sun 2004). Water pollution has also been linked to the phenomenon of 'cancer villages': communities located near major industrial sites with abnormally high rates of cancer (Slezak 2013). As outlined in the previous chapter, food contamination in China remains a major problem, too. Some of this contamination is deliberate, aimed at increasing profits, such as the baby milk formula incident in 2008 (*Guardian*, 22 January 2009).

Other food safety issues are the direct result of pollution: cadmium-tainted rice, the cause of the outbreak of *Itai Itai* in Toyama, has been found across southern China (*New York Times*, 21 May 2013).

These problems are (largely) endemic to the Chinese mainland. The primary source of concern about China's impact on the security of the everyday in Japan is transboundary air pollution. China's air pollution has received extensive media attention in recent years, usually accompanied by iconic images of a smog-enveloped Beijing or Shanghai. The primary health risk is the concentration of atmospheric particulate matter (PM), specifically particles less than 2.5 micrometres in diameter (PM 2.5). All industrialized states suffer from high rates of PM pollution, but levels in China far exceed those recorded elsewhere. The EU, US and Japan all regulate PM 2.5 emissions, with limits ranging from 15 to 35 micrograms per cubic metre. Although these are regularly exceeded in major urban areas, annual averages of PM 2.5 concentrations in European and North American cities rarely exceed 30 micrograms. Beijing's annual average, according to Chinese authorities, was 89.5 micrograms in 2013, with fifty-eight days of heavy pollution reported. The US embassy in Beijing also records PM 2.5 levels – an annual average of 103 micrograms (Andrews 2014). Although the readings recorded by the embassy and the Chinese authorities, along with their definitions of 'hazardous,' differ dramatically, both have registered readings well in excess of 500 micrograms. Similar conditions can be found in cities across China. PM 2.5 and below are particularly damaging to health, causing respiratory illness and exacerbating existing respiratory conditions. This kind of ambient air pollution has also been linked to coronary events (i.e. heart attacks) even at levels lower than the relatively strict EU regulations (Cesaroni *et al*. 2014).

The extreme levels of air pollution have a number of causes. As mentioned, export-orientated manufacturing drives the Chinese economy and helps secure the position of the CCP. China is the world's largest energy consumer, and coal provides 69 per cent of its energy (US Energy Information Administration 2014). Unlike oil, of which China is a net importer, coal deposits are abundant in China and every year dozens of new coal-burning power plants go online. Their various emissions include carbon dioxide, the prime cause of climate change, as well as sulphur dioxide and nitrogen dioxide. These compounds not only contribute to PM 2.5 concentrations but also cause acid rain. Beijing has introduced tougher regulations, as seen in the shutting down of energy inefficient plants and requiring the installation of desulphurization systems. Notwithstanding, the continued rapid increase in energy consumption has outpaced the implementation of emission reduction regulations (Wang and Hao 2012). Automobile exhausts, especially diesel fumes, are another important source of emissions contributing both to acid rain and PM 2.5 concentrations. Car ownership levels continue to rise dramatically, and China is now both the world's largest car producer as well as the largest new car market (International Organization of Motor Vehicle Manufacturers 2014; Bloomberg, 1 February 2013).

Japan's location immediately to the west of China and the Eurasian mainland means that, during winter, cold air from the continent is blown across the Sea of Japan and the East China Sea. Spring also sees high concentrations of pollutants thanks to *kōsa* or the yellow dust phenomena, in which dust storms in desert regions of China and Mongolia result in high volumes of fine sand and other soil matter entering the atmosphere. Some of the fine matter continues on its journey across the Korean peninsula and Japanese archipelago. *Kōsa* is hardly a new or unique phenomenon: the historical records in Korea documented the phenomenon as early as two thousand years ago (Chun *et al*. 2001), whilst southwest Europe experiences a similar phenomenon thanks to sand and dust blown up from the Sahara desert. The difference is that today the journey across central and East China passes over major cities and industrial areas, with the result being that the fine matter absorbs some of the pollutants, exacerbating the spread of Chinese-originated PM 2.5 particulates. The first scientific confirmation that pollution emanating from China was reaching Japan came in 1989 (Brettell 2007). Since then it has gradually developed into a major risk for the security of the everyday, and has become intimately associated with the whole notion of the China threat.

5 Regional environmental cooperation

Even before transboundary acid deposition was confirmed, Japan was already assisting China with its own increasingly severe acid rain problems. As early as 1977 Japan sent its first environmental delegation to China, and from 1988 environmental aid was included in the ODA loan programme (Cui 2011). The same year also saw the establishment of China-Japan Friendship Centre for Environmental Protection, celebrating the tenth anniversary of the 1978 Treaty of Peace and Friendship. Thus, 1988 can be seen as a watershed in the development of serious bilateral environmental cooperation between the two states. Throughout the 1990s various agreements and communiques were signed, together with a variety of projects implemented across China. These projects operated from the formal state level down to the non-governmental organization (NGO) level, as seen in the Model City Plan in Chongqing, Guiyang and Dalian and the Obuchi Fund to promote afforestation (Cui 2011). Meanwhile, both in terms of the grants and loans provided to China through ODA, environmental assistance occupied an increasingly large share. This kind of unidirectional environmental assistance was not particularly controversial, as China benefitted from Japanese financial and technological assistance, whilst Japanese companies enjoyed access to a major market for environmental industry.

Politically, the establishment of the Acid Deposition Monitoring Network in East Asia (EANET) was a more difficult step. EANET was the result of Japan-sponsored expert and advisory meetings running from 1993 until the formal inauguration of the network in 2000. As the title suggests, its mission was (and still is) to monitor acid deposition in East Asia. Importantly, it was a Japanese initiative, and has largely been funded by Japan – it was originally headquartered in Niigata. Hypothetically the network might monitor transboundary acid deposition originating in Japan and moving elsewhere in the region; the reality is that Japan was 'keen to demonstrate that an increasing percentage of the acid rain falling on the country originates in the industrial districts of north China and Korea' (Triendl 1998: 426). Although Vice Premier Zhou Jiahou did acknowledge that China might play a role in transboundary pollution in 1992, overall China has been reluctant to admit that it is responsible for pollution in other states (Brettell

2007, Drifte 2005).[2] The seven-year gap between the first meeting and the formal start of the network was a result not only of this suspicion, but also of disagreements between the member states about its funding, as well as the 'seriousness, extent, and causes of the problem' (Miyazaki 2011: 59). Although South Korea and other states joined the network in its preliminary phase, Seoul has long been suspicious of Japan's motives in terms of regional leadership (Brettell 2007), whilst China remained an observer until 2000. Despite its painful beginnings, EANET has marked some degree of success, as illustrated by the regional standardization of monitoring techniques, training of experts from the thirteen different participant states, and the institutionalization of interstate meetings on acid deposition (Drifte 2005; Miyazaki 2011). Still, EANET's mission remains simply monitoring of the problem, not implementing solutions to it.

EANET is not the only regional environmental programme; in fact, in a region famous for the absence of deep international institutions, the environment is a relatively safe, 'soft' sphere for cooperation. Yet EANET and other smaller-scale programmes such as the Long-range Transboundary Air Pollutants in Northeast Asia face the same problems: they are aimed primarily at monitoring, not implementing mitigation measures. At the political level, the Tripartite Environment Ministers Meeting (Japan, South Korea and China) has been held annually since 2000, and provides a relatively high-profile forum for dealing with environmental risks, as well as enabling cooperation to continue even when other bilateral exchanges are frozen. On a practical level the meetings have not yet had any serious achievements to date (Shin 2015).

As mentioned earlier, Japan's environmental ODA programme occupied an increasingly large percentage of the overall ODA – increasing from 2 per cent in 1995 to 65 per cent in 1999 (Arase 2006). Japan's environmental ODA is not unproblematic: as with the rest of Japan's ODA, it was Tokyo-centric and often had no follow-up support or evaluation. Moreover, ODA loans had to be repaid – though Arase notes that grants were actually the least effective form. In reforestation programmes, for example, the Chinese side reported that 'the Japanese seem only interested in planting large numbers and care not enough about the actual survival of the trees' (Arase 2006: 101). Most interestingly, even as the risk of transboundary pollution has increased, Japan's ODA to China has continued to fall. As part of the response to the China threat, Japan's ODA loan programme to China was dramatically scaled back, and finally terminated in 2008 (Drifte 2006). The ODA discourse came to be dominated by assertions by both politicians and media outlets, which emphasized the contradiction of providing aid to a country that was embarking on a major military modernization programme and which represented a serious threat to Japan. According to Japan's own ODA white paper (Miyazaki 2013), the end of the loans coincided with the Beijing Olympics to symbolize China's own economic and social development: in other words, China is now self-sufficient and can look after itself. Today, China is repaying those loans such that the flow of money is now firmly from China to Japan at a rate of about one billion US dollars per year (MOFA 2014). The white paper goes on to

Transboundary pollution 51

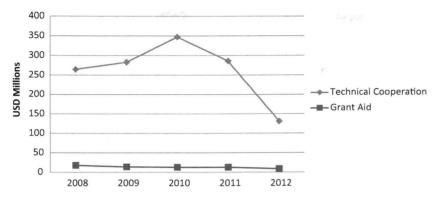

FIGURE 2.1 Technical cooperation and grant aid to China
Source: MOFA (2014: 1)

note that the other two forms of ODA, namely technical cooperation and grant aid, would be 'limited to address common challenges faced by both countries that may directly affect the lives and safety of Japanese nationals . . . that are beneficial to Japan' (MOFA 2013: 113). Yet, since 2008, both of these forms of ODA have also declined. As Figure 2.1 indicates, this fall-off has accelerated dramatically for technical cooperation, whilst grant aid is on a slow decline. Those projects funded by the technical cooperation budget, by far the larger of the two, are primarily focused on the environment and health. Examples of these plans include forestation technology dissemination, water management and nitrogen oxide emission control.

6 Media coverage

This reduction in direct environmental assistance correlates inversely with both the increase in the risk of pollution affecting China *and* with the dramatic increase in the coverage of both the Chinese pollution problem and the related risk of transboundary pollution for Japan. Throughout the entire 1990s the leading Japanese newspapers, *Asahi Shimbun* and *Yomiuri Shimbun*, carried only seventeen articles in total featuring the terms 'China' *(Chūgoku)* and transboundary pollution *(ekkyōsen)*.[3] However, the following decade saw this number jump to eighty, whilst in the short four years since 2010 there have already been seventy-nine published. These numbers are extremely conservative, as transboundary pollution is a technical term in Japanese, as in English.[4] Coverage of China's own pollution problem reaches a saturation point every spring, and the coverage tends to note the possible effects on Japan. As early as 1989 the news magazine *Aera* published an article on the possibility of Chinese acid rain falling on Japan, outlining in depth the risk of Chinese pollution – particularly sulphur dioxide – and noting the cautious approach taken by the then Environment Agency – as of 2001 the Ministry of the Environment (MOE) – which was careful not to place the blame squarely on China (29 August 1989). However, the media were generally less circumspect than the government. Throughout the 1990s the lack of desulphurization technology in Chinese coal power plants was increasingly linked to acid rain in Japan. As early as 1991, the *Yomiuri Shimbun* published an article on acid rain in which it extolled the deep link between the Japanese race and Japan's forests, noting how the Japanese use wood for everything from chopsticks (specifically mentioning the consumption of rice) to housing (30 July 1991). The same article pointed to the ability of Japanese soils to neutralize acid rain, but expressed worry that the soils would reach a limit, and pointed to transboundary pollution from China as requiring serious countermeasures. In this way, the environmental risk from China was portrayed as not only environmental, but somehow deeper, potentially affecting Japanese national identity.

In recent years the coverage has become far more emotional and rhetorical and the issue has played into the conventional China threat narrative, with some of the more radical nationalists criticizing both the media and government for colluding to withhold information about the extent of the risk posed by transboundary environmental pollution. This has echoes of the *gyōza* case, when the Fukuda administration came under fire for being seen to prioritize Sino-Japanese relations over the security of the everyday for Japanese citizens. For example, Sakai Nobuhiko (former professor at the University of Tokyo and head of the Japan Institute of Nationalism Studies) castigated the *Asahi Shimbun* for publishing an article in which the author (Mori Harufumi) notes that, without actual data on how much of the pollution in Japan is coming from China, it is difficult to accuse China and to ask the Chinese government to clean up its act (Sakai 2013). Sakai states that the media have deliberately hidden the real data, and accuses the *Asahi* in particular of being '[an utter enemy] to Japan.' The right-wing *Sankei Shimbun* has also been critical of both China's and Japan's handling of the risk of pollution, both domestic and transboundary. In an editorial in March 2014, for instance, *Sankei* strongly rejected the idea that Japan should be involved in any kind of transfers for China's pollution, since Japan was the victim of China's pollution – quite the opposite, the newspaper argued, China should be paying Japan compensation (*Sankei Shimbun*, 3 March 2014). The editorial also noted that the pollution was a result of China's prioritization of military modernization and economic growth.

Of course, neither *Sankei* nor Sakai is representative of the mainstream media opinions. The issue has been widely covered in both the dailies and the more 'liberal' or 'progressive' news magazines such as *Aera, Sunday Mainichi* and *Shukan Asahi*. Although the tone in these outlets is less harsh, it is still remarkably alarmist. For example, a *Sunday Mainichi* article from 2013 on the risk of pollution, headlined 'Chinese air pollution PM 2.5 eroding the archipelago!,' featured the classic images of the mask-wearing residents of Beijing and went on to describe the 'black snow' falling in Zao, a tourist site in northern Japan famous for its 'snow monsters' – trees covered in snow which look like monsters (*Sunday Mainichi*, 24 February 2013). In fact, the area is not covered in black snow; rather, particles in the snow are released when it melts. Yet 'black snow' falling in a major tourist resort generates a more impressive impact. Two months later *Shukan Asahi* published an article headlined 'Arsenic and mercury are flying to Japan!' The article details the detection of these elements, as well as other particles, in various sites across Japan, and questions the awareness (in Japan) of Chinese transboundary pollution together with the sense of crisis in Japan (*Shukan Asahi*, 10 May 2013). A further indication of the extent of the change in Japanese coverage of the issue comes in the form of a 2013 article in the *New York Times* (24 April 2013). The article outlines the situation in Yakushima, a heavily forested island in southern Kyushu, which is also a World Heritage Site. The article notes how scientists warning of damage to the trees on the island were ignored for years, but have suddenly found a more receptive audience because of the 'national health scare over rising levels of potentially dangerous airborne particles . . . that many now believe were produced by China.' Although the article details the extent of pollution in 'smog-belching China,' it also notes that the scientific consensus on tree die-off is that it is a result of deer overpopulation and an insect infestation – and that the phenomenon pre-dates China's economic take-off.

7 Conclusion

What is striking about the coverage in both the more right-of-centre and the more mainstream outlets is the constant recital of China's environmental pollution in the context of the risk and potential harm to Japan, despite the lack of evidence. Even in the *New York Times*, many column inches are devoted to China's emissions, even though the article acknowledges – in half of one sentence – that the scientific consensus points to other causes. Moreover, as scientists note, and the media occasionally add as a qualifier, the primary source of PM 2.5 particles in Japan at the moment remains domestically-produced car exhaust. In this way, China has been constructed as a source of environmental risk to Japan and its citizens. Yet, as we saw earlier in this chapter, and as with all industrialized states, Japan has a long history of pollution. Thousands died from preventable pollution diseases as the state prioritized the risks that threatened to hamper economic growth above all else, despite the actual harm from pollution to the security of the everyday for thousands of Japanese citizens. Furthermore, the state colluded with business to avoid dealing with lethal pollution issues, resulting in even more victims. The situation in China, then, is not so dissimilar to the situation in Japan in living memory.

Indeed, the aforementioned *Sankei* editorial mentions the tragic case of an eight-year-old girl from Jiangsu province who was diagnosed with lung cancer, which has distinct echoes of school children collapsing in Tokyo schoolyards in the 1950s and 1960s, and the many child victims of the petroleum refinery in Yokkaichi. Furthermore, as some of the media coverage admits, this research merely confirms that particles originating in China have been detected in Japan. Specifying the quantity of those particles from China is an entirely different matter. Despite the lack of scientific evidence, the basic assumption is similar to that outlined in the chapter on food risk: China equals dirty, Japan equals clean. This is precisely what scientists problematize: in the words of Professor Shima Masayuki of the Hyogo College of Medicine, it is simply 'not the case that China is dirty and Japan is clean' (quoted in *Sunday Mainichi*, 24 February 2013).[5] The point here is not to dismiss the very valid concerns of Japanese citizens regarding the potential harm to the security of the everyday of Chinese transboundary pollution, nor to suggest that the media do not shoulder a responsibility to cover the issue. Instead, this chapter has aimed at putting the risk posed by pollution from China, and in particular the response to this risk, into context. There is an irony inherent in the relationship between the increasingly alarmist coverage of China's pollution problem and the decrease in technical assistance and grant aid to mitigate precisely the same problem. Similarly, the critical coverage of Chinese environmental pollution belies an historical amnesia evident also in the food risk chapter. The environment is one area where all states in East Asia can cooperate – a potential win-win. Japan has the historical experience, it has the technology and it has the motivation to address the risk from transboundary pollution. The association of transboundary pollution with the China threat may hinder cooperation in one of the clear 'win-win' spheres of international relations in East Asia (Wishnick 2009). This would be both an environmental and a political tragedy.

Notes

1 For an account of the deterioration of relations and the effects of perceived anti-Japanese sentiment, see Gustafsson (2015).
2 China takes a similar attitude to CO2 emissions, pointing out that other states ought to take more responsibility for climate change since they have been emitting large quantities of CO2 for much longer.
3 From 1 January 1990 to 31 December 1999, using Nikkei Telecom database.
4 Differentiating between media coverage of Chinese pollution in China and Chinese pollution affecting Japan is problematic, given the huge coverage of Chinese pollution in Japan.
5 Interestingly, this quote rounds off an article which is entirely focused on how bad the pollution is in China and the high risk this puts on Japan.

References

Andrews, Steven (2014) "China's air pollution reporting is misleading," *China Dialogue*, 27 March. Available online at: https://www.chinadialogue.net/article/show/single/en/6856-China-s-air-pollution-reporting-is-misleading. Accessed 11 March 2014.

Arase, David (2006) "Japanese ODA policy toward China: The new agenda," in Peng Er Lam (ed.) *Japan's Relations with China: Facing a Rising Power*, Abingdon, Oxon: Routledge, pp. 92–106.

Brettell, Anna (2007) "Security, energy, and the environment: the atmospheric link," in In-taek Hyun and Miranda Schreurs (eds) *The Environmental Dimension of Asian Security: Conflict and Cooperation over Energy, Resources, and Pollution*, Washington DC: United States Institute of Peace Press, pp. 89–113.

Broadbent, Jeffery (1999) *Environmental Politics in Japan: Networks of Power and Protest*, Cambridge: Cambridge University Press.

Cesaroni, Giulia, Francesco Forastiere, Massimo Stafoggia, Zorana J Andersen, Chiara Badaloni, Rob Beelen, . . . Annette Peters. (2014) "Long term exposure to ambient air pollution and incidence of acute coronary events: prospective cohort study and meta-analysis in 11 European cohorts from the ESCAPE Project," *BMJ*, 348: f7412.

Chun, Youngsin, Kyung-On Boo, Jiyoung Kim, Soon-Ung Park, Meehye Lee. (2001) "Synopsis, transport, and physical characteristics of Asian dust in Korea," *Journal of Geophysical Research: Atmospheres*, 106, 16: 18461–69.

Committee on the Medical Effects of Air Pollutants (2010) *The Mortality Effects of Long-Term Exposure to Particulate Air Pollution in the United Kingdom*, Health Protection Agency. Available online at: https://www.gov.uk/government/uploads/system/uploads/attachment_data/file/304641/COMEAP_mortality_effects_of_long_term_exposure.pdf. Accessed 1 November 2014.

Cui, Shunji (2011) "Peace and reconciliation through environmental cooperation: changing the image of Japan in China," *Peace and Conflict Review*, 5, 2: 41–53.

Drifte, Reinhard (2005) "Transboundary pollution as an issue in Northeast Asian regional politics," Asia Research Centre Working Paper No. 12. Available online at: http://www.lse.ac.uk/asiaresearchcentre/_files/arcwp12-drifte.pdf. Accessed 4 November 2014.

——— 2006 "The ending of Japan's ODA loan programme to China – all's well that ends well?" *Asia Pacific Review*, 13, 1: 94–117.

Gustafsson, Karl (2015) "Identity and recognition: remembering and forgetting the post-war in Sino-Japanese relations," *Pacific Review*, 28, 1: 117–38.

Hall, Derek (2009) "Pollution export as state and corporate strategy: Japan in the 1970s," *Review of International Political Economy*, 16, 2: 260–283.

The Harvard Crimson (1971) "Smog over Mt. Fuji," 11 November. Available online at: http://www.thecrimson.com/article/1971/11/11/smog-over-mt-fugi-pbtbokyoseven-year-old-seiichi/. Accessed 27 April 2014.

International Organization of Motor Vehicle Manufacturers (2014) *Production Statistics 2014 Q2*. Available online at: http://www.oica.net/category/production-statistics/. Accessed 20 October 2014.

Kraemer, Kenneth L., Greg Linden and Jason Derek (2011) "Capturing value in global networks: Apple's iPad and iPhone," Irvine: Personal Computing Industry Centre, University of California Irvine. Available online at: http://mansueto.files.wordpress.com/2011/10/value_ipad_iphone.pdf. Accessed 5 November 2014.

Lewis, Alastair (2014) "Smog cloud is the same old pollution with a Saharan twist," *The Conversation*, 2 April. Available online at: http://theconversation.com/smog-cloud-is-the-same-old-pollution-with-a-saharan-twist-25164. Accessed 10 May 2014.

Lin, Jintai, Da Pana, Steven J. Davis, Qiang Zhang, Kebin He, Can Wang, . . . Dabo Guan. (2013) "China's international trade and air pollution in the United States," *Proceedings of the National Academy of Sciences of the United States of America*, 111, 5: 1736–41.

McCurry, Justin (2006) "Japan remembers Minamata," *The Lancet*, 367, 9505: 99–100.

Miyazaki, Asami (2011) "Between the theory and policy: environmental networking the East Asian Way," *Ritsumeikan International Affairs*, 9: 51–80.

——— (2013) "Japan's Official Development Assistance White Paper 2013," Ministry of Foreign Affairs Website. Available online at: http://www.mofa.go.jp/policy/oda/white/2013/pdfs/020203_1.pdf. Accessed 7 May 2014.

——— (2015) "Japan's foreign policy and transnational environmental risks," in Sebastian Maslow, Ra Mason and Paul O'Shea (eds) *Risk State: Japan's Foreign Policy in an Age of Uncertainty*, Farnham: Ashgate.

MOFA (2014) "Japan's ODA Disbursement's to China," Ministry of Foreign Affairs Website, April 1. Available online at: http://www.mofa.go.jp/policy/oda/data/pdfs/china.pdf. Accessed 5 May 2014.

Rosenbluth, Frances and Michael F. Thies (1999) "The political economy of Japanese pollution regulation," paper presented at the *Annual Meetings of the American Political Science Association*, Atlanta, 2–5 September. Available online at: http://www.yale.edu/leitner/resources/docs/1999-01.pdf. Accessed 29 May 2014.

Sakai, Nobuhiko (2013) "We cannot afford to see PM 2.5 pollution indifferently," GFJ Commentary, April 26. Available online at: http://www.gfj.jp/e/commentary/130426.pdf. Accessed 1 April 2014.

Shin, Sangbum (2015) "Environmental policy in East Asia: institutions in comparative perspective," in Paul G. Harris and Graeme Lang (eds) *Routledge Handbook of Environment and Society in Asia*, Abingdon, Oxon: Routledge.

Slezak, Michael (2013) "China takes steps to clean up 'cancer villages,'" *The New Scientist*, 26 February. Available online at: http://www.newscientist.com/article/dn23212-china-takes-steps-to-clean-up-cancer-villages.html#.U1-ENPmSyVM. Accessed 6 May 2014.

Sun, Giufan (2004) "Arsenic contamination and arsenicosis in China," *Toxicology and Applied Pharmacology*, 198, 3: 268–71.

Toyama Prefectural Itai-Itai Museum (2014) "About the Itai-Itai disease," the Itai-Itai Disease Museum Website. Available online at: *http://itaiitai-dis.jp/lang/english/disease/index.html*. Accessed 7 June 2014.

Triendl, Robert (1998) "Asian states take 'first step' on acid rain," *Nature*, 392, 6675: 426.

US Energy Information Administration (2014) "Country Analysis Brief: China," 4 February. Available online at: http://www.eia.gov/countries/analysisbriefs/China/china.pdf. Accessed 15 June 2014.

Walker, Brett (2010) *Toxic Archipelago: A History of Industrial Disease in Japan*, Seattle: University of Washington Press.

Wang, Shuxiao and Jiming Hao (2012) "Air quality management in China: issues, challenges, and options," *Journal of Environmental Sciences*, 24, 1: 2–13.

Wilkening, Kenneth E. (2004) *Acid Rain Science and Politics in Japan*, Cambridge, MA: The MIT Press.

Wishnick, Elizabeth (2009) "Competition and cooperative practices in Sino-Japanese energy and environmental relations: towards an energy security 'risk community'?" *Pacific Review*, 22, 4: 399–426.

3
EAST CHINA SEA DISPUTE

1 Introduction

> When a nation prone to changing the status quo surpasses nations honouring the status quo in military power, that nation is in effect launching an attack on those nations, making the most of the opportunity to claim and solidify its new territory. In terms of commonly accepted military analysis, China definitely is a very serious threat to Japan.
>
> (Sakurai 2013)

In the introduction to this part of the book we saw how the 'China threat' has developed over the past twenty years. Originally peripheral and confined primarily to those on the far right, it has gradually moved into the mainstream and is now propounded by prominent politicians in both the LDP and the DPJ. The recalibration of risk in regard to China has to a great extent developed as a result of the mutually reinforcing relationship between the 'China threat' theory and the East China Sea maritime and territorial dispute over the Senkaku/Diaoyu Islands. As a result of both international maritime law and straightforward geography the maritime and island disputes have become essentially inseparable. This chapter focuses specifically on this combined territorial risk, outlining the process through which China's claim to the territory has been recalibrated from a minor to a grave risk for Japan.[1] It also shows how this recalibration has produced a tough, non-negotiable response. Although the 'no-negotiation' policy has been designed to prevent certain potential harms to Japan, it has actually had the effect of both precluding any real progress on the dispute whilst simultaneously producing harm across a wide range of issues, from diplomatic relations to Japanese economic interests in China. Because the history of the dispute is complex and contested, the chapter begins with only a very brief background sketch of the dispute, outlining the key issues of relevance. It then outlines how the risk was recalibrated and reconstituted throughout the 1990s and 2000s and how this recalibration has produced Japan's response to the risk. The chapter then shifts focus to the potential and actual harm associated with the risk, considering the value of the disputed territory and the possibility of a Chinese occupation and contrasting this with the actual harm to, among other things, diplomatic and economic ties. The chapter finishes by considering the potential implications of the dispute not only for Japan but for the region as a whole.

2   Background

The territorial dispute itself revolves around a small chain of uninhabited islands located in the East China Sea, north of both the Yaeyama Islands of Okinawa Prefecture and Taiwan. This island chain – known as Senkaku Shōto in Japan, and Diaoyudao in China – consists of a handful of tiny isolated islands and rocks which historically have served as a navigational aide and occasional refuge for fishermen. Japan incorporated the islands during the First Sino-Japanese War in 1895. Tokyo insists that this incorporation was separate from and unrelated to the cession of Taiwan to Japan following victory in the war later that year, whereas China insists that the islands were taken as part of Taiwan, and therefore should have been returned following the defeat of Japan in World War II. In the early part of the twentieth century the islands were temporarily inhabited by workers in a newly constructed stuffed bird and *katsuobushi* (tuna flake) factory (*Aera*, 21 October 1996). Abandoned during World War II, the islands were administered by the US as part of Okinawa until its reversion to Japan in 1972. However, just a few years prior to the reversion a survey was published suggesting that the seabed of the East China Sea, including the waters around the islands, might harbour vast quantities of oil and gas (Emery *et al.* 1969). Soon after both China and Taiwan announced formal claims to the islands, the US declared that although it did not take a position on ultimate sovereignty of the islands, it was returning their administrative rights to Japan. To this day the US maintains the same position, meaning that the islands are covered by the Treaty of Mutual Cooperation and Security, which includes the treaty obligation to defend them were they to be invaded by a third party.

To further complicate the issue, the dispute is tied up in a broader maritime dispute over a large swathe of the East China Sea itself. The islands are located in the disputed zone, and also have the potential to generate their own, albeit more limited, maritime territory. Under the United Nations Convention on the Law of the Sea (UNCLOS), states can claim an Exclusive Economic Zone (EEZ) of up to 200 nautical miles (UNCLOS 1982). This EEZ consists of, among other things, rights over the water column and mining rights to the seabed. Beyond the EEZ, states can claim a continental shelf, where it exists, as far as 350 nautical miles from the coast, which grants rights to the seabed only. China has an extensive geographical continental shelf extending beyond the 200 nautical mile

EEZ, and this overlaps with Japan's claimed EEZ. To complicate matters even further, the disputed islands lie in this disputed zone and they could theoretically generate their own 200 nautical mile EEZ. Legally, the issue is rather murky; however, for our purposes it is sufficient to state that the two disputes are deeply interlinked and both sides have some foundation to their maritime and territorial claims.[2]

3 Risk construction, recalibration and response

The dispute was quietly shelved by both sides following the 1978 Peace and Friendship Treaty and remained more or less dormant until 1992, when China announced a law defining its territorial seas, which included the islands. Whilst this triggered Japanese diplomatic protests, when Prime Minister Miyazawa Kiichi of Japan met Jiang Zemin, the general secretary of the CCP, the pair agreed that nothing had changed and the dispute remained shelved. However, within a few days the Japanese MOFA announced that the dispute had not been shelved, but rather claimed no dispute existed – the islands were Japanese territory.[3] This marks the beginning of the 'no dispute exists' position taken by the Japanese government, which continues to this day (Drifte 2013). Still, the issue remained quiet and there was little political debate or media coverage of the issue (see Figure 3.1). In the National Diet the issue was raised only a handful of times in the subsequent years, and each time the government's reaction was straightforward. For example, in 1993 when questioned on the issue in the Diet, the head of MOFA's Asia section, Ikeda Tadashi, stated that, regardless of China's claims, Japan enjoyed effective control not only over the islands but also the disputed waters, thus there was

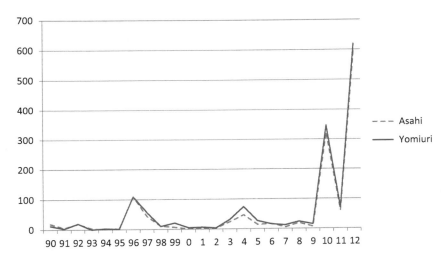

FIGURE 3.1 Number of articles with 'Senkaku' in the title
Sources: Yomiuri Shimbun and *Asahi Shimbun*, 1990–2012

no need to 'pointlessly' damage Sino-Japanese relations (Ikeda Tadashi, Foreign Affairs Committee, 22 November 1993). Even after the 1992 incident, few Japanese considered the islands of consequence: a 1988 *Yomiuri Shimbun* opinion poll saw the islands ranked as the least important issue in bilateral relations, whilst a similar 1992 poll found the islands ranked second from bottom (*Yomiuri Shimbun*, 25 September 1988, 13 September 1992).

The ratification of the UNCLOS by both China and Japan in early 1996 brought the issue of overlapping East China Sea claims – and by extension the islands – back onto the agenda. Later that year a number of activists, first from Japan then later Taiwan and Hong Kong, landed on the disputed islands. The Japanese activists claimed that they were doing this to protect the islands, and that a Chinese invasion of the islands would be *'dai ippo'* – the first step – in the invasion of Okinawa, and perhaps ultimately of Japan itself (interview, Nakama Hitoshi, 22 April 2011). In 1997 two prominent LDP politicians joined the right-wing activists in attempting to publicize the issue and recalibrate the risk: Nishimura Shingō together with Ishihara Shintarō set sail for the disputed islands, with Nishimura actually landing and planting a flag. The pair issued a statement denouncing the government for not taking a more assertive stance on the dispute and later that year Nishimura set sail once again, only this time his boat was intercepted by the JCG. Then prime minister Hashimoto Ryūtarō publicly criticized Nishimura and a criminal investigation was initiated to see if he or his accomplices had committed any crimes. At this stage the Hashimoto administration did not consider the territorial risk to be serious and made statements downplaying the dispute whilst emphasizing the need for positive Sino-Japanese relations.

However, pressure was building from both state and societal actors who sought to recalibrate the territorial risk and alter the government's response. Nishimura teamed up with right-wing academic Odamura Shirō, then president of Takushoku University, to organize a bipartisan meeting of Diet members, which produced a resolution calling on the Hashimoto administration to take a 'resolute' stance. These state and societal actors were less interested in the disputed islands because of any deep and historical symbolic importance to Japanese national identity. Nor did they make dramatic gestures or otherwise involve themselves deeply in Japan's other territorial disputes, even over territory that actually was deeply symbolic and important to Japanese national identity. Rather, the dispute was intimately related to anti-Chinese sentiment and right-wing conservatism. Nishimura himself was fired as vice defence minister in 1999 after making highly controversial comments about rape and nuclear weapons (*Japan Times*, 20 October 1999). Following a rehabilitation of sorts, he later joined Hashimoto Tōru and Ishihara Shintarō's Japan Restoration Party *(Nippon Ishin no Kai)* only to be expelled after making statements about the 'swarms' of South Korean prostitutes in Japan (*Japan Times*, 21 May 2013). Meanwhile, Ishihara has provocatively attempted to derail Sino-Japanese relations on a number of occasions, as discussed below.

The domestic pressure grew in tandem both with an increased Chinese presence in the disputed waters – still under effective administrative control by Japan – as well as other regional events as outlined earlier, such as the third Taiwan Strait crisis, underground nuclear testing and China's ongoing military modernization. These issues were used by those pushing the China threat theory, and ultimately led to a recalibration of territorial risk and a corresponding change in Japan's response. The policy of prioritizing bilateral relations over the dispute was altered in 1999, not by the prime minister or his cabinet but via an internal LDP committee which suspended a package of ODA loans to China over what was described as the research vessel 'incursions.' During the Koizumi administration (2001–6) Sino-Japanese relations entered a deep freeze, primarily over historical issues, although Koizumi's government did implement some comparatively assertive measures in the dispute, such as leasing some of the islands and recognizing a controversial lighthouse built on one of the islands as an official beacon. Still, the territorial dispute was not the primary source of Sino-Japanese friction during the Koizumi administration. Ironically, considering the state of Sino-Japanese relations when he left office, not only did Koizumi reject the China threat theory – publicly at least – but as we saw in the introduction to this part of the book, he went as far as to say that China was not a 'threat' but an 'opportunity' (*Asahi Shimbun*, 28 December 2005).

After Koizumi, Japan saw three LDP prime ministers come and go in quick succession, and for the most part the dispute was relatively quiet during their tenures. The chapter on food risk outlined how both the first administration of Abe Shinzō, as well as the subsequent administration of Fukuda Yasuo, attempted to mend bridges even after public opinion had shifted against China. Events took a surprising turn after the DPJ came to power following a historic election victory in 2009, comprehensively defeating the LDP and forming a government under Prime Minister Hatoyama Yukio. The Hatoyama administration's foreign policy was based on the idea of reintegrating Japan back into Asia – an 'Asia pivot' – through the development of multilateral institutions, most notably a proposed 'East Asian Community.' This Asianist streak was matched by a desire to rebalance the US–Japan alliance, in particular reducing the number of US troops stationed in Okinawa, as outlined in Part III. However, a combination of incompetence, inexperience and US intransigence led to the failure of the attempted foreign policy shift and Hatoyama's resignation only nine months after taking office (Hughes 2010; O'Shea 2014). The new administration, under Kan Naoto, abandoned the 'Asia pivot' and focused on domestic issues. However, as we saw in the introduction to this part of the book, the new foreign minister, Maehara Seiji, was a prominent China hawk and advocate of the China threat theory.

In late 2010, shortly after the Kan administration took office, the dispute flared up dramatically when a Chinese fishing trawler collided with JCG patrol vessels in disputed waters near the islands. Whereas agreed practice was to deport Chinese citizens arrested in the disputed zone – as even Koizumi had done in 2004 – the captain was detained for over two weeks whilst a file was prepared for the local prosecutors. Maehara personally visited the local JCG base in Ishigaki, Okinawa, announcing that there was no dispute and the issue would be dealt with under Japanese domestic law (Kyodo, 16 September 2010). China reacted with a range of measures, including the suspension of ministerial and other exchanges, and there were widespread anti-Japanese demonstrations in cities across the country (Hagström 2012). After Chief Cabinet Secretary Sengoku Yoshito took over the incident from Maehara, the captain was quickly released and gradually the dispute calmed (*Japan Times*, 23 October 2010). The following month Isshiki Masaharu, a JCG officer, leaked a video of the incident on YouTube, which was broadcast and analysed repeatedly on Japanese television. He claimed that he acted in response to Japan's weak stance on the dispute, which served to encourage Chinese aggression, and that he hoped the video would force the government to take a stronger line on the dispute (*Sankei Shimbun*, 6 September 2011). It seems likely that the departure from standard practice and precedent was orchestrated by China hawks within the DPJ. This created a major incident in which China responded with relatively severe measures. Meanwhile there was massive media coverage of anti-Japanese protests in China – as well as the YouTube video – which seems to indicate that the Chinese trawler deliberately rammed the JCG patrol vessels. In this way, the Japanese response to the territorial risk contributed to its ongoing recalibration, as Chinese actions – themselves triggered by Japan's breaking an agreement – apparently vindicated those seeking a tougher stance on the territorial dispute.

Less than two years later another China hawk, Ishihara Shintarō – who, as mentioned above, had participated in the 1997 trip to the islands – triggered a new crisis this time as governor of Tokyo. In April 2012 he announced plans for the metropolitan government to purchase the islands in order to 'protect' them as well as plans for stationing civil servants and constructing buildings (*Japan Times*, 18 April 2012). Whereas in 1996 when Ishihara first became involved in the dispute public interest was low, by 2012 a major recalibration had taken place such that the public fund set up to pay for the purchase received over 1.4 billion yen in donations. The DPJ government, now under Prime Minister Noda Yoshihiko, intervened and purchased the islands rather than allow Ishihara to gain control over them and provoke further flare-ups. However, from the Chinese point of view Japan acted to unilaterally alter the status quo of the dispute. The purchase triggered another wave of anti-Japanese street protests, whilst China stepped up its activities in the disputed waters, for the first time sending regular maritime surveillance patrols into the islands' territorial waters.

The timing of Noda's purchase was far from optimal, taking place two days after the prime minister had met Chinese president Hu Jintao, after which Hu was apparently under the impression that Noda would find an alternative solution (*Japan Times*, 20 November 2012). This poor timing served only to exacerbate an already difficult situation, although it is likely that the only way to prevent a flare-up was to find an alternative solution – the purchase at any time would have caused controversy. Indeed, it appears that even the US was privately urging Noda not to purchase the islands in order to prevent a major incident (*Japan

Times, 10 April 2013). However, Noda himself was no Asianist, leaning instead to a more traditionally conservative foreign policy: for example in 2004 during a flare-up in the dispute he proposed and passed the first ever lower house resolution calling on the Koizumi administration to take more steps to maintain Japan's 'inherent territory,' whilst criticizing China's claim as having 'no foundation' (*Asahi Shimbun*, 25 March 2004, 26 March 2004).

The change in Japan's calibration of and response to the territorial risk posed by China has been nothing short of dramatic. This is not to say that it took place in a domestic vacuum. Although the issue was seized upon by state and societal actors, including activists and politicians, a confirmation bias was at work: Chinese actions in the dispute often played into the China threat theory narrative, reconfirming the risk framing outlined here. China has gradually transformed the status quo of the disputed waters: once effectively controlled by Japan, they are now a sovereignty grey area (O'Shea 2012). In particular, China's severe responses in 2010 and 2012 could be cited as proof of precisely the kind of risk to Japan that China was supposed to present. As Figure 3.1 shows, these incidents were covered in an unprecedented manner in the media, and as Figure 0.1 shows, they correlate with all-time lows in Japanese public opinion toward China. However, although China's response was severe and led to further escalation in both 2010 and 2012, Japanese actors also played important roles in instigating and escalating both incidents. The Chinese fishing trawler did appear to ram the JCG patrol vessels, but Japan also broke an existing understanding in its moves to prosecute the trawler captain. The 2012 purchase took place not in retaliation to any specific Chinese act and thus was seen from the Chinese side as a unilateral Japanese move to strengthen its position in the dispute. Yet regardless of the complex interplay involved in the instigation and escalation of both incidents, China's behaviour was interpreted as confirming the risk recalibration, raising it even, to require a firmer Japanese response.

Japan's response, then, has moved from downplaying the dispute in the early and mid-1990s, to a more assertive position from approximately 1999 onwards, and finally to an assertive, arguably even provocative stance after Hatoyama's resignation. One key element of this response has remained the same since 1992: the 'no dispute exists' line. This precludes the possibility of negotiations, let alone a resolution of the dispute, and China has repeatedly called on Japan to acknowledge the dispute (*Japan Times*, 22 June 2013; *People's Daily Online*, 15 October 2012). Were Japan to acknowledge the dispute, so the logic goes, it would only reward Chinese pressure tactics and lead to further assertive measures. Moreover, acknowledging the dispute would harm Japan's bargaining position (although technically a bargaining position can only exist in a negotiation, which cannot take place without acknowledgement of the dispute). There may be an element of truth in this logic; however, as the next section shows, the risk approach adopted in this book expands the scope of harm, enabling us to consider this territorial harm in the context of the broader harm Japan's response to the territorial risk has caused.

4 Harm

As outlined in the introduction to this book, our focus here is not only on the construction and recalibration of risk, but also on the materialization of harm, both in terms of the manifestation of the risk itself as well as harm which may be caused by the response to the risk. In the case of territorial risk, the manifestation of the risk as harm has to some extent already taken place: where once Japan enjoyed relatively exclusive control over the disputed waters, China's policy of gradually increasing its presence has at this point greyed the issue of sovereignty and effective control. But what is the actual harm suffered by Japan as a result of this manifestation of risk? And what are the other potential harms that Japan's response is designed to mitigate? The obvious answer is loss of the disputed territory to China, but this requires elaboration: what are the islands and the surrounding waters worth? What are the other potential harms associated with Japan's response – specifically, what harms are actually consequences of Japan's approach? This section outlines the variety of actual and potential harm represented both by China's claims to and actions in the disputed maritime and island territories in the East China Sea as well as the actual and potential harms generated by Japan's response to the territorial risk.

4.1 Symbolic harm

We saw that China has gradually asserted control over the disputed waters but we have yet to consider the value of these disputed waters. The vast quantities of hydrocarbon deposits suggested by the 1968 survey never materialized. There are gas deposits; however, because of the distance and geographical obstacles to extraction and transportation they are of relatively less value to Japan (Drifte 2008). Perhaps more importantly, the current global fracking boom has caused a fall in global gas prices, reducing their value to both states. Indeed, the relative unimportance of the undersea deposits to Japan is highlighted by Japan's decision to refrain from exploration in the region until as recently as 2005, even as market actors (oil companies) petitioned for permission to test drill (see O'Shea forthcoming for a detailed discussion). Whilst the hydrocarbons may be of less consequence, the East China Sea has been described as 'one of the best fishing grounds in the world,' and represents an important food source for both Japan and China, as well as Korea and Taiwan (Nagamatsu 2009). In fact, the Chinese name for the disputed islands means 'fishing platform,' while the Japanese name of the largest island means 'fishing island.' Still, the dispute is not about fish: all littoral states have enjoyed access to the East China Sea over the past decades, and this is unlikely to change in the foreseeable future. The 2013 fishing agreement between Taiwan and Japan is an example of how the parties involved can continue to share the fisheries despite the fiery nationalism involved. Meanwhile the islands themselves are small, uninhabited and of almost no intrinsic economic value. In sum, the primary harm associated with the recalibration of risk is not economic harm.

Neither is the harm strategic: the size and location of the islands means that they are strategically of little significance (O'Shea forthcoming), and in any case the likelihood of a Chinese occupation of the islands remains very low (see below). Despite this, certain actors in Japan have suggested that the islands are strategically important, the logic being that China could use them as some form of base directed at Japan (Nishihara 2012). This ties into the broader idea of China as a threat to Japan, and suggests that the importance of 'protecting' the islands is not so much about the islands themselves as it is about standing up to China. The *'dai ippo'* remarks referred to earlier, in which a Chinese invasion of the disputed islands becomes the first step in an eventual invasion of the entire Japanese archipelago, are illustrative. The idea that China would eventually invade and subjugate Japan is usually associated with far right-wing activists. Right-wing politicians echo these sentiments, as mentioned in the introduction to this part of the book: in 2012 the head of the newly founded Japan Restoration Party *(Nippon Ishin no Kai)*, Ishihara, stated: 'We need to say no to China when necessary because I don't want Japan to be like Tibet, which has fallen under Chinese power' (*Japan Times*, 21 November 2011). Needless to say, a Chinese invasion of Japanese territory with the subsequent subjugation of Japan that would become an autonomous region of China is difficult to conceive of in the foreseeable future. In the end, then, the harm involved here is actually *symbolic* harm.

As we have seen, in the early 1990s the islands were of little concern to most Japanese citizens. However, the growth of the China threat theory together with the increasing media coverage of the dispute, not to mention the implementation of China's own policy on the islands, moved the dispute to centre stage. The dispute gradually made its way into school textbooks, with the islands introduced as 'our country's inherent territory' (*Asahi Shimbun*, 30 September 2006). Events such as the 2010 collision incident, together with the increasing maritime 'incursions,' led to the perception that Japan's sovereign territory was being invaded because of Japan's 'weak-kneed' response, and that Japan should stand up to China (Lhuillery 2012). This was visible not only in the usual places, such as Internet bulletin board 2-Channeru, but also in letters to newspapers and in general mainstream public discourse (*Asahi Shimbun*, 9 March 2006). This potential symbolic harm has developed, then, as a contrast between Japan appearing 'weak' and China appearing 'aggressive,' leading to questions about Japan's prestige, reputation and self-image. Links were even made between Japan's perceived weakness in the dispute and apparently completely unrelated fields: for instance, Takesada Hideshi, a Japanese professor at Yonsei University in South Korea, warned that 'a weak-kneed response will lead to similar results in other fields. China, for instance, may gain the upper hand in patent fights and other bilateral and regional disputes' (cited in Lhuillery 2012).

Whilst aspects of the territorial risk have materialized as harm, the harm of Chinese research or maritime patrol vessels operating in the disputed waters is very different from a Chinese occupation of the islands. The discussion of risk in the introduction to this book drew attention to how, theoretically speaking, an 'objective risk' is an oxymoron, and certainly the purpose of this book is not to make predictions. This does not, however, preclude all analysis of probabilities, specifically the probabilities of the materialization of the harm which forms the basis of the construction and recalibration of the risk under analysis; indeed, analysis indicates that the likelihood of a Chinese occupation of the islands is low for several reasons (O'Shea forthcoming). To start with, the economic value of the disputed territory is far less than originally expected and China is already developing existing East China Sea gas fields. Perhaps of more consequence is the coverage of the islands by the US-Japan Security treaty, meaning that the US would be obliged to defend them were China to act. For all the talk of China's military modernization, however, the combined strength of the Japan and US militaries is – and will remain for the foreseeable future – far greater than China's.

Perhaps more important than the deterrent effect is the fact that the fallout from a Chinese occupation of the islands would be particularly damaging. China is engaged in similar disputes in the South China Sea with the Philippines, Vietnam, Malaysia and Brunei, all of which follow events in the East China Sea closely. Since 2008, events in these disputes have tarnished the carefully crafted image of China's 'peaceful rise,' replacing it with the narrative of China's 'new assertiveness' – although questions remain as to what extent China has in fact become increasingly assertive (Johnston 2013; Jerdén 2014). Indeed, as we saw in the preceding section, in 2010 and 2012 China can be considered to have reacted to, rather than initiated, both of the crises involving the dispute. Regardless, the narrative of China's 'new assertiveness' is now in ascendancy with the result that China's reputation has taken a bruising and regional states remain wary of its intentions. In this context, the regional repercussions of an occupation of the islands would be devastating. China's economic growth is dependent upon exports, and the CCP's continued leadership is partially dependent upon providing economic growth (Downs and Saunders 1998). The regional instability in the aftermath of any such occupation would seriously damage both China's economy and, by extension, the position of the CCP – regardless of any short-term nationalism 'bump' (see below).[4]

4.2 Responses to harm

Despite the preceding analysis demonstrating the low probability of a Chinese occupation of the islands, this chapter has shown how the territorial risk has been recalibrated throughout the 1990s and especially since the 2000s, leading to a tougher response, which culminated in the 2010 and 2012 incidents. This risk recalibration and corresponding response has produced separate forms of harm, some of which are related to the harm the original risk was constructed to mitigate, whilst others are unrelated and appear to be unintended consequences. Perhaps the most obvious is the economic harm: the images of Chinese protesters attacking Japanese-branded cars and smashing Japanese restaurants (albeit many Chinese-owned) were broadcast around the world during the 2010 and 2012 incidents. In the 2012 incident Japanese businesses in China lost approximately US$120 million in property damage (Katz 2013).

The reality for both states is that their economies are deeply intertwined and interdependent. Moreover, this interdependency goes beyond a simple investment/consumption relationship, where Japan invests in China and the Chinese supply Japanese consumers with goods. Rather, the two economies are more deeply integrated, particularly in terms of production interdependence (Katz 2013). This economic relationship has shifted substantially over time: in the early 1990s Japan held all the cards as the major source of capital and technology for China's developing economy. Today, the tables have turned and there is a perception in China that 'Japan needs China more than China needs Japan' (Tiberghien 2012). However, the integrated nature of Sino-Japanese production means that China's economy is dependent not only on Japanese capital or technology but that entire production chains operate at the cross-border level. Still, private Chinese boycotts have been initiated – public ones would violate international trade laws – and various sectors of the Japanese economy have suffered. Chinese tourists have become an important market not only for Japan but also for the rest of Asia as well as Europe, and since 2010 and especially 2012 there has been a massive fall-off in the number of Chinese tourists travelling to Japan, some months showing an almost 50 per cent reduction in numbers compared to the same month the year before the 2012 incident (*The Japan Times*, 13 March 2013). Similarly, boycotts of Japanese products hit Japanese exports to China, with a 20 per cent overall decrease in the months after July 2012, with car sales being the worst-hit sector (Katz 2013).

The harm of the response to the territorial risk is not confined to the economic realm. Diplomatically, Japan has suffered harm as a result of its increasingly hard-line approach to the dispute. At first glance this might seem counter-intuitive, as Japan shares a territorial risk from China with several South and Southeast Asian states, and this shared risk has led to increased security cooperation and has arguably improved Japan's standing with states such as India, the Philippines and Vietnam. On the other hand, in its immediate neighbourhood Japan's approach to the dispute has undoubtedly caused it diplomatic harm closer to home. As mentioned earlier in the chapter, Taiwan also maintains a claim on the territory, and events in the dispute have frequently caused problems in Japan-Taiwanese relations. In fact, Japan is involved in territorial disputes with all of its neighbours in Northeast Asia: in the middle of the 2010 incident, Russian president Dmitri Medvedev made a historic visit to the Northern Territories/Kuril Islands, which have been under Russian administrative control since 1945 but which are also claimed by Japan.[5] To this day Japan refuses to formally end World War II by signing a formal peace treaty until Russia returns the islands. Medvedev's visit triggered a flare-up in Russo-Japanese relations, and afterwards he flew to Beijing to meet Chinese president Hu Jintao. The pair issued a joint statement criticizing Japan's position on historical issues, a clear reference to both territorial disputes (*Yomiuri Shimbun*, 29 November 2010). Meanwhile, Japan also disputes South

Korean control of a number of rocks in the Sea of Japan. As with the Senkaku/Diaoyu Islands, this dispute has become deeply symbolic and stirs up strong nationalist passions in Korea, to the extent that it has become the symbol of both Korean nationalism and anti-Japanese sentiment (Cha 1999). It is no exaggeration to say that these territorial disputes play a major role in Japan's continued separation from its immediate Asian neighbours, as discussed in the introduction to this book.

We saw in the previous section how Hatoyama, prime minister of the first DPJ administration, came to power with a foreign policy aimed at the reintegration of Japan into the region through the development of an East Asian community. Subsequent administrations have seen Japan's diplomatic relations with all of its Northeast Asian neighbours deteriorate while US-Japan relations have been strengthened. Indeed, although Hatoyama sought to reduce the burden of US troops on Okinawa, the recalibration of the territorial risk since 2010 has provided a powerful legitimating argument for the continued presence of US troops, and the Futenma relocation remains at a standstill (see Part III). This is despite the fact that, as pointed out in the introduction to the book, the marines deployed in Okinawa represented a forward fighting force rather than a defensive one. Thus, whilst Japan may be developing its security relations with South and Southeast Asian states such as India and the Philippines, it remains adrift from its nearest neighbours. The recalibration of territorial risk appears to be increasing this distance. Finally, on a human level the handling of the dispute by both governments has had highly negative consequences for interpersonal Sino-Japanese relations, as shown in Figure 0.1, and as evinced in the scale of the anti-Japanese protests in 2010 and 2012.

5 Conclusion

This chapter has traced the recalibration of risk with regard to the East China Sea territorial and maritime disputes. We saw that even after Japan shifted its position from 'shelving' to 'no dispute' in 1992, the risk recalibration remained relatively low despite the best efforts of both state and societal actors, such as right-wing politicians and activists, to publicize the issue. The dispute began to garner more attention after the turn of the millennium as domestic pressure on the Japanese government mounted in tandem with increased Chinese activity in the area and increased media coverage of the dispute. Yet it was not until the 2010 collision incident that China's behaviour in the dispute came to be widely seen as a grave risk to Japan's 'inherent territory.' To be sure, China's behaviour during the 2010 and 2012 incidents was unprecedented, yet both instances had their genesis in Japanese actions: the moves to prosecute the Chinese captain contravened a previous understanding, whilst the 2012 island purchase was a successful attempt by Governor Ishihara to derail Sino-Japanese relations. The irony here is that Japan's response to the territorial risk confirmed the ongoing recalibration, as the Chinese responses – themselves triggered by Japan's initial moves – vindicated those seeking a tougher stance on the dispute.

The East China Sea dispute is now the major source of bilateral friction in the Sino-Japanese relationship, and there is no question that Chinese actions have contributed to recent tensions, as illustrated by China's declaration of a new Air Defence Identification Zone in November 2013. Indeed, to an extent the risk represented by China's claim on the territory has become manifest, as China has successfully blurred the sovereignty issue and repeatedly changed the status quo. However, a key issue that is often overlooked in the discourse on the dispute is, what is the actual harm associated with this risk? What is the disputed area worth? As we saw in this chapter, the estimations of undersea oil and gas deposits have been dramatically revised down. The islands are tiny, of little historic or geographic importance or interest, and of little intrinsic value. Rather, they have a symbolic value which has grown in tandem with the deterioration of bilateral relations. Moreover, although China has blurred the sovereignty picture, its approach to the dispute is clear: a slow, long-term attempt to change the status quo. The rhetoric of a Chinese invasion, used by nationalists such as Ishihara, overlooks the fact that it is highly unlikely that China would occupy the islands for a variety of reasons, such as reputation, economic repercussions and the US–Japan alliance.

Thus the chapter argued that the harm which such nationalists refer to is in fact symbolic harm, associated with the idea that Japan's approach is 'weak,' whilst China is 'aggressive,' and that unless Japan stands up to China it will just reward and reinforce Chinese aggression. However, we saw that this is not the only harm associated with the dispute: both sides have suffered economic harm in a variety of fields, including both the tourist and the automobile industries. The recalibration of territorial risk has also played a role in the 'China threat' theory as outlined in the introduction to this part of the book – indeed the two appear to be in a mutually reinforcing relationship. In this way there is a much broader harm to the security of the everyday involved, visible in the expression of violent anti-Japanese sentiment in China as well as in Japanese perceptions of China and the Chinese – as demonstrated in the other three chapters of this part of the book. This leads us to the most serious potential harm: war. This chapter has argued that the likelihood of a Chinese occupation of the islands is low. However, that is not the only possible trigger for war. Indeed, a wide variety of Japanese media outlets have published various scenarios in which a small incident could spiral into a serious conflict (*Japan Times*, 7 December 2013). The preceding discussion of harms, potential and real, would fade into insignificance were any such conflict to take place.

Notes

1 Although not the focus of the chapter, Taiwan also claims the islands on same basis as China.

2 For a detailed analysis of jurisprudence and the East China Sea dispute, see O'Shea (forthcoming).
3 In recent years the question of whether the dispute was in fact 'shelved,' and the precise definition of the meaning of this term, has become a source of controversy. The current Abe administration, along with prominent opposition politicians such as Maehara Seiji, insist that the term 'shelved' was not used in 1978 or in 1972 (during the normalization negotiations), and that in fact the dispute was never shelved. This is part of the Japanese government's 'no dispute' position, since to admit shelving would imply admitting that there was something to shelve. Conversely, Nonaka Hiromu, former LDP chief cabinet secretary, who was a witness to the 1978 discussions, insists that he personally heard Prime Minister Tanaka Kakuei use the word 'shelve' during the 1972 normalization negotiations (*Asahi Shimbun*, 4 June 2013).
4 For a more detailed assessment of the likelihood of militarized conflict, see O'Shea (forthcoming).
5 For a risk approach to the Northern Territories dispute, see O'Shea (2015).

References

Cha, Victor (1999) *Alignment Despite Antagonism: The United States-Korea-Japan Security Triangle*, Stanford: Stanford University Press.

Downs, Erica Strecker and Philip C. Saunders (1998) "Legitimacy and the limits of nationalism: China and the Diaoyu Islands," *International Security*, 23, 3: 114–16.

Drifte, Reinhard (2008) "Japanese-Chinese territorial disputes in the East China Sea: Between military confrontation and economic cooperation," LSE Asia Research Centre Working Paper no. 24. Available online at: http://www.lse.ac.uk/collections/asia ResearchCentre/pdf/WorkingPaper/ARCWorkingPaper24Drifte2008.pdf. Accessed 1 February 2014.

——— (2013) "The Senkaku/Diaoyu Islands territorial dispute between Japan and China: between the materialization of the 'China threat' and Japan 'reversing the outcome of World War II'?" NISCI Discussion Papers, No. 32, May. Available online at: http://international.uiowa.edu/files/international.uiowa.edu/files/file_uploads/drifte_senkaku_article_1.pdf. Accessed 1 December 2013.

Emery, Kenneth O., Yoshikazu Hayashi, Thomas W. C. Hilde, Kazuo Kobayashi, Ja Hak Koo, C. Y. Meng, . . . Sung Jin Yang. (1969) "Geological structure and some water characteristics of the East China Sea and the Yellow Sea," Economic Commission for Asia and the Far East, Committee for Co-ordination of Joint Prospecting for Mineral Resources in Asian Offshore Areas Technical Bulletin, 2: 4–41.

Hagström, Linus (2012) "'Power shift' in East Asia? A critical reappraisal of narratives on the Diaoyu/Senkaku Islands incident in 2010," *Chinese Journal of International Politics*, 5, 3: 267–97.

Hughes, Christopher W. (2010) "The Democratic Party of Japan's new (but failing) grand security strategy: from 'reluctant realism' to 'resentful realism'?" *Journal of Japanese Studies*, 38, 1: 109–40.

Jerdén, Björn (2014) "The assertive China narrative: why it is wrong and how so many still bought into it," *Chinese Journal of International Politics*, 7, 1: 47–88.

Johnston, Alastair Iain (2013) "How new and assertive is China's new assertiveness?" *International Security*, 37, 4: 7–48.

Katz, Richard (2013) "Mutually assured production: why trade will limit conflict between China and Japan," *Foreign Policy*. Available online at: http://www.foreignaffairs.com/articles/139451/richard-katz/mutual-assured-production. Accessed 1 November 2013.

Lhuillery, Jacques (2012) "Japan's island disputes show malaise," *The China Post*, 21 August. Available online at: http://www.chinapost.com.tw/commentary/afp/2012/08/21/351660/p1/Japan's-island.htm. Accessed 9 September 2013.

Nagamatsu, Kimiaki (2009) "By-catch discards from a bottom trawl in the East China Sea," *Journal of National Fisheries University*, 58, 1: 73–82. Available online at: http://www.fish-u.ac.jp/kenkyu/sangakukou/kenkyuhoukoku/58/01_10.pdf. Accessed 30 August 2013.

Nishihara, Masashi (2012) "Japan should stand firm on the Senkaku Islands dispute," *AIJSS-Commentary No. 164*, 6 November.

O'Shea, Paul (2012) "Sovereignty and the Sino-Japanese maritime and territorial dispute," EIJS, Stockholm School of Economics Working Paper No.240, September 2012. Available online at: http://swopec.hhs.se/eijswp/papers/eijswp0240.pdf. Accessed 1 December 2013.

——— (2014) "Overestimating the 'power shift': the role of the United States in the failure of the Democratic Party of Japan's 'Asia pivot,'" *Asian Perspective*, 38, 3: 435–59.

——— (2015) "Static risks and Japan's policy on the Northern Territories," in Sebastian Maslow, Ra Mason and Paul O'Shea (eds) *Risk State: Japan's Foreign Policy Processes in an Era of Uncertainty*, Farnham: Ashgate.

——— (forthcoming) "How economic, strategic, and domestic factors shape patterns of conflict and cooperation in the East China Sea Dispute," *Asian Survey*.

Sakurai, Yoshiko (2013) "How should Japan protect the Senkaku Islands from possible Chinese military attack?," Yoshiko Sakurai Official Web Site, Column. Available online at: http://en.yoshiko-sakurai.jp/2013/06/04/5412. Accessed 4 November 2013.

Tiberghien, Yves (2012) "Misunderstandings, miscommunication, and mis-signaling Senkakus thru Chinese eyes," *The Oriental Economist*, December.

UNCLOS (1982) United Nations Convention on the Law of the Sea, 1982. Available online at: http://un.org/Depts/los/convention_agreements/texts/unclos/closindx.htm. Accessed 8 April 2015.

4
IMMIGRATION AND THE DEMOGRAPHIC CRISIS

1 Introduction

In July 2014 the Japanese Supreme Court determined that non-Japanese nationals with permanent residency status are ineligible for welfare benefits. The case had been taken to the highest court in the land by an eighty-two-year-old ethnically Chinese resident, born and raised in Japan, who had been previously denied benefits by her municipality. In practice, the decision as to whether or not to provide these benefits remains up to the local municipalities; however, the ruling served to illustrate the precarious position of the hundreds of thousands of non-Japanese residents living out their lives in Japan, and to highlight their marginalization and lack of full legal and social rights. Moreover, with Japan facing a looming demographic crisis, the case raised serious questions as to Japan's attitude to migrant labour – only a month previously Prime Minister Abe Shinzō had appeared on television stating that 'in countries that have accepted immigration, there has been a lot of friction, a lot of unhappiness both for the newcomers and the people who already live there' (*Financial Times*, 2 June 2014). To emphasize his anti-immigration stance, the prime minister held up a white sign with a large red 'X.' Immigration is a controversial issue in all industrially developed democratic states and ultimately the decision to either welcome or strictly regulate immigration is one determined by the citizens of the state and their representatives. This chapter however does not *a priori* take the position that Japan should or should not relax its strict immigration policy; rather it focuses on how immigration – and immigration from China, in particular – has been constructed as a risk to the everyday security of the population, as illustrated by the framing of Chinese immigrants in the context of crime and public safety.

The chapter begins with a discussion of multiculturalism and the 'myth of homogeneity,' followed by a short history of Chinese immigration to Japan, which focuses on Chinese immigrants' socio-economic status and treatment from the late Meiji period to today. We then move to the issue of crimes committed by Chinese immigrants, and especially how this risk has been recalibrated beyond any statistical correlation with actual crime statistics. After this we discuss how the strict immigration policy – the result of the response to this highly calibrated risk – has resulted in harm to Chinese immigrants and to Japanese citizens themselves. Finally, the chapter concludes by considering the extent of the potential social and economic harm to which Japan has exposed itself as a result of the combination of a strict immigration policy coupled with a rapidly aging society. Although this final section goes beyond the narrower focus on China, we return to the question of Chinese immigration in the conclusion, noting the win-win possibilities of Chinese immigration for both states, whilst maintaining a realistic perspective on the difficulties it might create. Focusing on Chinese immigration makes sense not only in terms of the perceived 'China threat' outlined at length earlier in this part of the book, but also because Chinese immigration is an understudied phenomenon – the Korean community in Japan has been the most researched to date because of its historical size and importance. However, since 1978 the number of Chinese immigrants has exploded and Chinese citizens are now the largest non-Japanese group in the country with 682,302 Chinese residents as compared to 519,737 Koreans as of December 2013.[1]

2 Immigration, multiculturalism and the 'myth of homogeneity'

It has become a cliché to argue that Japan is today a 'multicultural society.' The scholarly effort to dispel the 'myth of homogeneity,' that is, the idea that the Japanese population was/is racially and culturally unique and uniform, risked reducing the concept of multiculturalism to meaning little more than variance within the population, something which Japan – as with any other state – has in abundance (Oguma 1995; Burgess 2007). Despite the rhetoric of *tabunka kyōsei* (multicultural co-existence), Japan is not particularly multicultural in form and absolutely not in policy: postwar state practice has been to tightly regulate immigration to ensure that few migrants arrive on Japan's shores, and those that do (1) are required by the labour market, and (2) are to return to their home countries after a period of time. Koreans and Chinese, by far the largest groups, represent a combined total of approximately 1 per cent of the population, and as outlined below most of these remain unnaturalized, thus without full civil, political or social rights (hereafter 'citizenship rights'). There are, of course, exceptions, such as the South American *Nikkei* (descendants of Japanese emigrants) who were invited to Japan in the 1990s, although this group of foreigners was invited precisely because the *Nikkei* were perceived not as foreigners but as ethnic Japanese. State policy is fundamentally anti-multicultural: rather than the 'ethnic pluralism' of settler countries such as the US or Canada, or the 'assimilation' which typified twentieth-century Britain and France, Japan, like Germany, engages in 'differential exclusion' in which immigrants are seen as a necessary evil required by the economy but are prevented from attaining full citizenship rights (Yamanaka 2008).

The result of this kind of immigration policy – and the even stricter policies operated under the Tokugawa Shogunate – is that Japan is not as culturally or ethnically diverse a state when compared to other similarly sized industrially developed democratic states such as the UK or France. To say that Japan is not multicultural in its immigration and citizenship policy is not to say that it is mono-ethnic or mono-cultural: in both the prewar and postwar periods Japan has attracted hundreds of thousands of immigrants, legal and illegal, and remains an attractive destination for nationals of many neighbouring countries – not to mention the older minorities, such as Okinawans and Burakumin. Yet despite the presence of these groups, the aforementioned 'myth of homogeneity' remains strong: in 2005 former prime minister and then minister of internal affairs, Asō Tarō (now current minister of finance) described Japan as being the only country on earth that has "one nation, one civilization, one language, one culture, and one race" (*Asahi Shimbun*, 16 October 2005). In 2008, then minister of education Nakayama Nariaki made similar comments (Reuters, 27 September 2008), as did one of his predecessors in the same ministry, Ibuki Bunmei, in 2007 (*Japan Times*, 26 February 2007). Although some politicians, notably Kōno Tarō, struggle against this myth, the reality is that it has long pervaded Japanese society and forms the everyday social context in which immigrants and long-term non-Japanese residents live their lives.

3 Chinese in Japan

Ethnic Chinese residents in Japan can be divided into two groups: the prewar 'oldcomers' and their descendants and the postwar 'newcomers' (Chen 2008).[2] The vast majority of oldcomers are the descendants of those who moved to Japan during the period after the Meiji Restoration until 1945 – though there had been a few thousand Chinese merchants based in Nagasaki during the Tokugawa period. These oldcomers tended to cluster around established Chinatowns, or at least in cities which contain these Chinatowns, such as Kobe, Yokohama and Nagasaki. After the 1871 Sino-Japanese Friendship and Trade Treaty, Chinese were granted extraterritorial rights in Japan in a similar fashion to Western residents and lived in the foreign settlements. However, by the end of the nineteenth century there was already a nationwide debate on Chinese immigration, which was played out using conventions that are familiar to us today: Chinese immigrants might outcompete Japanese workers, introduce bad habits and lax morals, and dilute Japanese blood, thereby compromising the traditional Japanese spirit (Yamawaki 2000). The parameters of the debate ranged from calls to expel all Chinese living in Japan to granting Chinese the same rights as citizens of Western states with whom Japan had signed treaties allowing freedom of movement, residence and occupation. In the end, the solution was somewhere in the middle: in 1899 the Meiji government introduced Imperial Ordinance No. 352, allowing Chinese immigrants to live and work within the foreign settlements but proscribing such activities beyond their gates.

Aside from the merchants, these prewar immigrants worked in a number of specific trades, commonly known as the 'three knives' or *san-ba-dao*: chef, barber and tailor (Dongying 2011). As the Japanese economy boomed in the 1920s, Japan's Chinese population began to increase, with both legal and illegal labourers making the journey across the East China Sea. However, the reception in Japan remained hostile. There were a number of labour incidents in which deadly fights broke out between the Chinese and their Japanese counterparts, and hundreds of Chinese immigrants were also killed in the aftermath of the Great Kantō Earthquake in 1923 (Yamawaki 2000). With the beginning of Japanese encroachment on the mainland, Chinese conscripted labourers were brought to work for Japan's war industries. Apart from these voluntary and forced labourers, after China's defeat in the First Sino-Japanese War (1894–5) many tens of thousands of students went to Japan as part of an effort by the Qing government to emulate Japan's successful modernization. Among these students were many who would later become key figures in China's tumultuous twentieth century, including Zhou Enlai and Chiang Kai-shek (Dongying 2011). As we will see shortly, a similar movement of students took place after the 1978 Treaty of Peace and Friendship and Deng Xiaoping's concomitant economic reforms.

At the beginning of the postwar era, as in the Meiji period, Japan had to determine the status of the Chinese and Koreans who remained resident in Japan but were not Japanese citizens. Those who remained were stripped of voting rights, welfare and pensions, and an alien registration system was implemented to regulate and govern the population (Chapman 2008). Despite this, today many of these oldcomers are business owners and part of the middle class – the old Chinatowns are no longer ghettos but tourist attractions (Chen 2008). The newcomers, those who arrived after 1978, are a more diverse group. With China's opening up came a major top-down drive to encourage students to study abroad. Today Chinese students can be found in large numbers in almost all affluent countries, and Japan has been the largest recipient of 'educationally-channeled Chinese migrants' (Coates 2013: 9). Their numbers include not only traditional university students but also vocational and language ones as well. Those with a high level of education have been able to secure stable and well-paid employment. Rather than live in ghettos, these Chinese reside in the suburbs of major cities alongside middle-class Japanese (Chen 2008). However, these elite students do not represent the majority of Chinese in Japan. A large number of students attend language schools, some of which are fronts that provide the students with an initial visa to enter the country, after which they join the labour market, usually working in sectors with low pay and poor conditions (Dongying 2011; Coates 2013).

The trainee programme *(kenshū seido)* – which ostensibly is to provide on-the-job training) – has also brought tens of thousands of Chinese labourers to Japan to work in low-skilled, low-paid jobs in more remote areas of the country where employers struggle to find local labour (outlined in more detail later in the chapter;

see also Chen 2008: 43). Individuals from both groups frequently overstay their visas and pose risks to regulation and governance by continuing to work illegally. Because they are illegal immigrants it is impossible to state their numbers with certainty: according to the Ministry of Justice (MOJ) the number of illegal Chinese immigrants has been decreasing steadily since 2004 (when there were over 30,000), whereas today the ministry estimates the number is as few as 7,807 (MOJ 2014), though these figures are likely to be conservative. Despite the different forms of visas and different motivations for entry to Japan, many of the risks and challenges faced by these newcomers are the same: Coates (2013) describes 'mobility' as the primary marker of these newcomers, 'rather than classificatory terms such as migrant, tourist, student or labourer' (2013: 7). That is to say, the migration motivations are varied and banal; it is not the case that millions of Chinese are desperately seeking to move to Japan at all costs. Chinese immigrants face similar risks and challenges and have similar aspirations regardless of their visa status, and as such Coates (2013) considers this 'mobility' as something best interpreted as a banal form of 'everyday practice' (2013: 8).

Similarly, despite their different legal statuses, both the oldcomers and the newcomers face common risks and challenges in their everyday lives in Japan. The pervasive myth of homogeneity erects obstacles to integration, whilst the perception of Chinese as criminals does not differentiate between pre- and post-war arrivals. Still, given their temporary status and circumscribed legal rights, the trainees, students and illegal immigrants obviously face more hurdles than the oldcomers. This is not to say that the oldcomers do not experience significant risks to the security of the everyday as a result of their status – after all, the eighty-two-year-old woman who lost her social welfare case in the Supreme Court was born in Japan in the early 1930s. Where necessary the rest of the chapter explicitly differentiates between the old and newcomers, otherwise the term 'Chinese immigrants' refers to both groups, regardless of birthplace or length of residence in Japan.

3.1 Chinese and other foreigner crimes

Japan has long been famous amongst criminologists for its remarkably low crime rate and is often described as 'the safest country in the world' (Leonardsen 2010: 6). Throughout the economic boom years it bucked the near universal trend of increasing crime rates correlating with increased urbanization and industrialization: whilst Western states saw sharp increases in crime in the postwar era, Japan's crime rate actually decreased from the 1950s until the 1990s. The maintenance of social and public order is the responsibility of the government in any state, and in Japan order has long been prioritized as a key public good, tied up in Japanese cultural norms and expectations. Thus it is unsurprising that immigrants, presumed ignorant of and unable to integrate into Japanese culture, would be feared as threats to social order and seen as likely to commit crime at a far higher rate than the Japanese themselves, in marked contrast to the US perception of crimes committed in Okinawa (see Chapter 10). Indeed, we have already noted that as early as the late nineteenth century Chinese immigrants were seen as a risk to governance and social order in Japan. Today *gaijin hanzai* or foreigner crime has become the major trope in the national discourse on immigration (Friman 2003), with Chinese crime often singled out as the most prevalent and heinous. Fear of immigrant or foreigner crime is hardly a Japanese phenomenon – the assumption that immigrants commit crime at a higher rate than the local population is more or less universal (Wortley 2009).

This section assesses the risk recalibration of Chinese crime in Japan by focusing on state and media actors. This is not to say that the generation of anti-immigrant sentiment is singularly a top-down process in Japan or elsewhere, but rather that in the Japanese context the state has historically played a major role in conditioning the public imagination of foreigners (Shipper 2005). This stretches back as far as the Tokugawa Shogunate and is evidenced in the words and deeds of the contemporary National Police Agency (NPA). Subsequently some media outlets have been vocal in their opposition to immigration as well as their desire to see closer governance of existing migrants. Conversely, at the societal level approximately 200 support groups have been set up by Japanese citizens to provide aid and information to immigrants – highly unusual given that in other states such groups are set up by the immigrants themselves (Shipper 2005). This section also considers how the state response to immigration in general and crime in particular serves to exacerbate the risks posed by immigrants, leading to further harm to Japanese citizens who are victims of these crimes as well as Chinese immigrants, the overwhelming majority of whom are law-abiding and simply wish to enjoy the security of the everyday.

Whilst Japan's crime rate was unusually low from the 1960s until the 1990s, it has increased since the bursting of the bubble as a result of growing *anomie* accompanying the two 'lost decades' (Leonardsen 2010). However, the perceived increase in the crime rate is far greater than the actual increase, with the risk of crime recalibrated by a combination of both the NPA and media actors together with the rise of victims' support movements (Hamai and Ellis 2006). Although cultural explanations are often cited by both Japanese and non-Japanese alike for the low crime rates in Japan, the reality is that favourable economic circumstances – exceptional economic growth coupled with a relatively equitable distribution of wealth – played a major role in keeping crime low (Leonardsen 2010). The high crime rates of the immediate postwar years support this claim, and the example of the methamphetamine or *hiropon* panic of the late 1940s and early 1950s serves to underscore how even then state and media actors attempted to single out immigrants as the culprits.

Hiropon refers to a brand name of medical methamphetamine, 'Philopon,' sold across Japan until 1945 (Alexander 2013).[3] Methamphetamines were widely used in the 1930s and 1940s by both military and civilian workers, and in the early postwar years usage spread across many sectors of society. In 1951 their use was restricted but black market imports, together with new production in clandestine laboratories, meant that they remained available. In the early 1950s *hiropon* addiction was involved in a number of heinous crimes, including the 1954 rape and murder of Hosoda Kyōko, a school child who was abducted when she left her classroom to use the bathroom (Kingsberg 2013). Although usage of *hiropon* amongst the US soldiers stationed in Japan was so high that the *Asahi Shimbun* labelled their military bases '*hiropon* bases,' the Supreme Commander for Allied Powers (SCAP) authorities as well as the Japanese bureaucracy and media sought to divert attention, instead focusing on China, which was depicted by some as a 'narco-state' (Kingsberg 2013: 146). Today North Korea is seen as the narco-state, as Chapter 8 makes clear (also see Chapter 10 for a discussion of US crimes in Okinawa). Although Koreans, Chinese, Americans and Japanese were involved in the drug trade, *sankokujin* (a derogatory term used to describe people from both China and Korea who remained in Japan after 1945) were singled out by both the police and the media as drug dealers. This was very much connected to the broader debate over the future of people from the former colonies in Japan (for details, see Morris-Suzuki 2006). Eventually, after an extensive and graphic anti-*hiropon* campaign, matched by harsh sentences for use and distribution, together with an economic upswing, the number of users began to decline.

The connection between foreigners, especially Chinese foreigners, and crime faded somewhat during the boom years only to be revived in dramatic fashion in the 1990s, as the era of *gaijin hanzai* began. As we have seen, the 1990s and 2000s saw a dramatic increase in the perceived risk of crime in general in Japan. This risk recalibration was partially produced by the police and the popular press. Hamai and Ellis (2006) describe the phenomenon as a 'moral panic,' and part of this process involved the perception that especially violent crimes such as murder were becoming commonplace, despite evidence that death from violence in the 1990s and 2000s was substantially lower than it had been in the 1980s (32). Nevertheless, overall crime did increase in post-bubble Japan, and so did crime by non-Japanese. Perhaps, unsurprisingly, the latter received a disproportionate amount of coverage. One study of coverage of 'foreigner crime' concluded that crime by non-Japanese was almost five times more likely to be reported than crime by Japanese (Mabuchi 2001).

Reporting on the *gaijin hanzai* phenomenon came in various flavours. On the lower end of the scale, it manifested itself simply as increased and disproportionate coverage of ordinary crimes committed by non-Japanese, as we have just seen. However, it was also adopted and developed by right-wing nationalists, especially those seeking to demonize China. Former Tokyo governor, current Diet member and leader of the Party for Future Generations, Ishihara Shintarō provides an illustrative example: in 1999 he stated that 'there are extremely large numbers of crimes committed by Chinese who are illegally in Japan,' before going on to say, 'I don't know how the Chinese government understands this, but rather than extending aid to the country that makes nuclear bombs, [Japan] should spend it on public safety in Japan and anti-Chinese criminal measures' (quoted in Akaha 2008: 9). This quote exemplifies the risk construction and multiple connections between the China threat and Chinese immigration. In Chapter 2 on environmental risks, we saw how environmental aid to China, which would serve to mitigate harm to Japanese citizens who may suffer harm as a result of transboundary pollution, was portrayed in terms of the China threat, thus making aid to China equivalent to funding the enemy and its military modernization. Here we see a similar process: China is the source of illegal immigrants who commit crimes against the Japanese. Japan should respond, then, by using its resources *against* these immigrants. In 2001 Ishihara used his *Sankei Shimbun* column to warn Japan of the dangers of Chinese immigrants and their genetic propensity to commit crime. In a tone reminiscent of the immigration debate at the close of the nineteenth century, he wrote that the kind of criminally disposed deoxyribonucleic acid (DNA) of Chinese people could spread throughout Japanese society, changing its fundamental nature (*Sankei Shimbun*, 8 May 2001).

Although (deliberately) controversial, Ishihara's extreme comments on Chinese immigration and crime do not make him an outlier. In 2003 Kanagawa governor Matsuzawa Shigefumi announced to an election rally that 'foreigners are all sneaky thieves' and noted the 'marked increase in the number of cases in which some foreigners . . . remain in the country illegally to commit heinous crimes' (*Japan Times*, 7 November 2011). A similar attitude appears to be pervasive within certain state agencies. The NPA and the MOJ statistics are used to make the linkage between foreigners and crime and are artificially inflated and selectively portrayed in order to 'convey the greatest sense of foreign threat' (Friman 1996: 971). Furthermore, although there are stand-out incidents such as the Fukuoka murders (outlined below), in reality approximately half of the recorded crimes committed by non-permanent resident foreigners involve visa violations (Shipper 2005). Visa-related crimes are not necessarily differentiated from crimes against persons or property; indeed, foreigners not carrying their alien registration card are subject to arrest as criminals. As with politicians, NPA officials also make deeply discriminatory remarks about the extent of non-Japanese involvement in crime. According to the deputy superintendent of Ueno police station, 'It is safe to assume that foreigners are committing a lot more crimes because unless you arrest them you never know' (*International Herald Tribune/Asahi*, 14 December 2002). Similar comments have been made by both local and high-ranking police officers, and often form the basis of local crime-fighting policy. Shipper (2005) cites an example of Tokyo metropolitan police posters captioned 'Apartment break-ins occur frequently. If you think [the person] is Chinese, call [the police at] 110. If you hear them speaking Chinese . . . call 110' (313).

The early to mid-2000s saw the peak of the *gaijin hanzai* boom, taking perhaps its most extreme form in a magazine published in 2007, *Gaijin Hanzai Ura Fairu* (Secret files on crimes by foreigners). The magazine was full of xenophobic rhetoric and graphically illustrated depictions of crimes committed by citizens of various nations, but especially Chinese. Of the six criminal cases outlined in the magazine, four were committed by Chinese, conveniently illustrated with a PRC flag beside each subheading. The 2003 murder of a Japanese family in Fukuoka by three Chinese students was covered over a six-page spread, in which the murderers were depicted as sadists extracting pleasure from their crimes, and ended by pointing out that this kind of action is unthinkable to Japanese people, leaving the reader with the rhetorical question, 'Is it because the accused are Chinese that they can so easily murder people?' The murder was undoubtedly both chilling and gruesome and played into the narrative framework of China – and by extension Chinese people – as posing risks to the everyday security of the Japanese people. Japan is hardly immune to shocking mass murder – we learnt in Chapter 1 of the curry poisoning murders in Wakayama in 1999 by a Japanese national – but the Fukuoka murder received blanket media coverage, no doubt precisely because the perpetrators were Chinese. Today the media hype around crime by Chinese immigrants has calmed somewhat, although this is partly because of the normalization of its disproportionate coverage. Chinese gangs have established themselves in Japan, and do account for almost half of the crime committed by non-Japanese residents (Rankin 2012). Contrary to media reports, however, for the most part these gangs are not part of high-level international crime syndicates, but rather are small-time criminals based in Japan.

In sum, state and media actors have successfully recalibrated the perceived risk of criminal activity by Chinese immigrants in Japan. Again, the association of immigrants or indeed ethnic minorities and crime is not unique to Japan; rather, the 'myth of immigrant criminality' is pervasive in immigrant-receiving countries (Wortley 2009: 349). Chinese immigrants do commit crime: Chinese gangs operate in Japan, and as in the Fukuoka case, Chinese nationals have been involved in heinous crimes against Japanese people. However, the perceived risk as portrayed in the media and as announced by politicians and state agencies bears little resemblance to the actual Chinese crime rate. It should be repeated that this goes for both crime committed by people of Chinese *and* Japanese descent, although again it is crime committed by the Chinese which is most disproportionately portrayed. The next section outlines how Japan's response to the risks posed by immigrants – such as crime and the loss of national identity – has produced an immigration system which propagates harm. This harm is experienced primarily by the immigrants themselves. As we shall see, the response mounted in order to regulate and govern crime, however, also produces harm for Japanese citizens, too.

4 Harm to Chinese immigrants

The state response to the risk of immigration in general, and Chinese immigration in particular, produces further harm to the security of the everyday for the immigrants. Everyday life for illegal immigrants involves uncertainty and risk. They live clandestinely, taking jobs with poor working conditions and long hours. Given the precarious nature of existence for many illegal immigrants – often the first to lose their job in a crisis – in post-bubble Japan, combined with the ongoing crackdown on illegal immigrants, many have turned to petty drug dealing to earn a living (Friman 1996). These illegals represent the street front of much larger Japanese-organized crime gangs. The street-level dealers face a far higher risk of arrest and prosecution than do the far more numerous behind-closed-doors *Yakuza* organizations that employ them. In simple terms, 'foreigners are more likely to be arrested for drug crimes than Japanese' (Friman 1996: 976). The fact that such foreigners, because of their precarious position, are more likely to turn to crime creates further harm to Japanese citizens themselves. Indeed, cross-national research indicates that levels of immigrant crime differ according to the treatment of those immigrants in the host society. States with higher barriers to entry, and which discourage permanent settlement, have higher rates of immigrant crime than more open states (Wortley 2009). Japan, with its system based on differential exclusion, therefore, experiences a higher rate at least in part as a result of how the immigration system itself is used to regulate and govern immigrants.

Beyond increasing the likelihood of crime, the response to this highly recalibrated risk continues to produce other harm for immigrants. Differential exclusion, the basis of the system which led to denial of social welfare benefits to the Chinese octogenarian outlined in the introduction to this chapter, is justified through the public attitudes to immigration, which themselves are partially a product of over-reporting by the media and misrepresentation by state agencies such as the NPA. The regulation and governance of non-Japanese through a differential registration system, where all non-Japanese, including permanent and second generation residents, are registered as foreigners, poses risks to the exercise of rights by immigrants and their offspring. Until 2012 foreigners were ineligible to apply for residency registration *(jūminhyō)*, with the result that foreigners marrying Japanese essentially did not exist. For instance, Chapman cites the example of Lee Hong-jun, a *Zainichi* Korean who married a Japanese woman and had two children. Since Lee was neither registered on the family register *(koseki)* nor the *jūminhyō*, he did not exist as the children's parent. He existed only on the alien registration card. The effect of this form of regulation and governance was that, in Lee's view, the state saw him as an unrelated man living together with a woman and her children (Chapman 2008).

Although Japan's immigration policy does allow the *Zainichi* Koreans and Chinese to remain indefinitely, albeit with restricted legal and political rights, the policy is fundamentally designed to regulate or indeed prevent the influx of potential permanent residents. As we have seen, the basic policy is to allow workers to enter Japan for a limited period and then to return to their home countries. The primary source of overseas workers is the trainee programme *(kenshū seido)*. A special temporary visa was set up in 1981 with relatively 'strict rules ensuring that only larger companies were eligible and that even these companies were limited in the number of trainees they could hire (Shipper 2008). Reforms in 1991 established the Japan International Training Cooperation Organization (JITCO), under whose auspices the trainees would be recruited and deployed within Japan (Shipper 2008). Initially envisaged as a genuine programme for the transfer of skills and technology to developing countries, the programme has morphed into a guest-worker system. The majority of participants come from China: in 2012 of the 44,897 admitted, 35,004 were Chinese (JITCO 2013).

Urbanization, together with Japan's strict policy for regulating and governing immigrants, had left small and medium sized companies located in peripheral regions facing a labour shortage. To this end, the trainee programme was modified to enable these companies to hire the trainees as effectively unskilled labourers (Tsuda 2001). Rather than learning skills to bring back to their home countries, the trainees were performing repetitive tasks in industries that failed to attract domestic workers because of their reputation as involving the three K's: *kitanai* (dirty), *kiken* (dangerous) and *kitsui* (demanding) (Shipper 2008). Furthermore, the trainee status meant that, since they were not regarded as regular employees, employers did not have to pay a full wage but rather a much smaller trainee allowance. In order to get into the programme potential applicants pay local brokers as much as US$7,300, and some employers confiscate passports, others charge high rents for tiny but mandatory accommodations, whilst still others simply withhold payment (US State Department 2014). Even more extreme, reports indicate that some workers are forced to work sixteen-hour shifts, are fined for toilet breaks, and have up to half of their pay lodged into bank accounts in their name but which they cannot access (Shipper 2008). Of course, not all trainees suffer these kinds of harm through the programme. However, even Japan's number one partner and ally, the US, has repeatedly criticized the programme in its annual Trafficking in Persons Report (US State Department 2014). The report states that trainees 'are subjected to conditions of forced labour' and that the programme lacks 'effective oversight or means to protect participants from abuse' (2014: 221–2). Coupled with the government's failure to address its sex-trafficking problem, the issues with the trainee programme resulted in the US giving Japan a 'tier 2' ranking, putting it alongside states such as Ethiopia and Haiti.

5 Demographic risks and economy

Japan's decision to maintain the trainee programme as a source of unskilled labour rather than initiate immigration reform is not only characteristic of its immigration policy as outlined thus far, but also provides a segue into the final section of this chapter: the demographic risks facing Japan and the policy options available to forestall massive economic contraction. The extent of Japan's population crisis has been the subject of much international media hyperbole, and declining fertility rates are hardly unique to Japan: industrially developed states across the globe have seen their fertility rates decline steeply, in most cases below replacement rates (the number of children required to maintain the present population). What makes the Japanese case particularly acute is the combination of the strict regulation and governance of immigrants and the long duration of the low fertility rate – it first fell below replacement rate in the late 1950s, and has remained below it since 1974 (UN Demographic Yearbooks, various years). As repeated attempts to stall the declining birthrate continue to fail, the government appears left with little choice but to open its doors to increasing numbers of immigrants simply in order to help to maintain its economy and provide care for its increasingly greying population. However, fierce resistance to immigration remains, with faith placed instead in solutions such as mechanization of care and introducing more women into the workplace.

Some Japanese agencies recognize that these measures are insufficient to avoid a nationwide crisis in the coming years. The National Institute of Population and Social Security Research (IPSS), a state research body under the MHLW, describes Japan as facing a future 'super-aged society . . . the first experience in human history' (Morita 2014). A recent IPSS report projected that Japan's population would fall from 128,057 in 2010 to 107,276 in 2040 (IPSS 2013) – a decrease of 16.3 per cent. Furthermore, the percentage of the population over sixty-five will increase from 23 per cent in 2010 to 36.1 per cent in 2040. In rural prefectures such as Akita and Kochi those percentages will reach 43.8 per cent and 40.9 per cent respectively. Currently, 11.1 per cent of Japanese residents are over seventy-five. Simply put, in a few years two out of every five Japanese residents will be over the current retirement age, and one fifth of the population will be already over seventy-five. The combination of extremely low immigration, high life expectancy and rapidly aging population means that the current population trends in Japan are unsustainable.

Earlier in the chapter we outlined the historical, and to some extent the contemporary, resistance to immigration. Recent survey research suggests that, despite the demographic pressures and associated potential harms (see below), the majority of Japanese remain fundamentally opposed to opening the door to more migrants (Richey 2010). Those who support immigration tend to encourage assimilation and have a more accurate understanding of the extent of immigrant crime, whilst those opposed tend to focus on 'essentialist difference' and are hostile to assimilation as 'it violates their belief in Japanese uniqueness,' as well as having exaggerated views of the extent of immigrant crime (2010: 197). Ironically, whilst elsewhere in the world assimilationist stances are unfavourably compared to multicultural ones in terms of support for immigration, in Japan assimilationism correlates positively with pro-immigration sentiment. Either way, surveys indicate that the general public remains opposed to immigration and this opposition is founded in both the fear of crime and the desire to preserve cultural identity (Richey 2010). Research does suggest that less hostile attitudes to immigration can be found amongst young people (Llewelyn and Hirano 2009), albeit in terms of population and representation they also make up smaller proportions with lower voter turnout.

The issue of elderly care in light of the rapidly aging population has prompted various state-level responses. A programme to import Filipino and Indonesian nurses has had very limited success because of tiny numbers and the difficulties involved in passing required exams administered in Japanese – the 2013 pass rate was below 10 per cent (*Asahi Shimbun*, 26 March 2013). The mechanization of elderly care through the development and utilization of robots has been put forward as an alternative to increased immigration. In fact in 2013 Prime Minister Abe Shinzō announced a plan for spending 2.39 billion yen to subsidize twenty-four companies with the aim of producing 'nursing care robot equipment' (*Japan Times*, 19 June 2013). Some robots are already in use in nursing homes: Paro, the therapeutic seal – a robot designed to provide emotional comfort – is used not only in Japan but also in Denmark (Denmark Technical Institute 2014). However, when it comes to more advanced caregiving, Japan is a pioneer. Humanoid robots such as Palro, capable of playing games and dancing, are also used in nursing homes. The money earmarked by the Abe administration is aimed at taking these robots beyond the provision of social and emotional contact to the actual delivery of physical care such as lifting as well as tracking the location of residents in care homes. Although some research shows that residents have responded positively to the kind of assistive social robots such as Paro and Palro, the evidence remains limited and inconclusive (Broekens *et al*. 2009).

The widespread introduction of robots in elderly care creates grave potential harm. In Akita in 2040, 28.4 per cent of the population will be over seventy-five. The government response to the elderly care issue – robots rather than immigration – generates a rather chilling image of a depopulated, aged and isolated rural Japan in which robot carers have replaced human contact. Sharkey and Sharkey (2012) identify several related ethical issues, from increased feelings of objectification to deception and infantilization. Although the authors conclude that, if used carefully, such robots could have positive effects, the fact remains that although 'someone in solitary confinement might benefit from being given a robot companion . . . they would benefit far more if they were offered a friendly social environment' (34). Furthermore, whilst inevitably robots will be used to provide basic care, the lack of human resources means they will eventually have to replace humans in other areas of employment, from convenience stores to local government offices. Apart from the further reduction of human contact this entails, the cold, hard economic fact is that robots are not consumers – they will not stimulate growth.

This leads us to another potential harm Japan faces in the coming decades: economic harm. By 2025 Japan's elderly dependency ratio will be substantially higher than any other country in the world: one elderly person will depend on two workers (Faruqee and Mühleisen 2003). Simulations based on current trends suggest that, from 2025 onwards, inflation adjusted Gross Domestic Product (GDP) will begin to decrease dramatically, also on a per capita basis, as the labour contraction will match the population contraction. Pensions and healthcare costs will require contributions to double over the next fifty years. Inevitably this will lead to reductions in public spending and investment and increases in both indirect and direct taxation, which will lead to further contractions in GDP. It will be impossible to maintain current living standards and will likely create the need to introduce new mechanisms of governance to address generational friction as the young are forced to shoulder the burden of supporting the increasing proportion of the elderly. Simulations on the effect of immigration on the Japanese economy suggest that, if Japan were to start admitting as many as 150,000 people per annum, this would have a major impact on living standards into the future (Shimasawa and Oguro 2010). Still, even with this relatively high level of immigration the government could not adequately provide welfare, and tax increases would still be required. More obviously, as this chapter has shown, such levels of immigration would be deeply unsettling for a large proportion of the Japanese population and would pose new risks in the regulation and governance of the population.

6 Conclusion

Imagining a Japan that opens its doors to immigration also requires imagining a source of all these immigrants. Despite its affluence relative to Southeast Asian states, Japan has a reputation as being a difficult society into which to settle. We have already seen the extent of the 'myth of homogeneity' and the widespread belief that immigrants would be unable to adapt to Japanese culture and norms. The Japanese language *is* very difficult – ranked by linguists in the most difficult language group, alongside Chinese. Indeed, we have already seen that the plan to import Filipino nurses failed because of the difficulties faced in learning the language needed to gain formal qualification as a nurse or carer. Moreover, as some Southeast Asian states become more affluent, they are beginning to witness their own decline in fertility rates. Malaysia, Thailand, Singapore and Vietnam are already below replacement levels. Indonesia is approaching replacement level. The governments of these states are unlikely to welcome the large-scale migration of their population, especially the more highly skilled workers, and this may produce diplomatic friction.

Here the conversation returns to China. Chinese immigrants in Japan do not face the same hurdles as, for example, Filipinos. The script is relatively easy for Chinese to read, making language learning far less time-consuming. Cultural barriers exist, of course, but are lower than those between Japan and Southeast Asia. Geographical proximity and multiple transport links allow for more mobility. Despite its own low fertility rate – largely a product of the now-relaxing one child policy – China is by all accounts overpopulated. As we saw in Chapter 2 (environmental risks) not only the cities, but even the countryside is heavily polluted. Supplies of clean water are decreasing as desertification increases. Cities are clouded in smog, and transport systems are crowded in the extreme. Property prices in many cities are beyond the reach of the average worker. Rents, too, are high. In short, life for many Chinese people is difficult. Chinese migration to Japan would then potentially benefit both countries.

Still, much of this chapter has outlined the difficulties faced by Chinese immigrants in Japan, many of which remain the same today as they were over one hundred years ago. It is unrealistic to expect these obstacles to disappear overnight. Indeed, as this part of the book has shown, the dominance of the 'China threat' narrative framework has led to increased demonization of China, its government and even its citizens. The various risks posed by Chinese immigration have been highly calibrated. Some market actors do advocate for increased immigration, most notably Keidanren, which regularly warns of the lack of domestic labour (*Japan Times*, 25 October 2014). However, both the state and societal spheres appear to largely share the same basic anti-immigration stance, despite the increasingly precarious demographic situation. This is partly a function of Japan's long history of seeking to minimize immigration, but also in the case of Chinese immigration, it is a function of the 'China threat.' China, for its part, has done little to ameliorate this. The patriotic education campaign and other state-sponsored nationalistic endeavours have produced a population with a strong anti-Japanese streak. It is perhaps wishful thinking, but it is possible that Chinese immigration to Japan could change this. Xenophobic and anti-immigration sentiment is almost always strongest amongst the individuals with the least contact with foreigners. Increased daily contact between Chinese and Japanese people has the potential then to improve mutual perceptions, at the same time as making a contribution to solving Japan's demographic crisis and even easing some of the difficulties in China. As with the possibilities for bilateral cooperation outlined in the environment chapter, the prerequisite for this win-win is delinking the everyday issues from the frosty state of bilateral relations.

Notes

1 Of the 681,402 residents, 648,078 are mainlanders whilst 33,324 are Taiwanese citizens. Part of the reason for the decline in the number of Koreans is the naturalization process, as Japan does not allow dual nationality and many of the second and third generation Koreans naturalize as Japanese (Ministry of Internal Affairs and Communications 2014).
2 They can also be divided according to nationality, i.e. Taiwanese or mainland. The number of mainlanders far outweighs the number of Taiwanese, and thus this chapter focuses on mainland immigration unless otherwise stated.
3 Methamphetamines were initially popular as they increased wakefulness and physical activity. At higher doses they can also induce euphoric highs – as well of course as subsequent extreme lows and severe withdrawal. It is also a highly addictive drug.

References

Akaha, Tsuneo (2008) "Immigration in Japan," paper presented at the *2nd Global International Studies Conference*, Ljubljana, 23–26 September. Available online at: http://www.wiscnetwork.org/ljubljana2008/papers/WISC_2008-430.pdf. Accessed 15 June 2014.
Alexander, Jeffrey W. (2013) "Japan's *hiropon* panic: resident non-Japanese and the 1950s meth crisis," *International Journal of Drug Policy*, 24, 3: 238–43.
Broekens, Joost, Marcel Heerink and Henk Rosendal (2009) "Assistive social robots in elderly care: A review," *Gerontechnology*, 8, 2: 94–103.

Burgess, Chris (2007) "Multicultural Japan? Discourse and the 'myth' of homogeneity," *The Asia Pacific Journal: Japan Focus*, 24 March. Available online at: http://www.japanfocus.org/-Chris-Burgess/2389. Accessed 8 November 2014.

Chapman, David (2008) "Tama-chan and sealing Japanese identity," *Critical Asian Studies*, 40, 3: 423–43.

Chen, Tien-shi (2008) "The increasing presence of Chinese migrants in Japan," in Shinji Yamashita, Makito Minami, David Haines, and Jeremy Edes (eds) *Transnational Migration in East Asia*, Osaka: National Museum of Ethnology, pp. 39–52.

Coates, Jamie (2013) "Everyday mobility: the normalization of China-Japan migratory flows and their 'everyday practice,'" *International Review of Social Research*, 3, 1: 7–26.

Denmark Technical Institute (2014) "Robotic sea's therapeutic effect on care," Danish Technological Institute Website. Available online at: http://www.dti.dk/services/robotic-seal-s-therapeutic-effect-on-care/26034. Accessed 8 November 2014.

Dongying, Fuji (2011) "A century of Chinese student migration to Japan," in Grace Liu-Farrer (ed.) *Labour Migration from China to Japan: International Students, Transnational Migrants*, London: Routledge, pp. 18–37.

Faruqee, Hamid and Martin Mühleisen (2003) "Population aging in Japan: demographic shock and fiscal sustainability," *Japan and the World Economy*, 15, 2: 185–210.

Friman, Richard H. (1996) "Immigrants and drugs in contemporary Japan," *Asian Survey*, 36, 10: 964–77.

—— (2003) "Informal economies, immigrant entrepreneurship and drug crime in Japan," *Journal of Ethnic and Migration Studies*, 27, 2: 313–33.

Hamai, Koichi, and Thomas Ellis (2006) "Crime and criminal justice in modern Japan: from re-integrative shaming to popular punitivism," *International Journal of the Sociology of Law*, 34, 3: 157–78.

IPSS (2013) "Regional population projections for Japan," National Institute of Population and Social Security Research.

JITCO (2013) "Todōfukenbetsu kokusekibetsu JITCO shien gaikokujin ginō jisshusei (1go) kenshūsei ninzū." Available online at: http://www.jitco.or.jp/about/data/y-trainee_nat.pdf. Accessed 2 September 2014.

Kingsberg, Miriam (2013) "Methamphetamine solution: drugs and the reconstruction of nation in postwar Japan," *Journal of Asian Studies*, 72, 1: 141–62.

Leonardsen, Dag (2010) *Crime in Japan: Paradise Lost?* Basingstoke: Palgrave Macmillan.

Llewelyn, James and Junichi Hirano (2009) "Importing human capital: contemporary Japanese attitudes to immigration," *Electronic Journal of Contemporary Japanese Studies*, 30 November. Available online at: http://www.japanesestudies.org.uk/articles/2009/Llewelyn.html. Accessed 29 August 2014.

Mabuchi, Ryogo 2001. "Shinbun hanzai hōdō ni okeru yōgisha no kokuseki – kokusekibetsu 'hanzaisharitsu' to no hikaku," lecture delivered at Nara University. Available online at: http://www.k3.dion.ne.jp/~mabuchi/lectures_nara/nwsppr_ntnlty.htm. Accessed 5 November 2014.

Ministry of Internal Affairs and Communications (2014) "Kokuseki-chiikibetsu zairyūshikaku (zairyū mokuteki) zairyūgaikokujin." Available online at: http://www.e-stat.go.jp/SG1/estat/List.do?lid=000001118467. Accessed 5 August 2014.

MOJ 2014 "Shutsunyūkokukanri wo meguru kinnen no jōkyō." Available online at: http://www.moj.go.jp/content/000105769.pdf. Accessed 4 August 2014.

Morita, Akira (2014) "Introduction" IPSS Website. Available online at: http://ipss.go.jp/pr-ad/e/eng/.

Morris-Suzuki, Tessa (2006) "Invisible immigrants: undocumented migration and border controls in early postwar Japan," *The Asia-Pacific Journal: Japan Focus*, August 30.

Available online at: http://www.japanfocus.org/-Tessa-Morris_Suzuki/2210. Accessed 29 July 2014.
Oguma, Eiji (1995) *Tanitsu Minzoku Shinwa no Kigen: Nihonjin no Jigazō no Keifu*, Tokyo: Shinyosha.
Rankin, Andrew (2012) "Recent trends in organized crime in Japan: Yakuza vs. the police, & foreign crime gangs – Part 2," *The Asia-Pacific Journal*, February 20. Available online at: http://www.japanfocus.org/-Andrew-Rankin/3692. Accessed 25 July 2014.
Richey, Sean (2010) "The impact of anti-assimilationist beliefs on attitudes toward immigration," *International Studies Quarterly*, 54, 1: 197–212.
Sharkey, Amanda and Noel Sharkey (2012) "Granny and the robots: ethical issues in robot care," *Ethics and Information Technology*, 14, 1: 27–40.
Shimasawa, Manabu and Kazumasa Oguro (2010) "The impact of immigration on the Japanese economy: a multi-country simulation model," *Journal of the Japanese and International Economies*, 24, 4: 586–602.
Shipper, Apichai W. (2005) "Criminals or victims? The politics of illegal foreigners in Japan," *The Journal of Japanese Studies*, 31, 2: 299–327.
—— (2008) *Fighting for Foreigners: Immigration and Its Impact on Japanese Democracy*, Ithaca: Cornell University Press.
Tsuda, Takeyuki (2001) "Reluctant hosts: the future of Japan as a country of immigration," Centre for Comparative Immigration Studies at the University of California. Available online at: https://migration.ucdavis.edu/rs/more.php?id=39_0_3_0. Accessed 13 July 2014.
US State Department (2014) *Trafficking in Persons Report*, Available online at: http://www.state.gov/documents/organization/226847.pdf. Accessed 10 June 2014.
Wortley, Scot (2009) "Introduction. The immigration-crime connection: competing theoretical perspectives," *International Migration and Integration*, 10, 4: 349–58.
Yamawaki, Keizo (2000) "Foreign workers in japan: a historical perspective," in Mike Douglass and Glenda S. Roberts (eds) *Japan and Global Migration: Foreign Workers and the Advent of a Multicultural Society*, London: Routledge, pp. 36–50.
—— (2008) "Japan as a country of immigration: two decades after an influx of immigrant workers," *Senri Ethnological Reports*, 77: 187–96.

PART II
Deconstructing the framing of North Korea

1 Introduction

The purpose of this part of the book is to elucidate how the Japanese government's state-led policy of securing the nation against risks identified with North Korea – constructed, mediated and recalibrated from what is portrayed as a highly salient and imminent cohort of threats – gives rise to harms that put the security of the everyday at risk for domestic actors. Whilst these include risk and harm at the state level, as well as those incurred by internal market-based actors, Part II continues to adopt the overarching approach of the book in emphasizing how the process of recalibrating risks at the state level disproportionately puts subnational actors' security of the everyday at risk as a result. The reasons for this are somewhat complex, but originate from the need for Japan to replace the former Soviet Union with a comparable challenge manifest in an enemy-state entity, which could be framed to produce a range of risks serving the interests of powerful actors intersecting the state, market and society in the post–Cold War era. These include maverick premiers, such as Koizumi Junichirō and the current prime minister at the time of writing, Abe Shinzō; extreme right-wing groups, represented by Satō Katsumi and the National Association for the Rescue of Japanese Kidnapped by North Korea (NARKN), or *sukūkai;* right-of-centre news media groups; and Japan's military-industrial complex – inclusive of its links to powerful commercial (mostly US) arms companies and associated political actors.

2 Context

Prior to normalization of relations with Seoul in 1965, Japan–North Korea relations were cautious but mostly constructive in terms of trade and social ties (Koh 2007: 38–41). In the decades that followed, however, Japan has been tilted towards emphasizing its enemy state vis-à-vis the North – as the de facto trilateral alliance between Seoul, Washington and Tokyo, in combination with post–Cold War structural changes effectively created a Beijing-Pyongyang block that is seen as counter to Japan's national interests (Sakurai 2007). In addition, North Korean brinkmanship has been interpreted as partly directed towards Japan – or at least having the potential to put Tokyo's national security at risk (Masaki 1995; Michishita 2009). This has included multiple actual harms, such as abductions, smuggling of illicit substances and incursions into Japan's EEZ (Black 2014), in addition to multiple missile tests and nuclear proliferation (Arms Control Association 2009).

Amongst these, Pyongyang's August 1998 Taepodong-1 test missile launch probably acted more than any other single event or action as the most significant catalyst in the processes driving Japan's post–Cold War shift in its foreign policy responses vis-à-vis North Korea. Specifically, it served to justify the shift to a hard-line policy against the various issues identified above concerning actions taken by the Pyongyang regime – and specifically identified with the Kim (Il-Sung, Jong-Il, Jong-Un) dynasty. As such, the preceding 1993 Nodong missile test, and the reaction by key actors to it, as well as the series of subsequent test launches, can be seen as a chronological barometer by which to examine how this process has created a potent set of socio-economic and political risks for the security of the everyday in post–Cold War Japan.

These risks have been contextualized internally in relation to a number of re-prioritized societal norms (antimilitarism, nationalism, developmentalism, etc.), which have influenced how new threats identified with North Korea have been mediated. As a result, they have not only exerted an impact upon Japan's relations with the three key states addressed in this volume, China, North Korea and the United States, but have also resulted in a disproportionate set of risks being posed to the everyday security of domestic actors associated with North Korea. The traceable transition of reactions to the series of North Korean satellite and missile launches between 1993 and 2012, therefore, underlines the fact that the Taepodong launch was by no means an isolated incident, and must be placed in the context of both precursory events and ongoing political discourse. Overall, these incidents and events have led to the recalibration of risks identified with North Korea. In this part of the book we examine how risks and harms stem from such discourses and are mediated between and amongst the state, market and society in Japan. Examination of such explains much not only about the change of Japan's rhetorical state-level stance, but also illustrates the extent of actual harms resulting from the changing responses to North Korea. These include not only the breakdown of normalization talks in the early 1990s between Japan and the DPRK; Pyongyang's withdrawal from the Nuclear Non-Proliferation Treaty (NPT), which sparked the so-called nuclear crisis of 1993–4; and increasing public and political attention regarding the abduction issue. This investigation into risk narratives also reveals the unequal side effects of the coverage by particular leading media corporations, in terms, for example, of harms inflicted upon the resident Korean community in Japan (and its associations) due to the negative framing of the DPRK.

3 Narratives on North Korea in Japan

The extant literature on relations with North Korea is dominated in Japan by realist-oriented authors (Endō 2011; Nishihara and Tsuchiyama 2010; Michishita 2009; Sakurai 2007; Izumi 1998). This is not surprising given the sphere of influence and subject matter. However, it is noteworthy that leading foreign scholars in this sub-field (Hughes 2009; Pempel 2010; Samuels 2007) have also tended to be predominantly (neo)realist in their approach to and assumptions about the topic. In one sense this merely reflects a theoretical bias within the discipline, but the result is that, with a number of notable exceptions, the focus of analysis generally becomes reduced to a discussion of threat perceptions which assess the DPRK's intentions and capabilities vis-à-vis Tokyo. Indeed, even the most insightful analytical concepts, such as the evaluation of the threat 'super-sizing' arguments (Hughes 2009), which identify the instrumentalization of deliberate threat inflation, still suffer from the limitations of analytical scope to which other realist-based works succumb.

In focusing almost entirely on North Korea's state-based strategies and the specific levels of threat assigned to tangible issues, as illustrated by missile launches, nuclear proliferation and the abduction issue, a broad range of influential processes, intersecting the state, market and society, are either relegated to a subsidiary role or neglected altogether. This results in disproportionate, reductionist assumptions influencing the analysis of Japan's responses, whereby national interest is often taken as being without sophisticated theoretical grounding or broader awareness. This even reaches the point where it is claimed that 'we are not using any theories,'[1] because *rational action* assumes only benefit for the Japanese state in essentially geostrategic or economic terms. In this section, we briefly critique how such *theoryless* theorists in Japan, who are a powerful driving force behind Tokyo's narrative on the DPRK, have fallen – or navigated via their own volition – into the constraints of a (neo)realist conceptual trap. We argue in this part that a more nuanced understanding and application of theories which identify and explain multiple sub-state actors and processes offer a valuable addition to the literature, similar to what we observed in the cases of Sino-Japanese relations (Part I) and US military facilities on Okinawa (Part III). This is particularly true in terms of illuminating how state-led risk mediation oft-times disproportionately puts the security of the everyday at risk for the very sub-state actors that the mediation is portrayed as being designed to protect.

Although potential economic gains for the DPRK are routinely expressed as a primary factor in Pyongyang's manoeuvres, they are usually assigned by realist-minded scholars to functionality and the understanding that any such agenda is driven by the power-political imperative of regime survival. This appraisal is typified by the scholars listed above in their tendency to evaluate Japan's options vis-à-vis Pyongyang by warning against being drawn into a North Korean–engineered game of competition over the future geo-political and economic battleground that will likely dominate Korean affairs. Indeed, in consecutive sections of his 2009 article for the *Korean Journal of Defense Analysis*, respectively entitled, 'Enhancing regime security' and 'A reconfigured equidistance policy,' Michishita states:

> Normalization of relations with the United States and Japan would be the single most important turning point for North Korea's security and foreign policy strategy. If this is achieved, North Korea's regime survival would be significantly enhanced.
>
> In this new strategic environment, North Korea would benefit from the reconfigured equidistance policy. . . . Regional rivalry between China and Japan, and South Korea's concern that their influence over the northern part of the peninsula might become too strong would benefit Pyongyang. If North Korea provides appropriate incentives, it might be able to draw Russia into this game as well. . . . The Japanese input would be particularly important because the Japanese have a lot of money but do not pose a political threat to the legitimacy of the North Korean regime.[2]

(2009: 115–17)

This kind of defensive-realist analysis pays scant attention to the interactive domestic influences in either state. Specifically, no explanation is provided of how external threats identified with the North's provocative actions are internalized and mediated between multiple actors.[3] In this respect, Endō assigns greater emphasis to the respective impact of internal political and social manoeuvring (at least within North and South Korea), but still falls short of accrediting it with more than a functional role which facilitates the manipulation of predetermined national interests and strategies. For instance, having already framed Pyongyang as the source of deadly harms in a preceding paragraph, Endō asserts:

> The international community – Japan, the United States and South Korea in particular – has so far repeatedly responded to Pyongyang's hard-line stance and escalating brinkmanship diplomacy with conciliatory policies yielding to domestic pressures in the countries concerned. This has at least made Pyongyang confident that its hard-line stance has paid off. Inserting apparently flexible stances between hard-line policies is a clever strategy by North Korea, and we should be prepared for a repeat of the pattern.

(2011: 1)

Therefore, despite Endō's recognition of 'domestic pressures,' by focusing only on the potential threat posed by the DPRK's power elite, the above statement also fails to accredit North Korea's own internal socio-political climate as a major factor in shaping policy. There is clearly a whole range of state-societal phenomena contingent upon Japan–North Korea relations that needs to be accounted for, including choices faced by policy elites on both sides as a result of being embedded within societal norms and the domestic market, as well as the pressure to counter threats to political survival. On the Japanese side, these are manifest not only in Japan's international identity and security status, as well as prospects for normalization of diplomatic relations with Pyongyang, but also in the potential harms posed to the security of the everyday for subnational actors such as resident Koreans and their organizations, precisely as a result of recalibrated risks targeting North Korea. In the predominant neorealist scholarship, there is also scant recognition of the fact that the threats being discussed bear no objective relationship to the probability of the harms apparently being responded to.

Nowhere is such a *mis*-calibration as evident as in the case of North Korean missiles. The potential threat of a missile is easy to mediate from the state to broader socio-political spheres, but the actual likelihood of being struck by – even an off-target part of – any missile/satellite launched from the North whilst in Japan is statistically miniscule. Yet, leading realist academics in Japan project growing concerns with regard to North Korea in this regard (Nishihara, 2011: 5–6). Hence, this arm of Japan's security establishment has, evidently, used the narrow framing of North Korean threats to veil a far more complex process of perception and interpretation which relates to it. This includes the governance of probabilities, as a means to govern power, contested by multi-levelled actors which intersect the state, market and society.

4 Structure of Part II

The four chapters following this introduction illuminate how policies justified as providing security for all in Japan are indifferent to their disproportionate effect upon the security of the everyday for a minority. It highlights how people are exposed to an unequal share of the risks arising from the implementation of state policy. This part also exposes how risks to future commercial activity and bilateral and regional relations have not been constructed or mediated in such a way as to allow them to gain precedence within the process of political contestation. The chapters address these points by examining how the framing of the various key issues identified with North Korea, as well as their associated resident Korean community in Japan, gives rise to additional or subsidiary risks, as well as potential and actual harm. In the case of North Korea, this is due predominantly to the process of risk recalibration itself – manifest as responses to missile testing (Chapter 5); abductions (Chapter 6); nuclear weapons programmes (Chapter 7); and financial remittances and narcotics smuggling, including multiple maritime incursions (Chapter 8). The chapters explore how risk has been constructed and recalibrated in the process of mediation between and amongst the Japanese state, market and societal actors responding to perceived external threats. The focus is, therefore, predominantly on the potential harm and the materialization of harm to the security of the everyday as a result of state-centric policies and approaches. For instance, we explore how targeting of North Korean incursions and illicit actions at the state level contributes to narcotics entering Japanese society through domestic criminal channels without regulation, and how domestic commercial enterprises are harmed as a result of the strangulation on remittances between Japan and the North.

In all, the chapters aim to offer a view of Japan's framing of North Korea not only from the perspective of the Japanese state countering an external enemy, and the actual harm inflicted upon Japan-DPRK and Japan-regional relations, but also as a risk to the security of the everyday for domestic actors within Japan. These two contrastive views of the risks born by North Korean actions and intentions divide opinion. This schism separates unequally a minority who have kinship, economic and political ties with the DPRK – or who recognize the potential gains to be made from a more convivial Tokyo-Pyongyang relationship – and the convergence of state, market and societal actors whose various interests are served by a sustained emphasis upon risks attributed to the North. As seen in Part I, comparisons can also be drawn between this phenomenon and the risks increasingly identified with China's (military-economic) rise.

This includes, but is not exclusively limited to, the contested threat inflation of North Korean actions and intentions in relation to a portrayed weakness in Japan's security deterrence capabilities, which serves to recalibrate the risks themselves into a salient, and arguably disproportionate, risk to the state. As acknowledged in Chapter 5, North Korea undoubtedly has the potential to strike Japan with a missile, but this is a narrative fallacy (Taleb 2007). The circular discourse between Japanese policymakers at the state level and media actors able to profit commercially from the story of framing a high-risk North Korea has all but neglected the unlikely motivation and negligible probability of Pyongyang actually seeking to launch an attack. In the interim, the construction of risks as a result of this discourse being trumpeted and reinforced through a process of confirmation bias (Gardner 2008) has been largely overlooked. Even when recognized to a minimal extent, for example by those critical of the establishment, the justification of Japan's recalibration of risk in response to threats sourced in North Korea has been allocated to state responsibility and geo-military prioritization – seemingly ignorant of the fact that ameliorating those risks purportedly includes the protection of *all* citizens and residents in Japan. Efforts to redress the unequal distribution of these risks and harms arising from the risk recalibration process itself offer the only way for stakeholders to resist this continued imposition of state-centric policies that put the security of the everyday at risk. However, with the power base of actors such as the resident Korean community and its traditional supporters being attacked economically, socially and politically, via the highlighted process of risk mediation, their ability to effectively contest political decisions affecting their daily lives becomes highly limited.

These diverse areas of risk identified with North Korea are also illustrative of how the recalibration and mediation of risk can lead to state, market and societal actors targeting elements which exhibit a high degree of discrepancy from their supposed potential harm. Narcotics smuggling, covered in Chapter 8, for example, has been incorporated into the North Korean framing, as posing a high risk to Japanese society, yet the importers and distributors of harmful narcotics are overwhelmingly native criminal organizations, such as the *bōryokudan*, or *yakuza*, and it is actually the state's inability to reduce the risks posed by such a high level of domestic organized crime that creates the need to deflect attention to the minimal amounts of illicit substances brought in from North Korea. Furthermore, as highlighted by the case of ecstasy and horse riding covered in the introduction to this book, it is often the state's failure to properly regulate and legalize narcotics that in one sense causes the greatest actual harm to both the national economy and society at large. In other words, it is the recalibration of risk, initiated by the state and mediated by market actors, such as mainstream media and vested interest groups, that results in these risks – apparently attributable to an enemy state such as North Korea – becoming more salient.

In addition to the above, the issue of North Korea abducting Japanese citizens, discussed in detail in Chapter 6, elucidates a further form of the risk, potential harm and actual harm nexus. Here the results of the recalibration process are comparable to those outlined above in terms of the actors affected but, as with nuclear proliferation, are based primarily on ideological risk, as opposed to risks tied to hard-power, external, geo-military threats. A key agenda item for the state in this case is the potential for North Korean abductions to represent a case study which demonstrates not only the violation of the human rights of Japanese citizens, but also of the state's sovereign power. Therefore, the broader narrative of risk is spread to allow a psychological link between, for instance, North Korean incursions and abductions and the risks posed to Japan's sovereignty by China's supposed expansionism in the East China Sea, dealt with in Part I.

The brief introductory discussion above, therefore, highlights the significance of multiple forms of risk – not only potential harms posed to the state of Japan, but also harms facing subnational actors within it. Specifically, it illustrates the constraints state-orchestrated risk recalibration places upon subnational actors' ability to counter potential resulting harms. Indeed, it is this process of mediation and recalibration pervading from the state, but oft-times becoming a circular or interactive discourse between actors intersecting the state, market and society, which presents the greatest likelihood of potential and actual harms being inflicted – commonly upon the security of the everyday for those whose safety the state claims as its primary objective. In the following chapters, the specifics of how this process has been realized, in relation to the cases alluded to above, are discussed, applying the discursive risk-based approach outlined in the book's introduction.

Notes

1   This was stated during a doctoral workshop at Jochi University in September 2010 by a leading political scientist and later supported at a government-backed, independent

research institute in Japan, in response to a participant question during a post-presentation panel discussion – querying what theoretical framework was underpinning policy analysis and implementation for contemporary North Korean affairs.
2 In the same article Michishita also discusses how responses should counter what he terms as Pyongyang's 'cybernetic decision-making' to refer to the DPRK's "cyclic application of adventurism and caution, coercion and dialogue" in its attempts to maintain regime survival (2009: 110–11).
3 The significance of this process is explicated further in the following chapter.

References

Arms Control Association (2009) "Chronology of US and North Korean nuclear diplomacy." Available online at: http://www.armscontrol.org/factsheets/dprkchron. Accessed 10 December 2013.
Black, Lindsay (2014) *Japan's Maritime Security Strategy: The Japan Coast Guard and Maritime Outlaws*, London: Palgrave Macmillan.
Endō, Tetsuya (2011) "How should Japan deal with North Korea?" AJISS Commentary. Available online at: http://www.jiia.or.jp/en_commentary/201103/29-1.html. Accessed 4 April 2011.
Gardner, Dan (2008) *Risk: The Science and Politics of Fear*, London: Virgin Books.
Hughes, Christopher W. (2009) "'Super-sizing' the DPRK threat: Japan's emerging security posture and North Korea," *Asian Survey*, 49, 2: 291–311.
Izumi, Hajime (1998) *Kitachōsen sono jitsuzō to kiseki*, Tokyo: Kōbunken.
Koh, Byung-chul (2007) *Between Discord and Cooperation: Japan and the Two Koreas*, Seoul: Yonsei University Press.
Masaki, Stuart K. (1995) "The Korean question: assessing the military balance," *Security Studies*, 4, 2 (Winter): 365–425.
Michishita, Narushige (2009) "The future of North Korean strategy," *Korean Journal of Defense Analysis*, 21, 1: 110–17.
Nishihara, Masashi (2011) "Japan's Defense Policy and the Asia-Pacific Region," Embassy of Japan in Canada (Lecture). Available on line at: http://www.ca.emb-japan.go.jp/2011_shared_images/Cultural%20Events/nishihara_lecture_text.pdf. Accessed 12 April 2015.
Nishihara, Masashi and Tsuchiyama Jitsuo (2010) *Nichibei dōmei saikō, heiwa anzen hoshō kenkyūjo*, Tokyo: Akishobo.
Pempel, Thomas J. (2010) "Japan and the two Koreas: the foreign-policy power of domestic politics," IGCC Occasional Paper, No.3, University of California: Berkeley.
Sakurai, Yoshiko (2007) *Nihon yo, tsuyoki kuni to nare*, Tokyo: Diamond.
Samuels, Richard (2007) *Securing Japan: Tokyo's Grand Strategy and the Future of East Asia*, London: Cornell University Press.
Taleb, Nassim (2007) *The Black Swan*, London: Penguin.

5
MISSILE TESTING

1 Introduction

From the first Nodong missile launch into the Sea of Japan in May of 1993, to the rounds of proclaimed 'satellite' test launches in April and December of 2012, and short-range rocket launches in May 2013, North Korea's sporadic missile test firings have punctuated its ongoing brinkmanship in the international arena. Nowhere has this exerted a more profound effect than in Japan, where the increasing range and sophistication as well as the proximate trajectory – flying over Japanese territory – have been used to justify a wide range of security-based initiatives stemming from Japanese lawmakers' recalibration of the potential risks posed by the North's actions (Mason 2014). This chapter explores how state-level mediation of these risks intensified most dramatically following the first Taepodong missile launch of 1998 and was then further escalated following multiple launches in 2006 and 2009. In each section the chapter then goes on to examine how, whilst the improbability of being struck even by a falling piece of missile has arguably remained largely constant, Japan's convergent right-of-centre policy community has been able to emphasize the risk of missile strikes by the North as a means to securitize a range of – supposedly related – spheres (Wada 2009) that have jeopardized the security of the everyday in each case.[1] These spheres have included the particular focus upon the DPRK's nuclear facilities and capabilities, covered in greater detail in Chapter 7, as well as the conflation with the abduction issue discussed in Chapter 6.

These elements, however, each only provide one readily identifiable aspect of the process that has enabled the Japanese state – as well as market and societal actors – to further facilitate stigmatization of North Korea both externally and within domestic sites of activity. In this sense, once again the harmful impacts of these processes can be observed in terms of the compounding of Japan's framing of North Korea as an 'enemy state' and the persecution of and prejudice towards North Korea's associated ethnic diaspora and agencies within Japan. These include Korean residents, schools and representative bodies, as well as concurrently having a knock-on effect that impacts upon international, particularly East Asian, spheres of influence across the Asia-Pacific (Global Security Newswire 2013). Detailed scrutiny of the pertaining strands of discourse, represented illustratively by Diet statements and news coverage, exposes how Japan's international and subnational reactions and responses to North Korean missile testing have been subject to processes of risk mediation. These responses intersect the state, market and societal spheres, and determine the construction, mediation and recalibration of associated risks. The evidence unearthed in this chapter leads to the conclusion that the resulting actual and potential harms – manifest in a loss of everyday security for individual actors such as those listed above – are found to be both under-emphasized and grievous.

2   What harms for whom in Japan?

The potentiality of risks incurred by Japan sourced from North Korean missiles is understandably the subject of ongoing debate. However, as prominent North Korea specialists, amongst others, have explained, Pyongyang does not even possess sufficient oil and other supplies to engage in war (Shigemura 2011). Nevertheless, it is clear that the DPRK is capable of launching, for example, a mid-range Nodong missile that could strike Japan with enough accuracy to land somewhere in Tokyo and cause untold damage. As noted by one of Japan's leading experts on contingency plans and policy for North Korean affairs, recent developments – particularly in terms of a comparison between the 2012 missile tests and previous launches – do point to a high likelihood that North Korea's missile capabilities have been substantially advanced in terms of how much harm they *could* inflict upon Japan (Michishita 2013). Factors suggestive of such include the relocation of the North's testing site from its traditional launch site on the East Coast to Ton Chan Yee on the West Coast; the fact that missiles were launched southwards – against the Earth's rotation (rather than, as usual, firing eastward with it); and the claims that a modified payload and miniaturization may have been achieved. The dedication of North Korea to its missile programmes per se, as well as to realizing the ability to use missiles to deliver nuclear warheads, has also been demonstrated. This is evinced, not least, by the fact that the DPRK was willing to risk launch-failure of this advanced technology at the time of Kim Il-Sung's anniversary – suggesting that the intention is to make the system operational at all costs (Interview A, 18 July 2013).[2]

Therefore, Japan's military and other security strategists have constructed the risks identified with North Korean missiles based on the argument that the DPRK could use missile technology effectively and relatively economically. Yet, such a course of action can be largely discredited with reference to the almost assured counter strike that Pyongyang would face from Japan and/or the US, in addition to the economic constraints faced by the North's impoverished military in operationalising any form of attack. Indeed, the reason for the North Korean's determination to develop advanced weaponry at all costs is actually to provide the deterrent of a counter-strike capability against Tokyo as a response to the potentiality of a US pre-emptive strike against the DPRK. Regardless of the actual risks, to counter the potential harm, Japanese lawmakers have justified the introduction of a $10 billion-plus mostly US-made BMD system (*The Wall Street Journal*, 9 December 2012). This carries the tacit understanding that Japan would then be positioned to both avoid the risk of being coerced into any conflict involving North Korea and the US, and or South Korea – as well as potentially assist its, de facto, southern ally.[3]

In terms of the recalibration of the North Korean missile risk, however, this cannot simply be relegated to state action that is distinct from public discourse – or, put another way, the analysis of 'what they do, not what they say.' For example, rudimentary analyses often assume simply that the state's convergent right-of-centre policy community exaggerated, or 'super-sized' (Hughes 2009) the risks posed by North Korean missiles in order to justify the introduction of lucrative BMD technology and other measures related to further militarization.[4] However, in fact, in the case of addressing the risks borne by North Korea's missile capabilities strategically, the state has in one sense been forced to tread more carefully in order to avoid fuelling increasingly anti-Korean discourse – associated with both halves of the peninsula – emerging in Japanese society and commercial media spheres. In this sense, there is a mediation process between and amongst state, market and societal actors that determines how risks are identified and recalibrated, which is articulated via discourse.

Within this, the combination of the negative framing of North Korea and increasing bilateral tensions between Japan and South Korea – fuelled by populist exclusionary nationalism – has created an environment in which market actors outside of the media are also less inclined to seek closer commercial relations with either of the two Koreas.[5] Such is further reflected by the mainstream sentiments within society towards the ROK, which have also deteriorated to a twenty-first century nadir (Cabinet Office, Government of Japan 2013). As a result, the state is readily able to persuade – and indeed gain support from – the market and societal sectors with regards to the maintenance of a hard line against North Korea. However, it is not necessarily provided with a politically palatable mandate to implement the strategic protection of South Korean security interests if they incur any risk to Japan.

Furthermore, these risk-calculating factors have also come to exert an influence over Japan's North Korea policy as a whole – whereby risks are hedged, partly against potential contingencies sourced in Pyongyang, but also, in the market sphere, as part of ongoing regional competition resulting from severe economic risks faced at the state level in Japan, China and both Koreas. The former can be seen in initiatives such as Iijima Isao's visit to Pyongyang, which sought progress on resolution of the abduction cases, perhaps as a first step towards reopening normalization talks, but did not include open dialogue on the North's missile programmes (*Asahi Shimbun AJW*, 2013). In this sense, whilst Japan seeks to remove any potential harm from Pyongyang's missiles through enhanced BMD capabilities, policymakers also appear to have understood the risk of regional isolation. Given Japan's current strained relations with the ROK and China – as well as the growing integration of those states – they have moved to reopen the lines of communication with North Korea to allow for the possibility of normalization, particularly as the salience of the abduction issue, discussed in Chapter 6, wanes. As one expert on Korea-Japan affairs noted in relation to South Korean speculation, particularly if missiles can be sidelined as an issue of dispute, Japan might offer the DPRK in the region of US$2 billion worth of aid or investment. This would effectively be a kind of down payment for reparations that would be agreed, as per the 1965 treaty signed with South Korea, as part of a normalization package (Interview B, 18 July 2013). In return, the North would reopen abduction cases, return home abductees still alive in North Korea or hand over agents involved in the abductions themselves.

3 Missiles as a risk to the security of the everyday

The process outlined above – whereby central actors intersecting the state, market and society in Japan converge upon a recalibration of risk as a function of responses to North Korean missile strikes – has been well documented within the IR and security studies literature (Hughes 2009; Hagström and Söderberg 2006; Samuels 2007; Mason 2014). However, as noted in the review of literature in the introduction to this book, the mainstream arguments have been based essentially around threat inflation theories and those of securitization (Buzan 1991). Building on these conventional contributions to the field, the sections below further highlight the significant distinction that needs to be drawn between risk and threat, and elucidate how the mediation of risk between actors in these different sections of Japan's policy making community has resulted in a misrepresentation of the challenge that North Korean 'missiles' pose to the security of the everyday in Japan, thereby obfuscating the actual harms the reaction to them has caused within domestic society and the market sphere.

The comparative cases of the May 1993 Nodong test launch and August 1998 Taepodong-1 launch illustrate the relevance of the phenomenon described above. It is not simply that the Taepodong-1 was inaccurately interpreted and portrayed as the greater threat – though this can certainly be argued with some justification – but also that the Taepodong-1 facilitated a conceptual reinterpretation of what risks were posed by North Korea. Most critically, the internalization of the risks identified with the Taepodong-1 was undertaken by a far more diverse range of actors in far greater volume. Hence, the mediation of the risk, between and amongst state, market and societal actors became greatly intensified (Mason 2014).

As already discussed in the introduction to the book, risk is mediated as a set of uncertain yet malleable cohorts of politicized choices, which are articulated via discourse. Within this, it is in the institutionalization of practices and their ongoing evolution that resulting policy directives are shifted towards a given norm (Wishnick 2009: 406–7). In the case at hand this is a norm that identifies North Korea as the unquestionable source of multiple and salient risks. The dramatic quantitative increase of media and Diet attention paid to risks associated with the regime in Pyongyang following the 1998 Taepodong-1 launch is evidence in itself that threat perceptions had been raised and risks would be recalibrated accordingly. The complexities of the process by which such a stark differentiation in response to the Taepodong-1 – i.e. from that witnessed in 1993 – was made, however, can only be fully elucidated through closer examination of how those risks were mediated via discourse.

3.1 Risk recalibration via discourse: the August 1998 Taepodong -1 missile launch

Discourse is illustrative in this case because it showcases how a specific risk was reinterpreted and how the focus of attention and perspective were redirected as an outcome – ultimately represented in state-centric policy responses that have endangered the everyday security of some of the individual citizens they are purportedly designed to protect. This is observable not only as a rise in perceived levels of risk, but in the content and (re)conceptualization of a given risk. Here, in contrast to the almost negligible and highly technical discussion and response to the 1993 test firing from within Japan, both Diet speakers and media editors were outspoken in their interpretation of the Taepodong-1, as representing a 'new risk.' This was despite neither the ability to predict a higher probability of harm being exacted as a result, or the identification of any major shift in North Korea's intentions towards Japan in the interim.

Therefore, the transformation in perceptions and portrayals of the risks supposedly brought about by the August 1998 test engenders the dynamic effect of risk mediation. Concretely, this was projected in terms of which actors were expected to bear responsibility and what subsidiary risks had to be taken in order to counter those identified with the Taepodong-1. This effectively spread the responsibility for these risks to incorporate everyone from individual citizens in Japan to regional cooperation and practices elicited from the surrounding Asia-Pacific powers. Such risks were then linked to Japan's identity as a coordinating and central structure in stabilizing the region (MOFA 2008: 9–11).

This effect was represented at the state level by a variety of prominent and influential figures. The thrust of such arguments and statements was represented by then minister of state, Takamura Masahiko, who not only asserted in his address to the Committee on Foreign Affairs and Defense that 'North Korea's missile launch directly affects Japan,' but immediately followed the assertion with an illustrative elaboration. This included an explanation of how the action also placed at risk the 'security and stability of the East Asia region, proliferation of Weapons of Mass Destruction (WMD) and efforts to promote non-proliferation' (Committee on foreign Affairs and Defense, 3 September 1998). Critically, in terms of contrasting isolated threat inflation with an illustration of how risk is used more actively in governance, he also appealed for the development of cooperative practices to deal with the risks manifest in ongoing responses – urging the 'international community to proactively participate in tackling this mutual issue, so as to move towards the stability and prosperity of the entirety of the international society.' In other words, Takamura was advocating the taking and prioritizing of a particular set of subsidiary risks internalized in each state, which it was claimed had arisen from the primary risks manifest in North Korea's launching of the Taepodong-1.

Consistent with the approach led by state representatives such as Takamura, a triple layered process of risk interpretation (internalization of threat/hazard), allocation (of responsibility for the risk) and action (taking of subsidiary risks) rapidly emerged. To this effect, the issue of Japan's (lack of) crisis management capabilities was repeatedly raised in the Diet – in terms of North Korean missiles being representative of how Japan's dysfunctional security apparatus was putting the lives and property of its people at risk. As former diplomat and deputy minister Takano Hiroshi remarked in the Committee on Foreign Affairs and Defense, assuming the DPRK's ability to strike Japan with a missile and Tokyo's inability to defend effectively against it because of organizational inefficiencies, 'it is remarkable that the head of the Defense Agency, which bears the responsibility for national defense, is making statements to this effect with regards to the vital role of crisis management that takes care of our citizens['] lives and property.' (Committee on Foreign Affairs and Defense, 11 December 1998).

In this regard, Diet speakers – increasingly from all major political parties across both ruling and opposition coalitions – alluded to the risk of non-action and immobilism as tantamount in itself to actively putting the security of the everyday at risk. Within this, North Korean missiles were also linked by state actors to the risks of mere uncertainty. As Minister of State Norota Hōsei contextualized during one session of the Committee on Foreign Affairs and Defense, 'As seen by North Korea's 31 August missile launch, our country is surrounded by an increasingly opaque set of circumstances'; he went on to urge the Japan Defence Agency to make every effort in addressing this situation, describing it as 'of upmost importance' (Committee on Foreign Affairs and Defense, 3 December 1998). In this way, whilst clearly an important distinction can be made between what central actors do and what they say, the examination of trends and usage of rhetoric in Diet discourse is highly illuminating in terms of how debates over risk come to be framed and contested. This is particularly relevant here because, ultimately, the centre ground of such contestation demarcated the perimeters within which policies could and would be framed in regard to the Taepodong. As discussed further below, it is oft-times precisely this enactment of policy stemming from a particular context of risk construction, framing and mediation which creates harmful side effects for the security of the everyday.

This pattern of risk recalibration formulated – partly at least – as a function of prominent discourse, was also articulated in the mainstream media. Here, too, risk once again served a crucial role in reshaping Japan's responses to North Korea and the challenges it was perceived to present to regional security as a whole. The *Asahi Shimbun*, which had previously been ridiculed for its sympathetic stance towards both Pyongyang and North Korean elements within Japan (interviews, *Asahi Shimbun* journalist, 27 August 2011; Deputy Director, Resident Korean Historical Research Centre, 8 February 2011) is particularly illustrative of how core public sphere discourse shifted – as much in the case of missile test firings as that of the abductions, covered in the next chapter. In an editorial shortly after the Taepodong-1 launch, entitled, 'The dangers of an unspoken power-monger – North Korea' (*Asahi Shimbun*, 8 September 1998), the newspaper directly identified and emphasized the risks arising from Kim Jong-Il as an unchecked, unchallenged leader, interpreting them as highly uncertain but all the more salient to Japan as a result. This marked the beginning of Kim's almost universal demonization within Japan and once again the risks were spread to incorporate responsibilities for key regional actors. These included the US, South Korea and China, with the prescribed action, even if less overtly asserted than the newspaper's peers and political counterparts in the Diet, being one of pro-action.

In addition to a measured shift in editorial stance, the paper provided its more proactive – and in one sense 'risk-mongering' – readers with a platform from which to assert a line well to the right of previous incarnations. Concordantly with other issues, this was epitomized by reference to the immobilism and impotence of the Japanese security apparatus, as being symbolic of how the security of the population was being put at risk by the state. This facilitated the advocating of a more assertive and proactive response, immediately made justifiable by the recalibration of risks attached to the North Korean Taepodong-1 missile. One commentator stressed critically and with evident sarcasm that 'with North Korea's missile delivery system this time bringing about a potential disaster . . . all of you in the Defense Agency are not even able to do your "main job" . . . so why not either disband or turn yourselves into a specialized disaster relief unit only?' (2 September 1998). Such sentiments are striking in terms of how they represent a societal actor interacting with market (news media) elements to echo state-level shifts in risk construction. Important though this process is, and continued to be – as seen in the cases of succeeding missile launches discussed below – the above statements, and numerous others, are also notable for their absence of concern for the potential harms that the process of recalibrating risk in response to North Korea might engender for the security of the everyday.

In the case of advocating a more proactive response, based on improved organizational and operational capabilities for the Japan Self-Defense Force (JSDF) and their governing agency (later to become ministry), it can be argued that the Taepodong-1 missile launch effectively served as the initial catalyst (Reuters 2013). This included taking a more assertive approach, flag-shipped by the importation of costly American BMD technology. In itself this is further illustrative of how risks, in this case primarily those of greater entanglement in US security interests, were deprioritized in relation to those identified with North Korean missiles. The potential harm of taking such steps can also clearly be linked back to the initial risks of further exacerbating regional concerns over Japan's remilitarization, as well as specific escalation of the bilateral strains Japan found itself in with North Korea. However, as illustrated succinctly by the selected examples above, the manner in which risks are constructed and recalibrated effectively – in this case relating to the Taepodong-1 – determines which contingent risks are prioritized, or even whether they are identified as risks at all, as well as any potential harms that may result as a by-product. When these are realized as actual harms, thereafter, policymakers and media editors alike – as well as large swathes of society at large – are then more able to explain them away as inevitable, rather than as a function of the risk recalibration process itself.

3.2 The July 2006 multiple missile launch

In violation of its agreed moratorium on missile launches, on 5 July 2006, North Korea launched an estimated seven ballistic missiles into the Sea of Japan. These included one Taepodong-2 long-range missile, which had been designed with the potential to strike targets along the US West Coast, but failed inside the first minute of its flight (CNN International.com, 2006). The other missiles tested were Soviet-derived shorter range scud-type units. All landed in waters hundreds of miles in distance from the Japanese archipelago and no collateral or other damage was incurred. Amid a barrage of international criticism, most staunchly from Japan's soon-to-be prime minister and then chief cabinet secretary Abe Shinzō, North Korea's state media claimed the test had been conducted lawfully as part of strengthening the country's military capabilities for the purpose of self-defence (*New York Times*, 4 July 2006).

In counter to the North's claim, the processes of risk recalibration and its resulting harms, outlined above, were very much extended and accentuated by Japan's reaction to the DPRK's resumption of multiple missile testing in the summer of 2006. Analysis of such also has to be further considered in the context of the launches taking place prior to the DPRK's first nuclear test – something which had an important combined influence, as discussed in the context of further launches, explicated below and in greater detail in Chapter 7. It is also relevant, however, that even prior to the nuclear devices being headlined, the test firings had a powerful impact on the immediately ensuing discourse – as well as the policy and countermeasures adopted as a result.

In the Diet, Abe led calls for the strongest possible measures to be taken against then leader Kim Jong-Il's Pyongyang regime. As detailed in Chapter 6, particularly in the case of Japan's responses to the issue of abductions, elements of Japan's identity, as well as everyday human and material assets, were being identified as at risk from North Korea's actions. It was this that provided Abe and others with an ideological tool to drive a discourse justifying punitive action against the North, whilst omitting any reference to consideration of other potential harms that might be incurred as a result. In an address to the Special Committee on Prevention of

International Terrorism, Abe asserted, 'This missile launch threatens our nation, and as the nation is threatened, surely we must stress this to the Security Council, and indeed it is our right to do so.' (Special Committee on Prevention of International Terrorism, 11 August 2006). By juxtaposing terms such as 'our nation' *(waga kuni)* and 'right' *(kenri)*, Abe infused an element of emotion and indignation that clearly exceeded the bounds of purely objective transfer of information about probable harms caused by the missile.

Preceding Abe's statement, then foreign minister Asō Tarō had already given a lengthy explanation of how the North's multiple missile test launch was the source of a range of risks – based partly on reference to the inclusion of a Taepodong, which had already been used to establish the construction of latent risks since the time of the August 1998 test. Asō's arguments included the echoed assertion: 'This missile launch is of direct consequence to our nation's security, and is extremely regrettable from the point of view of peace and security in the international community, as well as preventing the proliferation of Weapons of Mass Destruction [WMD]' (Security Committee, 6 July 2006). He went on not only to justify the instantaneous implementation of various sanctions, thereafter restricting the flow of goods and finances to and from the North, but also trumpeted the idea of dangerous information coming out of all areas of the DPRK, and urged citizens not to risk travelling to North Korea.

In the above sense, the concepts of conflation and spreading of constructed risks from a single state source to a multiplicity of harms inflicted upon the security of the everyday are consistently observed. Indeed, it is these elements of the process which often result in the greatest actual harms, because punitive measures affect those not involved – in this case with developing missile technology in North Korea. Abe's and Asō's inclusions of a degree of emotive terminology, as well as mention of WMD proliferation and travel to the North, may seem relatively subtle in this regard. However, Abe in particular was also at the forefront of making the far more dubious connection between missiles and abductions, as well as nuclear issues, bundling all three together with further references to the direct and indirect risks posed to Japan. Nowhere was this implemented within the Diet to greater effect than in Abe's statements to the Special Committee Concerning the Problem of Abductions by North Korea, where in one session, for example, a lengthy passage was devoted to detailed explanation of the multiple missile launches. Therein, the combination of missile, abduction and nuclear issues was again stressed and North Korea's actions of July 2006 were attached to them with a description as being of 'ultimate obligatory concern' *(kiwamete yūryo subeki mono)* (Special Committee on North Korean Abduction Issue and Related Matters, 10 July 2006). Once again, government statements and sanctions from the Diet in reaction to the test firings were, in the main, unchallenged in emphasis by opposition parties – and were further echoed in mainstream media reactions.

The majority of Japan's right-of-centre news media sources, represented by the *Yomiuri Shimbun*, for example, were unsurprisingly bellicose in their responses to the North's resumption of missile testing, as well as being outspoken in their support for sanctions to be applied in 2006 (*Yomiuri Shimbun*, 6 July 2006). However, in terms of selling news, the conflation and extension of issues are standard practice; and, in Japan's case, a standardized and mostly politically uncontroversial perspective is also supported by the convergence of the Press Club system and direct ties among large media corporations (Lynn 2006; Krauss and Pharr 1996). The impact of an extensive recalibration of risk in response to North Korea, however, particularly in terms of how the process of recalibration was not considered a risk, is again made more evident by examination of the traditionally more liberal *Asahi Shimbun*.

As was spotlighted in the case of leading lawmakers in the Diet, the *Asahi* was more notable for the risks that it chose not to highlight than those that did find extended coverage throughout its pages. In this sense, whilst editorials stuck by the newspaper's long-held principle of advocating dialogue with the North, no open opposition – or even allusion of inherent risks to the security of the everyday – was made with regards to the imposition of sanctions. Indeed, a hard-line response was assumed and the inclusion of risks attached to missile, nuclear and abduction issues aggregated (6 July 2006: 3). Furthermore, a far more vocal and hard-line sentiment from contributors to the paper was, as in the case of previous North Korean actions such as the abductions, given prominent coverage – once again illustrating how media sources' selection of events exerts social influence and shapes the discourse that it is deployed to articulate. In a piece written precisely to encourage a tough stance on North Korea as a response to the missile firing, one office worker contributed to the *Asahi*'s pages by introducing the idea of DPRK-focused regional tactics as having become a 'dangerous game'; the worker went on to assert: 'Our country too must take a robust attitude and absolutely must not ease economic sanctions that limit and prohibit trade, remittances and such like until the nuclear, missile and [abduction] issue[s] and the like have been fully resolved' (6 July 2006). Such sentiments selected from its readers by the *Asahi*, therefore, exhibit precisely the features expressed by the *Yomiuri* and its right-leaning counterparts in terms of recalibrating the risks posed by missiles in order to construct and mediate multiple potential harms from a single source. Such came without mention of either the non-existent actual harm inflicted by the July tests themselves or the potential harm that could be caused by such a mediation of the risk.

3.3 Missile tests, 2009–2013

Following the escalation of regional tensions brought about by reaction to North Korea's first underground nuclear test in October of 2006, dealt with in Chapter 7, the already extensive recalibration of risk that had taken place in Japan was taken to new levels in response to the resumption of further missile tests throughout 2009 and again in 2012 and 2013. Although the details – and trajectory – of each test differed somewhat in nature, Pyongyang again made reference to its sovereign rights in improving its self-defence capabilities and, in the 2012 case, testing of an acclaimed satellite. Amid a barrage of international complaint and protest, the unit was evaluated to be another enhanced capability missile. As with previous DPRK missile firings the risks were interpreted by Tokyo as salient, though no actual harms were inflicted. In this sense, responses from the Japanese state, market and society were produced in a context of already firmly established hostility towards the North – something that had combined a range of emotional and tangible risks which included abductions, nuclear testing, maritime incursions and illicit financial activities and narcotics smuggling, as well as the more recent, 2010, cases of the Cheonan naval vessel sinking and shelling of Yeonpyeong Island in South Korea. All of these aspects were attributed higher salience with each successive missile test.

With the aforementioned advocates of a hard line against North Korea, Asō and Abe, at the helm of the Japanese government at the time of the North's missile tests in April and July of 2009, December of 2012 and May of 2013 respectively, the already outlined processes of sourcing an increase in risks attached to North Korean missiles – in contrast to actual harms inflicted – and seemingly recalibrating them for the purposes of galvanizing national sentiment and political capital, were clearly evident. Of greater interest, however, in terms of understanding the extent of the recalibration process, is the response witnessed to the missile launch of April 2012, when the now opposition DPJ coalition was in power. This is particularly salient in terms of demonstrating how the security of the everyday for actors such as the ethnic Korean community and its representative bodies, as well as others out of sync with mainstream sentiment, became marginalized to the point where even a full change of governing administration did little to relieve the harmful effects of the risk recalibration process. This lack of shift in rhetoric and outlook under the DPJ-led government was also expressed clearly in the prevailing, interactive discourse of Diet speakers and media outlets.

For instance, in a session of the Foreign Affairs and Defence Committee, having explained the extensive operations and deployment of the JSDF that had been utilized to prepare for a potential missile launch, Defense Minister Tanaka Naoki did state that absolutely no damage had been incurred. However, in the same session he and Foreign Minister Genba Kōichirō both went on to use rhetoric very similar to their post-1998 predecessors and successors of the LDP when describing the North's actions, with Genba also referring to the test as 'grievous provocative behaviour that destabilizes the peace and security of the region including our own country' (Security Committee, 17 April 2012). In this way, the construction of a high-risk framing of North Korean actions was sustained and the political tide of firm stance and practical imposition of sanctions at both United Nations (UN)-led and unilateral levels were continued.

Likewise, in the by then well-established pattern of voicing the opinions of a readership portrayed as at once more militant and right-leaning than the editors of the paper to which they were contributing, the *Asahi Shimbun* gave column space to a disgruntled citizen complaining that Japan's politicians were not doing enough to quickly counter the risks from the North. The comparison was made to European states in concluding that 'as much as possible, and as rapidly and accurately as able, [European states] have the crisis management capability to try and reach people and warn them. This is just what Japanese politicians lack' (19 April 2012). This expression of both the gravity of risks – identified as crisis-level – posed by North Korean missiles and the suggestion that the Japanese state could do more to pro-actively counter them, rather than any suggestion that the probability of risks had been overplayed, is recurrent. As with previous North Korean missile launches, the *Yomiuri Shimbun* and other leading news media agents were also consistent in this portrayal, and the phenomenon of cross-referencing various issues was also widespread (*Yomiuri Shimbun*, 18 April 2012). This swathe of mainstream discourse intersecting the state, market and society left any dissenting voices, including those of actors most at risk of incurring actual harms, isolated and marginalized.

3.4 Missiles and the risks of actual and potential harm

Evidently, it is highly problematic to accurately measure the causal link between mainstream discourse that articulates a recalibration of risk in response to North Korean missile test firing and the actual and potential harms that are manifest as a result. However, the fact that Japan has based its programme of official multilateral and unilateral sanctions, as well as a range of measures targeting North Korean actors and their associates in Japan, on responses to the series of post–Cold War missile tests conducted by the DPRK does not seem in doubt. Indeed, in the most self-evident examples, the fast-tracking of a collaborative BMD programme was justified with respect to the 1998 Taepodong-1 launch, and the adoption of UN Resolution 1695 – pushed for most prominently by Diet members in Tokyo – was stated as a direct response to the North's 2006 missile launches (MOFA 2006). Additionally, as explained further below, commercial market actors such as Keidanren have also shifted their political weight behind a tougher line. As resident Korean community leaders have attested (Interviews C and D, 17 July 2013 and 20 July 2013, Tokyo), whilst sanctions themselves have been directed at the North Korean state, the negative impact that such actions have had, in terms of reducing the security of the everyday for Korean residents on suspicion of aiding and abetting the regime in Pyongyang, has been significant.

In addition, the strangulation of remittances and punitive financial measures taken against organizations such as Chōsensōren (General Association of Korean Residents in Japan), Korean schools and Korean-run pachinko parlours, not to mention individual citizens of Korean origin, has had a highly discriminatory effect on those living within the legal bounds of Japanese law, as well as on Japan's societal and security authorities' practices. Whilst much of the stigmatization of Koreans and the extralegal harms inflicted as a result have been linked to the emotive issue of abductions and the highly sensitive issue of nuclear development, missiles have served most powerfully to direct policy in this area. In conflation with these elements, missiles have also provided a recurring theme by which state, market and societal actors in Japan are repeatedly reminded of the uncertainty of risks sourced within the DPRK.

The recalibration of risk in this sense has, as witnessed across the sources of discourse analysed above, not taken into account the cumulative negative effect of harms it is bringing about. Indeed, at the state level, the uncertainty of missile technology has been used – once again in tentative connection to other risks such as those posed by WMD – to evince the potential for North Korea to inflict untold damage upon Japan (MOD 2013: 19; Quinones 2006). Yet, by framing and mediating such risks in this way, successive administrations have continued to jeopardize the security of the everyday for the victimized ethnic minorities within its borders – apparently as a result of missile technology being developed by a seemingly unrelated regime in Pyongyang.

Finally, as will be discussed further throughout Chapter 7, Japan's particular reaction to nuclear development and testing practiced by the DPRK in the post–Cold War era has witnessed the full spectrum of state, market and societal actors intersecting Japan's policymaking apparatus. These actors have also been manoeuvred by the state's own interactive process of risk recalibration in response to missiles. Thereby, for example, state actors and their political representatives cannot be seen to do other than prioritize the potential harms of a missile strike, however unlikely. Similarly, societal opinion suggests these potential harms are prioritized above the actual harms to the security of the everyday as outlined above. In addition, market actors, such as Keidanren and other commercially driven stakeholders, have switched their position in relation to North Korea. This mostly moves them to adopt policies where the risk of investment in the DPRK's reforming economy is considered as too grave compared to allowing areas such as Japan's state military-industrial complex to suffer as a result of risks attached to missile strikes being recalibrated downwards. The factor of lucrative BMD technology being shared with the US also means that American market actors are at risk of suffering losses should Japanese lawmakers and business leaders change their evaluation of probable harms in favour of a less proactive response to missiles fired across the Sea of Japan.

It remains to be seen to what extent these commercial risks have been accurately calibrated in relation to their potential harms. However, as some of the most staunchly right-wing – and therefore supporting of a hard line against the DPRK – commentators in Japan have suggested themselves, China is slowly but surely economically colonizing large areas of North Korea (Sakurai 2007). As such, where China colonizes and exploits the North's resources, Japan is missing an economic opportunity. This is in terms both of missed commercial opportunities and also of the potential for the fostering of socio-political ties that could prove beneficial at an unknown juncture in the future.

4 Conclusion

In essence, from the first Nodong launch to the pivotal 1998 Taepodong-1 test firing over Japanese territory (and its successors launched into the Sea of Japan in 2006, 2009, 2012 and 2013), North Korea's missile launches have formed a central part of Japan's construction, framing and recalibration of risks identified with the DPRK. We have as a result witnessed a series of unilateral and multilateral sanctions and UN resolutions imposed and pushed for by the Japanese government and its allies and security partners in response. Such measures have not only served as a key element in worsening Japan–North Korea relations, but have also been part of a regional interaction between Tokyo, Washington and other stakeholder states that has seen a harmful deterioration in negotiations designed to reduce the isolation of North Korea. This has also compounded the complexities of how the risks are internalized in a form that adversely affects the security of the everyday for sections of Japanese society associated with the North.

What is more, at the domestic level, missile launches have played a major role in intensifying the negative depiction of North Korea, *per se*, and more subtly, the Korean community as a whole. They have also contributed to actual harms for those businesses, organization and individuals who require cross-border travel or financial transactions – including Japanese citizens with relatives in the DPRK. However, these and other harms inflicted as a function of the risk recalibration process have been deprioritized vis-à-vis a combination of issues that are given greater salience by the mainstream of state, market and societal actors. Not least this has been justified with regards to the additional risks identified with Pyongyang's growing nuclear capability. This issue, therefore, forms the central focus of Chapter 7, which explores how the combination of abduction, missile and nuclear issues has consolidated the processes identified above.[6]

Notes

1. The initial concept of securitization highlighted how the range and extent to which risks are identified and recalibrated into salient security concerns seemingly bear little correlation with the actual and potential harms that are being securitized (Buzan 1998).
2. Because of the politically loaded nature of the content, interviewees' identities have mostly been kept anonymous throughout. Please contact the author or publisher if further details are required.
3. Regardless of increased political tensions and the lack of an official Japan-ROK alliance, in geo-military terms Japan effectively operates with the US as an ally of South Korea.
4. As noted by respected Japan defence expert, Michishita Narushige (interview, 18 July 2013), Japan has already 'remilitarized,' now holding the fifth most capable military in the world, making the debate on Japan's remilitarization somewhat redundant. Indeed, as Michishita argues, if Japan is not militarized, nor is either of the Koreas or most other states both regionally and globally.
5. This has also been manifest in commercial risks faced by Korean enterprises within Japan, such as shops and pachinko parlours in the ethnic minority districts of major cities (*Japan Times*, 6 December 2013).
6. The additional – and mostly complementary – influences of abductions and nuclear issues are dealt with in Chapter 6 and Chapter 7 respectively.

References

Asahi Shimbun AJW (2013) "Insight: Abe adviser's visit to Pyongyang irritated allies but did little." Available online at: http://ajw.asahi.com/article/asia/korean_peninsula/AJ201307080091. Accessed 29 December 2013.

Buzan, Barry (1991) *People States and Fear: An Agenda for International Security Studies in the Post-Cold War Era*, London: Pearson Longman.
Cabinet Office, Government of Japan (2013) "*Gaikō ni kansuru yoron chōsa, zu 14 kankoku ni taisuru shinkinkan.*" Available online at: http://www8.cao.go.jp/survey/h25/h25-gaiko/zh/z14.html. Accessed 2 January 2013.
CNN International.com (2006) "U.S. officials: North Korea tests long-range missile." Available online at: http://edition.cnn.com/2006/WORLD/asiapcf/07/04/korea.missile/. Accessed 21 August 2013.
Global Security Newswire (2013) "Japan's new military build up seen as response to North Korea, China." Available online at: http://www.nti.org/gsn/article/japans-new-military-buildup-seen-response-north-korea-china/. Accessed 24 November 2013.
Hagström, Linus and Marie Söderberg (2006) "Taking Japan–North Korea relations seriously: Rationale and background," *Pacific Affairs* 79, 3: 373–85.
Hughes, Christopher W. (2009) "'Super-sizing' the DPRK threat: Japan's emerging security posture and North Korea," *Asian Survey*, 49, 2: 291–311.
Krauss, Ellis S. and Pharr, Susan J. (eds) (1996) *Media and Politics in Japan*, Honolulu: University of Hawaii Press.
Lynn, Hyung-Gu (2006) "Vicarious traumas: television and public opinion in Japan's North Korea policy," *Pacific Affairs*, 79, 3: 483–508.
Mason, Ra (2014) *Japan's Relations with North Korea and the Recalibration of Risk*, Abingdon, Oxon: Routledge.
Michishita, Narushige (2013) "Can a missile defence system defend Japan?" *The Straits Times* (Singapore), 15 May: 28.
MOD (2013) "Defense of Japan 2013." Available online at: http://www.mod.go.jp/e/publ/w_paper/2013.html. Accessed 22 August 2013.
MOFA (2006) "Statement by Mr Taro Aso, Minister for Foreign Affairs, on the adoption of the United Nations Security Council Resolution 1695 on the launch of missiles by North Korea." Available online at: http://www.mofa.go.jp/announce/announce/2006/7/0716.html. Accessed 21 August 2013.
—— (2008) *Japan's Disarmament and Non-Proliferation Policy* (Fourth Edition), Tokyo: Ministry of Foreign Affairs of Japan.
Quinones, Kenneth (2006) "North Korea's missile launches declare Kim Jong-Il's strategic decision to the international community," *Sekai*, 756 (September): 82–100.
Reuters (2013) "Japanese defence ministry reviewing 'buy Japan' policy." Available online at: http://in.reuters.com/article/2013/11/11/japan-defence-idINL4N0IW3DN20131111. Accessed 23 November 2013.
Sakurai, Yoshiko (2007) *Nihon yo, tsuyoki kuni to nare*, Tokyo: Diamond.
Samuels, Richard (2007) *Securing Japan: Tokyo's Grand Strategy and the Future of East Asia*, London: Cornell University Press.
Shigemura, Toshimitsu (2011) *Kim Jong-Il no kōkeisha*, Tokyo: Besuto Shinsha.
—— (2011) "*Nihonteki orientarizumu to kokusaikankei*," *Waseda Asian Review*, 9: 24–9.
Wada, Haruki (2009) "Japan-North Korea relations: a dangerous stalemate," *The Asia-Pacific Journal*. Available online at: http://www.japanfocus.org/-Wada-Haruki/3176. Accessed 3 November 2014.
Wishnick, Elizabeth (2009) "Competition and cooperative practices in Sino-Japanese energy and environmental relations: towards an energy security 'risk community'?," *The Pacific Review*, 22, 4: 401–28.

6
ABDUCTIONS BY NORTH KOREA

1 Introduction

The state-sponsored abduction of Japanese citizens by North Korean agents during the 1970s and 1980s served to facilitate a comprehensive recalibration of risks associated with the regime in Pyongyang across state, market and societal spheres in Japan (Mason 2014; Umeda 2007). This involved a process of logrolling by convergent domestic actors as well as the reframing of the North at the state level as an entity posing more than mere military challenges to Japan (Solingen 2007: 57–81). The process saw leaders (particularly Koizumi Junichirō and Abe Shinzō in his first period in office, 2006–7) seeking to utilize the issue to demonstrate their strength of leadership in the face of the risks that purportedly challenged Japan's sovereignty and identity, but were also portrayed as putting at risk the security of the everyday for individual Japanese citizens. This was combined with public backing and, ultimately desperate, support from organizations representing the interests of the families of abductees – once again highlighting the internalization of internationally located risk into the domestic domain. These included the *Kazokukai*, which gained popular support as a victims group manipulated by and in collusion with far rightist groups, to leverage the abduction cases as a means to mobilize anti-Korean sentiment and grassroots exclusionary nationalism, including the NARKN (*Japan Times*, 15 April 2003).[1]

The recalibration of risk at the state level, however, did little to affect the already negligible risk of citizens being kidnapped off Japan's northern coastline by agents from the DPRK.[2] Rather, those within Japan who actually faced the greatest potential and actual harms as a result of reactions to the issue were ethnic Korean citizens and their representative organizations, such as *Chōsensōren*, who became targeted on the largely erroneous grounds that they were somehow aiding and abetting state-sponsored terrorism – in the form of organized abductions (Chapman 2008).

This chapter, then, seeks to analyse how the disparity between risk framing via the recalibration of external risks, and harm to the security of the everyday that results from the recalibration process itself, is manifest in Japan's responses to state-sponsored abductions by North Korea. After first revisiting the emergence of the abduction cases as a salient issue in Japan, the chapter examines how risks related to abductions by North Korea have been mediated for strategic purposes by an intersection of state, market and societal actors, including politicians, civil society groups and market-based media actors. This examination is followed by an account of how risks have also come to be recalibrated as a greater source of ideational harm, in terms of reinforcing and defending individual identities and conceptions of citizenship. After going on to document how this recalibration process has inflicted actual harm upon Korean residents and others, the chapter concludes with a discussion of how the abduction issue has been conflated to the point where actors associated with both halves of the Korean peninsula are targeted via a complex interaction of contested political and ideological interests within Japan.

2 Before abduction was a risk

One of the first points that should be emphasized when analysing Japan's recalibration of risk with regards to the abduction of Japanese citizens by North Korea is the discrepancies in the timing of the events. Most pertinently, during the 1970s and 1980s, when the abductions actually took place, the risks to Japanese citizens were barely identified at all.[3] In other words, at the only time when there was even a minimal statistical possibility of a Japanese citizen being abducted by the DPRK's secret agents, no state, market nor societal actors in Japan had identified North Korea as posing a salient geo-political or ideological risk to Japan in any kind of pronounced or recognizable form. Of course, it can be argued that the most significant actors within Japan, such as those able to direct and transfer information via mass media, were yet to be fully convinced of the risks (*Asahi Shimbun*, 11 February 2008). Nevertheless, it is remarkable how a mostly retrospective issue – as there is no longer any substantial probability of being abducted – has gained such attention across state, market and societal spheres in Japan.[4] As this chapter, and this part of the book as a whole, goes on to demonstrate, this is emblematic of how processes of risk recalibration can work to profoundly affect domestic actors as a function of foreign policy issues. This is in stark distinction from the probabilities of actual and potential harm. In this sense, such processes are shown to be decoupled from the threat perceptions that they are typically attached to by political actors and other stakeholders.

The emergence of the abduction cases within public discourse first came to full prominence via the state as Japanese investigators concluded in 1997 that the North Korean side had been economical with the truth regarding an investigation into the remains of eleven suspected abductees, who were allegedly abducted between 1977 and 1983 (MOFA 2002). This was then rapidly escalated as a cause for Japanese concern following the Taepodong-1 missile launch of 1998. Indeed, though far less overt than later combinations of missile and abduction issues mediated under state management, the conflation of the two issues – as being associated with a high-risk framing of the DPRK – can be seen to have originated as the formulaic pattern that characterized Tokyo-Pyongyang relations at that time (Mason 2014). However, the impact that this began to exert, in terms of inflicting actual harms, was first felt primarily at the sub-state level. In essence, the abductions' emergence as a politicized issue, acted in combination with the geo-military concerns (also covered below and further in Chapters 5 and 7) to hamper efforts to restart bilateral normalization talks – and therefore to secure not only improved diplomatic but also social and economic exchanges as a result (Maslow 2013).

One of the often under-emphasized factors in the sourcing and construction of risks identified with the abduction cases, however, is its relation to how risks are attached not only to North Korea or the Kim-led regime, but to the Korean peninsula and populace as a whole. As confirmed by a number of specialists in the field (Interviews C, A and E, 17, 18, 23 July 2013), in one sense the abduction issue allowed a historical prejudice, already felt strongly within Japan against Koreans both inside and outside of its borders, to be justified and made politically acceptable. This psychological connection between state-sponsored abductions committed by agents from the DPRK and Koreans as a whole came as the result of how risks sourced from North Korea became framed. The abduction issue was central to this because it added the emotional and ideational elements lacking in the less emotive risks internalized from the perceived threats of missiles, nuclear weapons or even maritime incursions, as covered in more detail below. This was also combined with a long period of extended growth that ended with the bursting of Japan's economic bubble in 1991, which had provided a level of affluence sufficient to provide elements of Japan's state, market and society with the impetus to reflect on perceived past wrongdoings and amend laws directed at reducing the risk of the *contamination* of Japan's population by resident Koreans.[5] This culminated in the removal of enforced fingerprinting of resident Koreans during the 1990s – with such a positive move to reduce discrimination being close to unimaginable in the current socio-political climate (Interview F, 20 July 2013).

In the above sense, prior to risks being recalibrated, Japan was unable to justify a derogative attitude towards Koreans or openly discuss the risks presented by Koreans' activities. Not least, this was because Koreans had previously been victims of racial profiling and Japanese discrimination and aggression (Lie 2008). The reversal of this perceived role as victim was made possible within Japan in the case of abductions by North Korean state agents, which became of central importance to reframing risks for instrumental purposes of identity reformation (Tanaka 2009: 217–19). In other words, there was motivation for the Japanese state authorities and leading media actors to orchestrate a discriminatory attitude towards resident Koreans as a function of these risks. Yet, the harm caused as a result of this process was disproportionate to the relatively tiny number of confirmed abductions.

3 Abductions and strategic risks

Consideration of the impact of North Korean abductions upon how risks have been recalibrated to serve strategic interests at the state level in Japan offers an important case study which further highlights the empirical significance, outlined in the introduction to the book, of the theoretical distinction between risks and the threats to which they are often attached (Luhmann 1996: 6). In no uncertain terms, as Funabashi Yōichi, chairman of the Rebuild Japan Initiative Foundation (RJIF) – a leading Japanese think tank that has been tasked with analysing likely crisis scenarios for Japan including the collapse of North Korea – asserted, "the abduction issue has changed Japan's political process radically" (Interview, 18 July 2013). It is largely understood, therein, that (1) right-of-centre political forces have utilized the abduction issue to spotlight other potential North Korean threats – such as missiles and nuclear proliferation (dealt with in other chapters) – and that (2) the mediation of these threats has exerted a negative influence upon bilateral relations. The extent of this process's harmful impact upon the ethnic Korean community in Japan (see below) has been less prominently covered, but the disparity in the consequences of risk mediation faced by ethnic Koreans as a result in itself reflects the inequality of risk governance – as discussed further in Part III of this book. However, what has not been carefully examined is how these aspects have been realized through an active process of risk recalibration. This cannot be fully explained solely by discussing threats, because, unlike risks, a threat cannot be an active choice. In other words, one cannot transitively *take* threats; they are limited only to identifiable, external sources of harm. Risks, on the other hand, represent choices that are both taken and incurred.

In this regard, policymakers and security managers have been willing to risk the future improvement of Japan–North Korea relations (Hagström and Söderberg 2006a) and a potential stake in any commercial developments that may result from economic market reforms under Pyongyang's new leadership. They have also come to sacrifice – in one sense as collateral damage – the ability of the state to protect its own resident population against the resulting risks and actual harms that materialize. For instance, this includes violent domestic discrimination, documented further below. Such 'boomerang' effects come partially as the result of strategic risk avoidance in relation to the abduction issue. Furthermore, this has been supported at the state level in view of the strategic argument that the risk of China's rise being mismanaged has to be prioritized before all such everyday security concerns by Japan in order to protect Japan's mid- to long-term interests. In this sense, to access and accurately analyse how political agency acts upon these issues we need to look beyond the limited scope of China or North Korea threat theories, to examine what risks are being both identified and taken as an apparent means to ameliorate contingent aspects of internal as well as international security dilemmas. This explains why issues with high political stakes but low geo-military risk, such as the abduction of Japanese citizens by North Korea, can be of such pivotal significance.

Additionally, we need to consider how the various risks posed to US strategic interests and regional stability have played a role in shaping how risks related to the abduction issue have been recalibrated in Japan (Defense Intelligence Agency 2012; Hughes 2009). Indeed, here, too, interstate strategic influence has been brought to bear on the process – without comparable attention being assigned to the everyday security of societal subsections. As explained in the following section, this is further complicated by individual politicians acting to secure their own short-term political interests or stockpile of political capital. In many cases Diet lawmakers are eager to be seen as maintaining a firm line on the abduction issue. This is something which causes a tension between the long-term strategic interests of Japan's policymakers and security managers in ameliorating risks through the alliance with the US, and the immediate need to appease and appeal to a consistently anti–North Korean electorate for which abduction remains the issue of greatest concern in relation to the DPRK (Cabinet Office Poll 2014).

Not least because of the timing, when North Korean nuclear issues were capturing centre stage across global media sources, Iijima Isao's May 2013 visit to Pyongyang is a striking case study in this regard. In a semi-official capacity, as a *goodwill messenger* from Prime Minister Abe Shinzō, Iijima's focus on resolving the abduction issue, without joint collaboration with Seoul or Washington, demonstrates the further complicating factor of risks relating to the abduction cases as a whole. In the case of Abe's dispatch of Iijima, he risked further souring regional relations in order to secure his own domestic support through an apparent show of leadership skills and indomitability on an issue from which the prime minister has long sought to extract political capital (Miller 2013).

4 Abductions as a political and market risk

In terms of the significance of the abduction issue - in relation to how risks are constructed, framed and mediated by Japan's state in a way that leads to harm to the security of market and societal actors - its greatest salience lies ultimately in the sphere of political risk. This stems particularly from the momentum of convergent agency (e.g. support groups for the victims' families, rightist political factions, mainstream media companies, etc.) that until Abe's second term in office created a climate within which no politician could gain political capital by pursuing a more moderate line towards the DPRK (Leheny 2006: 167; Hagström and Söderberg 2006b: 382–3). In other words, in terms of political survival, the short-term risks of being seen as either conciliatory towards North Korea or insensitive to the Japanese victims of North Korean abductions (or both) have inevitably been considered greater than the mid- to long-term risks manifest in allowing Japan's deadlocked bilateral relations with Pyongyang to endure.

Indeed, as one former Japanese government negotiator with North Korea pointed out, the abduction issue's political toxicity likely still has longevity in this sense because until it can be convincingly proven that all abductees are in fact dead or accounted for, the issue will re-emerge every time North Korea test fires a missile or nuclear device, or raises its level of hostile rhetoric towards Japan (Interview C, 17 July 2013). The result is that overt downward recalibration of risks identified with the North by politically motivated actors bears the potentially severe consequence of being discredited. Indeed, Prime Minister Abe has only been able to gain political capital from a more moderate line in his second term in office because of his entrenched image of being tough on North Korea. As developed further in Chapter 7, the interactive process between key state and media actors and the conflation of abduction, missile and nuclear issues, represent the structural cornerstones for how risks framed against North Korea have been recalibrated and explain why a range of harms continue to be inflicted upon the security of the everyday as a result.

However, it should also be stressed that the impacts of both waning media-based market and societal interest in the abduction issue, as well as the greater influence of worsening Japan-ROK relations, have in fact played significant roles in shaping a recalibration of risk downwards in response to the abductions cases themselves in recent years (Takashima 2006). This is driven not least by a perception within both state and commercial (such as Japan's large business groups, or *zaikai*) spheres that a deterioration of relations with South Korea is not such an extreme risk for Japan as might at first be assumed. The reasoning behind this is based on the idea that Tokyo-Seoul trade relations are well established and not easily damaged, as well as the advantage to media outlets to be able to create a new Korea narrative, this time directed at the peninsula's southern half, that will sell, as interest in the North, and particularly abductions, wanes.[6] Here again, then, the intersection of state-market interests in risk governance comes largely at the disregard of localized risks to livelihoods or businesses adversely affected by such changes to the existing Korean risk narrative.

5 Abductions and the risks to identity

When considering the actual and potential harms posed to everyday security in response to the issue of North Korea's state-sponsored abductions, the relevance of identity looms large. In this sense, the sourcing, construction, framing and recalibration of risk is less obvious, but salient nonetheless. This is so not least because of the abduction issue's malleability, particularly as a practical means by which to transform Japan's status from aggressor to victim (Tanaka 2009: 217; Hanssen 2011: 65–6). Prior to the emergence of the abduction issue, without a means by which to vindicate state-level behaviour, Japan's policymakers continually faced the risk of being discredited as insensitive, provocative or racist if criticizing Korean actions. This stemmed in one sense from a national sense of guilt that was felt at state and, perhaps more critically, at societal levels and maintained Japan's identity as that of aggressor, based on its colonial history on the Korean Peninsula. However, through what one leading former journalist on the issue described as a process of 'psycho-engineering' (Interview G, 18 July 2013), those on the right of Japan's political spectrum were able to remove this risk to self- and state identity and replace it with a risk constructed around threats to identity and victimization, based on the unlawful actions of the DPRK's agents. This state-level risk recalibration was then transposed to the individual level of citizens, as somehow representative of a collective national identity.

As alluded to in the introduction to this book, the articulation of this process is expressed clearly via mainstream political and media discourse. This is particularly evident with reference to an outspoken prioritization of the abduction issue by parliamentarians, which became intensified following the September 2002 Pyongyang summit and admission by Kim Jong-Il that state-sponsored abductions did indeed take place. The ensuing recalibration process was backed by a media tailwind, but was led at the state level by prominent politicians such as former and present prime ministers, chief cabinet secretaries and defence ministers, including, among others, Koizumi Junichirō, Abe Shinzō, Asō Tarō and Ishiba Shigeru. However, emotive language was used to evince the substantial emotional harm caused to Japanese abductees' families as a result of abductions – and to defend national identity. Such language was used not only by these elite figures, but by a broad range of actors from the political upper echelons in the months that followed Koizumi's September 2002 meeting with Kim. The thrust of this was exemplified by coalition, *Kōmeitō*, party representative Araki Kiyohiro, who spoke on 23 October 2002 to the main session of the Diet; he said, 'We ourselves are torn apart when thinking of [the victims' and their families'] indescribable pain and anguish.' Araki, as a case in point, then immediately went on to discuss this abstracted suffering in relation to 'the primary responsibility of the state being the defence of its citizens' lives and property.' Hence, he both linked the risk of potential and actual personal emotional harm to national sentiment and material loss.[7]

The subtle shift in the framing of North Korea within Japan – in terms of its impact upon how risks to political identities were recalibrated – is also evident from opposition members. This has been particularly noticeable when coming from those who would be expected to be more sympathetic towards Pyongyang, and can be seen in the context of a rapidly declining leftist influence in Japanese politics and society after the end of the Cold War and the perceived failure of Soviet-led socialist systems (Christensen 1994: 597–7; Steel and Kabashima 2010). Reaction by the Communist Party of Japan (JCP) in the same session (as Araki above) of the Diet, for example, is illustrative in this respect. Indeed, with political capital at risk for anyone seen to be soft on a hostile North Korean regime culpable for state-sponsored abductions, Representative Ichida Tadayoshi was quick to both reiterate comments made by the likes of Araki and then prime minister Koizumi in confirming staunch criticism of Kim Jong-Il's regime, as well as reaffirming his party as being 'in a state of complete separation from the Communist Party of North Korea' (Main session, 23 October 2002). In this way, the growing prominence of the abduction issue came to be a key game-changer in terms of demarcating the internal ideational risks to political identities. The framing of these risks could then be credibly sustained – without risking long-term damage to reputations and, ultimately, popular support.

Similarly, leading Japanese media sources also contained a plethora of indirect references to identity in their reactions to the emerging revelations attached to North Korean abductions. Once again, as observed within political circles, the conflation of issues relating to risks to the security of the everyday with national sentiment and geo-military threats was a prominent feature of how the risk recalibration process took hold. Concurrently, in terms of this intersecting the state, market and society, elements of this particular ideological reconceptualization within the media were visible across a broad spectrum of political alignments, which ranged from the staunchly rightist *Sankei Shimbun* to the traditionally left-leaning, or at least liberal, *Asahi Shimbun*. For example, the *Yomiuri Shimbun*, which along with more extreme rightist media actors such as the *Sankei Shimbun* played a leading role in promoting the abduction issue, highlighted not only the emotional suffering of the victims but also the shock and distress of the Japanese leaders and negotiators. In other words, all fellow Japanese nationals, including Koizumi and Abe, were apparently victimized in collective suffering following the revelations of state-sponsored abductions by the North that came to light at the summit. Indeed, the sudden emergence of risks that were tangible, yet uncertain in their overall consequences, was even specifically juxtaposed by the newspaper in contrast to the prime minister's assertion that the summit was 'more of a chance than a risk' (*Yomiuri Shimbun*, evening edition, 18 September 2002). This was as if to demonstrate how in fact there were serious risks of a multifaceted (e.g. socio-emotional and geo-political) nature that had been made apparent via the abduction issue coming fully into perspective. In concordance, *Yomiuri* editorials painted a picture of a reframed North Korea – embodying an identity that was at once harmful to vulnerable Japanese citizens and a risk to national security (*Yomiuri Shimbun*, 19 September 2002).

As with the political rivals in the Diet, spotlighted above, convergence towards the recalibration of risks associated with the abductions cases – not least in terms of being posed or framed against a specific identity – was also present in Japan's major competing media outlets. This was to varying degrees, but exhibited comparable aspects across the commercial sectors, particularly with regards to leading national newspapers. In this respect, the *Asahi Shimbun*, often accused of being overly sympathetic towards the North, and nicknamed *Chōnichi Shimbun* (a word-play reusing the characters in its title to mean 'Korea-Japan Newspaper') by those on the political right, was quick to rebuff the risk of being identified as soft on North Korea. Measures to ensure it could avoid such an association again revolved partially around identity – and the everyday security of its commercial viability if risking a softer line on the DPRK. One aspect of this involved emphasizing its position as a voice of the people and Japanese society, including giving coverage to reader comments that highlighted the harms inflicted by the DPRK (*Asahi Shimbun*, 19 September 2002).

Similar sentiments expressed by prominent domestic politicians and others were also profiled (*Asahi Shimbun*, 20 September 2002), suggesting the *Asahi*'s awareness both of the risk to its own societal identity, as well as its core commercial interests, should it be too closely associated with DPRK sympathizers. This was then expressed in the perceived need to emphasize a shared emotional outpouring at national and individual levels. The conflation of these concepts with the geo-military issues of missile and nuclear programmes (discussed in Chapters 5 and 7) was, therefore, in one sense realized through a process in which key actors in Japan's political and media elites juxtaposed individual and national identity with risks presented by the DPRK.

6 Harms resulting from abductions

Evidently, the abduction (in addition to forced immigration and naturalization) of Japanese citizens from their place of residence in Japan to North Korea by Pyongyang's agents represents a clear and hard-to-dispute form of actual harm. However, as expressed in the introduction to this part of the book, there have been a range of other actors adversely affected as a result of reactions and responses to these state-sponsored criminal acts. Far less well-documented and publicized in Japan, for example, is the immeasurable impact that Tokyo's state-led response to the North's abductions has had upon the ethnic Korean community. This form of actual harm inflicted upon directly unrelated actors in Japan comes as a result of the ensuing process of reaction to and recalibration of risks that are cognitively (rather than logistically) associated with the abduction issue. The abductions are central in this regard because they are far more emotive than the objective threats of missile or nuclear capabilities identified with Pyongyang, but can be conflated with those and other issues associated with the North as a negative entity (see also Chapters 5, 7 and 8). The result, in terms of potential and actual harms, is that all elements connected with Korea identified as a single whole have been stigmatized in Japan – bringing a range of life-changing risks and actual damages to economic, social and political organizations and actors. Indeed, as stated by one prominent leader of the ethnic Korean community in Tokyo, the situation for the so-called *Zainichi*, or resident Koreans, is now in its worst state in sixty years (Interview H, Ebisu, 17 July 2013).

These harms include a number of somewhat notorious incidents, such as the stoning of Korean school buses and the targeting of the General Association of Korean Residents in Japan, *Chōsensōren*, through punitive measures that restrict its ability to trade and operate businesses, extending to the removal of special school fees and tax exemptions (Maslow 2013: 1; Tokunaga 2011). In addition, until its recent partial removal under the current Abe administration the imposition of a comprehensive trade embargo and other sanctions meant that all those connected to North Korea, such as relatives, were also effectively unable to travel by land or sea to the DPRK and are still unable to send more than intercepted letters to their loved ones on the far side of the Sea of Japan. The above are all as a direct result of sanctions imposed by the Japanese state.[8] However, the particularly constructed nature and narrative of the abduction issue in regards to how these measures are justified is also noteworthy here. This has been something which both local and national authorities, as well as a plethora of media actors and lobbyist groups, have emphasized as purportedly inflicting harmful consequences on families in Japan.

Other harmful *side effects* to the security of the everyday resulting from Japan's obsession with North Korean abductions are diverse and serious for those actors most affected, though they are rarely deemed newsworthy – once again highlighting the inequality of state and sub-state risk narratives. Japanese citizens with relatives in the North, for example, are no longer able to travel short-term to visit them or even send basic supplies such as medicines. In addition, published materials from the DPRK cannot be imported. This is a legal restriction that may ostensibly be deemed justifiable in order to prevent the North's regime from influencing a young generation of ethnic Koreans in Japan. However, not least in terms of reopening a more wide-reaching dialogue between the two countries on the abductions and other related issues, such as Japan's wartime behaviour, the restriction of literary imports from North Korea can surely only be seen to exacerbate distrust and miscommunication. Further, the targeting of Korean schools and organizations was extended under the current Abe administration to include the removal of fee exemption status at prefectural (Kanagawa, Saitama, Hiroshima, Tokyo and Osaka) and, increasingly, city levels of local government – supported by ministerial decree (Interview H, Ebisu, 17 July 2013).

Given the tangible harms being inflicted upon the security of the everyday in the cases documented above, it is clear that discourse mediating the issues identified with the abductions cases has played a major emotive role in bundling risks associated with all actions sourced from Pyongyang in Japan (Mason 2014; Wittig 2005). The resulting momentum, and extent of harms inflicted thereafter, has meant that those most affected, such as the *Zainichi* Koreans, have been forced to take a range of measures in an attempt to avoid the risks of further harm being suffered. It is striking in this regard that, other than some mostly fruitless attempts to publicize the current plight of resident Koreans through the mass media and cultural exchanges, there has been extremely little concerted effort to counteract *en masse* – by either the Korean community as a whole or individuals within it. Likewise, little has been done by legal entities, or other law enforcement authorities such as the police, to counter discriminatory actions that have led to these harms.[9]

Rather, as noted by one community representative (Interview I, Ikebukuro, 17 July 2013), the *Zainichi* are simply 'enduring it' *(gaman shiteiru)* in relation to the disproportionate burden of state-centric security that they are being forced to face in their daily lives. This includes finding ways around punitive economic sanctions, removing the term *'chōsen,'* or 'Korean' (or replacing it with *'kan,'* pertaining to South Korea – though this too is becoming less effective) from school buses and Korean restaurants, and in some cases naturalizing to Japanese citizenship or moving elsewhere. According to on-site interview accounts and supporting opinion poll data (*Mainichi Shimbun*, 19 August 2014), this is because the risks of reprisal, revenge or further persecution are considered to be higher if any kind of proactive countermeasures are taken, as opposed to the ability to limit the harm currently posed through the kinds of risk aversion measures listed above. In that regard, the decision of the Korean Residents Union in Japan *(Mindan)* representatives to finally take the matter of hate speech to the United Nations Human Rights Committee shows to just what a critical extent the problem has escalated (*Japan Times*, 30 August 2014).

7 Recalibrating complex risks connected to the Korean community

Ethnic Koreans in Japan have not, of course, remained entirely passive towards the current onslaught of discrimination and oppression being witnessed, but are in one sense trying to counter a socio-political, state-led risk narrative that runs against them. This has been outlined by the NGO Network for the Elimination of Racial Discrimination (ERD Net 2012). However, the process that undergirds such in the senses outlined above can be traced not only to historical prejudice directed at the Korean peninsula as whole, which is oft-times the result of risks perceived to emanate from an increase in Korean influence within Japan, but also, more specifically, to political repositioning and recalibration of specific risks, such as the abductions.

These harms have been brought about partly as a result of the disproportionate framing of the abduction issue, but are manifest in a broader context of responses to long-term economic stagnation and political neo-liberalization. As noted by one leading analyst (Interview J, 23 July 2013), a key aspect of this process is the destruction and disintegration of the left-leaning and old-form liberal parties in Japan with which Korean resident groups had a natural affinity and alliance (Steel and Kabashima 2010; Stockwin 2008). Indeed, the weakening of the left as a whole has given both a right-of-centre ruling party, in Abe's LDP, and right-wing extremists a mandate to attack (both figuratively and literally) resident Koreans in relation to issues attached to both the North and South.

Nevertheless, recent efforts have been made within the community to utilize the overextension of this directive in order to reinstate a sense of the *Zainichi* identity as, once again, victims rather than aggressors – and hence reposition the risk of Japan, at state and societal levels, being discredited for carrying out persecution (Mason 2013). Indeed, in tandem with more moderate political forces, representatives of the resident Korean community have already begun to make use of statements that are unpopular with the Japanese population as a whole – such as those made with regards to 'comfort women' by Osaka governor, Hashimoto Tōru, which put Japan's reputation at risk (BBC News Asia, 2013). However, we must note that there are limits to the extent such actors are able to recalibrate risks in their own favour. This is not least because of the inequality between state and sub-state risk governance illustrated throughout this book. Hence, as with the relative failure seen in North American and European anti-globalization movements, the influence that non-governmental groups can now hold over the political process at the state level is often minimal. This is particularly so given the Abe administration's more powerful mandate following lower and upper house election victories in 2012 and 2013 (Interview K, 23 July 2013).

Furthermore, as can be seen from the recent emergence of 'hate speeches' being given on a regular basis in areas with a high proportion of ethnic Koreans in Tokyo (Shinōkubo) and Osaka (Tsuruhashi), the continuing bilateral tensions between Japan and South Korea are, in effect, sustaining the risks already associated with North Korea (*Japan Times*, 6 December 2013). This is occurring most prominently via the abduction issue, to conflate a negative portrayal of the peninsula as a whole. In this regard, there has been cross-fertilization of risks sourced from the framing of the abduction issue into a more openly generalized persecution of all Korean elements.

In addition, the recent shift more towards a particular targeting of South Korea, even ahead of the North, by elements within Japan – and its combined effect in terms of stoking exclusionary nationalism on both sides of the Sea of Japan – has the potential to further increase the extent of actual harms in this area. As one leading journalist pointed out (Interview L, 24 July 2013), it only takes one fight to break out at a hate speech rally – and there have already been multiple confrontations – where someone is struck and killed to spark major unrest. There is a dearth of official crime statistics dedicated to hate crimes against *Zainichi*, but another security specialist at a leading think tank described the situation as a disaster, as both Tokyo and Osaka saw large increases in the number of hate speech gatherings in 2012–3 (*Japan Times*, 4 August 2014). This type of activity, he suggested, is to the point where despite the limitations of operating within a democratic state, the authorities need to work with media and NGOs to quell a deteriorating scenario in terms of ongoing harms and increased risk of violent escalation. Once again, these are state-orchestrated risks in origin, particularly as Japan lacks a legal basis to break rallies up, but these risks impact upon the security of the everyday for individual citizens (Interview M, 25 July 2013).

The harms to the Korean community in Japan have also been compounded by state actors, or those who inform them, continuing to prioritize risks such as those associated with the unlikely possibility of social uprising and unrest, for instance. Indeed, as the head of one government-funded think tank remarked, when asked about the risk of further harms that might be inflicted upon Korean residents, 'Is there a risk? Oh, you mean of the Koreans causing trouble?' The same representative also quickly went on to discuss the risk of trained North Korean agents still living within the Korean community in Japan, who might be mobilized by Pyongyang at any time in order to inflict harm by way of coordinated terrorist acts (Interview N, 24 July 2013). Such statements highlight how politicized and open to reinterpretation the narratives of risk and harm in relation to Korea and Korean residents have become. Moreover, this is further exacerbated by the protracted deterioration of relations between the Park administration in Seoul and her counterparts in Tokyo (Interview O, 24 July 2013).

8 Conclusion

This chapter has, then, elucidated how the state response to the abduction of Japanese citizens by North Korean agents in the late 1970s and 1980s has exerted an important influence over the articulation of risks associated with both halves of the Korean peninsula by the Japanese population at large. It has also revealed how risks identified with Koreans as a whole have continued to be sourced, constructed and recalibrated in Japan, resulting in an oft-times highly disproportionate distribution of actual and potential harms. This has involved a complex process of political and ideological contestation over risk governance, which impacts heavily upon the security of the everyday at local levels. This incorporates using hate speech at demonstrations in areas populated by large numbers of ethnic Koreans, as well as local council members, regional governments and opposition politicians seeking to gain political capital and personal or national prestige through powerful expressions of a particular anti-Korean rhetoric.

In the above sense, despite the relative waning of interest in the abduction issue at the commercial (market) media level, the possible harms that may have been inflicted upon the individual citizen, in the case of abductees for instance, continue to be officially prioritized ahead of both the risks posed to the entire ethnic community of *Zainichi* Koreans and, ultimately, interstate regional relations as well. Indeed, this appears to be understood with respect to the deprioritizing of Japan–South Korea relations and in spite of recent moves by the Abe administration seeking a resurrection of normalization talks with the DPRK. The continuation of an essentially hard line and the inability of government authorities to effectively disentangle themselves from the abduction issue, whether actively seeking to or not, mean that the state continues to play a central role in inflicting an array of harms, internally, at both ideological and physical levels. North Korea's ongoing nuclear proliferation and testing has intersected and punctuated this process in the post–Cold War context; how Japan has constructed and recalibrated the risks attached to these highly symbolic – as well as potentially deadly – weapons and the resulting harmful effects, therefore, forms the basis for discussion in Chapter 7.

Notes

1 National Association for the Rescue of Japanese Kidnapped by North Korea (NARKN) is the group previously led by Satō Katsumi. Originally a leftist activist, Satō converted to nationalistic right-wing extremism because of his own personal experiences relating to North Korea.
2 The government of Japan identifies seventeen abductions of Japanese citizens by North Korean agents, all of which reportedly took place between 1977 and 1983 – making the statistical likelihood of being abducted during the post–Cold War era almost non-existent.
3 For a full list and documentation of the confirmed abductions cases, see Headquarters for the Abduction Issue, Government of Japan (2011).
4 It should be noted that an awareness of the suspicion of North Korean abductions was present across leading media outlets some years earlier – and was given coverage,

particularly in combination with the 1993–4 nuclear crisis, by those on the political right of the spectrum (see *Sankei Shimbun*, 30 July 1994).
5   Most notably this relates to the colonial (1910–41) mistreatment of Koreans by the Japanese state.
6   Moreover, it was stated by one leading analyst (interview, 23 July 2013) that negotiators in the upper echelons of Japan's political elite had grown 'tired' of what they felt were their best efforts to improve relations with Seoul – and were now more concerned about trying to improve Japan-China relations at whatever risk to letting ROK-Japan relations fall by the wayside. This has become a further sticking point in Japan-China-ROK summit meetings as well, as both *junior partners* (Japan and the ROK) feel that if China is on board the other party will, essentially, have to follow.
7   The reference to risks posed to life and personal property is also key in terms of Japan as being identified as victim – rather than as the perpetrator of colonial aggressions and material exploitation, for which it is expected to accept responsibility for and pay compensation for as part of any normalization process with the North.
8   The now tight restrictions imposed on remittances and other goods are dealt with in greater detail in Chapter 8.
9   One exception to this state-led unwillingness, seemingly linked to negative perceptions of all elements sympathetic towards North Korea in Japan – that in itself being a phenomenon linked closely to public opinion on the abductions issue – has been the recent lawsuit in favour of Kyoto Chōsen Gakuen – a North Korean-allied school. This saw the anti–North Korean group, known as *zaitokukai*, restrained and fined over ¥12m for racist defamation (Fujiwara 2013).

References

BBC News Asia (2013) "Japan WWII 'comfort women' were necessary." Available online at: http://www.bbc.co.uk/news/world-asia-22519384. Accessed 20 August 2013.
Cabinet Office Poll (2014), "*Gaikō ni kansuru yoron chōsa: Kitachōsen e no kanshin jikō*". Available online at: http://survey.gov-online.go.jp/h26/h26-gaiko/2-1.html. Accessed 17 February 2015.
Chapman, David (2008) *Zainichi Korean Identity and Ethnicity*, Abingdon, Oxon: Routledge.
Christensen, Raymond (1994) "Electoral reform in Japan: how it was enacted and changes it may bring," *Asian Survey*, 34, 7: 589–605.
Defense Intelligence Agency (2012) "Annual threat assessment: statement before the Senate Armed Services Committee." Available online at: http://www.dia.mil/public-affairs/testimonies/2012-02-16.html. Accessed 23 November 2013.
ERD Net (2012) "Report on the hate speech against minority communities in Japan." Available online at: http://www2.ohchr.org/english/bodies/cerd/docs/discussion/TD28082012/NetworkJapaneseNGO.pdf. Accessed 19 November 2013.
Fujiwara, Gakushi (2013) "Kyoto court bans 'hate speech' around school for ethnic Koreans," *Asahi Shimbun, AJW*. Available online at: http://ajw.asahi.com/article/behind_news/social_affairs/AJ201310070090. Accessed 17 November 2013.
Hagström, Linus and Marie Söderberg (eds) (2006a) *North Korea Policy: Japan and the Great Powers*, New York: Routledge.
——— (2006b) "Taking Japan-North Korea relations seriously: rationale and background," *Pacific Affairs*, 79, 3: 373–86.
Hanssen, U. A. Rynning (2011) "Changes in Japanese attitudes toward North Korea since '9/17,'" MA thesis (unpublished), University of Oslo. Available online at: https://

www.duo.uio.no/bitstream/handle/10852/24204/Hanssen.pdf?sequence=1. Accessed 5 November 2014.

Headquarters for the Abduction Issue, Government of Japan (2011) "Individual cases: 17 abductees identified by the government of Japan." Available online at: http://www.rachi.go.jp/en/ratimondai/jian.html. Accessed 26 October 2013.

Hughes, Christopher (2009) "'Super-sizing' the DPRK threat: Japan's emerging security posture and North Korea," *Asian Survey*, 49, 2: 291–311.

Leheny, David (2006) *Think Global, Fear Local: Sex Violence and Anxiety in Contemporary Japan*, Ithaca: Cornell University Press.

Lie, John (2008) "Zainichi recognitions: Japan's Korean residents' ideology and its discontents," *The Asia-Pacific Journal*, 11. Available online at: http://japanfocus.org/-John-Lie/2939. Accessed 10 December 2013.

Luhmann, Niklas (1996) "Modern society shocked by its risks," *Social Sciences Research Paper* (Occasional Paper) 17, Hong Kong: University of Hong Kong Social Sciences Research Centre.

Maslow, Sebastian (2013) "Japan, North Korea and the abduction issue," *East Asia Forum*. Available online at: http://www.eastasiaforum.org/2013/07/05/japan-north-korea-and-the-abduction-issue/. Accessed 16 November 2013.

Mason, Ra (2013) "Exclusionary nationalism in Japan: the dangers of institutionalized racism," *Asahi Shimbun, AJW Forum*. Available online at: http://ajw.asahi.com/article/forum/politics_and_economy/east_asia/AJ201310040032. Accessed 17 November 2013.

—— (2014) *Japan's Relations with North Korea and the Recalibration of Risk*, Abingdon, Oxon: Routledge.

Miller, J. Berkshire (2013) "Abe's North Korean riddle," *The Diplomat*. Available online at: http://thediplomat.com/flashpoints-blog/2013/06/02/abes-north-korean-riddle/. Accessed 2 November 2013.

MOFA (2002) "Outline and background of abduction cases of Japanese nationals by North Korea." Available online at: http://www.mofa.go.jp/region/asia-paci/n_korea/abduct.html. Accessed 26 October 2013.

Solingen, Etel (2007) *Nuclear Logics: Contrasting Paths in East Asia and the Middle East*, Princeton: Princeton University Press.

Steel, Gill and Ikuo Kabashima (2010) *Changing Politics in Japan*, Ithaca: Cornell University Press.

Stockwin, James A. A. (2008) *Governing Japan: Divided Politics in a Resurgent Economy*, Malden: Blackwell.

Takashima, Nobuyoshi (2006) *Rachimondai de yugamu nihon no minshushugi: ishi wo nageru nara watashi ni nage yo*, Tokyo: Supeisu Karō.

Tanaka, Hitoshi (2009) *Gaikō no chikara*, Tokyo: Nihon Keizai Shimbun Shuppansha.

Tokunaga, Risa (2011) "Racism in Japan: exclusion of Korean Schools from the high school fee exemption policy," *Voices from Japan*, 25 (March): 32–4.

Umeda, Masaki (2007) *"Kitachōsen no kyōi" to shūdanteki jieiken*, Tokyo: Kōbunken.

Wittig, Alexandra (2005) "Evolving perceptions of North Korea in the post-Cold War era as reflected in the Japanese media," MA thesis (unpublished), University of Cambridge.

7
NUCLEAR TESTING

1 Introduction

North Korea's escalation of nuclear development fluctuated considerably throughout the 1990s as the government sought to maintain a deterrent to potential external intervention. The leadership was preoccupied in particular by the interpretation of US intentions, on the one hand, whilst at the same time seeking to increase trade, investment and aid with a range of regional states, not least Japan, on the other. This period was followed in the twenty-first century by the North's testing of nuclear devices in 2006, 2009 and 2013. Japan's highly sensitized position with regards to nuclear issues – as the only state to suffer nuclear warfare – meant that Pyongyang's provocations in this sphere were rapidly recalibrated as salient risks; indeed, in one sense, up to the potential level of the annihilation of humankind by leading political figures and media actors in Tokyo (*Asahi Shimbun*, 28 May 2009). As detailed below, Japan's hyper-sensitivity to nuclear risks was further compounded following the North's 2013 nuclear test, on account of the socio-political fallout from the Fukushima nuclear plant crisis in the wake of the Great East Japan Earthquake of March 2011. Market actors, such as major media companies, as well as vast swathes of society, joined this consensus led by the state, which acted to further reinforce the framing of North Korea (which was associated with the missile and abduction issues as discussed in Chapters 5 and 6). Once again the gulf between risks has been stark in terms of the limited potential harms being inflicted at the level delineated by the state, and those actually hindering the ability to progress normalization of regional and bilateral relations, including denuclearization of the Korean Peninsula. The contingent impact upon the security of the everyday for ethnic Koreans in Japan is one of the outcomes of the framing of North Korea in this way.

Having established the processes of risk construction, framing and recalibration identified through examination of the prevailing public sphere discourses, unpacked in Chapters 5 and 6, this chapter analyses the nuclear issue to contextualize the extent of the shortcomings in theories of deterrence. This enables us to further explain how ideology and identity construction at the state level take precedence over *probability* and the security of the everyday within leading political and media discourses. Once again such discourse is examined as a means by which to access and assess how policymaking has been informed by processes of risk recalibration. The aim here is to further illustrate how actual and potential harms for the Japanese state and its population have been brought about as much by ideological immobility as deliberate over-calibration of risks that relate to Pyongyang's nuclear development. In other words, the chapter primarily demonstrates the extent to which the concerns over North Korean weaponry by policymakers and security managers are a function of Japan's post–Cold War identity. This includes aspects of anti-nuclearism, but also anti-communism, and is additionally intertwined with the at-times contradictory roles of economic and ideological leaders in East Asia. At the same time, victims are a major concern in terms of actual harms inflicted by US nuclear weapons and potential harm that might be incurred via a North Korean attack or accident. In this sense, there has been a complex confluence of ideas and identities that once again intersect the state, market and society. The theoretical application of risk to the empirical discourse that articulates this nexus, therefore, adds value to the study of not only Japan–North Korea relations, but also provides a further nuanced elucidation of the internalization processes involved. Ultimately, the chapter reveals that the political energy, societal investment and monetary cost required to construct and mediate the risks attached to the North's nuclear development is in itself the cause of considerable potential and actual harm to the security of the everyday in Japan.

2 The risk of a nuclear strike against Japan

As some analysts (Michishita 2013; Endō 2013) have concluded, a nuclear strike by North Korea, whilst an extremely unlikely contingency, is not strictly impossible in terms of the estimated capabilities being developed by Pyongyang. In addition, the nuclear capacity of a combined North Korea and China alliance – particularly given Beijing's leasing of land that reaches the Sea of Japan with the possibility of a naval as well as commercial port being built – must be considered.[1] The first risk identified is based on the premise that North Korea would not be willing to test its highly limited and (proportional to its GDP) expensive plutonium unless it believed it had made progress in its bomb-making technology at each stage. Therefore, every test is claimed by predisposed actors in Japan to represent a likely genuine advancement in the DPRK's nuclear power, rather than being interpreted as largely a political move within Pyongyang's existing tactics of regional brinkmanship.

In this sense, the device tested in 2009 was considerably more powerful, at an estimated four kilotonnes, than that detonated in 2006, which reportedly only reached around one kilotonne (Medalia 2010). The subsequent test, conducted in

February 2013, was not only even more powerful but, as alluded to in Chapter 5, preceded by high-risk missile launches. This is suggestive that, in accordance with both US intelligence and North Korean claims, missile and nuclear miniaturization programmes are being coordinated in such a way as to be able to simultaneously threaten the US mainland, South Korea and Japan. Despite a lack of conclusive evidence to support the above argument, its probability, if confirmed, would mean that theoretically there is a risk of a nuclear device being attached to a Japan-bound missile – however crude or inaccurate – with the subsidiary risk of thousands of Japanese lives being lost. This represents the ultimate risk to the security of the everyday in Japan. In this sense, defence analysts are able to source nuclear risks in North Korea and argue that without an appropriate capability to defend against them, Japan faces the risk of being coerced by Pyongyang into, for example, either normalizing relations or again becoming the victim of nuclear war (Michishita 2013). Having framed this risk in the form outlined above, particularly those supporting a strengthened Japanese military deterrence are always able to claim that this nuclear contingency should be prioritized above the amelioration of other potential harms. In any case, it is possible to claim that there is no way to prove a causal relationship between the process of risk recalibration in response to North Korea and the actual harms being incurred as a result, such as stagnated diplomatic ties, regional isolation and discrimination against resident Koreans. In addition, the risks of escalating regional tensions and/or further worsening relations with North Korea via such internalization processes can be subordinated based on the argument that, *however* unlikely, the risk of nuclear annihilation must be prioritized above all others.

However, whilst the analysis of these kinds of external threats in terms of deterrence is not without merit from a purely geostrategic perspective, the narrowing of focus in this way does not fully consider a far broader range of risks that intersect not only state security but also other areas of the market and the security of the everyday for a variety of societal stakeholders as well. As such, if only considering how to improve state defence systems and deterrents to lower the already low risk of a North Korean nuclear strike, in effect the risks borne by the other areas affected as a result are being further recalibrated themselves to a lower level – one which is not necessarily relative to the actual harms being exacted as a result.

As discussed in Chapter 5, the recalibration of geo-military risks framed against North Korea has already had a serious negative impact upon the security of the everyday for the resident ethnic Korean population in Japan, in terms of both increased risk and incurring of actual harms. Particularly in the case of nuclear issues, however, there are also evident risks created by this recalibration process that are internalized from the Japanese government's international relations, especially those with states within the East Asia region. This is the case not simply as a function of worsened or stagnated relations with Pyongyang, but also by way of how Japan is affected by US pressure, and Japan's own strained relations with China and, potentially, South Korea.[2] In addition, consolidation of practical strategic and tactical interoperability with the US is likely to increase concerns over Japan's longer-term aims of military expansion and fortification. This is compounded by the Abe administration's proactive rhetoric with regards to revising or, as achieved, reinterpreting the antimilitarist constitution to allow the exercise of collective self-defence and the revision of terminology used to identify the JSDF (*Wall Street Journal*, 18 July 2013). Ultimately, as predicted by the deputy head of the Korean History Research Centre in Tokyo (interview, 17 July 2013), the above also paves the way for Japan to develop its own nuclear capability within the next twenty years. This is something which, when combined with uncompromising statements from Japan's leading political actors with regards to historical issues, also carries the risk of further aggravating tensions with South Korea and pushing Seoul increasingly towards bandwagoning with China – a tendency which has already begun to be observed at state and market levels and has further potential impacts on the security of the everyday for a range of related actors.[3]

3 US pressure and strategic risks for deterrence

As suggested in Chapter 6, the US' interpretation of risks in East Asia and Japan's relationship with the Korean Peninsula serve to limit the recalibration of risks identified with Pyongyang. This has been evident in the sphere of nuclear proliferation even more than in the abduction issue, and is also linked to the US' displeasure at Japan's administration being seen to increasingly distance itself from South Korea, another key regional ally for both parties.[4] Somewhat ironically, this has also meant that the US is effectively providing the counter-balancing force against a regionally perceived risk that Japan, particularly under the second Abe administration, may become too muscular in its drive to reassert a leading international role. As one of the leading authorities on Japanese domestic politics noted (Interview P, 18 July 2013), this has been compounded by the political left having been substantially weakened in Japan over the past six decades and most of the leading opposition parties now in one sense being 'off-shoots of the [ruling] LDP.' It is, therefore, a serious concern for the current US administration that Japanese leaders such as Abe, Asō Tarō and Ishiba Shigeru continue to push a hard line in East Asian foreign policy to the point of aggravating relations with South as well as North Korea. This has also coincided, where deemed necessary, with the Japanese government's overruling of domestic concerns about the security of the everyday being put at risk from the nuclear fallout of the Fukushima disaster (Freund 2013).

Evidently it is highly problematic to claim that the Fukushima meltdown and radiation leak has been conflated to any large degree with risks posed by North Korea's nuclear programmes, but it has certainly reinforced the image of nuclear issues as bearing tangible risks. In that sense, the renewed fears of risk from nuclear power have given fresh impetus to voices calling for a resumption of the Six Party Talks (SPT), as well as those highlighting the danger of a comparable nuclear accident in the DPRK (Interview Q, 6 December 2013). In this sphere, too, the US plays a pivotal role in shaping how Japan is able to construct risks vis-à-vis North Korea. This stems from the fact that the US prioritizes nuclear and missile issues over those of abductions when identifying risks sourced from the DPRK (*Asahi Shimbun AJW* 2013a). In this sense, the US has supported the imposition of punitive sanctions against Pyongyang in so far as they act as a deterrent in curtailing the risk of the North pushing to develop further nuclear weapons – particularly those that could be miniaturized and attached to missiles that could reach the US mainland. In one regard, making use of this impetus, Japanese administrations have been able to capitalize on US concerns by attaching their own sanctions to a so-called comprehensive *(hōkatsuteki)* approach to North Korean risks and issues. This has allowed Japanese lawmakers to include Pyongyang's state-sponsored abductions in addition to nuclear proliferation as a justification for the recalibration or risks and contingent countermeasures.

Nevertheless, the role of US agency should not be underestimated in terms of how Japan has constructed risks attached to North Korea's nuclear programmes, including how the risks have been internalized as a function of ideology, as discussed below. Not least, this comes with the basic understanding that the US-Japan security alliance was consolidated during the Cold War in response to the perceived nuclear threat from the former Soviet Union (Nakamura 1985). Since the conclusion of the Cold War the US-Japan security relationship has sought to find new justifications for increased interoperability and the maintenance of up-to-date military capabilities. This has largely been as part of the US' attempt to maintain its powerful influence in the Western Pacific and contain a rising China (Hughes 2006; McCormack 2007; Zhou 2013). North Korea has provided an extensive element of justification for this process. Hence, the recalibration of risk in response to Pyongyang's nuclear programme may have been utilized to somewhat differing effect by the two alliance partners, but the reinforcement of Cold War perceptions, principles and practices has been achieved through it. Indeed, the association of the North with left-leaning elements in Japan has led to the left being further targeted by the US. This in turn has contributed to the discrediting of the left within Japan under mostly continuous US-aligned LDP administrations and, perhaps most significantly, powerful bureaucratic institutions such as the MOFA.

4 Nuclear tests as a risk to national identity

There are many, particularly on the more militarist side of the political spectrum, who would argue that Japan's stern responses to North Korean nuclear development are well founded (Katsumata 2014), and indeed that they are even understated – particularly with regards to the potential for Japan to revise its constitution. Such standpoints have been expressed by those at the very top of the policymaking elite both explicitly and implicitly (BBC 2006; Asō Tarō, Foreign Affairs Committee, 27 October 2006; Abe Shinzō, Main Diet Session, 14 October 2014). The precursors to this more open discussion of such can be traced to actions throughout the Cold War, namely those by the US and Japan, through covert as well as overt means, which sought to secure a deterrent against the threat of Soviet-led aggression. These actions were implemented through secret importation, via US nuclear naval dockings at Japanese ports (*Japan Times*, 17 May 2012). However, given the low probability of nuclear warfare and the extent to which other issues, such as missiles, are sufficient to allow 'risk entrepreneurs' to recalibrate the risks identified with North Korea, Japan's specific reaction to nuclear proliferation requires further attention. This also goes beyond the established rhetoric of Japan's 'nuclear allergy' (Aldrich 2012: 2–5). In reality one of the greatest risks posed to Japan by Pyongyang's nuclearization of the Korean Peninsula originates in the protection of Japan's identity – both as a 'peace state' and as a preeminent representative of non-proliferation. This goes beyond state-level projection of such to the very heart of Japanese society – and in this sense the security of the everyday. The recalibration of this risk is something which was reflected clearly in Japan's reactions to the North's nuclear tests between 2006 and 2013.

5   Reaction to the 2006 nuclear test

Japan's recalibration of risk in response to North Korea's first nuclear test was extensive in both qualitative and quantitative terms. Indeed, as a single event that affected Japan's responses to and relations with the DPRK it was exceeded only in overall scope and velocity by Japan's reaction to revelations of state-sponsored abductions, unearthed by former Prime Minister Junichirō Koizumi's summit meeting with Kim Jong-Il (Mason 2014). The magnitude of Japan's reaction was in part, as argued in the analysis of responses to the abduction issue (see Chapter 6), because of the emotive power of it being nuclear, as compared even to missiles (see Chapter 5) or other illicit activities perpetrated by North Korea and its agents in Japan. The nuclear risk contains powerful ideological aspects that further evinced this particular risk, however indirectly, as being linked to Japanese identity at both state and societal levels, which are intrinsically anti-nuclear.[5]

As also demonstrated in the cases of abductions and missiles – as well as Japan's territorial disputes, discussed in Part I – the form and trajectory of how risks are recalibrated is well expressed in the pertinent mainstream discourse, represented by Diet members and national newspaper coverage. In the Diet, the issues of nuclear testing and abduction were again brought together. Opposition figures were as outspoken and fervent in their linkage of such risks as their LDP counterparts in power (Main Session, *honkaigi*, 10 October 2006). This was further exemplified by DPJ shadow minister, Watanabe Shū, who, in also making reference to Cold War issues that reasserted Japan's position in a rivalry with the former Soviet-led communist powers, asserted that 'it is obvious that North Korea is up to something in the way it tries not to let Japan make this or that statement, based on the potential to greatly disturb history. Who knows how much history will be moved, but when diplomatic negotiation moves substantially, it is absolutely essential that Japan is not driven into a corner' (Special Committee on North Korean Abduction Issue and Related Matters, 7 December 2006). Here,

Watanabe's use of both reference to history and Japan as being cornered into a weaker position, therefore, internalizes the risks of abduction and nuclear testing – the primary topic of his address – into issues of Japan's regional position and the risk that the government might find itself victimized by Pyongyang as a result of historical guilt.

News media reaction was similarly focused on the powerful emotive impact – as well as the risk of potential harms – brought about by the nuclear nature of the North's October 2006 test. As observed in the case of the Taepodong-1 missile test launch, covered in Chapter 5, the *Asahi Shimbun*, for example, also showed an unprecedented form of risk recalibration in response to the underground detonation. This took the form of a clear profiling of North Korea in juxtaposition to Japan. The manner of such went well beyond mere discussion of the probable or even potential harms that could be inflicted upon the lives of Japanese citizens and their property. At the outset of a lengthy editorial two days after the test, outlining how risks posed by the North's nuclear testing should be stopped, the paper referred to the DPRK as 'Japan's closely neighbouring dictatorship . . . a country that has twisted international rules in even dirtying its hands with state-crimes such as abductions and terrorism.' This highly emotive branding of the North was then contrasted with Japan's identity as 'a victim-state of bombings which has felt the tragedy of nuclear power with its own skin' (*Asahi Shimbun*, editorial, 11 October 2006). In this way, both the positioning of contrasting identities as well as the discussion of potential risks borne by nuclear weapons served to delineate the parameters within which the issues were discussed. In the case at hand, then, this left little room for coverage of the harms of such portrayals themselves and their contingent prioritization of risks – including those that can have a negative impact upon the security of the everyday, as we have already seen.

Consistent with the discourse covered in the chapters above, more traditionally right-of-centre newspapers, such as the *Yomiuri Shimbun*, were similarly expressive in their construction of risks as representing a strong ideational element attached to the identities of Japan and North Korea. This was illustrated in particular detail by a commentary article that painted the regime in the DPRK and, by inference, a broader swathe of North Korean actors, as being somehow deceitful in their concealment of the risks that were posed by the Pyongyang power structure. It described how 'they have thrown away their rhetoric of being a "peaceful country" and are now bearing their sharpened claws. This is the true face of the rogue state as the Kim Jong-Il regime throws off its cape and reveals its true form' (*Yomiuri Shimbun*, 24 October 2006). Once again this colourful language, using descriptions that would not be out of place in popular horror-genre fiction, served to construct and perpetuate a narrative within the discourse. This depicted Japan as at risk of being further victimized and manipulated at the state level, but with the harms being unequally distributed among citizens. The same article exemplified this on the grounds that the North was in some way unfairly demanding, hypocritically, that Japan should acquiesce, stating that, 'they asserted that "with this our country has been recognized as a peace-loving state" and retorted that "Japan should behave appropriately."'' The use of a North Korean quote here, portraying the DPRK erroneously claiming itself as a righteous victim in juxtaposition to Japan, demonstrates how the sophisticated framing of motives was articulated in the Japanese public sphere.

In the above sense, reaction to the first North Korean nuclear test in October 2006 exhibited similar features to that witnessed in response to the abduction cases, by way of injecting an emotive and oft-times identity-based aspect to the sourcing and construction of risks pertaining to the DPRK. It also allowed for a further conflation of issues, which became deeply ingrained in light of the nuclear test – as abduction, nuclear and missile issues were established as quite openly linked and containing interrelated risks. As in the cases of both articles cited above, and countless others published by the *Asahi, Yomiuri* and Japan's other leading dailies, the market-led advantages of such a compounding were clearly maximized as a way to inform a composite focus on North Korea as a whole. This made use of the DPRK as a ready-made *villain*, being the source of risks that were rapidly recalibrated by state, market and societal elements. As discussed in the penultimate section of this chapter, it is this recalibration of risks initiated via discourse as a response to the 2006 test which tightly linked an ideologically based construction of abduction, missile and nuclear issues and consolidated the state's ability to engage and formulate policy accordingly. The reaction that ensued towards the following tests was, therefore, based on the said comprehensive, or *hōkatsuteki*, approach which left minimal credibility for voices outside of the mainstream. This also limited the resistance of actors that suffered direct harm as a result and served to nullify the influence of those concerned about the ongoing damage that has resulted for Japan's regional relations and security of the everyday.

6 Reaction to the 2009 nuclear test

The sense of an already established rhetoric and *modus operandi* with respect to the level and form in which risks were evaluated following North Korean nuclear testing had, then, become clearly delineated by the time of the DPRK's second nuclear test in 2009. In this regard, conversely, partially because of the lack of 'novelty value' of the first test occurring in 2006, the ability of Japanese policymakers and other societal groups – such as the NARKN – to actually recalibrate risks beyond levels already expressed in the discourse and policy provisions pertaining to the 2006 case was limited. However, the test came at a time when incumbent Prime Minister Asō Tarō was searching for any means possible to demonstrate strong leadership – in a desperate attempt not to lose the upcoming 2009 lower house election – and hence his and his party's mostly unbroken postwar grip on power. As a function of this domestic political need, it would seem, Asō sought to deflect negative public attention onto North Korea and was quick to seize upon the test, which in combination with the missile tests conducted immediately preceding and succeeding it, became a viable means for him to try and garner greater electoral support (*Chūō Nippō*, 9 June 2009).[6]

The combination and conflation of the July 2009 missile launches and the North's second nuclear test on 25 May of the same year was certainly utilized extensively by the Asō administration. In the Diet, leading ministers, such as then foreign minister Nakasone Hirofumi, repeatedly referred to all three issues in sessions of the Committee on Foreign Affairs and Defense that followed the weapons tests. In so doing, the highly sensitized issue of the abductions became included in discussions over technical risks perceived to emanate from the missile and nuclear programmes (Nakasone, Committee on Foreign Affairs and Defense, 4 June 2009). The extent to which this was the overwhelming understanding across the political spectrum was highlighted both by the opposition's equal willingness to combine issues in the same breath and unwillingness to attack the government on its anti-North Korea stance. In this respect, lawmakers normally determined to counter the government at every turn were critical only of specific details in how the government sought to ameliorate the risks – rather than the direction of North Korea policy itself. This was epitomized by opposition spokesman Takemasa Kōichi, when he spoke to the Foreign Affairs Committee members: 'The government has made it clear that it does not accept [North Korea] as a nuclear state, and of course I agree absolutely.' Similarly, the conflation of issues was also present, as he went on to seemingly arbitrarily allude to, 'speaking of abductions, the nuclear and missiles, including how to deal with this kind of country.' In other words, a conflated framing of North Korea was reemhasized by adding abductions and missiles to the nuclear issue (1 July 2009). Hence, with almost total acceptance across both houses of the Diet, not only for the recalibration of risk in response to North Korean weapons testing but also their continued framing of North Korea as a combined package of abductions, missiles and nuclear issues, the lack of credence given to arguments that might seek to emphasize the harm to the security of the everyday manifest in the promulgation of this interactive political process becomes self-evident.

Similarly, news coverage of the cocktail of missiles and nuclear testing conducted over the spring and summer of 2009 left little room for reflection on how Japan might contain risks in a pragmatic and isolated form. Rather, news outlets primarily opted to emulate the construction of a kind of compound risk sourced from this combination of elements identified with the single entity of the DPRK. The *Asahi Shimbun* had reported in 2006, referring to comments made by the then head of the defence agency, Kyūma Fumio, that, 'if North Korea miniaturizes a nuclear weapon and attaches it to a ballistic missile, it will become a major threat,' going on to express how the combination of Pyongyang's potential missile and nuclear capabilities represented 'Japan's greatest "nightmare"' (*Asahi Shimbun*, 11 October 2006). In reaction to the May 2009 test, the *Asahi* maintained this basic rhetoric, but in an editorial shortly after the test also made specific mention of the combination of nuclear and abduction issues as representative of the North's comprehensive identification as a negative reference point. This built on the recalibration of risks first witnessed after the 1998 Taepodong-1 launch, constructed as new risks perceived to emanate from that event. The piece stated that

'North Korea's nuclear testing and abduction problem have to be considered as critical threats' (*Asahi Shimbun*, 26 May 2009).

It is also pertinent to note that the editorial referenced above had already alluded to the North in quite emotive terms in order to create a sense of a hostile external entity juxtaposed with Japan's own identity. This included expression of "a feeling of increasingly strong indignation" as well as advocating actively 'pursuing the increased isolation of North Korea' (*Asahi Shimbun*, 26 May 2009). Of course, only so much can be read into the subtle phrasing of editorial comments, but when considering the stance of the *Asahi* as a high-quality left-leaning newspaper, the emotive – identity-based – nature of the rhetoric directed at North Korea illustrates how risks were recalibrated in response to nuclear testing. Moreover, it highlights how major newspapers intersect state and domestic spheres in this regard – so that national ideology is portrayed as representative of the security of the everyday for the population.

The *Yomiuri Shimbun*'s reaction to the 2009 nuclear test followed the same tack as the *Asahi*, although in terms of its evaluation of the resulting risks and potential harms, an additional shift was made. In the editorial which immediately followed the detonation, attention was first brought to the claim that 'the carrying out of a nuclear test linked to the miniaturization of nuclear weapons makes clear how North Korea is fervently intent on acquiring nuclear missiles as soon as possible.' However, in addition to the types of negative framing outlined above, the same article also stated that 'normalization with a nuclear armed North Korea is out of the question' (*Yomiuri Shimbun*, 26 May 2009). This strong statement highlights the extent to which any potential harms likely to be incurred as a result of hard-line responses to the North's nuclear development and testing were not even mentioned when asserting the sacrifice of possible normalization between the two countries.

7 Reaction to the 2013 nuclear test

Japan's response to a third nuclear test by North Korea in February 2013 was less bellicose than on earlier occasions. A more dramatic reaction was expected by those who see Prime Minister Abe as a right-wing hawk, with deep-seated hatred for North Korea. Indeed, as mentioned above, Abe first came to power both as leader of the LDP and then prime minister on the back of a highly emotive, anti–North Korean, election campaign. He also comes from a lineage of right-of-centre Japanese political leaders. However, in his second incarnation as Japan's elected leader, Abe has demonstrated a high degree of pragmatism, suggesting he has greater awareness than previously given credit for in understanding the potential harm that can be done to regional and bilateral relations should he take too hard a line. Conversely, he has shown little concern for the domestically located stakeholders whose security of the everyday has been put at risk – once again demonstrating the unequal distribution of risk framing in this sphere.

In the Diet, as observed in Chapters 5 and 6, the recalibration of risk in response to North Korea had already been realized, so cross-party debate focused almost entirely on what measures could be implemented or reformed in order to further deter the DPRK. Little or no mention was afforded, therein, to re-evaluating the actual harms brought about by Tokyo's previous responses in 2006 and 2009. Abe also reinforced the cross-usage and association of risks linked to the DPRK by discussing them in the context of other terrorist threats and problem cases, such as the war in Syria and regional terrorism. Within this, in an address to the main session of the Diet conducted to relay his dealings at the Group of Eight (G8), he reinstated the extent to which North Korean affairs were identified as of pressing concern – with reference to both nuclear and abduction issues as well as risks posed by the DPRK's missiles. The prime minister also asserted:

> Particularly in the case of North Korea, I led the discussion, stressing the message that we do not recognize the DPRK as a nuclear state, North Korea must not behave provocatively and must adhere completely and unwaveringly in implementing United Nations resolutions, as well as at the same time gaining understanding and support from all countries on the importance of resolving the problem of abductions cases.
> (Abe Shinzō, Main Diet Session, 24 June 2013)

Thereafter, Matsuda Manabu of the Japan Restoration Party gave his support to the strength of the prime minister's statement on North Korea. Matsuda's reconfirming of a hard-line stance is in line with his party's rightest rhetoric. The lack of any major critique from opposition leaders, when the LDP's leading lawmakers raised the North Korean nuclear test in the context of a firm hand used as deterrence against a range of salient risks, further evinces how a full and comprehensive recalibration of risk in response to North Korea had taken place. It also highlights the neglect of actual harms that Japan's state and market-led actors have overseen.

News media reaction to the 2013 nuclear test was also comparable to the preceding tests of 2006 and 2009. However, in the case of the *Asahi Shimbun*'s post-test coverage, a further recalibration of risk was made. In addition to the already established discourse on miniaturization being re-stated, one editorial stated, for example, that 'if they really do succeed in miniaturizing a nuclear war-head and are able to attach it to a long-range ballistic missile, the security environment of the Asia Pacific will change fundamentally' (*Asahi Shimbun*, 13 February 2013). Following lengthy discussion of the identified risks present in dealing with the nuclear threat posed by North Korea, the editor concluded his piece with the prescriptive assertion: 'We must not succumb to "nuclear blackmail" from North Korea. It has got close to the stage where in the worst case scenario we have to seriously consider measures to defend ourselves. A new threat awareness is needed' (*Asahi Shimbun*, 13 February 2013). This construction of a new set and level of risks sourced from the miniaturization of North Korea's nuclear weapons was echoed by the *Yomiuri Shimbun*'s editorial statement: 'There is no doubt that North Korea is closer to operationalizing a nuclear missile'; the statement also asserted that 'with regards to the deteriorating security environment, Japan must work with the United States and others to strengthen its deterrence capabilities vis-à-vis North Korea' (13 February 2013). Once again, it is striking that the only concern substantially voiced and given major credence by both papers was that relating to the risk of harms inflicted by the North launching a nuclear missile at Japan. The actual harm as well as the potential for harm to be realized in other spheres, created predominantly by the risk recalibration process itself, is in this way almost entirely omitted from discourse covering the 2006, 2009 and 2013 nuclear tests.

8 Harms from North Korean nuclear risks

As in the cases of abductions and missile testing, the high profile assigned to risks pertaining to North Korean nuclear testing, and particularly its combination and conflation with the former, has clearly had a negative impact in terms of harms inflicted upon the security of the everyday for ethnic Koreans in Japan. These three issues combined have evidently also had a cumulative effect, though it is hard to extrapolate the exact extent to which each has influenced the other two. The results have included the further tightening of sanctions and other restrictive legal measures, but the nuclear factor has also, as outlined by those on the intellectual arm of the community (Interviews C, D and R, Tokyo, 17 July 2013; Tokyo, 20 July 2013; Kōbe, 23 July 2013), provided an additional source for Japanese lawmakers, media editors and sub-national groups to shift Japan's identity. This predominantly takes the form of Japan as a victim, moving away from its stigmatization as a past aggressor in relation to Korea. In this sense, a conflation – or at least association, which is potentially harmful in itself – of Japan's nuclear victimization at the end of World War II, with that of North Korean nuclear development, has been directly and indirectly linked to abduction and missile issues. This combining of issues, therefore, means that anything with Korean connotations in Japan incurs both practical – by way of violence and discrimination (Asia Pacific Human Rights Information Center, 2013) – and ideological harm.

Japan's national identity and political diversity has also been negatively influenced by this multiple recalibration of risks sourced in North Korea. In the case of Pyongyang's nuclear testing, one of the most salient areas brought into question as a direct result is Japan's security stance and capabilities. In the wake of nuclear tests in 2006, for instance, Asō Tarō, now deputy prime minister and finance minister (then foreign minister), was among the first of several leading right-of-centre political figures in Japan to promote the idea of a debate on Japan's development of a nuclear deterrent. Unlike the almost universal recalibration of risks witnessed across state, market and societal spheres in response to the nuclear testing itself, however, the foreign minister's assertion that 'in one sense it is important to thrash out all kinds of debates when a neighbouring country has acquired nuclear weapons' (Main Session, October 2006) brought immediate negative reaction, as Japan's more liberal political and media actors recognized the risk that such a debate could lead to Japan's nuclear armament. The *Asahi Shimbun*, for instance, slammed those involved – headlining an editorial with 'Debate on 'nukes':

Foreign Minister's spiel is inappropriate' (20 October 2006). In this sense, whilst the *Asahi* and other more left-leaning actors had been forced to distance themselves from their progressive roots, and contingently any association with North Korea, the potential harm of nuclear armament was seen as extreme enough to counter its imposition.

Conversely, however, in one sense it is striking that risks attributed to North Korea's nuclear development were seen to be constructed and recalibrated to a high enough level that outspoken right-of-centre media (including the *Yomiuri Shimbun*) and political actors were given a mandate to voice their proactive stance on the matter, without fear or risking credibility, political capital, and commercial sales and readership. In other words, the recalibration of risk in response to North Korean nuclear testing brought about what can be construed as the harmful erosion of Japan's antimilitarist postwar national identity (*The Economist* 2013). In addition, use of the nuclear issue, as observed above, as a further reason for stalling progress on bilateral normalization between Tokyo and Pyongyang has a negative impact in the market sphere. This is exacerbated by sustaining and reinvigorating the imposition of sanctions, which virtually nullifies any potential for Japanese commercial enterprises to gain a foothold – in one sense further putting the security of the everyday at risk for these independent market actors, as a function of state policy.

9 Conclusion

In essence, then, this chapter has elucidated how North Korea's nuclear testing between 2006 and 2013 has been combined with missile and abduction issues in mainstream discourse to both realize and mediate a compressive recalibration of risk in response to the DPRK. Primarily as a by-product, this has also meant the inflicting of serious harms on the security of the everyday for sections of Japan's own population. As well as the consequent suffering of ethnic Koreans, this recalibration of risks acts as an impediment to future commercial market potential and has a mostly negative impact upon Japan's broader national identity, which intersects state and sub-state spheres.[7]

As with the issues of abductions and missiles, the ethnic Korean community in Japan has felt the full force of these harmful side effects at the societal level – as a targeted scapegoat for Pyongyang's apparent ills. The effects of the state-led recalibration process are therefore clear, but Japan's disproportionate – in comparison to the probability of harms alluded to – recalibration of North Korean–sourced nuclear risks has also clearly impacted upon its international relations, particularly within the East Asia region, adversely affecting political processes such as the SPT. In the market sphere, too, Japan's risk recalibration has also prevented moves to reduce sanctions and renew or increase investment in North Korea, hence constraining potentially lucrative commercial activities for domestic stakeholders. In the final chapter of this part of the book, how the recalibration of risks has spread from the core issues of nuclear proliferation, abductions and missiles to those of less well-publicized areas of concern, and the harmful consequences that have been once again disproportionately inflicted upon the security of the everyday as a result, are brought to light.

Notes

1 Unofficial reports suggest that the port of Rason in northern North Korea will be developed for use in China's military operations in the Western Pacific (*Asahi Shimbun AJW* 2013b).
2 It was noted by one analyst (Interview C, 17 July 2013) that South Korea's movement away from a more convivial relationship with Japan was represented clearly in the order of state and diplomatic visits conducted by Seoul following the election of Park Un-Hye – i.e. with Japan falling behind not only the US, but also China in the order.
3 Much has been made of China's state-led commercial initiatives which have led to burgeoning trade with South Korea in recent years, but in contrast to this trend, current polls have shown that the South Korean public feels more should be done by leader Park Un-Hye and her administration to rebuild bridges with Japan (Russell Mead 2013).
4 This was highlighted by the recent trilateral meeting brokered by the US amongst leaders Barack Obama, Abe Shinzō and Park Un-Hye, on the sidelines of the Nuclear Security Summit, designed to ease tensions between the two Asia-Pacific neighbours (Panda 2014).
5 This understanding relates to Aldrich's explanation of the 'nuclear allergy' (2012: 2), rather than official policy – as represented by the use of nuclear power in Japan's energy industry. From 2006 to 2011 Japan met up to 30 per cent of its energy demand via nuclear power (World Nuclear Association 2014).
6 The *Chūō Nippō* is the Japanese language edition of the *Korea Joongang Daily*.
7 In addition to the widespread emergence of anti-Korean demonstrations, led by extremist groups such as the *zaitokukai*, 'hate speech' has entered the popular media lexicon, and some independent studies have identified a marked increase seen in the use of xenophobic language amongst Japan's online communities (*Japan Times*, 13 April 2013).

References

Aldrich, Daniel P (2012) "Post-crisis Japanese nuclear policy: from top-down directives to bottom-up activism," *Asia Pacific Issues*, 103: 1–10.
Asahi Shimbun AJW (2013a) "Insight: Iijima called on North Korea to return Japanese abductees immediately." Available online at: http://ajw.asahi.com/article/behind_news/politics/AJ201305190028. Accessed 26 August 2013.
––––––– (2013b) "Russia, China go head-to-head with development of North Korean port." Available online at: http://ajw.asahi.com/article/asia/korean_peninsula/AJ201309240064. Accessed 13 April 2014.
Asia Pacific Human Rights Information Center (2013) "Rise of hate speech in Japan." Available online at: http://www.hurights.or.jp/archives/focus/section2/2013/12/rise-of-hate-speech-in-japan.html. Accessed 5 September 2014.
BBC (2006) "Japan's Aso urges atomic debate." Available online at: http://news.bbc.co.uk/1/hi/world/asia-pacific/6061620.stm. Accessed 7 February 2014.

Economist, The (2013) "North Korea's nuclear test: fallout." Available online at: http://www.economist.com/news/asia/21571938-chagrin-his-neighbours-young-despot-appears-determined-continue-his-familys-atomic. Accessed 26 August 2013.
Endō, Tetsuya (2013) *"Kitachōsen no kaku, misairu kaihatsu: kako, genzai, mirai,"* Occasional report, Tokyo: Kokusai Mondai Kenkyūjo.
Freund, Alexander (2013) "No quick end to Japan's nuclear power." Available online at: http://www.dw.de/opinion-no-quick-end-to-japans-nuclear-power/a-16659572. Accessed 7 February 2014.
Hughes, Christopher W (2006) "The political economy of Japanese sanctions towards North Korea: domestic coalitions and international systemic pressures," *Pacific Affairs*, 79, 3: 462–6.
Katsumata, Hiro (2014) "East Asian security dynamics and the recalibration of risk in Japanese foreign policy," (comments as discussant for panel), ISA Annual Convention, Toronto, 26 March.
Mason, Ra (2014) *Japan's North Korea Relations and the Recalibration of Risk*, Abingdon, Oxon: Routledge.
McCormack, Gavan (2007) *Client State: Japan in the American Embrace*, New York: Verso.
Medalia, Jonathan (2010) "North Korea's 2009 nuclear test: containment, monitoring, implications," Congressional Research Service (CRS) Report for Congress, Washington: CRS.
Michishita, Narushige (2013) "Changing military strategies and the future of the U.S. Marine presence in Asia," Executive Office of the Governor Policy Report, Naha: Okinawa Prefectural Government.
Nakamura, Kenichi (1985) *"Soren kyōiron kara no dakkyaku,"* *Sekai*, 473 (April): 56–73.
Panda, Ankit (2014) "Obama, Park, Abe meet to discuss North Korea, regional security," *The Diplomat*. Available online at: http://thediplomat.com/2014/03/obama-park-abe-meet-to-discuss-north-korea-regional-security/. Accessed 12 April 2014.
Russell Mead, Walter (2013) "South Korea rejects talks with Japan." *The American Interest*, 4 November. Available online at: http://www.the-american-interest.com/blog/2013/11/04/south-korea-rejects-talks-with-japan/. Accessed 8 February 2014.
World Nuclear Association (2014) "Nuclear power in Japan." Available online at: http://www.world-nuclear.org/info/Country-Profiles/Countries-G-N/Japan/. Accessed 8 February 2014.
Zhou, Jinghao (2013) "US Containment frays China's nerves," *Global Times*. Available online at: http://www.globaltimes.cn/content/827508.shtml#.U0pvqVsvDDU. Accessed 14 April 2014.

8
DRUGS AND MONEY

1 Introduction

The importation of drugs and remittance of illicit funds by North Korean agents, activities which are carried out in collaboration with Japanese organized crime syndicates (*yakuza*), represent a further diversification of potentially grievous risks identified with the DPRK by the Japanese state. Furthermore, as in the cases of missiles, abductions and nuclear proliferation discussed in Chapters 5, 6 and 7, the mediation of these risks results in harms to the security of the everyday. Because of Japan's draconian laws on the importation and usage of narcotics, and stigmatization of all recreational substance usage, Pyongyang's apparent involvement in such activities has allowed actors seeking to instumentalize the negative framing of the country for political purposes to add an additional form of risk.[1] This has been compounded by the DPRK's association with drug production, other than alcohol and tobacco, which is viewed as inherently dangerous and deviant, particularly given its domestic association with organized crime in Japan (Kurōzu appu gendai 2003). This framing is manifest in the portrayal of potential harm to the everyday security of Japanese society. Therein, having recalibrated security risks related to missile and nuclear testing, as well as the framing of state-sanctioned abductions by North Korea (see Chapters 5–7), as threatening Japanese sovereignty and identity, Japan has also linked narcotics smuggling to the DPRK in the minds of its citizens.

The purpose of this chapter is to examine how the drug risk is constructed, framed and mediated in combination with fears of Pyongyang's other illicit financial activities, in the sense of North Korea being the deliberate perpetrator of Japan's social evils. How this is represented by drug proliferation sourced from the North and illicit remittances sent to the DPRK is a point of particular concern. These aspects of risk construction are understood in the context of Japanese society's inability to overcome a historically based identity that can be traced back to the emperor's reinstatement of power following the Meiji Restoration. Ultimately, this has produced a predominant world-view whereby Japan constructs risks identified with an ongoing rivalry against neighbouring states. In that sense, by highlighting the diversity of risks identified with North Korea, this chapter also builds on the understanding of how Japan has recalibrated risks in response to China, examined in detail in Part I of this volume, as part of a contextual process that is directed at the state level across the East Asia region – but produces harm for subsections of sub-state stakeholders.

As noted in the book's introduction of the portrayal of the risks of ecstasy usage in the UK, it is partly the illegalization and recalibration of risks associated with recreational drugs which causes the greatest actual harm. Indeed, in Japan's case, too, the disparity between the risk's mediation, in terms of portrayed risks posed to Japanese society by North Korean narcotics imports, and those faced by loss of freedom, livelihood and social reputation, as the result of even one-time usage of marijuana, for instance, is severe. The fact that Japan imports multiple recreational chemical substances illegally from North Korea, and that in unregulated form these are the cause of considerable social harms, is well documented and virtually undeniable (Perl 2007: 4–6). However, the DPRK is only one of a number of narcotics producing states within the Central and East Asia regions which has the ability to supply Japan's domestic demand, and competes, albeit seemingly effectively, for the multi-sourced, unofficial, Japanese market.

As with the other cases addressed in Part II of this volume detailing recalibrated risks sourced in North Korea, the conflation and compounding of multiple risks into the single framing of Pyongyang's apparently covert and hostile actions is a central theme. In the case of narcotics smuggling this has been closely tied into both maritime incursions, which have reportedly included seizures of illegal drugs when intercepted (JCG 2003), and financial remittances sent to North Korea. Here, the suspicion is that the DPRK is administering the state-sponsored production of narcotics and profiting from Japanese consumption of them in order to fund other military and nuclear projects. These activities combine a geo-political threat, which has been constructed into risks incurred primarily by the state, with the potential for harms being exacted upon the security of the everyday in Japan as a result of drug use. The illustrative examples of media reports and Diet statements spotlighted in the following sections of this chapter demonstrate the qualitative realization of this process through a recalibration of the risks posed.

2 Drugs as conflated risks identified with the DPRK

Once again, the emergence of a conflated risk narrative has been realized in a temporal context where once none existed. The case of Japanese authorities' counter drug-policing measures highlights this point. On 29 November 1991, for instance, it was reported by the national broadcaster (NHK) that a small North Korean goods vessel entering Onahama port in Fukushima Prefecture had been intercepted and searched by the JCG as part of an operation to prevent the importation of narcotics. The emphasis within the report was focused largely upon avoiding misinterpretation, and repeatedly alluded to the acting JCG officer's strenuous efforts to deny any persecution or biased treatment of the vessel and its crew on the grounds of them being North Korean. Conversely, representatives of the General Association of Korean Residents in Japan (*Chōsensōren*) – acting effectively in an unofficial diplomatic capacity – took it upon themselves to visit the JCG headquarters and lodge a complaint to the effect that intrusive tactics had been deployed because, they claimed, the vessel was from the DPRK (NHK News, 29 November 1991). No mention of the incident was made in any of the main or committee sessions of the Diet that followed and little coverage was afforded to related issues across the spectrum of Japan's national newspapers.

In contradistinction to the Onahama case, by the late 1990s, national TV stations (including NHK) and Japan's leading broadsheets had both begun to emphasize the extent to which the importation of drugs from North Korea was putting the Japanese population at risk. This included using high-profile overseas examples to illustrate the salience of the challenge faced in enforcing security to counter it. NHK, for instance, covered the story of two North Korean diplomats being arrested in Egypt for smuggling large quantities of lysergic acid diethylamide (LSD) – linking the issue directly to suspected state-orchestrated narcotics smuggling by the North into Japan (NHK News, 11 July 1998).[2] In continuance of this narrative, in just over a decade later we saw a shift in what could be legitimately portrayed on Japanese state television as a high risk, including a multiple conflation of associated risks, as illustrated by a report on 25 April 2010 entitled: 'Drugs and counterfeit currency: Carried out by the authority directly affiliated to Kim.' Not only did this piece unequivocally target a personalized character profiling – i.e. a demonized state leader, Kim Jong-Il – but also discussed in detail the alleged risk of drug trafficking and money laundering. These issues were framed as being part of a coordinated illicit programme of activities, which 'also included channelling funds for nuclear development and such like' (NHK News, 25 April 2002). Risks related to North Korea's narcotics trading were also taken up within the Diet, with neoconservative members, such as Yamamoto Ichita, inserting the issue in an initially unrelated discussion of the North's illicit activities channelled through the Bank of Macao (Yamamoto, Committee on Foreign Affairs and Defense, 27 April 2010). In stark contrast, minimal voice was afforded to non-state stakeholders, such as those in the resident Korean community who might have sought to provide greater balance to this portrayal. Indeed, even *Chōsensōren* was publicly largely silent on the matter.

3 Risk recalibration and the framing of North Korean narcotics

The above discussion demonstrates two points of particular interest in terms of the narrative of Japan's recalibration of risks and how it relates to specific security issues and resulting harms. First, the initially almost conciliatory attitude of the Japanese authorities in expressing their neutrality towards North Korean nationality in the Onahama case exposes how the risk to Japan's state image, being perceived internationally and domestically as fair and unbiased, was then deemed of equal or greater priority than that of state duties to enforce the law.[3] Second, in contrast, the assertive reaction of *Chōsensōren* in representing the North Korean crew, and protesting their case as discriminatory, highlights the extent to which the organization was able to operate at the subnational level from within Japan to protect the everyday security of resident Koreans. This is almost unimaginable in the present climate, which further evinces the extent to which *Chōsensōren* has been harmed by the process of Japan's state and market mediation and recalibration of risk. This is observable, as illustrated throughout this part of the book, via state and market actors' comparative assertions, which include Japan's publicly and commercially funded television stations and right-of-centre political actors.

Now, following the transition to the new Pyongyang leadership under Kim Jong-Un, North Korea continues to be implicated consistently by policymakers (Diet sessions: Kusakawa, Committee on Land, Infrastructure, Travel and Tourism, 27 May 2010, Koike, Budget Committee, 1 February 2012), media editors (*Yomiuri Shimbun, Mainichi Shimbun, Sankei Shimbun*, editorials, 2012–14, etc.) and other subnational and bureaucratic actors (Ministry of Finance 2011) in Japan as a key source of narcotics entering the domestic market. As such the drug risk is identified as a source of potential harm to the security of the everyday in Japan, and is also associated with broader illicit financial activities, discussed further below, and the potential funding of weapons programmes, alluded to above. In the latter case, the central premise rests upon the double inference that North Korea is an essential component of Japan's growing domestic drug problem and that the profits from such are at risk of being channelled into weapons programmes and other areas that put Japan's security further at risk. However, even if sanctions and other measures directed at North Korea were to be effective in nullifying its drug trade with Japan altogether, this would not ameliorate the risk of narcotics being illicitly imported into the country. Rather, another state or combination of subnational sources including, for instance, international terrorist groups and foreign students, would likely increase their existing proportion of the trade to fill the short-fall currently not filled by the DPRK. Indeed, even in terms of regional sources, the Japanese archipelago's biggest suppliers of narcotics are in fact the African continent (*Yomiuri Shimbun*, 12 November 2008), followed by China (Aquino 2013).

Critically, the fact that North Korea is singled out in multiple spheres by state, market and societal actors within Japan, as the source of so many potential harms, gives rise to an inability to construct and frame specific risks, such as those relating to narcotics usage and distribution, accurately. For instance, arguably the greatest risks to drug users in Japan, as elsewhere, include misinformation, contamination of substances and equipment, and the monopoly over distribution held by criminal organizations that are often violent. If policymakers were able to educate state and sub-state actors more effectively in differentiating to a greater extent between a variety of illegal drugs, control and regulate their usage, and open lines of communication between Japanese and North Korean authorities, the risk of harms being inflicted as the result of ingesting narcotics from the DPRK in Japan would surely be greatly reduced.

In addition, the ability of authorities, such as the JCG and NPA to engage more proactively with comparable representative North Korean organizations, including official bodies in the DPRK as well as *Chōsensōren* and, for example, its affiliated Pachinko parlours and owners within Japan is critical in terms of actually reducing the risks to potential consumers of North Korean drugs. Such initiatives might give rise not only to better narcotics regulation on both sides of the Sea of Japan, but also contribute towards affecting a bottom-up process of re-engagement at the state level – thus indirectly reducing national security risks. The potential for Japan to invest in pharmaceutical research in North Korea and encourage the manufacturing of medicinal drugs, though as yet a long way off, would also offer a potential means by which to reduce these permeable security risks, particularly in terms of their association with directly or indirectly funding weapons programmes and the production of counterfeit currency. While the concept of Tokyo and Pyongyang cooperating to manufacture socially acceptable chemical products for domestic consumption within Japan, including regulated drug usage, may seem far-fetched, it should be evident from the discussion above that the biggest risk posed to Japan by North Korean narcotics is likely not one manifest in an imminent international security threat. Rather, the issue of greatest salience is actually how to recalibrate the risks associated with concerns such as drug importation without losing credibility – and political capital as a result.[4] As it stands, the continued framing of the DPRK as a state-funded drugs shop, feeding its profits into weapons programmes on the back of Japanese users, continues to be one of several impediments blocking improvement of bilateral relations, as well as indirectly inflicting ongoing harms upon those it proclaims to protect, i.e. the citizens of Japan (Metropolitan Police Department 2013).

The most obvious causes for this identification of risks sourced in North Korea have already been highlighted through the case studies discussed in earlier chapters of Part II. However, there are two additional highly potent interstate influences upon the process of risk mediation that relate to narcotics importation from the North in Japan. Both contribute substantially to constructing risks that have been recalibrated to produce harmful internal effects. The first pertains to the stigmatization of foreign residents and particularly short-term (Asian) immigrants, *per se*, and can be described as blurring – or at times conflating – in terms of an approximation of various risks identified with North Korea and China (see Part I). The second factor is that of US foreign policy interests and their exercising through ministries and law enforcement agencies, such as the State Department and military (in cooperation with the JCG, JSDF, and other administrative bodies in Japan) – not least, it can be argued, in order to maintain a controlled hostility directed towards the DPRK from Japan. The impact of each of these elements is illustrated briefly in the section below.

3.1 East Asian foreigners and US foreign policy

In recent years, the stereotyping of (East Asian) foreigners as being synonymous with high-risk activities – or somehow more likely to be implicated in criminal behaviour than those of native Japanese background – has caused multiple harms as the result of the recalibration processes already outlined. In the case of drug distribution and usage this has largely been associated with Chinese criminal gangs, as alluded to in Part I of this book, but the approximation of the "foreign criminals" concept has facilitated blurring and spreading effects whereby North Korea is included within the risk-set as a potentially harmful source of foreign crime – despite its very distinct regional role and lack of fully native foreign residents in, or visitors to, Japan. The results, as in the case of abductions, missiles and nuclear development, outlined earlier in Part II, include a detrimental effect upon bilateral relations and harmful violence inflicted upon resident Koreans. However, this also contributes to a broader region-wide impression of Japan as a xenophobic and institutionally exclusive state and society, which in itself poses risks to Japan's ability to gain greater credibility and trust within East Asia as a whole.

Media coverage is highly illustrative in this respect and can actually be traced as far back as the aftermath of the 1999 suspicious ship incursion, discussed further below, with regards to cross-referencing multiple nationalities, which include North Korea, into a single frame of drug-related risk. The mediation of risks constructed from this synthesized source gathered pace thereafter. For instance, the traditionally liberal *Asahi Shimbun* followed the lead of more generally right-of-centre national and regional newspapers in identifying the 'China-North Korea route' for illegal drug importation that was to be dealt with primarily through tackling 'organized crime organizations and groups of Iranians' (2 March 2000). The association of various foreign nationals – including Chinese and North Koreans conflated as one – with criminality and the proliferation of risk is self-evident. In the years since, scant attention has been assigned to the potentially negative impact of this portrayal, or the harm exacted as a result. Conversely, the focus has been warped towards ameliorating the risks posed to law enforcement agencies, such as the JCG, when attempting to curtail maritime narcotics smuggling outside of Japan's territorial waters. Indeed, the impetus has been shifted in the state authorities' favour via inferred or direct criticism of political forces, such as the Social Democratic Party, which has opposed operationalizing the Maritime Self-Defense Force (MSDF) to reduce the risk of inflicted damage in hostile exchanges during any such operations (*Asahi Shimbun*, 29 November 2009).

In addition to the conflated East Asian stereotyping outlined above, there has also been a complementarily – in terms of risk recalibration against the North – renewed interoperability-drive between US-Japan security forces, illustrated by state-level responses to perceived nuclear and missile risks discussed above (MOFA 2013). In combination with US Senate and Japanese Diet rhetoric and actions, such as sanctions directed towards North Korea's drug trade, this strengthening of the US–Japan alliance leads to the conclusion that US pressure is also a significant factor in preventing any moves within Japan towards a less combative recalibration of risks in response to Pyongyang's state-led narcotics operations. From the US side, a hard line in cooperation with Tokyo and in response to portrayed risks identified with North Korean–sourced narcotics in East Asia has been made evident throughout the past decade. Indeed, the rationale for such was expressed in the International Narcotics Control Strategy Reports (US Department of State 2003).[5]

In combination, then, Japan's construction and framing of North Korean drug trafficking operations as a salient risk provides a further illustrative case study of the dynamic form in which risk as domestic and international phenomena can provide a powerful exposition of the disproportionate nature of resulting harms. It also reinforces the argument that it is oft-times the state-led recalibration of risk itself that creates the most significant internal harms – in many cases exceeding the potential harm of the risk supposedly being countered. In the case of drugs entering Japan from North Korea, this is not limited solely to exacerbating stagnant bilateral relations and inflicting further discrimination upon ethnic Koreans in Japan. It also puts drug users in Japan at risk, in the sense that Japan's responses to North Korean narcotics smuggling – as part of a decidedly strict law enforcement policy against recreational substances – has led to sustained hyper-illegality and a perceived integration with Japan's own organized crime gangs (Kurōzu appu gendai 2003). It can also be seen to be preventing more open and measured usage, licensing and treatment that would reduce the risks for users seeking to protect their everyday security.

Furthermore, although drug trading and distribution activities led by Japanese organized crime groups has increased in recent years (Rankin 2012), such trade with North Korea has actually become limited to increasingly remote and covert means. These include trafficking with Korean prostitutes and the sending of electronically tracked, dissolved crystal methamphetamine in plastic bottles, which is picked up by narcotics dealers off the Sea of Japan coast, boiled off, and commercialized (Mizoguchi 2011). The disproportionate – relative to other industrially developed states – risk of harsh punishment for even one-time usage of predominantly low-risk drugs, such as cannabis and ecstasy, also has the counterproductive effect of driving the street price up to the point where actors outside of Japan are more willing to risk smuggling because of the higher incentives (Ministry of Justice 2011).

In essence, with state-societal stereotyping and US pressure also influencing how narcotics-related risks are mediated, a range of resulting harms have been created that are problematic to counter. In the next section, the discussion moves to a comparable process of framing, momentum and external pressure that can be observed in the intersecting areas of financial remittances and maritime incursions.

4 Maritime incursions and remittances: the risk of funding North Korea

As with the abductions issue, North Korea's multiple incursions into Japanese maritime territory – most often identified with special operations boats entering

Japan's EEZ in 1999 and 2001 – are viewed by policymakers and security managers as not only a security risk, and the potential source of narcotics trafficking, but as a violation of sovereignty, too. Indeed, the issue of maritime incursions combines entanglements of many elements of the multifaceted process of risk recalibration in response to North Korea. The comparative state responses to the two incidents either side of the start of the twenty-first century illustrate this process, with North Korean activity being comparable in both cases, but the Japanese reaction being far more assertive in the latter. The potential risks which the JCG was willing to prioritize and take in the 2001 case were, yet again, striking when contrasted with the probability of harms being exacted by the relatively weak North Korean vessels. This included an incursion into China's EEZ by the JCG and the unprecedented firing of live rounds by the Japanese ship (Gotō, Ogawa and Shigemura 2005). Such was viewed as justified in order to counter perceived risks to Japan's sovereignty and society (as a result of narcotics on the boat entering Japan), as well as proactively facing a challenge to its maritime security perimeter.

In terms of the conflation process outlined above, inclusion of narcotics and counterfeit currency (discussed further below) into portrayals of the challenge posed by the incursion of 2001 is highly illuminating of the risk recalibration process when contrasted with coverage of the preceding incident two years earlier. In March 1999, when Japanese authorities were alerted to suspicious activities being carried out by an unidentified North Korean vessel off the coast of the Noto Peninsula, the reaction was slow and cumbersome. The vessel was chased, but escaped into North Korea's EEZ, upon which the Japanese crew abandoned its pursuit. Coordination of the operation to track and chase the North Korean ship between the JCG and MSDF was stilted and ineffective. However, although limited concerns over these capabilities were raised both in the media and Diet, in one sense the lack of resolve in capturing or disabling what was very likely a 'spy-boat' sent by Pyongyang reflected the erratic, and predominantly minimal, motivation of both Japan's maritime defence authorities to do so (*Asahi Shimbun*, 4 July 1999). Certainly, there was little discussion of potential narcotics importation or money-laundering risks that could have been associated with the small Korean ship – not least because such a clearly conflated narrative was then yet to be created.

In contrast, the JCG's exchange of fire and consequential sinking of a comparable vessel in December of 2001 drew a far more vitriolic Japanese reaction – and what is more served to create a platform for the developing narrative of North Korea as a source of illicit drugs and counterfeit money.[6] The incident itself and the raising and public display of the sunken vessel the following year caused a flurry of Diet and media commentaries (*Mainichi Shimbun*, 31 December 2001; Black 2014). However, what is of even greater significance when critically analysing its effect, is the ongoing linkage between the diverse risks that were identified with the North Korean special operations boat – as representing a single challenge to Japan's security. For example, in 2003, almost two years after the maritime confrontation in the East China Sea, the *Yomiuri Shimbun* carried a series of commentary pieces, collectively entitled 'Stop it! Smuggling from the North' (*tate! [kita]*

mitsuyu), which discussed topics such as 'Drugs, counterfeit dollars and illicit remittances . . . funds for weapons development?' (*mayaku, gidoru, fuseisōkin . . . heikikaihatsu shikin ka*) (*Yomiuri Shimbun*, 8 June 2003). There is no great revelation to the fact that the *Yomiuri* is a right-of-centre newspaper and uses a variety of means by which to inflate, or at least emphasize, potential security threats. This is usually, as in the case of North Korea's illicit activities, achieved by juxtaposing external illegality and the risks it poses to Japan's national defence capabilities. Even so, its total recalibration of risks framed against the conflated unitary actor of North Korea is striking in this case, particularly in terms of presenting a narrative that supports it – even in the face of worsening the security of the everyday for certain sections of Japanese society. The 2003 series, referenced above, for example, referred extensively to an incident involving Australian authorities' pursuit and capture of a small North Korean vessel carrying narcotics within the so-called Golden Triangle to unspecified destinations (*Yomiuri Shimbun*, 8 June 2003). However, by adding discussions of Pyongyang's links to international crime syndicates, US claims relating to the North's production of forged American currency, and of Japan being North Korea's primary market for illicit substances, a whole range of risks were focused into a single narrative of potential harms coming from North Korean activities. In other words, this narrative articulated multiple risks that intersected state, market and societal spheres in Japan.

In the above sense, it is this risk narrative that allows for the re-application of risk in its transitive form (active choice + uncertainty) – thereby allowing it to be recalibrated and instrumentalized (Taleb 2007). This has been critical for the JCG, whereby the potential risks posed to state security by North Korean maritime incursions have come to be prioritized above the potential risk to interstate relations as well as everyday security, manifest in, for example, intrusion into a neighbour state's (e.g. China) EEZ or even armed conflict – as was the case when the JCG commanders calculated the risks of engaging fire with the North Korean vessel in December 2001 (Gotō *et al*. 2005: 78–91). The acceptance of this shift in risk construction and framing was thereafter supported by leading political figures and became recognized and standardized within mainstream discourse. This can be observed by qualitative examination of both Diet speakers and news media coverage pertaining to the period that immediately followed the confrontation in the East China Sea – and the quantitative volume of such sources that disseminates this discourse (Mason 2014).

For example, the fact that, partly as a result of the armed confrontation with the North Korean 'spy-boat' in 2001, the Special Committee Concerning Provisions for Contingencies of Military Aggression was convened is illustrative in itself of the process and formalizing of the higher-risk status Japanese policymakers and security managers assigned to the DPRK. However, in addition to the wealth of more overt statements representative of the almost unanimous support given to Japan's 'proactive' response to the 2001 incident, more subtle responses are highly illuminating in terms of exposing how risks became recalibrated. For instance, when tasked with explaining the 'spy-boat's' operations, the minister in charge, Uruma Iwao, noted that he could not confirm details on the grounds that to do so would reveal how security forces in Japan were operating to counter operations vessels sent by the North (Special Committee on Responses to Armed Attacks, 8 May 2002). In other words, security risks pertaining to the covert operations posed by North Korea came to be prioritized above concerns of risking a public or political backlash because of a perceived lack of transparency by state authorities.

Media stories of the time mirror this politicized recalibration of risk – and again subtle items provide some of the most telling illustrations. In one opinion piece carried by the *Asahi Shimbun* (27 December 2001), for example, the author at first seems to be cautioning the unruly actions of the JCG, but later discusses the need for Japan to ensure total control of such marine areas and to be clearer about what the JCG can consider within its jurisdiction under international law. This highlights a number of underlying assumptions with regards both to what the JCG can and should be allowed to consider its defendable territory, beyond the immediate bounds of the territorial waters of the Japanese archipelago. This is also reflected by news media coverage across the board, which rather than focussing on, for example, the potential costs of retrieving the vessel, instead focussed on when and how the boat would be brought up from the sea depths (NHK News, 9 May 2002). This represents how the risk of alienating sections of the public, by incurring arguably unnecessary expenses to retrieve the North Korean vessel accused of spying, was outweighed by the risk of allowing any kind of maritime incursion directed by Pyongyang into Japanese territorial waters.

In the case of remittances, Japan has also come to frame North Korea as the potential source of economic risks, once again recalibrated through a state-led process which has embedded the concept of financial transactions sent from Japan to the DPRK within the context of a growing set of uncertain but serious potential harms being posed to Japan's state, market and societal spheres. This portrayal developed in tandem with North Korea's nuclear proliferation, and was implemented, in some cases directly and illegally (see Fukushima Mizuho's 14 May 1999 accusations in the Diet), in order to target the DPRK's domestic economic power base in Japan. At the practical level, a conceptual link was made which centred upon the connections between Korean-run pachinko parlours and *Chōsensōren*. As Fukushima asserted, however, with regards to the calculated implementation of responses to such perceived risks, 'This documentation clearly amounts not to an investigation, but the planned creation of a problem in order to stop remittances being sent.' In this sense, the process of risk recalibration was being driven both overtly and covertly by state actors at subnational as well as international levels.

This process was expedited by portrayal of the image that actors such as Korean Pachinko parlour owners and their affiliates were sucking wealth out of Japan and investing it in the regime in the North, which was then redirecting the funds towards nuclear programmes. Ironically, as a result of punitive sanctions taken against such Korean businesses and agents in Japan, it is arguably Japanese citizens, with relatives in North Korea, who have suffered the greatest actual harm. In addition to the constraints on sending personal remittances, this harm comes in the form of restrictions on movement, which deny access for visiting and the granting of visas, as well as the prohibitive and exponential rise in prices charged by the North Korean authorities to grant limited, short-stay, family visits (interview, deputy director, Research Centre for the History of Korean Residents, Tokyo, 17 July 2013). In addition, the constraints placed upon bilateral financial transactions between the two states have further hampered commercial activity and investment on both sides of the Sea of Japan.

5 Mediating responses to risk, threat and harm

The cases above of North Korea – mostly indirectly – putting Japan's security of the everyday at risk through maritime incursions and illegal remittances, highlight the value added of risk as a tool for critically analysing the underlying processes in Japan's relations with the North. This is significant because, as outlined in the introduction to this book, threat perceptions are regularly readjusted or recalibrated depending on a range of tangible potential harms and politicized interests, but have a limited conceptualization as exactly that – i.e. identifiable external sources of harm. Risk, conversely, better explains the recalibration process because it has a transitive form and is centred around the idea of rational, justifiable or calculable choices – not only the potential harms that they stem from. Put simply, risks are taken as well as borne. One cannot *take* a threat.

The above is particularly relevant in terms of illustrating the construction of dominant narratives which can be mediated through the projection of risk. In other words, no figures are given for the likelihood and extent of drug abuse and health risks supposedly posed to Japanese citizens, or for the extent remittances to the North are related to forged currency or channelled into weapons programmes. Yet, the synchronized coverage of international state authorities' identification of 'risks' in all these areas with the one entity, 'North Korea,' facilitates the adoption of a narrative that evinces a serious, multifaceted challenge to the security of the everyday in Japan. The actual harms that have been created as a result of this process are then neglected almost entirely and the potential harms disproportionately (re)calibrated in line with political aims rather than probable outcomes.

As alluded to in Chapter 5 and Chapter 7, following the Taepodong-1 launch of 1998 and nuclear test of 2006, for instance, punitive economic measures directed against North Korea have largely been ineffective (Yoshida 2008: 252). In this regard, it can be argued that from the time of Japan's initial imposition of sanctions and logistical restrictions, with the acclaimed potential to disrupt commercial activities, risks have been inaccurately identified as threats and dealt with, ineffectively, on that basis. Evidently, this assertion is supported not least by the lack of a substantive correlation between the imposition of sanctions applied by the government of Japan and the level of economic productivity and growth exhibited by the DPRK.[7] What is more, even the reported decline in commercial exchanges in the post–Cold War period between ethnic Koreans in Japan and the DPRK can actually be attributed extensively to Japan's protracted economic malaise from as early as the turn of the century (Elliot 2003). In addition, this can be put into the context of North Korea's overwhelming comparative reliance upon China and South Korea as trade partners that dwarf Japan's contribution to the North's ailing economy (Koo and Lim 2013). Therefore, the increased severity of Japan's unilateral and multilateral (primarily via UN resolutions) economic sanctions imposed against Pyongyang can be seen to have only had a limited impact upon any potential risk of funds being directed towards, for example, nuclear and ballistic weapons programmes that might ultimately target Japan. Indeed, Abe's recent drive to improve Pyongyang-Tokyo relations via the easing of such sanctions shows the awareness by the government itself of the lack of their efficacy.

Nevertheless, multiple additional sanctions were implemented in the wake of missile and nuclear tests conducted by the DPRK in 2006 and 2009, with the justification that this would tighten the economic noose around the Kim regime's neck and prevent the risk of illicit funds being misdirected to harmful effect. However, in the current economic climate, in which financial and budgetary concerns relating to trade have a tendency to take immediate and pressing precedence, the actual harms created by this recalibration and response to the supposed risks of weapons funding should be apparent. Whilst, as noted above, it is the negligible size of trade relations between Japan and North Korea that limits the impact of Japan's sanctions, the potential for expansion in this area is extensive and most pertinent to other rival states – such as China and South Korea (Hagard and Noland 2008). In other words, as North Korea's economy is liberalized under the market reforms already being put in place by Kim Jong-Un's regime, Japanese investors are at risk of suffering the harm of being ostracized (as is normally the case for politically alienated or opposed actors) from ongoing resource extraction and related service sector developments, as well as any other economic benefits associated with investment in the DPRK's potential economic growth.

6 Conclusion

In sum, North Korea's narcotics smuggling and other economic activities have, in terms of objectively calculable probabilities, posed a limited range, volume and degree of risks to Japan's state security and society. Yet, Tokyo's construction, framing and mediation of these portrayed risks has brought about a situation that threatens potential harms to the security of the everyday, as seen from the perspective of individual economic and social stakeholders. Furthermore, it has already inflicted actual harm upon a minority of individuals in the Korean community and ethnic Japanese citizens whose personal circumstances have left them exposed to the movement of Pyongyang and Tokyo's exchanges. In this sense, then, Japan's continued recalibration of risks as an economically based reaction to missile and nuclear tests by North Korea, discussed in the earlier chapters of Part II, has in itself created a climate where the improvement of Japan's comparatively minimal trade relations with the North are impeded by Japan's framing of the DPRK as the source of – albeit indirect – economic and societal risks. These risks are regularly sourced in narcotics smuggling and remittances by actors intersecting Japan's state, market and society. Therefore, by alienating itself from the regime in Pyongyang, policymakers and security managers have been left in a situation where Japan faces commercial damage on the international scene, relative to rival states in the region. Japan's position as such is also inextricably linked to Japan's sustained emphasis on bilateralism with the US and maintenance of that security alliance, as well as the construction of regional security risks that are manifest as a function of its presence.[8]

Indeed, in the above sense, the manner in which the historical structural environment of the East Asia region has shaped Japan's construction of risks across all spheres cannot be underestimated. As stressed by the head of the History Museum of Japanese-Koreans (interview, 20 July 2013), many analysts argue that Japan has long perceived unification of the Korean peninsula as one the greatest risks to its preeminent position in the region and would view a unified Korea as a major rival in geostrategic and economic terms (see also Sakurai 2007).[9] This position is, of course, closely linked to the posture of the US and bilateralism, *per se*, but for all the talk of hedging risks borne by North Korea's weapons programmes with normalization efforts via messengers, such as the recently dispatched envoy, Iijima Isao (Mason 2013), there is a sense in which Japan can been seen at both state and societal levels to be engaging with Korean risks as whole. This is further evident – in contrast to the targeting of illegal drugs and money identified with Pyongyang – in the almost total lack of punitive measures being taken against those discriminating against resident ethnic Koreans in Japan from both halves of the peninsula. This can be put further into context if one imagines, for example, Japan allowing weekly hate speeches to take place against American, or even Chinese, immigrants in the same form that are currently being permitted by the Japanese police authorities against ethnic Koreans, as noted above.

The actual harms being inflicted upon the regional status quo, bilateral relations with Pyongyang and the everyday security of resident Koreans and their relatives in Japan are severe. In one sense they are also warped by Japan's failure to overcome a historically based identity – traceable from the emperor's reinstatement of power after the Meiji Restoration – that produced Japan's world-view of constructing risks identified with a competitive rivalry between itself and its neighbours. This has facilitated indefensible levels of discrimination and persecution of Koreans and other foreigners (Asia Pacific Human Rights Information Center 2013), which is exacerbated intensively at times of economic downturn and geostrategic loss alike, not least because of the need for someone or something to blame for personal hardships. As one elderly *Zainichi* recalled (Interview S, 20 July 2013) in relation to how Japanese viewed defeat in World War II, 'They used to say, "we can put up with losing to the American's, but can't bear to see the Koreans acting as if they own the place." (*sic*)' Circumstantially, of course, the legacy of how the subsequent US occupation came to shape all aspects of Japan's regional relations, including identification and recalibration of risk, is plain to see.

Drugs and money 155

The influence of how risks continue to be unequally distributed as a result of US forces still stationed in Japan forms the basis for discussion in Part III of the book to follow.

Notes

1 The narcotics-related penalties in Japan include: a prison sentence of between one and ten years, a fine of up to 5,000,000 yen and deportation orders with no return to Japan for five to ten years (MHLW 2013).
2 It is noteworthy that this inflammatory piece directed at North Korea's drug-trafficking activities was carried even prior to the September 1998 Taepodong-1 missile test launch, which witnessed a vociferous reaction across all sectors of the state, market and society (see Chapter 5). Since the incident took place during a Diet recess, the political reaction is more problematic to discern in this case.
3 The incident fell within the period of Japan's initial normalization talks with the North between January 1991 and November 1992.
4 This is highlighted not only by responses from politicians, but also state authorities, such as the conflated line given by police, who refer to, 'things like theft, smuggling and drugs from countries such as China and North Korea' (Ibaraki Prefectural Government 2011: 1).
5 This continues in contrast to the US' own domestic scaling back of minimum mandatory sentences for minor drug-related crimes, as outlined by Attorney General Eric Holder, in his address to the American Bar Association's House of Delegates (Merica and Perez 2013).
6 The sinking itself was caused not by shots from the JCG, but was due to a self-destruct device being detonated by the North Korean crew, who then jumped overboard into the water.
7 For discussion of the overall inefficacy of sanctions applied by regional powers upon North Korea, see Frank (2006). For insight into the domestic determinants of Japan's North Korea policy in this sphere, see Hughes (2006).
8 By removing the DPRK from its list of state sponsors of terrorism in 2007, a move vehemently opposed by Tokyo, the US also enabled itself, in contrast to Japan, to reduce the risk of freezing out North Korea in the market sphere – e.g. in such case as its isolated position towards Western commercial organizations were to change.
9 It was also noted that, in one sense, this stems from the fact that after the end of World War II, Japan's postwar fate and *modus operandi* were effectively decided by the San Francisco Peace Treaty of 1951 and then concluded during the Korean War (1951–3), when there was no consideration of the interests of either of the two engaged Koreas or the US' rivals in that proxy war, namely China and Russia (Soviet Union).

References

Aquino, Faith (2013) *Japan Daily Press*. Available online at: http://japandailypress.com/japans-largest-source-of-smuggled-drugs-traced-to-africa-2531150/. Accessed 13 September 2013.
Asia Pacific Human Rights Information Center (2013) "Rise of hate speech in Japan." Available online at: http://www.hurights.or.jp/archives/focus/section2/2013/12/rise-of-hate-speech-in-japan.html. Accessed 5 September 2014.
Black, Lyndsay (2014) *Japan's Maritime Security Strategy: The Japan Coast Guard and Maritime Outlaws*, London: Palgrave Macmillan.

Elliot, Kimberley A. (2003) "The role of economic leverage in negotiations with North Korea," DPRK Briefing Book, Nautilus Institute. Available online at: http://nautilus.org/publications/books/dprkbb/sanctions/dprk-briefing-book-the-role-of-economic-leverage-in-negotiations-with-north-korea/#axzz2fGUQHZ1K. Accessed 18 September 2013.

Frank, Ruediger (2006) "The political economy of sanctions against North Korea," *Asian Perspective*, 30, 3: 5–36.

Gotō, Mitsuyuki, Kazuhisa Ogawa and Toshimitsu Shigemura (2005) *"22/12 Kōsaku-sen tsuiseki jūgeki dokyumento"* in Nishioka Tsutomu, Kazuhisa Ogawa, Mitsuyuki Gotō, Toshimitsu Shigemura, Yoshikazu Shimizu and Duk-min Yun (eds), *Kitachōsen mondai o seiri suru go fairu*, Tokyo: Jiyu Kokuminsha, pp. 78–91.

Haggard, Stephan and Marcus Noland (2008) "North Korea's foreign economic relations," *International Relations of the Asia Pacific*, 8, 2: 219–46.

Hughes, Christopher (2006) "The political economy of Japanese sanctions towards North Korea: domestic coalitions and international systemic pressures," *Pacific Affairs*, 79, 3: 455–81.

Ibaraki Prefectural Government (2011) *"Kenmin no koe."* Available online at: http://kouchou.pref.ibaraki.jp/kotyo/hp_iken_syousai.php?vUKE_NO=02220116&PHPSESSID=6dbaeb8218b8098022e35e05e62bacad. Accessed 5 September 2014.

Japan Coast Guard (JCG) (2003) *"Kaijō ni okeru saikin no hanzai jōsei ni tsuite,"* Available online at: http://www.kantei.go.jp/jp/singi/hanzai/dai1/1siryou3.pdf. Accessed 15 February 2015.

Koo, Soo-kyung and Lim Ji-hye (2013) "Why do China and South Korea trade with North Korea?" *East Asia Forum*. Available online at: http://www.eastasiaforum.org/2013/08/17/why-do-china-and-south-korea-trade-with-north-korea/. Accessed 14 September 2013.

Kurōzu appu gendai (2003) *"Kitachōsen to bōryokudan: kakuseizai mitsunyū no jittai."* Available online at: http://www.nhk.or.jp/gendai/kiroku/detail_1774.html. Accessed 14 August 2014.

Mason, Ra (2013) "Time for Tokyo to change track on North Korea," *AJW Forum*. Available online at: http://ajw.asahi.com/article/forum/politics_and_economy/east_asia/AJ201308060024. Accessed 6 August 2013.

——— (2014) *Japan's North Korea Relations and the Recalibration of Risk*, Abingdon, Oxon: Routledge.

Merica, Dan and Evan Perez (2013) "Eric Holder seeks to cut mandatory minimum drug Sentences," CNN. Available online at: http://edition.cnn.com/2013/08/12/politics/holder-mandatory-minimums/index.html. Accessed 18 September 2013.

Metropolitan Police Department (2013) *"Yakubutsu ni kansuru dētā."* Available online at: http://www.keishicho.metro.tokyo.jp/seian/yakubutu/toukei.htm. Accessed 5 September 2014.

MHLW (2013). Available online at: http://www.mhlw.go.jp/english/wp/wp-hw3/dl/3-03.pdf. Accessed 2 September 2013.

Ministry of Finance (2011) *"Kakuseizai mitsuyunyū tekihatsu ken ga kako saikō o kiroku."* Available online at: http://www.mof.go.jp/customs_tariff/trade/safe_society/mitsuyu/cy2011/ka240206.pdf. Accessed 11 September 2013.

Ministry of Justice (2011) *"Heisei 23-nen hanzai hakusho,"* (White paper), Tokyo: Ministry of Justice.

Mizoguchi, Atsushi (2011) *Yamaguchi-gumi doran!!* (Revised Edition), Tokyo: Take Shobo.

MOFA (2013) "Telephone Talks between Foreign Minister Fumio Kishida and US Secretary of State John Kelly." Available on line at: http://www.mofa.go.jp/announce/announce/2013/2/0212_05.html. Accessed 18 February 2015.

Perl, Raphael F. (2007) "Drug trafficking and North Korea: issues for U.S. policy," CRS Report for Congress, released 25 January. Available online at: http://fas.org/sgp/crs/row/RL32167.pdf. Accessed 6 November 2014.

Rankin, Andrew (2012) "21st-century yakuza: recent trends in organized crime in Japan: Part 1," *The Asia-Pacific Journal*, 10, 7, 2 (February). Available online at: http://www.japanfocus.org/-Andrew-Rankin/3688#sthash.vgPIyH1x.dpuf. Accessed 12 September 2013.

Sakurai, Yoshiko (2007) *Nihon yo, tsuyoki kuni to nare*, Tokyo: Diamond.

Taleb, Nassim (2007) *The Black Swan*, London: Penguin.

US Department of State (2003) International Narcotics Control Strategy Report (INCSR). Available online at: http://www.state.gov/j/inl/rls/nrcrpt/2003/. Accessed 27 July 2013.

Yoshida, Yasuhiko (2008) *"Kitachōsen" saikō no tame no 60 shō: nicchō taiwa ni mukete*, Tokyo: Akashi Shoten.

PART III
Internalizing the US–Japan alliance in Okinawa

1 Introduction

The overarching theme of Part III of this book is how the risk posed to the security of the everyday by Japan's alliance with the United States (US) has been internalized in Okinawa. Whilst the four chapters following do not address directly the question of the efficacy of the deployment of US troops in the prefecture as a deterrence against potential external enemies such as China and North Korea, discussed in Part I and Part II of this book, the evidence presented here does challenge the government's state-centric security policy by demonstrating concretely how a minority of the national population bears a disproportionate share of the risks, potential harm and actual harm associated with the deployment of foreign troops in the archipelago and the implications of this unequal distribution for governance. Each chapter in its own way aims to elucidate how the government's security policy, focused on external threats and risks, engenders domestic risks to the security of the everyday, as manifest in potential harm and actual harm for the local population.

The location of American troops in the prefecture results in part from the historical legacy of the US victory in the 1945 battle of Okinawa as well as the US occupation of Okinawa as a 'semi-colony' from 1945 to 1972, but also from the national government's policy of promoting the concentration of US bases in the prefecture. The forward deployment of US troops in Japan is the quintessence of the alliance between these two Pacific powers. From the signing of the original Bilateral Security Treaty between the United States of America and Japan in 1951 through to the treaty's revision as the Treaty of Mutual Cooperation and Security between the United States and Japan in 1960 to its extension in 1970 and continuation to this day, the security policy of Japan has remained rooted in the alliance, combined with national forces – from 1954 onwards the JSDF or SDF. Integral to decades of military cooperation across the Pacific is Article VI of the 1960 treaty, granting the use by American land, air and sea forces 'of facilities and areas in Japan' or, in the 1951 treaty, by US 'land, air, and sea forces in and about Japan.' As US forces, facilities and areas remain to this day clustered together in the prefecture, especially on the main island of Okinawa, the security of the everyday is exposed disproportionately to the risks and harms produced as a consequence of the treaty and the alliance more generally.

Thus, the four chapters following this introduction illuminate how a policy trumpeted as providing security for all is premised on a minority of the national population being exposed to a disproportionate and unequal share of the risks arising from the implementation of a state-centric security policy. During the Cold War, the opposition Japan Socialist Party and other critics of the alliance constructed a risk narrative centred on how the deployment of US forces in Japan could act as a 'magnet,' potentially causing harm to Japanese security as a result of America's enemies becoming Japan's enemies, too. In contrast, for the government and many others, the risk of foreign invasion by communists would exist irrespective of whether or not US forces were deployed in Japan: the deterrence offered by the alliance was simply the best way to ensure security for the national population. But the costs of this policy to the security of the everyday remain as a source of harm at the local level, which can pose a problem for the national system of governance. The local population's dissatisfaction with the current state of affairs is evidenced in the lower level of support in Okinawa for the security treaty with the United States as a means to protect Japan. For instance, an NHK poll in 2012 showed that only 53 per cent of the pollees in Okinawa agree that the treaty is contributing to Japanese peace compared with 75 per cent on the main islands (Kōno and Kobayashi 2012: 8). As far as the US bases in the prefecture are concerned, a 2012 poll carried out jointly by the *Asahi Shimbun* and *Okinawa Taimuzu* found 86 per cent of pollees in favour of reduction or complete withdrawal of the bases on Okinawa compared with 72 per cent on the main islands, and 37 per cent of Okinawan pollees compared with 24 per cent on the main islands calling for complete withdrawal (*Asahi Shimbun*, 9 May 2012). In other words, a salient difference exists between the main islands and Okinawa, with main islanders less enthusiastic about the complete withdrawal of the bases from the prefecture, no doubt partly because of the risk of their relocation elsewhere in Japan – perhaps even in their own neighbourhood.

2 The legal framework: Status of Forces Agreement (SOFA)

One of the reasons for the local resistance to the continued presence of the American eagle in the prefecture is the existence and operation of the US-Japan Status of Forces Agreement (SOFA). The SOFA prescribes the legal framework to be used in addressing how the manifestation of risk as harm – for instance, military accidents as well as rape, burglary and other incidents allegedly committed by US military personnel – is to be dealt with in Japan. The SOFA came into force with the original treaty in 1952 and the revised treaty in 1960. *Ad hoc* revisions have been carried out over the years in the context of these two agreements, with accidents and incidents now coming under the legal purview of the 1960 SOFA, formally the agreement under Article VI of the Treaty of Mutual Cooperation and Security between Japan and the United States of America (US-Japan security treaty), regarding facilities and areas and the status of United States Armed Forces in Japan (Ministry of Foreign Affairs 1960).[1]

The SOFA signed in 1960 remains basically the same as the previously negotiated US-Japan administrative agreement signed in 1952, as 'the content of the agreement was almost unchanged in 1960, except certain rules concerning criminal proceedings or cost sharing for the compensation for civil damage to residents in Japan' (Honma *et al*. 2001: 375).[2] With the formal reversion of Okinawa to Japan in May 1972, the 1960 agreement has henceforth been 'applied to Okinawa under the same condition as to any other area of Japan' (Honma *et al*. 2001: 376).[3] Given the US occupation of the prefecture at the time the SOFA was first signed in 1960, however, the agreement only applied to US forces in mainland Japan, not Okinawa. In other words, since 1972 the SOFA has been extended to US military outposts originally constructed without any restrictions and to US military forces having enjoyed the prerogatives of history for twenty-five years without any constraint imposed by the bilateral agreement, whatever the current misgivings and criticisms of the SOFA among the local population. For such reasons, the revision of the SOFA has been called for on numerous occasions by local political leaders, activists and others, as illustrated by the 1995 decision of the prefectural assembly to pass a unanimous resolution requesting both governments to review the agreement (Okinawa Prefectural Government 2008: 82–3).

Whilst the exact contents of the SOFAs the US maintains with a range of other countries differ, their uniform purpose is to set in place a legal framework for US military forces when in a foreign country as visiting forces (for discussion, see Flynn 2012 and Stone 2006; in Japanese, see Honma 1996; Ryūkyū Shimpōsha 2004). That is, the SOFA details the legal foundation for the basing of US troops in Japan and the jurisdictional rights, competencies and frameworks for both parties in the case of US military accidents and incidents committed by US service personnel, US civilian contractors, and their families *(Beigunkōseiin)*. As far as the incidents of crime are concerned, the jurisdiction of the two parties is affected by the location and status of the individual suspected of committing the crime, such as whether the suspect was on- or off-base as well as on or off official duty when the unlawful act was committed.[4] The law of the United States and, within limits, the law of Japan apply on-base, although neither of the two sides appears to have sought over the decades to 'compile a list of which laws [of Japan] apply, which do not, and whether the application is dependent on whether the actor was a member of the US armed forces or a civilian or a national of Japan' (Honma *et al*. 2001: 397). As far as off-base crimes are concerned, the SOFA severely constrains the ability of the Japanese authorities to exercise their primary jurisdiction in arresting and prosecuting US military suspects in Japanese legal space.

In the case of more fraught cases, such as murder, rape and other heinous crimes allegedly committed by American military personnel and others, the operation of the SOFA leads to widespread local concern and criticism, with critics charging that the agreement fundamentally undermines Japanese sovereignty and gives US forces at least some degree of extraterritoriality. Or, to illustrate the point more colourfully, 'All servicemen in Okinawa know that if after committing a rape, a robbery, or an assault, they can make it back to the base before the police catch them, they will be free until indicted even though there is a Japanese arrest warrant out for their capture' (Johnson 2004). In other words, whereas the local population is exposed to the potential risk of harm from US military personnel when off-base, as in the case of rape, robbery or assault, the perpetrators of these crimes bear little risk of being punished by the full weight of the law of the land because of the unequal legal framework between the two countries under the SOFA.

In the more than half century since the signing of the 1960 agreement, a limited number of revisions to the SOFA have been implemented on an *ad hoc*, informal basis, such as the strengthening of the custodial rights of the Japanese police before the indictment of the accused.[5] The most recent amendment is the agreement of the US to submit a monthly report to the Japanese government listing the punishment meted out (or not) for the crimes committed by US service personnel from January 2014 onwards, whereas until this revision was implemented only the final outcomes of US courts-martial were reported (*Yomiuri Shimbun*, 8 October 2013). Or, to put it another way, for the first time the US government has agreed to supply data on how the military deals with all of the crimes suspected of being committed by service personnel in Japan.[6] In short, the wording of the US-Japan SOFA remains exactly the same as when the agreement was signed in 1960, that is, essentially the same as in 1952, except for minor modifications being implemented in an *ad hoc* manner, mostly in response to local pressure in the face of US crimes.[7]

In this way, the operation of the SOFA has been modified as a result of grassroots pressure in Okinawa, but the efficacy of such local action remains under severe constraint because of the power of the United States and the central government as well as the unswerving commitment to the maintenance of the alliance by policymakers and security managers. To start with, a long-standing, informal agreement exists between the two governments stating that Japan will 'waive its primary right to exercise jurisdiction except in case of "special importance" to Japan' (Honma *et al*. 2001: 387). This agreement is buttressed, bolstered and sustained by the operation of a two-pronged US policy: to gain a waiver of charges brought against US military personnel suspected of crimes, on the one hand, and to maximize US jurisdiction in Japanese legal space, on the other (Flynn 2012). Maximization implies a proactive US approach, which seeks 'to obtain release of cases to the US through a combination of non-indictments, US investigation of crimes involving alleged US perpetrators, lapse of time to present a notice of intent to indict, and, if necessary, waivers of cases already under indictment' (Honma *et al*. 2001: 388). Needless to say, even for the supporters of the deployment of US forces in Okinawa, the abstract notions of the erosion of sovereignty and extraterritoriality highlighted by critics take on concrete form and meaning in such US attempts to insulate suspects from the application of Japanese law, especially when the crime has been committed off-base.

The above discussion of the SOFA sets the essential context for the following four chapters, as the accidents and incidents occurring in Okinawa are subject to the existence and operation of this agreement. The concrete operation of the SOFA will become clear as we proceed in the following chapters to take up military accidents (Chapter 9), military incidents such as crime (Chapter 10), as well as environmental degradation (Chapter 11) and noise pollution (Chapter 12). Whilst the approach in each chapter differs, and the implications of the SOFA are of greatest relevance in Chapter 10 on crimes committed by US service personnel off-base, the overriding purpose of our investigation is to shed a penetrating light on how the existence and operation of these military outposts of US power, in the context of the SOFA, pose risks to the security of the everyday in Okinawa and, where relevant, the implications of the construction, framing and recalibration of risk for governance. In some cases, the chapter explores the source of the risks and how risk has been constructed, framed and mediated in the process of different actors responding to the US military presence, whether the actor is the state or grassroots activists. In others, the focus is on the potential harm and the manifestation of risk as actual harm as a result of the operation of the bases or behaviour of US military personnel. In all, the four chapters offer a critical view of the operation of the alliance, not from the perspective of US forces as a deterrent against potential external enemies, but rather as the internalized source of risk, potential harm and actual harm to the security of the everyday for the local population. Whilst, as seen above, support for the alliance and the deployment of US forces in the prefecture is in no way to be denied, these two contrastive views of the alliance are at the heart of the division between a state-centric view of security among national policymakers and security managers and the focus on the security of the everyday in Okinawa discussed in the following chapters.

3 Divergent views of US military outposts

The salience of this divergence is evident in comments made by Prime Minister Abe Shinzō in response to the proposed relocation within the prefecture of the Marine Corps Air Station Futenma to Henoko, Nago city, discussed in different sections of the following chapters (for an overview, see Wright 2010). What the prime minister says below serves to underscore three fundamental differences between the national and the local in their views of national security policy and the alliance. To start with, the prime minister's matter-of-fact statement reveals his view that 'the responsibility for security policy lies with the state' (*Okinawa Taimuzu*, 10 March 2013). True, national governments do indeed hold the reins of power and responsibility for national security policy, but the way Japan's security policy has been instrumentalized over the past decades means the local population in Okinawa continues to be exposed disproportionately to the risks posed by US military deployments. This can be seen in the percentage of American bases in Okinawa: 74 per cent are located in a prefecture making up no more than 0.6 per cent of Japanese territory. So although the prime minister arrogates to the national government the right to be the sole arbiter of a state-centric security policy, Okinawan subnational political authorities at the prefectural, city, town and village levels, along with a large percentage of the local population, refuse to accept a policy giving them no say over the risk to the security of the everyday posed by US deployments. The Abe government's policy of disregarding the ongoing concerns of the local population became particularly salient following his administration's decision to forge ahead with the transfer of the Futenma base to Henoko, despite the 2014 re-election of the mayor of Nago, Inamine Susumu, who is staunchly opposed to the relocation. Even though, for those wedded firmly to a state-centric view of security, the Okinawans may appear to be no more than a voice crying in the wilderness; their efforts to redress the unequal distribution of the risks and harms arising from US deployments in the prefecture offer them the only way to resist the continued imposition of a governance system distributing the risk and harms of the bases so unequally within the national community.

Second, the prime minister states that he must 'build trust' with Okinawa by 'carefully explaining state policy' (*Okinawa Taimuzu*, 10 March 2013). This seems to presuppose that local leaders and citizens have failed to understand the reason for the planned relocation of the Futenma base within the prefecture rather than their fundamental disagreement over a state security policy leading to the construction of a new base in Okinawa. Put bluntly, the prime minister is calling for the prefecture to accept the ongoing need for the US to deploy bases and troops in Japan, on the one hand, but to continue to acquiesce in their unequal distribution in Okinawa, on the other. The reason for the government's determination to maintain the unequal distribution of risks in Okinawa is straightforward: the reluctance of other prefectural governments to accept the risks, potential harm and actual harm posed by the transfer of Futenma to elsewhere in Japan. It is not a lack of understanding to be overcome by building trust and explaining state policy, but rather a call on the government to share more equitably amongst the national population the risks arising from a security treaty meant to secure the whole nation. The fundamental difference in viewpoint is well captured by the former governor of Okinawa, Ōta Masahide, when he declared:

> Whenever the Japanese government opens its mouth, it cannot stop stressing how the security treaty is essential in order to protect the life and property of the Japanese nation in accordance with the national interest. However, many prefectures do not wish to share the burden and obligation of the treaty by themselves. As a result, tiny Okinawa has been forced to accept the heavy burden arising from the security treaty for more than half a century, [and] Okinawans have been exposed to risks *(kiken)* to their lives on a daily basis, and are unable to carry on a peaceful life.
>
> (quoted in Maedomari 2011: 170)

The third point is the prime minister's perspective on how Futenma functions; namely, he claimed, the base must be relocated within the prefecture because 'the deterrent power of the US Marines is essential for the peace and stability of Japan and the Asia-Pacific region' (*Okinawa Taimuzu*, 13 March 2013). However, the transformation of the external security environment represented by North Korea's development of nuclear weapons and the rise of China has led the two countries in 2006 to agree on the redeployment of marine forces to Guam under the US-Japan Realignment Roadmap. Although the original time scale of 2014 has slipped to the 2020s, the proposed transfer of the marines itself, whether implemented or not, undermines the premise of their centrality as a deterrent needing to be located in Okinawa. As the mayor of Nago reminded us after his election victory, 'Former Defense Minister Morimoto once said there is no military reason for the bases to be in Okinawa. It's just more politically expedient and easier to have them in Okinawa' (Inamine 2014).

The above division over a state-centric security policy and the security of the everyday is not to suggest an anti-American streak runs through the Okinawan body politic, nor to claim any widespread objection to a close partnership with the US, *per se*. (Indeed, the vast majority in Okinawa could be best described as more anti-base and anti-Tokyo than anti-American.) Our purpose is rather to emphasize how many Okinawans remain sceptical of the logic of deterrence and baulk at the unequal distribution of the risks associated with the government's state-centric security policy, even if most remain supportive of the alliance with the United States, *per se*. What matters at the local level is the amelioration of the risk to the security of the everyday by a redistribution or dismantling of the US military outposts in the prefecture. The following four chapters aim to demonstrate how the system of governance is vulnerable to continued local resistance as a result of the risk, potential harm and actual harm arising from the existence and operation of the bases and the behaviour of US troops in the prefecture.

Notes

1 In addition to the US-Japan SOFA, the Japanese government is party to the United Nations Command (UNC)-Japan SOFA. This covers non-US visiting forces (US forces personnel assigned to the UNC are covered by the US-Japan SOFA) assigned to the UNC. The UNC has a presence in Japan because of the ongoing role it plays on the Korean peninsula, where the North and South still remain formally at war. See Honma *et al*. (2001: 390).

2 Between 2004 and 2013 the Japanese government contributed 380 million yen (of a total of 1.5 billion yen) that was paid out for accidents and incidents by US service personnel and civilian workers in Japan as a whole. Of the 9,962 accidents and incidents, approximately 48 per cent took place in Okinawa (*Japan Times*, 13 August 2014).

3 As Honma *et al*. (2001) note, however, Okinawa's reversion to Japan was on the basis of the 1969 joint communique between Prime Minister Satō Eisaku and President Richard Nixon, but 'it cannot be defined clearly . . . what such application means' (377). Of greatest concern is whether the separate Exchange of Notes in 1960, which stipulated 'prior consultation' on changes in US equipment as part of the treaty negotiations and attached to Article VI, usually interpreted to mean prior consultation on the

introduction of nuclear weapons into Japan, applies to Okinawa, given the existence of a secret agreement between the two governments: 'In the secret agreement, the Japanese government pledged that the government should reply "Yes" in the Prior Consultation when it is necessary for US forces in Okinawa to bring any nuclear weapon into their bases for the purpose of deterring any danger against the peace and security of Korea or Taiwan in particular' (Honma et al. 2001: 377; also see 412). In short, if this secret agreement makes an exception of Okinawa, do any others? For the relevant documents and discussion of the secret agreement, see Wampler 2009.

4 For further details, see Honma et al. (2001: 402). For instance, so long as the member of US military forces in question is travelling directly to and from his or her residence to the place of duty, this is part of 'official duty.' The alleged offender's commanding officer determines whether the incident took place on 'official duty,' although this can be challenged by the Japanese side.

5 Following the 1995 protest against the rape of a school girl (see Chapter 10), the 25 October 1995 Joint Committee Agreement on Criminal Jurisdiction Procedures strengthened police powers.

6 This change will no doubt be welcomed by the victims and their families but is still constrained by the need to gain the consent of the US perpetrator in order to protect individual privacy (*Mainichi Shimbun*, 8 October 2013). It was seen by the media as part of the battle over the relocation of the Futenma Marine Air Station to Henoko (*Mainichi Shimbun*, 8 October 2013; *Sankei Shimbun*, 8 October 2013).

7 It was announced in December 2013 that, for the first time, the government was investigating the possible revision of the SOFA (*Sankei Shimbun*, 13 December 2013).

References

Flynn, Jonathan T. (2012) "No need to maximize: reforming foreign criminal jurisdiction practice under the U.S.-Japan Status of Force Agreement," *Military Law Review*, 212 (Summer): 1–69.

Honma, Hiroshi (1996) *Zainichi Beigun Chiikyōtei*, Tokyo: Nihon Hyōronsha.

Honma, Hiroshi, Dale Sonnenberg and Donal A. Timm (2001) "United States Forces in Japan: a bilateral experience," in Dieter Fleck (ed.) *The Handbook of the Law of Visiting Forces*, Oxford: Oxford University Press, pp. 365–416.

Inamine, Susumu (2014) "Okinawan resistance against construction of a new US Marine base," speech at the Foreign Correspondents Club of Japan. Available online at: https://www.youtube.com/watch?v=tvuaFHQ1Nfc. Accessed 5 November 2014.

Johnson, Chalmers (2004) *Three Rapes: The Status of Forces Agreement and Okinawa* (Japan Policy Research Institute, Working Paper No. 97, January). Available online at: http://www.jpri.org/publications/workingpapers/wp97.html. Accessed 29 November 2013.

Kōno, Kei and Toshiyuki Kobayashi (2012) "Fukki 40 nen no Okinawa to anzen hoshō," *Hōsō Kenkyū to Chōsa* (July): 2–31.

Maedomari, Hiromori (2011) *Okinawa to Beigunkichi*, Tokyo: Kadokawa.

Ministry of Foreign Affairs (1960) Agreement under Article VI of the Treaty of Mutual Cooperation and Security between Japan and the United States of America, regarding Facilities and Areas and the Status of United States Armed Forces in Japan. Available online at: http://www.mofa.go.jp/mofaj/area/usa/sfa/pdfs/fulltext.pdf. Accessed 25 November 2013.

Okinawa Prefectural Government (2008) *Okinawa no Beigun Kichi*, Okinawa Ken Chiji Kōshitsu, Kichi Taisakuka, Naha: Okinawa Prefectural Government.

Ryūkyū Shimpōsha (ed.) (2004) *Nichibei Chiikyōtei no Kangaekata: Gaimushō Kimitsu Bunsho*, Tokyo: Kōbunken.
Stone, Timothy D. (2006) "U.S.-Japan SOFA: a necessary document worth preserving," *Naval Law Review*, 53: 229–58.
Wampler, Robert A. (2009) "Nuclear Noh drama: Tokyo, Washington and the case of the missing nuclear agreements." Available online at: http://www2.gwu.edu/~nsarchiv/nukevault/ebb291/. Accessed 8 July 2014.
Wright, Dustin (2010) "Impasse at MCAS Futenma," *Critical Asian Studies*, 42, 3 (September): 457–68.

9
MILITARY ACCIDENTS

1 Introduction

The deployment of US military personnel, weaponry and the infrastructure to support them produces risks for the everyday security of Okinawans living side by side with the outposts of American power. As touched on in the introduction to Part III of this book, Okinawa hosts nearly three-quarters of US military installations, despite the prefecture being no more than 0.6 per cent of the land area of the Japanese archipelago. Published works in both Japanese and English on the historical and contemporary role of US military bases in general as well as in the prefecture are substantial (in English, see Calder 2007; Cooley 2008; Lutz 2009; McCormack and Oka Norimatsu 2012) but most do not employ a conceptual framework enabling us to consider as a whole the multitude of ways in which America's military presence impacts on the everyday security of the local population. This first of the four chapters making up Part III demonstrates how the internalization of these military facilities poses risks, potential harm and harm to everyday security arising from US military accidents in the prefecture.

The existence and operation of US military installations means that America plays a dual role in Okinawa: first, as a mediator of external risk for the security of the national population; but, second, as a mediator of internal risk causing *insecurity* for the local population. As detailed in the introduction to the book, by employing the concept of risk we are able to contrast clearly how a state-centric security policy focused on external threats and risks exposes the local population to potential harm and harm including death, injury and physical damage as well as emotional stress and trauma as a result of the crashes, mishaps and mechanical failures of US planes and helicopters at the military heart of the alliance. The purpose of this chapter is to provide concrete examples of these military accidents before proceeding to an examination of military incidents in Chapter 10, environmental degradation in Chapter 11 and noise pollution in Chapter 12.

More specifically, this chapter focuses on how the risk of military accidents has been constructed, framed and recalibrated as potential harm in Okinawa by linking new accidents to the memory of historical accidents impacting on the security of the everyday. The chapter thus starts out by providing an historical overview of the range and type of military accidents from the early years of the American occupation and the changes taking place after the reversion of Okinawa to Japan in May 1972. The first section demonstrates how living side by side with American forces for nearly seventy years is accompanied by harm for the local population. The following three sections then take up the potential and actual harm arising from cases of aircraft accidents and local anxiety about them. The second section examines the case of the August 2004 crash of a US Marine CH-53D Sea Stallion transport helicopter in the grounds of Okinawa International University in Ginowan city. The third section considers the case of the August 2013 crash of a US Air Force HH-60 rescue helicopter inside the marines' Camp Hansen near Ginoza village. In contrast, section four addresses the risk of potential harm rather than the manifestation of risk as harm resulting from the new deployments in 2012 and 2013 of the MV22 Ospreys to Marine Corps Air Station Futenma in Ginowan city. In each of these three cases, the focus is on how subnational political authorities and the local population in Okinawa have responded discursively and in terms of praxis to the risk and harm arising from the actual and potential military accidents as well as on the details of the events themselves. It underscores how the memory of military accidents causing death and injury during the American occupation of the prefecture have shaped the local population's response to the risk of present-day military activities and the deployment of new weaponry in the prefecture. The conclusion summarizes the discussion and draws out the implications of military accidents for our understanding of risk to everyday security in the context of governing Okinawa, highlighting how an end to unequal risk in Okinawa and the logic of governance is countered by a logic of deterrence by policymakers and security managers.

2 Historical overview

The history of military accidents in Okinawa can be traced back to the years of the American occupation of the prefecture from 1945 to 1950 and the United States Civil Administration of the Ryukyu Islands, 1950–72. A wide range of accidents involving military personnel and weaponry has taken place over the years, with the most serious in terms of death or injury to the local population occurring before reversion in 1972. At one end of the risk spectrum are automobile accidents involving US service personnel and local inhabitants, as these would not have occurred without the American military presence on the islands.[1] The point can be illustrated by a 1963 case, when a vehicle driven by a US serviceman struck and killed a twelve-year-old student on his way home from school. A US military court martial found the driver not guilty of an offence, provoking widespread protests. In another case a traffic accident in 1970 involving a US soldier caused a public disturbance in Koza city (present-day Okinawa city): seventy-three US military vehicles were burned in response, illustrating the 'magma' under Okinawa.[2] Other military accidents have included stray bullets, as in the case of a local man killed by a stray bullet in 1964 whilst gathering shells on Kuwae beach, Chatan town, demonstrating how living in such close proximity to the bases poses the risk of harm to everyday security. In the post-reversion period, no such fatalities or serious physical injuries of locals have occurred from US military accidents, except through automobile accidents involving military personnel, but these earlier accidents have become embedded in the discourse and popular memory of the risk posed by the US military presence in Okinawa.

At the other end of the spectrum is the manifestation of risk as harm resulting from the crashes and mishaps of military aircraft.[3] The prefectural government maintains an up-to-date record of such accidents dating back to the first recorded cases at the start of the occupation. In the post-reversion period, a total of 540 accidents have occurred, including forty-three crashes, albeit without local fatalities (Okinawa Prefectural Government 2013a: 104). The accidents during the pre-reversion period included fatalities and serious injury, as in the death of one Okinawan and the injury of three in Yomitan village, August 1950, when a US military aircraft dropped a refuel tank in the garden of a private dwelling. The last military accident before reversion involving the death or injury of local inhabitants occurred in 1968, when a B-52 bomber crashed at Kadena Air Base injuring four local inhabitants. In the post-reversion period, forty-four aircraft accidents have occurred, although none has involved the death or serious physical injury of any of the local population. The risk posed by the potential harm of such aircraft accidents, however, remains centrally part of the Okinawan discourse on the American military presence in the prefecture.

Indeed, the memory of one of the most serious and evocative military accidents to take place in Okinawa is of the crash of a US F-100D fighter into Miyamori Elementary School (present-day Uruma City Miyamori Elementary School) in 1959. The fighter accident caused the death of eleven children and six others as well as a large number of injuries. It has become the most poignant military accident in the popular memory of Okinawans. In a prefectural poll conducted by the *Ryūkyū Shimpō*, for instance, the pollees selected the accident as the seventh most important in Okinawan history out of twenty events from a multiple choice questionnaire (the pollee selected three out of twenty), suggesting the way the memory of military accidents from the past continues to impact on present-day perceptions of risk for Okinawans (*Ryūkyū Shimpō*, 2007: 36). The school has kept the memory alive through the construction of a memorial on the school grounds, an annual remembrance ceremony and other activities, including the plan to establish a museum focused on the event (see Hook forthcoming).

As the city continues to suffer from the risk of potential harm from aircraft accidents, the memory of the 1959 crash has been employed by city officials as a source to construct a risk narrative of future military accidents or mishaps occurring in Uruma city. A number of statements issued by city officials illustrate the way current accidents are embedded in a discourse linked to the memory of the Miyamori crash. For instance, in a 2006 statement issued by the city assembly – sent to the prime minister and other Japanese and US officials – protesting the January crash in the sea nearby of a F-15 fighter from Kadena Air Base, the city noted that '[this] is a major incident which brings back the memory of the fatal accident that occurred in our city when in 1959 a jet crashed into Miyamori Elementary School and the fatal accident in 1961 when a jet crashed into a private dwelling' (Uruma City 2006).

Attempts have been made over the years to reduce the risk of military accidents arising from the US presence in the midst of the Okinawan community, the most significant being the actions taken as a result of the Special Action Committee on Okinawa (SACO). SACO was established by both the US and Japanese governments in November 1995 in response to widespread protests in the wake of the rape of a local school girl by three US military personnel (see Chapter 10). Illustrative of the concrete efforts made is the decision announced in the final SACO report of December 1996 to stop live ammunition practices over Prefectural Highway 104 and to move them to the main islands (Ministry of Foreign Affairs 1996a).[4] Despite the implementation of such changes, however, outstanding issues – such as fields and crops being inadvertently set alight through military activities and the potential for other aircraft accidents to occur – remain on the agenda, indicating how the US presence will continue to impact on the security of the everyday in Okinawa.[5] Crucially, such reduction in the risks posed does not address the structural inequality between Okinawa and the main islands at the heart of US deployments.

3 Sea Stallion helicopter crash

One of the most serious crashes in the years following the reversion occurred in August 2004 when a CH-53D Sea Stallion heavy assault transport helicopter from the Marine Corps Air Station Futenma crashed into the grounds of Okinawa International University, Ginowan city. Located immediately next to the university, the air station is scheduled to be relocated to the Henoko district of Nagano city because of the risks posed, but opposition to relocation within the prefecture remains strong, despite the decision of the Abe Shinzō administration to push forward with the plan, as touched on in the introduction to Part III.[6] In a concrete way, the crash confirmed how a military installation located in the midst of a city continues to pose a risk to the population, but the national and local responses to the crash revealed a divergence in views between mainland policymakers and the prefecture. The point is illuminated by the visit to the crash site of the foreign minister in the then Koizumi Junichirō cabinet, Machimura Nobutaka. Rather than focus his concern on how the crash had impacted on the everyday security of the local population, the foreign minister revealed the same sort of divergence in view illustrated by Prime Minister Abe Shinzō in the introduction to Part III when he praised the pilot of the Sea Stallion for avoiding a more serious crash

(*Ryūkyū Shimpō*, 16 October 2004). In other words, the alliance with the United States is based upon the built-in risk of the local population in Okinawa potentially suffering harm.

Although no deaths or serious physical injuries occurred on campus nor among the local residents of Ginowan as a result of the crash,[7] emotional as well as material harm was suffered by both. The main emotional harm related to trauma, post-traumatic stress disorder, anxiety and stress, especially among the university's staff and students. A survey by the university's psychology department, for instance, found a majority of the administrative and academic staff suffering from some form of stress (Okinawa International University 2004). The material impact was physical damage to the university, including the need to rebuild the main building, as well as to remove contaminated soil, replant burned trees and other such remedial work. This obviously disrupted the operation of the university as well as the learning environment of the students. Outside the campus, seventeen houses and thirty-three vehicles were damaged as a consequence of the flying debris.

Most significantly, the crash brought the local officials and residents face-to-face with the concrete operation of the SOFA (see the introduction to Part III for details on SOFA). Indeed, the US response to the crash, not only the crash, *per se*, exacerbated the intensity of the local reaction (Eldridge 2008–9a; Eldridge 2008–9b). In particular, the marines cordoned off the campus for four days, evoking a sense of Okinawa as still being under American occupation, even though the proclaimed aim of the action was to reduce the risk to the local population, that is, 'minimize danger and protect lives' (US Embassy Tokyo 2004). This not only prevented the staff and students from accessing the campus, but also limited the role local government officials and the police could play. A heightened perception of the risk of radiation contamination spread among the inhabitants when US service personnel were seen using Geiger counters, but examination of the soil by the university and the prefectural government once the cordon was cleared found no evidence of radiation at a level impacting on health (Arakaki 2005). The decision by the marines to resume flights of the Sea Stallion shortly after the accident, despite a lack of full information on the cause of the crash, was viewed locally as a disregard of local anxiety and the everyday security concerns of the local inhabitants.

The crash of the Sea Stallion was embedded in a discourse of the risk to the local population of suffering future fatalities, serious physical injuries or other harm from aircraft accidents as well as of the need to reduce the risk of future accidents. The voices of city officials, students and residents heard at the Ginowan City Resident Rally shortly after the accident illuminate how the risk and harm from the crash affected local lives (Ginowan City 2004). The Ginowan response was framed in the context of the ongoing controversy over the closure and relocation of Futenma. As discussed in further detail in Chapter 11, the 1996 SACO agreement proposed the return of Futenma within five to seven years, but because of local opposition over the proposed site of the new base, this timetable had not been implemented by 2004 (Ministry of Foreign Affairs 1996b). Protests against the crash and the relocation involved staff and students at the university and others affected by the crash, activists, and local and prefectural officials and residents. Put simply, the protests sought to achieve one recurring request, 'the prompt closure of the Futenma Air Station,' as stated by the president of the university (Okinawa International University 2004). At the political level, the mayor of Ginowan, Iha Yōhei, took the initiative to press for the closure and relocation of the base. He not only played an active role as the local mayor, but also the Ginowan city assembly issued a statement condemning the crash and calling for the return of Futenma. Other local assemblies in the prefecture followed Ginowan's lead so that, by the end of August 2004, over thirty had joined in the protest (*Ryūkyū Shimpō*, 29 August 2004).

At a press conference on the ninth anniversary of the crash in August 2013, the mayor of Ginowan, Sakima Atsushi, used the occasion to build a discursive link between the memory of the crash and the implementation of the 1996 SACO agreement (Ginowan City 2013). As the date for the closure of the marine air base is still to be settled, despite the passage of seventeen years, Sakima renewed his call for the governments of both Japan and the United States to close and return Futenma as soon as possible. He claimed that, just as at the time of the 2004 crash, the local residents and the wider Okinawan population want the two governments to "quickly implement a policy to eliminate the danger of the base and reduce our burden" (Ginowan City 2013). As we will see in Chapter 11, the ongoing protest against the relocation of the base to Henoko, supported by a majority of the prefectural population, which calls for Futenma to be moved outside of the prefecture or outside of Japan, means Prime Minister Abe's commitment to implement the move to Henoko will only take place in the face of the strong opposition at the local level. The risk, potential harm and harm resulting from the continued operation of the Futenma air station, evoked by the memory of the Sea Stallion's crash, is thus a narrative of resistance against the central government's policy on base relocation (McCormack and Oka Norimatsu 2012).

4 Pave Hawk helicopter crash

The most recent aircraft accident in Okinawa occurred in August 2013 during a military exercise, when a Kadena-based Air Force HH-60 Pave Hawk rescue helicopter with four military personnel on board crashed and burst into flames at the central training area, Camp Hansen, next to Ginoza village, with one fatality and three injuries among the four members of the crew. The crash site was close to the dam supplying water to the village, a short distance from the highway and within a couple of kilometres of the residents of Ginoza village. No deaths or injuries were suffered among the local population, but as the resolution of the prefectural assembly highlighted, 'a major disaster' could have occurred (Okinawa Prefectural Assembly 2013). The accident brought back the memory of the "enormous fear" generated at the time of the crash at Okinawa International

University (Okinawa Prefectural Assembly 2013). In the same way the Sea Stallion crash illuminated how the marines were able to cordon-off the university crash site under the SOFA, this time Kadena Air Base issued a NOTAM (notice to airmen), which is used to warn other pilots of risks and potential hazards along a flight route. In effect, the notice prevented the local and national media from flying over the site of the crash as part of their efforts to collect data and images for their reportage (*Ryūkyū Shimpō*, 8 August 2004).

The harm from the crash included anxiety about the presence or not of radioactive helicopter parts, the general emotional stress caused by the accident itself, and environmental pollution, as discussed in Chapter 11 (*Okinawa Taimuzu*, 8 and 9 August 2013). As far as radiation is concerned, the Okinawa Defense Bureau confirmed to the village head that strontium 90 was not present, although helicopter parts did contain thorium 232.[8] The issue of radioactivity was high on the agenda for the villagers because of the crash site's proximity to the dam supplying water to local households, but tests of the water and the ground in the village proved negative.

Following the accident, the prefectural assembly submitted a resolution to the two governments protesting the crash and calling for the publication of the accident's cause before the resumption of HH-60 flights. At the local level, resolutions calling for the grounding of helicopter flights were passed promptly by the assemblies of Kadena town, Kin town, Onna village and Ōgimi village as well as Ginoza village, and the official representatives of these communities delivered the protests in to the Okinawa Defense Bureau (*Ryūkyū Shimpō*, 10 August 2013). In addition, Ginoza villagers organized a protest rally calling for the cessation of flights (Ginoza Village 2013).[9]

Despite the local protests, the same type of helicopter was in the air eleven days after the crash without the cause of the accident being announced. At the societal level, the resumption of flights caused emotional harm by exacerbating the Okinawans' distrust of the central government and the US military, with the local mayor of Kadena town deploying emotive language by calling the decision 'outrageous' (*Ryūkyū Shimpō*, 17 August 2013. Also see *Okinawa Taimuzu*, 17 August 2013). The local feeling was summed up in an editorial in the *Okinawa Taimuzu*: 'The action puts excessive priority on the military, ignoring the lives and daily lives *(kurashi)* of the prefectural inhabitants. How long can this unreasonable situation continue, where even the most basic request cannot be accepted? It is impossible to suppress our strong misgivings and anger' (13 August 2013). Japanese government officials sought to gain local acquiescence in the risk posed by flight resumptions by disseminating a counter narrative on the benefits of the HH-60 deployments in Okinawa in the context of the US military's response to the harm arising from the March 2011 Great East Japan Earthquake, when the HH-60 was active in search and rescue missions. This discursive tactic is clearly evident in the statement of Minister of Defense Onodera Itsunori, who evoked the memory of US support at the time of the disaster when he reminded everyone that the Pave Hawks had played 'an important role in Operation Tomodachi emergency rescue activities at the time of the Great East Japan Earthquake,' on announcing his acceptance of the resumption of flights by the HH-60 even though the US had still to clarify the cause of the crash (*Asahi Shimbun*, 16 August 2013).[10]

Similarly, when the head of Ginoza village presented the resolution of the village rally protesting the accident and the resumption of flights to the director of the Okinawa Defense Bureau, the latter responded: 'Considering the importance of the role the HH-60 plays under the US-Japan security treaty in carrying out operations for the purpose of search and rescue, as the government we understand the resumption of flights' (*Ryūkyū Shimpō*, 8 August 2004). In other words, this narrative logic was used to juxtapose latent goodwill towards the role of the HH-60 with the manifest ill will towards the helicopter as the cause of the crash and potential future harm by the resumption of flights by the same type of helicopter.[11] For the local inhabitants, however, the resumption of the Pave Hawk flights without a full explanation of the reason for the crash was nothing other than to confirm the government's state-centric security policy of disregarding the voice of Okinawans and local concerns about everyday security.

5 Osprey deployments

The deployment of twelve MV-22 Osprey tiltrotor aircrafts to Marine Corps Air Station Futenma during October 2012 and a further twelve by September 2013 generated widespread protest and the dissemination of a narrative focused on the unequal distribution of the burden of US bases and the new risks to everyday security faced by the local population.[12] The crash of the HH-60 led to a halt in the movement of the second batch of Ospreys from Iwakuni to Futenma in August 2013, although the transfer soon resumed after a short delay. The intersection of the crash and the deployment of the Osprey led Prime Minister Abe to indirectly acknowledge the risk to everyday security faced in Okinawa by stating that his priority was the 'daily life *(seikatsu)* of the residents,' of Okinawa, whilst remaining fully committed to the security treaty under which the US deployments and military accidents occur. This is a concrete manifestation of how the state is recalibrating the risk posed by US military deployments *within* Okinawa rather than addressing the fundamental problem of recalibrating the risks posed throughout Japan by the existence and operation of the security treaty. By pushing forward with the agreement to transfer the MV-22 to a new base in Henoko, not out of the prefecture, the Abe administration is maintaining the unequal distribution of US deployments and the risk to the security of the everyday this policy implies (*Mainichi Shimbun*, 12 August 2013).

The risk and potential harm posed by the deployment of the Ospreys to Futenma is not because of a military accident involving an Osprey in Okinawa, which unlike in the above two cases has not occurred, but rather relates to inherent questions about the airplane's safety, the record of crashes and mishaps elsewhere in the world and the fear and anxiety among the local population of a similar military accident taking place in Okinawa. To start with, the aircraft's inherent safety has been questioned in the wake of a number of crashes, hard landings and mishaps, including the aircraft's lack of an autorotation function in an emergency (G2mil 2003). Even though improvements to the Osprey have been implemented over the years, the question for the local population still remains, 'What if?' (*Okinawa Taimuzu*, 2 September 2013). With the deployment of the MV-22 at a marine air facility located in the middle of a city, surrounded by residential housing, schools, hospitals, businesses and so on, the potential harm should a crash occur is clear. The point was reinforced with news suggesting that the potential use of school grounds for emergency landings by the Osprey was being considered (*Okinawa Taimuzu*, 2 September 2013).

Local concerns over the risk posed by the deployment of the Osprey have increased in the wake of a number of recent accidents occurring just before or after the arrival of the aircraft in Japan. In April 2012, for instance, a Marine Corps MV-22 crashed when participating in a military exercise in Morocco, killing two marines and seriously injuring the two pilots. The accident was found to be the result of pilot error, leading the marines' deputy commander for aviation to declare the Osprey: 'solid, safe' (Majumdar 2012). Then, during a routine training exercise in June 2012, a US Air Force HV-22 went down in Florida injuring five on board. The crash report says the fault was due to the pilots not keeping enough distance from other Ospreys (United States Air Force, 2012; Whittle 2012). Following that, in August 2013 an Osprey from Marine Corps Air Station Miramar near San Diego burst into flames on making a 'hard landing' in the desert near Creech Air Force Base in Nevada, a rank A 'crash' according to later reports.[13] As demonstrated in the latter case, the training environment in the United States and the base in Okinawa clearly pose different risks, given the dense population around the Futenma base. As prefectural assembly member Nishime Sumie stated: 'In the US residential housing is not located in the vicinity of the base. It is a completely different situation to Okinawa' (*Shimbun Akahata*, 13 September 2013). A freedom of information request by *Akahata* found the MOD to be concerned in early 2013 that, should an Osprey accident occur, the situation was such that it 'might lead to a protest movement demanding the removal of all bases' (24 August 2014). For the Japanese government, of course, the proposed move of Futenma to a newly constructed base at Henoko offers a way to reduce the risk of an accident occurring in Ginowan, as flights would take place in a less populated part of the island. Nevertheless, as it stands, the flights have increased at Futenma, from 888 in the first year (October 2012 – September 2013) to 1,453 in year two (October 2013 – September 2014) (*Ryūkyū Shimpō*, 1 October 2014).

The subnational political authorities and the local inhabitants again deployed protest as a way to highlight their response to the increase in risk posed by the deployment of the Osprey to Futenma. Illustrative is a June 2012 call made by the Ginowan local assembly to the US marines and the US consulate in Naha to cancel the deployment (Ginowan City 2012). Then, in September 2012, a major protest rally was called, with approximately 100,000 people participating. This was followed by the executive committee of the rally, along with the prefectural assembly and all of the forty-one subnational political authorities in Okinawa, submitting a petition *(kenhakusho)* to the prime minister in January 2013 calling on him to '(1) immediately revoke the deployment of the Osprey and call off the deployment of the additional twelve aircraft scheduled to be deployed. . . . Also, to immediately withdraw the plan to deploy the special operations transportation aircraft CV-22 Osprey to Kadena Air Base. (2) close and remove MCAS Futenma, and renounce the plan to relocate it within the prefecture' (Executive Committee for the Okinawa Prefectural Citizens' Rally 2013).

A range of protests has been in evidence following the deployments, including four citizens carrying out a hunger strike in front of Ginowan city hall in August 2013, although a city official made clear the protest could not be permitted (*Okinawa Taimuzu*, 24 August 2013). In an attempt to address the unequal distribution of US deployments, the Okinawan group Sōzō is pressing for the agreement of other prefectures to accept military training of the Osprey. In September 2013, for instance, the group sent a request to the remaining forty-two prefectural governors to accept the military training of Ospreys in their own prefecture following earlier requests to Shizuoka, Aichi, Oita and Yao city, Osaka. Whether the request will lead to any change poses a political challenge for prefectural governors, but the narrative deployed in the reply from the governor of Oita draws attention to how Okinawans' concern with the unequal distribution of the risk from US deployments has taken hold, as the prefecture 'already hosts live ammunition training by the marines, and increasing the burden even further is a difficult situation' (*Sankei Shimbun*, 3 September 2013). As a first step, joint training exercises in October 2013 and then in 2014 between the US and Japanese forces in Shiga Prefecture and Kōchi Prefecture included the participation of the Osprey (*Asahi Shimbun*, 16 October 2013, 29 January 2014). Indeed, in line with reducing the burden on Okinawa, by July 2014 the Osprey was involved for the first time in flights to Atsugi base in Kanagawa Prefecture and can be expected to be operated in other parts of Japan (*Asahi Shimbun*, 15 July 2014). This reduces the risk of military accidents in Okinawa, at least to some extent, in line with the Abe government's aim to thereby facilitate the move of Futenma to Henoko (*Tokyo Shimbun*, 16 July 2014). As far as the safety of the Osprey is concerned, however, as Governor Nakaima Hirokazu previously pointed out, "The anxiety *(fuan)* of the prefecture's population has not at all been swept away" (*Nihon Keizai Shimbun*, 7 September 2013).

6 Conclusion

The above discussion of military accidents in Okinawa has concentrated mainly on the examples of the risk of aircraft accidents, potential accidents and crashes as these are integral to the risk narrative and praxis of the local inhabitants. The manifestation of risk as harm from military accidents was most salient during the period prior to reversion, when death and serious injury, as illustrated by the aircraft crash at Miyamori Elementary School, became embedded in discourse and popular memory through dissemination and annual commemorations of the event (Uruma City 2009). In the post-reversion period, harm has manifested mainly as emotional stress and anxiety as well as the physical damage caused by military accidents. But subnational political authorities and the local community have kept the memory of the harm caused by earlier accidents alive, and the memory acts as a source for constructing the risk of future military accidents. In this sense, the risk narrative on military accidents has helped to shape the nature of the local population's response to the risk of present-day military activities and the deployment of new weaponry in the prefecture. So why continue to protest, despite the lack of deaths and serious injury to the local population from military accidents?

Three points are germane. First, despite the reversion of Okinawa to Japan in 1972, the central government policymakers and security managers still continue to expose the prefectural population to a disproportionate and unequal level of risk from US deployments in the post-reversion period, as illustrated by the crashes at Okinawa International University and Camp Hansen as well as the risk of a potential crash posed by the 2012 and 2013 deployments of Ospreys to Futenma air station, the 'world's most dangerous base,' in the words of Donald Rumsfeld, former US secretary of defence (*Ryūkyū Shimpō*, 13 August 2013). This means the security of the everyday for the local population is at disproportionate risk from the US military presence in Japan. As we have seen here and will see in later chapters, the Abe administration's commitment is to recalibrate the risk in Okinawa by moving the Futenma base to Henoko. The joint US-Japan training exercises in Shiga and Kōchi prefectures and other prefectures as time passes aim to help facilitate the transfer. If this decision is implemented, despite strong local opposition, then as a consequence the risk from aircraft accidents in Okinawa may be reduced because of the impingement of the new base on a hamlet rather than a city. But the state's mediation of risk in this way does not address the fundamental problem: the call to reduce the risk of US bases in Okinawa, not by moving the functions of Futenma to elsewhere in the prefecture, but by moving them to elsewhere in Japan or outside of Japan altogether. Even though a reduction in the exposure to risk in Okinawa was implemented in the summer of 2014 when the KC-130 extended range tanker (for aerial refuelling) was transferred from Futenma to the Iwakuni base in Yamaguchi Prefecture (*Tokyo Shimbun*, 15 July 2014), the structural inequality between Okinawa and other prefectures remains as a result of a state-centric security policy focused on the maintenance of a disproportionate number of US military installations in Okinawa.

The second point builds on the first. As the deployment of Ospreys to the Futenma air station demonstrates, rather than the risk and potential harm of military accidents decreasing as a result of government policy, the opposite has occurred instead. The reason for this is straightforward: the reluctance of other prefectures to accept the deployment of risky American aircraft. Whilst the call for other parts of Japan to shoulder more of the burden of US deployments offers a potential way to recalibrate risk from the perspective of the Okinawans, any redeployment of the Osprey to other electoral districts is a vote loser, not a vote winner, indicating how the mediation and recalibration of risk remain at heart a question of governance. In this sense, the risk of military accidents in Okinawa poses a fundamental question for Japanese democracy: how should the government distribute to the few the risks of a security treaty claimed to be for the benefit of the many?

The final point is the different logic of risk employed by many in Okinawa, on the one hand, and the central government policymakers and security managers in Tokyo and Washington as well as on the ground in Okinawa, on the other. When the Okinawan population asks rhetorically, 'Just how much insecurity *(fuan)* are you asking us to shoulder in carrying on our daily lives?' (*Okinawa Taimuzu*, 15 August 2013), the logic unfolds in Okinawa as the logic of governance: the government's duty is to protect the life and property of the citizen. Inhered in this logic is the political requirement of the central government to take action to address the risk and potential harm to everyday security faced by citizens as a result of US deployments in the prefecture. But this hardly ever happens, except around the edges of risk, as exemplified by the transfer of live ammunition practice to the main islands. Rather, a military accident occurs, and subnational political authorities and citizens protest, deploying a risk narrative calling for the military operation to cease – or at least to postpone flights until the cause of the accident is ascertained and steps are taken to correct any faults. The resumption of risky flights without the cause of the accident being announced erodes the trust of the Okinawans in the process of governing as well as causes emotional if not physical harm.

However, a counter logic of risk is deployed by the US military and accepted and disseminated by policymakers and security managers in Tokyo and Washington as well as on the ground in Okinawa. More precisely, the resumption of flights as soon as possible after an accident symbolizes the supremacy of the logic undergirding the logic of national governance: state-centric security. This logic is crystalized in the statement made by Brigadier General Hecker following the crash of the HH-60 in Camp Hansen: resuming flight training is essential, he said, in order to 'fulfill our commitment to the mutual defense of Japan' and to maintain 'peace and stability in the East Asia region' (Hecker 2013). So the protests in Okinawa continue not simply as a result of a counter-posed logic of risk as well as governance, but also because of a greater commitment to the security of the everyday – as distilled in the life and well-being of the community – than to the national security of Japan as represented by reprising military exercises.

In a sense, central government policymakers and security managers, on the one hand, and the subnational political authorities and local inhabitants in Okinawa, on the other, have produced a 'theatre of risk' as a mechanism for playing out the quintessential problem of governance. It accentuates how the risk of military accidents has been countered with discursive practices and protests, but the performance remains basically the same, with no settlement of the fundamental question of how to resolve the governance of the unequal distribution of risks and the burden of US forces locally in the context of a state-centric security policy. In the next chapter we move on to investigate how the theatre of risk is played out in another area of Okinawan life affecting the security of the community: military incidents.

Notes

1 US military personnel, civilians working for the military, and their family members *(Beigunkōseiin)* accounted for 3 per cent or less of automobile accidents resulting in death or injury in Okinawa between 1990 and 2012. In 2011, for instance, the 176 accidents involving all of the above categories accounted for 2.6 per cent of the total number of these accidents, with three deaths recorded. See Okinawa Prefectural Government (2013b), p. 109. It should be noted that, both on- or off-base, US drivers eighteen or older can obtain a USFJ-4 EJ, US Forces Japan operator's permit by producing a valid US driver's license and attending a driver's improvement course if under twenty-six years of age. For full details, see US Marines (undated).
2 The city of Koza and the village of Misato were amalgamated on 1 April 1974 to form the new city of Okinawa. The city is still often referred to as Koza by the local inhabitants.
3 Our focus is on the impact of military accidents on the local population.
4 For details of the number of rounds fired annually between 1973 and 1997, see Okinawa Prefectural Government (2013b), p. 100, showing a total of 33,100 bullets and 180 incidents.
5 For details, see Okinawa Prefectural Government (2013b), pp. 103–6.
6 The proposed transfer of the Marine Air Station Futenma to Henoko, which helps to elucidate the different perceptions of risks by Okinawa, the Japanese government and the US government and military, is addressed in Chapter 11.
7 The timing of the crash, when most students were not attending classes, helped to avoid a disaster. Of the three crew members on board, one was seriously injured and two sustained minor injuries. The site of the crash next to the university and the swift action of a number of the marines on the base, who scaled the two fences between the base and the university in order to rescue their comrades, helped to ensure their survival.
8 Kadena Air Base informed the Okinawa Defense Bureau that, as thorium 232 occurs in the natural world, it will have no impact on the environment. See *Ryūkyū Shimpō*, 9 August 2013 and *Okinawa Taimuzu*, 9 August 2013.
9 The participants were asked to wear red at the rally as an expression of local anger.
10 As Brigadier General James B. Hecker of 18th Wing Command, Kadena Air Base, commented, 'The unit involved in the accident was in fact the same unit that launched five HH-60s and 51 rescue personnel in less than three hours of the tsunami hitting the Tohoku area in the March 11, 2011 Great East Japan Earthquake and tsunami, participating in what later became known as Operation Tomodachi. The unit flew 55 missions and logged 310 flight hours supporting our Japanese brothers and sisters in the disaster area. They helped to deliver about 1.4 tonnes of food, water and medical supplies to the locations that needed them' (Hecker 2013).
11 Of course, this does not mean Okinawans do not appreciate the support from the marines in responding to the earthquake. It was the motivation for the founding of the Osprey Fan Club. See US Marines (2012).
12 Twelve Ospreys were expected to be deployed in August 2013 following the twelve the previous October but one remained in Marine Corps Air Station Iwakuni, Yamaguchi prefecture, as of September 2013. The reason was not disclosed (*Ryūkyū Shimpō*, 8 September 2013).

13 Minister of Defense Onodera Itsunori stressed the safety of the Osprey based on the low number of rank A accidents, but following the crash in Nevada highlighted that, rather than safety or operation, rank A referred to the financial cost of the crash. As the *Okinawa Taimuzu* commented, this seems contradictory (4 September 2013).

References

Arakaki, Takeshi (2005) "Okinawadai nado ni yoru Dojō Osen Chōsa," in Kurosawa Ariko (ed.) *Okikokudai ga Amerika ni Senryō sareta Hi*, Tokyo: Seidosha, pp. 84–101.
Calder, Kent E. (2007) *Embattled Garrisons: Comparative Base Politics and American Globalism*, Princeton: Princeton University Press.
Cooley, Alexander (2008) *Base Politics: Democratic Change and the US Military Overseas*, Cornell: Cornell University Press.
Eldridge, Robert D. (2008–9a) "Anatomy of a crash: local reactions and official responses to the 2004 Futenma helicopter accident and its aftermath (1)," *Kokusai Kōkyō Seisaku Kenkyū* 13, 1: 135–45.
—— (2008–9b) "Anatomy of a crash: local reactions and official responses to the 2004 Futenma helicopter accident and its aftermath (2)," *Kokusai Kōkyō Seisaku Kenkyū* 13, 2: 15–25.
Executive Committee for the Okinawa Prefectural Citizens' Rally Against Osprey Deployment (2013) Okinawa prefectural assembly, municipalities and municipal assemblies petition. Available online at: http://kenmintaikai2012.ti-da.net/e4331515.html. Accessed 8 September 2013.
G2mil (2003) "Why the V-22 Osprey is unsafe." Available online at: http://www.g2mil.com/V-22safety.htm. Accessed 4 September 2013.
Ginowan City (2004) Okinawa Kokusai Daigaku Kōnai e no Beigun Heri Tsuiraku Jiko ni tsuite (8 October). Available online at: http://www.city.ginowan.okinawa.jp/pageRedirect.php?url=/2556/2581/2582/3905.html. Accessed 3 September 2013.
—— (2012) Beigun Kichi Futenma Hikōjo e no MV-22 Osupurei no Haibi ni Danko Hantai suru Ketsugi Gian. Available online at: http://www.city.ginowan.okinawa.jp/DAT/LIB/WEB/1/370ketugi.pdf. Accessed 3 September 2013.
—— (2013) Okinawa Kokusai Daigaku e no Beigun CH-53D gata Heri Tsuiraku Jiko kara 9 nen, Shichō komento. Available online at: http://www.city.ginowan.okinawa.jp/organization/kichisyougaika/sisei/base/05/okiuheli9nen.html. Accessed 3 September 2013.
Ginoza Village (2013) Ginoza Sonmin Taikai. Available online at: http://www.vill.ginoza.okinawa.jp/archives/7594. Accessed 3 September 2013.
Hecker, James B. (2013) "Friendship shines after Okinawa crash," *Inside Kadena*. Available online at: http://www.kadena.af.mil/news/story.asp?id=123361103. Accessed 3 September 2013.
Hook, Glenn D. (forthcoming) "The American eagle in Okinawa: contested memory and the unfinished war."
Lutz, Catherine (ed.) (2009) *The Bases of Empire: The Global Struggle against US Military Posts*, New York: New York University Press.
Majumdar, Dave (2012) "Morocco USMC MV-22 Osprey Crash due to Pilot Error," Flightglobal, 17 August. Available online at: http://www.flightglobal.com/news/articles/morocco-usmc-mv-22-osprey-crash-due-to-pilot-error-375617/. Accessed 3 September 2013.
McCormack, Gavan and Satoko Oka Norimatsu (2012) *Resistant Islands: Okinawa Confronts Japan and the United States*, Lanham, MD: Rowman and Littlefield.

Ministry of Foreign Affairs (1996a) The SACO Final Report December 2, 1996. Available online at: http://www.mofa.go.jp/region/n-america/us/security/96saco1.html. Accessed 2 September 2013.

Ministry of Foreign Affairs (1996b) The SACO Final Report on Futenma Air Station (An integral part of the SACO final report) December 2, 1996. Available online at: http://www.mofa.go.jp/region/n-america/us/security/96saco2.html. Accessed 2 September 2013.

Okinawa International University (2004) Statement by the president of Okinawa University regarding the USMC helicopter crash and request for the closure of USMC Futenma Air Station. Available online at: http://www.okiu.ac.jp/gaiyou/fall_incident/data/info26(state1104).pdf. Accessed 2 September 2013.

Okinawa Prefectural Assembly (2013) "Beigun HH60 Hericoputa-Tsuiraku Jiko ni kansuru Kōgi Ketsugi," 12 August. Available online at: http://www.pref.okinawa.lg.jp/site/gikai/h250812ikenketugi.html#ketugi. Accessed 2 September 2013.

Okinawa Prefectural Government (2013a) "Futenma Hikōjo no Kikensei," 23 August. Available online at: http://www.pref.okinawa.lg.jp/site/chijiko/chian/futenma/risk.html. Accessed 2 September 2013.

—— (2013b) *Okinawa no Beigun oyobi Jieitai Kichi (tōkei shiryō shū)*, Okinawa Ken Chiji Kōshitsu, Kichi Taisakuka. Available online at: http://www.pref.okinawa.lg.jp/site/chijiko/kichitai/documents/h25-1_1.pdf. Accessed 28 August 2013.

Ryūkyū Shimpō (2007) *Okinawa Kenmin Ishiki Chōsa Hōkokushō*, Naha: Ryūkyū Shimpō.

United States Air Force Aircraft Accident Investigation Board Report (2012), CV-22B, T/N 06–0032, 13 June. Available online at: http://breakingdefense.sites.breakingmedia.com/wp-content/uploads/sites/3/2012/08/afsoc.pdf. Accessed 4 September 2013.

United States Embassy, Tokyo (2004) Background Brief on CH-53 Helicopter Accident, 27 August. Available online at: http://japan2.usembassy.gov/e/p/tp-20040827–61.html. Accessed 2 September 2013.

United States Marines (undated) III Marine Expeditionary Force Marine Corps Installations Pacific. Available online at: http://www.mcipac.marines.mil/LivinginOkinawa/DrivingonOkinawa.aspx. Accessed 29 August 2013.

—— (2012) III Marine Expeditionary Force Marine Corps Installations Pacific. "Osupurei Fuan Kurabu ga Futenma Hikōjo o Kengaku," 24 July. Available online at: http://www.okinawa.usmc.mil/News/130724-osprey.html. Accessed 12 September 2013.

Uruma City (2006) Beigun F-15 Sentōki Tsuiraku Jiko ni kansuru Ikensho, January. Available online at: http://www.city.uruma.lg.jp/DAT/LIB/WEB/1/h180117ikensho.pdf. Accessed 1 September 2013.

—— (2009) Beigun Jettoki Tsuiraku Jiko o Tsutaeru. Available online at: http://www.city.uruma.lg.jp/4/3346.html. Accessed 1 September 2013.

Whittle, Richard (2012) "AFSOC Crash Report Faults Understanding of Osprey Rotor Wake," *Breaking Defense*. Available online at: http://breakingdefense.com/documents/afsoc-crash-report-faults-understanding-of-osprey-wake-effects/. Accessed 2 September 2013.

10
MILITARY INCIDENTS

1 Introduction

The existence and operation of US military installations in Okinawa are dependent upon US service personnel carrying out their official military obligations, but their dual role as soldiers both on- and off-duty leads to not only the occasional accident, as seen in Chapter 9, but also incidents, the second reason for the ongoing opposition to the bases in Okinawa. Such 'incidents' are not simply a question of the statistical frequency of service personnel committing crimes impacting on the security of the everyday for Okinawans, but rather how the offences carried out by these overseas warriors can at times give rise to a breakdown in relations with the local community and damage the relationship between Japan and the United States.[1] The most serious incidents recorded by the prefectural police, 'heinous crimes' *(kyōakuhan)* such as murder, arson, rape and robbery, are at the heart of the matter for central government policymakers and security managers as well as for the local population.

The overwhelming majority of military personnel deployed in Okinawa live in gated communities separated from the local society by a physical barrier. As far as breaking the law is concerned, however, the barrier should be regarded as a permeable boundary, with soldiers frequently crossing the line between the base and the local community. The SOFA discussed in the introduction to Part III means that the fences dividing the military personnel and their families on the inside from Okinawan society on the outside serve to inscribe two different legal spaces as far as criminal offences are concerned. Of course, not all service personnel live on-base, as in the case of GIs marrying and living locally, as well as other members of the military moving off-base into Japanese legal space (Forgash 2009).[2] But the crucial point to note is that these 'little Americas' behind the barricades function legally in a different way from other parts of Japan. In this sense, barbed wire and railings symbolize not only physical separation, but also the co-existence of two legal jurisdictions and the challenge to Japanese sovereignty posed by the operation and application of the US legal system in Japan.

The chapter starts by providing a broad-brush historical overview and context for the off-base crimes committed by the actions of some of the (mainly young) soldiers deployed in these overseas outposts of American power. The third section goes on to examine briefly a number of the recent cases of crime committed by Americans in the prefecture, highlighting how the concerns of the local population remain ongoing. The fourth section then moves away from the crimes themselves to examine the response to the crimes at the local level and by the US military. It spotlights how, despite the efforts made, crime perpetrated by the US military remains a risk to the security of the everyday in Okinawa. The fifth section explores the case of the 1995 rape of a school girl by three US military personnel, which led to widespread protests against US deployments in the prefecture. It illuminates the catalytic role heinous crimes can play in the politics of US bases in Okinawa. The conclusion summarizes the discussion and draws out the implications of military incidents for our understanding of risk to everyday security, underscoring how, in the context of the SOFA, the governance of Okinawa involves two states, Japan and the United States.

2 Historical overview and context

To start with, the role of US service personnel when off-base includes a range of collaborative activities between the communities on both sides of the fence aimed at generating support in Okinawan society for US military deployments. These activities aim to promote the US military as a good friend and neighbour (Yoshida 2007: 130–48). Illustrative is the participation of the marines in over 2,000 community events throughout the year, including beach clean-ups, music festivals, sports days, and so on (US Marines 2012). From this perspective, the wrongdoings of US soldiers when off-base erode the positive image of US-Japan amity being nurtured by these communal activities and are thus of concern to the supporters of the deployment of US forces in Okinawa as well as to the opponents. It is these wrongdoings by off-base US military personnel, more than anything else, which underscore how US troops in Okinawa pose a risk of potential and actual harm to the everyday security of the local community.

The history of off-base incidents represents a wide spectrum of crimes, misdemeanours and wrongdoings carried out by US military and civilian contractors and their families. At one extreme can be found heinous crimes such as murder and rape and at the other minor crimes such as shoplifting and drunk and disorderly conduct. More than any other offence, rape and other forms of sexual violence by US soldiers causing physical and emotional harm to local females stir a particularly strong response among the prefectural population and more widely in Japanese society. These incidents of sexual violence and other crimes committed by US military personnel and others are recorded and published by the Okinawa

Prefectural Police. The data show that the overall number of offences committed has declined in the more than five decades since the reversion of Okinawa to Japan in 1972. In that year, 233 cases of arrest involving a total of 250 US service personnel were recorded by the prefectural police, whereas in 2010 the number was 71 cases of arrest involving 71 members of the armed forces. In 2012 the number totalled even fewer cases, 54 cases of arrest, involving 54 personnel. The highest number of cases of arrest in the post-occupation period was 342, recorded in 1977 (Okinawa Prefectural Police 2010, 2011, 2012). In the specific instance of rape, there were 127 cases of arrest between 1972 and September 2012, involving 144 service personnel, illustrating how sexual violence at times involves more than one suspect. These numbers obviously do not include cases where no arrest was made or when charges were not brought by the victim (*Shimbun Akahata*, 24 October 2012).[3] What is more, although the two local newspapers, *Ryūkyū Shimpō* and *Okinawa Taimuzu*, report in detail the murders, rapes, robberies and other crimes involving the arrest of US soldiers off-base, locals believe the total number of criminal offences is much greater than the reported numbers, especially insofar as sexual assault is concerned.

As these figures clearly show, the number of arrests of US service personnel has declined considerably over the years, leading US officials to compare the small percentage of wrongdoings carried out by soldiers off-base with the crimes committed by residents in the prefecture. The point was made by Ambassador Tom Schieffer (2005–9) in the following May 2008 statement, when he highlighted the lower risk of crime posed by US soldiers compared to Okinawans: 'A few military personnel in Japan have acted badly. At the same time, the overwhelming majority of American servicemen and women are performing their service here with honor and distinction. Crime rates within the military are substantially less than those in the civilian population, and we should remember that before condemning all for the actions of a few' (United States Embassy 2008). The same point was trumpeted by a US State Department official when US Secretary of Defense Donald Rumsfeld visited Okinawa in November 2003: 'The per capita crime rate for U.S. personnel in Okinawa is lower than that of the local populace' (United States Department of Defense 2003). But what these stark comparisons between US soldiers and local Okinawans fail to take into account are a number of differences between the two sides, such as the omission of crimes committed by US service personnel on the military bases themselves (for details, see Yoshida 2007: 169–74). What is more, whilst soldiers acting badly in Okinawa may be seen by central government policymakers and security planners as nothing more than the collateral damage or 'negative externalities' of maintaining the alliance with the United States (Weyand 2012: 407), from the perspective of the victims of these crimes and the critics of US bases, the wrongdoings of soldiers are instead concrete examples of the risks posed by US military forces to the security of the everyday in Okinawa. Indeed, when a crime is committed by one of the US soldiers deployed in the prefecture, especially a heinous crime, this reveals how the risk is actually manifest as harm to the local population. In other words, the security of the everyday is at risk in Okinawa precisely because American soldiers are an essential ingredient in a state-centric security policy which ignores, deflects or underplays the cries of Okinawans to rid the prefecture of the bases, not simply because local Okinawans behave badly, too.

3   Recent cases

Despite the decline in the number of offences committed and the low overall rate of recorded criminal activity carried out by US military personnel, civilian contractors and their family members, Okinawans continue to be exposed to the risk of harm from the crimes still carried out when Americans are off-base in the Okinawan community. Several recent examples of the arrest of US soldiers for alleged wrongdoings illustrate how the existence and operation of the military bases seem to be linked ineluctably to off-base crimes. Indeed, what is striking about the examples given below is their occurrence at the time a military curfew was active. In one case, the curfew had been ordered by the commander of US Forces Japan in response to the arrest of two US service personnel on suspicion of sexual violence against a local woman in October 2012.

In November 2012, a marine from the Futenma air station was arrested off-base on suspicion of unauthorized entry into an apartment. A female friend of the owner called him to say that she had arrived to find 'an unknown foreigner asleep in the apartment' (*Ryūkyū Shimpō*, 19 November 2012). In another case in December 2012, an American marine from Camp Hansen was arrested on suspicion of unlawful entry onto the veranda of an apartment in Naha at around 04.30 in the morning. The incident came to light when the twenty-year-old daughter of the owner, who did not know the suspect, saw him on the veranda. On being arrested the marine declared, 'I made a mistake as it looked like the house I used to live in when I was in Columbia' (*Ryūkyū Shimpō*, 29 December 2014). In a similar case, in May 2013, an airman from the Kadena Air Base was arrested following an emergency call from a woman at home in her apartment. She rang to report that, at around 07.30, the soldier, who was unknown to her, had entered her apartment (the door was unlocked) without her knowledge, and simply repeated 'friend, friend' when asked what he was doing trespassing (*Okinawa Taimuzu*, 5 May 2013). Finally, in a case in November 2012, an airman from Kadena Air Base was arrested for breaking into a local home in Yomitan around 01.30 in the morning. Once in the apartment he allegedly struck a thirteen-year-old school boy, who at the time was asleep with the rest of his family, and smashed the television set (*Ryūkyū Shimpō*, 3 November 2012).

Whilst the risk of potential harm and the harm inflicted in the above cases was limited, the arrest of soldiers for violent sexual assault calls attention to how serious harm to local females can result from crimes comited by US servicemen as well. Indeed, the curfew mentioned above was ordered further to the arrest of two soldiers from Naval Air Station Joint Research Base Fort Worth, Texas, on suspicion of sexual violence off-base during a visit to Futenma base. The twenty-year-old woman who was raped was also robbed and injured in the attack in a parking lot near her apartment. The victim was on her way home close to where the accused had been drinking in the early hours of the morning (*Ryūkyū Shimpō*, 17 October 2012). In this way, sexual crimes are a risk to the everyday security of Okinawan females, as discussed in more detail below in the 1995 case of the rape of a twelve-year-old school girl.

4 Response to military incidents

During the long history of the American occupation of the prefecture and the more than fifty years following the reversion of Okinawa to Japan, the actions of the local population through rallies, protests, sit-ins and other forms of grassroots direct action, together with the official action taken by local policymakers and politicians, have been at the heart of the response to crimes committed by US service personnel. These have often gone hand in hand with the official response by the police, courts and central government policymakers and security managers on both sides of the Pacific. Whilst these grassroots, local actions give salience to the risk and harm posed by US forces in the prefecture, at the same time their aim is to promote change in the bilateral relationship between Japan and the United States, as illustrated by continuing efforts to improve the SOFA.

The risk and harm to the security of the everyday remains central to many of the actions taken at the local level, as seen in the way popular activists framed the issue of a US military crime at the time of the July 2000 G8 summit in Okinawa. In this case, a soldier was arrested after entering an apartment and allegedly committing a sex crime involving a middle school aged girl who was asleep with the rest of her family. Local critics contrasted the way this US soldier had been able to unlawfully enter the apartment and harm the everyday security of a child with the state-centred security measures implemented for the G8 summit. For instance, in the protest statement addressed to Prime Minister Mori Yoshirō and President Bill Clinton, the Group Opposed to the Heliport Base at Nago *(Nago heripōto Kichi Hantai suru Kai)* framed the crime in the context of the stringent security measures put in place in preparation for the G8:

> Taking account of the needs of the summit over 10,000 members of the police force have been sent from all over Japan to Okinawa. On the prefecture's main island over thirty inspection posts have been set up on a twenty-four hour basis. In an area near the summit, every house has been investigated by the police, checking the number of family members, how many cars, and the family members living in mainland Japan. For those with family cemeteries, people are being asked to check on a regular basis to ensure no-one is hiding there. It is under these strict conditions . . . the incident occurred.
>
> (Nago Heripōto Kichi Hantai suru Kai 2000)

In this way, the extra police presence aimed at state-centred security was seen as doing nothing to prevent the harm to the everyday security of a child by US military servicemen in Okinawa.

In the recent case of the arrest of the two service personnel from Fort Worth, local activists organized rallies and issued protest statements. This can be seen, for instance, in the statement of the Anti-US Base Network, which called for 'justice for the victim of the October 16 gang rape' (Anti-US Base Network 2012). Similarly, the prefectural assembly adopted unanimously a protest resolution sent to the prime minister, defence minister, foreign minister, US ambassador to Japan, commander of US forces in Japan and commander of US naval forces in Japan. It highlighted how voices in the prefecture were calling for 'full withdrawal' of US military installations; criticized the measures taken by US forces, such as education for the good behaviour of the troops and curfews as 'ineffective'; and stated that Okinawans had 'passed the limits of endurance' (*Ryūkyū Shimpō*, 22 October 2012).

At the same time, the formal process of the law is set in motion by the arrest of the US suspects. In line with the SOFA and the 1996 SACO agreement, which aims to improve the SOFA's operation, some of these offences are investigated by the Japanese police and prosecuted under Japanese law (SACO 1996). In this case, the two Fort Worth servicemen were taken into custody by Japanese police immediately after the incident so no need arose to activate the SOFA and request the US military to transfer the suspects to the Japanese authorities. The Naha District Court then held a trial at which both of the defendants pleaded guilty to rape and robbery. Both of them received custodial sentences, with one sentenced to ten years and one to nine years in prison (*Okinawa Taimuzu*, 19 March 2013).

Further, the reform of the Japanese judicial system in May 2009 now means that Okinawan society is represented in certain criminal trials, as local citizens act as lay judges under the new system. That is, six lay judges and three professional judges make up the judicial panel charged with reaching a verdict in these trials. The first member of US forces in Japan ever to be tried under the new system was a marine accused of the assault and robbery of a taxi driver at the Naha District Courthouse. The motive for his crime seems to have been 'to show he was macho enough to be accepted for Marine Corps special operation duty' (*Stars and Stripes Okinawa*, 29 May 2010). The verdict of the five women and one man making up the lay judges, together with the professional judges, was to sentence the accused to three to four years in prison. Reports after the judgement suggest that, at least as far as this trial is concerned, the lay judges were not influenced directly in their judgement by the presence of US military installations in the prefecture, as one of the women lay judges stated: 'While I do not have a good impression of the US forces due to the base issue, I was not swayed by my emotions as an Okinawan resident in the deliberations' (cited in Furukai 2011: 797). This change in the legal system to one involving lay adjudication thus provides a new opportunity for Okinawan society to play a role in 'effective judicial oversight of the actions and conduct of US military forces in the prefecture' (Furukai 2011: 798). In this way, the new judicial system aimed mainly at the trial of Japanese suspects provides a means for the local population to have some voice in responding to the manifestation of risk as harm by US service personnel, although the problem remains how the security of the everyday is at risk especially of such violent offences.

Indeed, as certain acts of criminality committed by service personnel are violent, personal injury and harm to society inevitably result from the risk posed by soldiers off-base. In such cases, compensation may be paid to the injured party. As an illustration, the 2006 case of a taxi driver assaulted and robbed in Okinawa city by two off-duty marines is instructive as it shows concretely how the operation of the SOFA impacts on the everyday security of Okinawans. The two marines were prosecuted for the offence in the courts and handed down custodial sentences. The victim, no longer able to work because of cervical sprain and post-traumatic stress disorder resulting from his injuries, sought justice through the courts. He was awarded approximately 28 million yen in compensation as a result of a civil suit and expected to receive his compensation in line with the SOFA and SACO agreement of 1996.

Nevertheless, the victim was not compensated as he had expected following the court case. Article 18, clause 6b of the SOFA deals with claims made against service members when not on official duty. It states that US authorities will 'decide without delay whether they will offer an ex gratia payment, and if so, of what amount.' Further to the improvements in the operation of the SOFA agreed in 1996, any issue that may arise concerning the amount of the compensation to be paid seems to have been addressed: 'In the past there have been only a very few cases where payment by the US Government did not satisfy the full amount awarded by a final court judgment. Should such a case occur in future, the Government of Japan will endeavour to make payment to the claimant, as appropriate, in order to address the difference in amount' (SACO 1996). In this case, however, the victim was forced to wait nearly five years to receive any compensation, despite the SOFA clause and the final SACO agreement (*Ryūkyū Shimpō*, editorial, 21 August 2013). In the end, the US agreed to pay 200,000 yen, approximately 7 per cent of the award by the court's legal judgement, with the remainder being left to the Japanese government to consider settling (*Ryūkyū Shimpō*, 21 October 2013).

In the above two cases, taking a marine to court for the 2010 assault and robbery of a taxi driver and paying compensation to a victim of a similar 2006 assault and robbery by two marines, we see examples of the responses made at the local level in the face of crimes causing harm to the security of the everyday in Okinawa. An alternative response is to tackle crime by reducing the risk of an offence being committed in the first place. One option adopted by US Forces Japan is to strengthen metaphorically the fence between the two communities by imposing a curfew on the soldiers. Of course, such restrictions on their access to the local community acknowledge the risk of lawlessness posed by US service personnel when off-base. Thus, the purpose of the curfew is to prevent, reduce or ameliorate crime by restricting the hours available to soldiers to commit a criminal offence, even though our discussion above of recent incidents underscored how curfews are not necessarily effective. Meanwhile, the use of a military curfew to tackle crimes commited by US servicemen illustrates how a comparison of the per capita crime rate of US service personnel and the local population in Okinawa is not as straightforward as the above quote by Ambassador Schieffer seems to suggest. As outlined in the introduction to the book, the probability of risk is only made relevant in relation to the framing of the risk, what is included and excluded. In this case, the rate of off-base wrongdoings would simply drop to zero without the presence of US soldiers in the local community.

As noted above, the most recent curfew was ordered in response to the rape by the two service personnel from Fort Worth. It was put in force by General Sam Angelella, commander of US Forces Japan, with effect from 23.00, 19 October 2012. The curfew policy

> applies to members of the United States Armed Forces when in Japan, which includes personnel temporarily in Japan. Off-installation curfew is in effect from 11 p.m. until 5 a.m. daily. During the hours of curfew, service members must either be: 1. On a U.S. military installation; 2. Off the installation in a private residence; 3. If on temporary duty (TDY/TAD) or on leave or pass, in their place of lodging, which may include a hotel room.
> (*Stars and Stripes Okinawa*, 21 October 2012)

Violations of this order are punishable under the Uniform Code of Military Justice.

In February 2013 the time limit was changed from 23.00 to midnight for service members below the rank of E-5 and the curfew was dropped altogether for higher rank soldiers, but in Okinawa an off-base ban on alcohol, introduced in December 2012, remained in force. The new rules meant

> service members below E-5 must be on a U.S. base, off-base in a private residence or lodging, or they must be performing duties to comply with the curfew. All service members must also complete sexual assault prevention and response training, as well as an orientation course on Japan prior to being granted liberty.
> (*Stars and Stripes Okinawa*, 13 February 2013)

In this way, the response of US Forces Japan to off-base crime was to restrict the opportunities for crime to be committed and to offer training and socialization, suggesting how the ongoing problem of off-base crime remained difficult to solve without the implementation of such measures. Indeed, the conclusion of the military authorities seems to be that, in order to ensure the security of the everyday for the Okinawan population, especially females, imposing restrictions on off-base activity is an ameliorative option, even if not a permanent solution given the predilection of some soldiers to breach curfew.

Finally, the prefectural police force has responded to the risk of crime by offering training and socialization of US forces and their families. The aim is to inculcate norms of obeying the law when off-base, thereby precluding the need to balance the different jurisdictional powers under Japanese law and the SOFA as well as reducing the number of offences. As an illustration, local law enforcement officers have been playing a role in tackling the risk of unlawful activities by juveniles. More concretely, since 2010 officers have been involved in a programme to prevent delinquency among the middle school and high school students of US service personnel. The programme was launched in the face of off-base criminal activity by juveniles. A November 2012 report of these training and socialization events called attention to how 'the recent reduction in crime committed by the family members of US service personnel includes the impact of these kinds of activities' (Okinawa Prefectural Public Safety Commission 2012). Local law enforcement officers have implemented measures to try to reduce the risk posed to the security of the everyday by the presence of US military personnel and their offspring. In this way, the measures adopted in order to respond to the ongoing problem of crime include training, socialization and curfews as well as the criminal justice system represented by the courts.

5 Response to 1995 rape of a school girl

Whilst the recent introduction of the lay judge system now provides the opportunity for societal engagement in the local response to criminal acts by US service personnel, civilian contractors and their families, the most significant mechanism for expressing local dissatisfaction historically has been by grassroots protests and rallies. More precisely, heinous crime, especially rape, has served as a catalyst for mass demonstrations and rallies against the wrongdoings of US service personnel as well as more broadly against the risk to the security of the everyday in Okinawa. As testified by the postwar history of Okinawa, local opposition to US bases tends to swell when such heinous crimes are committed by US soldiers (Maedomari 2011: 191; Tanji 2006). Indeed, the 1995 abduction and rape of a twelve-year-old school girl by three off-duty US service personnel and the mass outcry against their crime was instrumental in forcing the two governments to launch the SACO process (Akibayashi and Takasato 2009). The culprits leased a van when off-base and then kidnapped the school girl. She was beaten, her mouth and eyes taped and her hands tied before being gang-raped. It was an incident that galvanized many in Okinawa to take to the streets, participate in mass demonstrations and join together in the prefectural rally of over 80,000 participants organized in protest (Vogt 2012).

The case illuminates clearly the role crimes such as rape can play in galvanizing societal action and how this action can contribute to a change in the status quo mechanisms for mediating the risk of off-base crime by US soldiers. The SACO process led the US and Japanese governments to agree 'to reduce the burden on the people of Okinawa and thereby strengthen the Japan-US alliance' (SACO 1996). At the same time, as touched on above, the US agreed to give 'sympathetic consideration to any request for the transfer of custody prior to indictment of the accused which may be made by Japan in specific cases of heinous crimes of murder or rape . . . and other specific cases it [Japan] believes should be considered' (Ministry of Foreign Affairs 1996).[4] Notwithstanding, the number of cases of pre-indictment turnover was rare until 2004, when an agreement on mutual concessions was reached, and the US agreed 'to be more flexible when granting pre-indictment transfer requests and Japan agreed to allow a U.S. representative to be present during all stages of interrogation of a pre-indictment transfer' (Stone 2006: 255). At the time of the 1995 incident, the US called on Article 17 of the SOFA and refused to surrender the suspects to Japanese judicial authorities.

Whilst individual and mass rape as an instrument of war is well documented (Enloe 2000), the rape of women in Okinawa appears as a corollary of the risk posed to the security of the everyday by the US presence in the prefecture: as the quintessential ingredient of state-centric security, the US forces are in Okinawa as visiting forces, not as instruments of war against an ally. Even though the recorded and documented numbers of rape are statistically small, the impact on the local community is immense as sexual harm not only represents physical violence against the female victim, but simultaneously symbolizes the way the everyday security, dignity and identity of the local population is compromised by the existence and operation of US military installations. These military installations act as a constant reminder of the existential risk posed to Okinawan identity (Siddle 2003). As *Stars and Stripes Okinawa* highlights, moreover, the rape of local females has the potential to impact on the high-level politics at the heart of the US–Japan alliance: 'Crime, particularly rape, remains a top reason why many have demanded reductions in the large U.S. military presence on the island, where most American troops in Japan are based' (25 February 2013). Such a statutory offence sets in motion a different political dynamic than other crimes, as the following statement makes clear: 'In the relative calm of retrospect, it is difficult to understand how the incident [1995 rape] could logically have resulted in a change to the criminal jurisdiction procedures set out in the SOFA' (Honma *et al.* 2001: 388, footnote 81). But it is not the logic of the incident so much as the rape of a child as emblematic of the asymmetric power relationship between Japan and the United States under the SOFA that helps to explain the change taking place in jurisdictional procedures. For the local population, and many others in Japan, the rape of the twelve-year-old symbolized the rape of the Okinawan body politic by the United States (Angst 2003: 138). More precisely, whether the perpetrators were officially on- or off-duty does not purge them of their intrinsic association with state-centric security, exposing the subordination of the Okinawan victim to the dual structure representing the exercise of power by the three US perpetrators through physical violence and the two governments through the SOFA.

The apology for the rape of the school girl expressed by Governor Ōta Masahide at the 1995 prefectural rally should be viewed in this context: his failure as the Okinawan governor to protect the child from sexual violence resulted from the *structural position* of the prefecture in the government's state-centric security policy focused on the US–Japan alliance, making his words representative of his concern for the everyday security of the wider community; as Kinkō Bokuzetsu stated: 'His apology was as the Okinawan governor *(gyōsei o atsukaru mono)* but these sentiments could not just have been those of the governor. I think those words of apology were directed from all adults – those who participated in the mass rally, those who, for whatever reason, could not participate – to the child victim and to the children who bear the burden of the future' (*Ryūkyū Shimpō*, editorial, 26 September 2007).

6 Conclusion

The above discussion has focused on how off-base military crime poses the risk of harm and actual harm to the security of the everyday in Okinawan society. What the SOFA and SACO make clear, however, is how risk in Okinawa is mediated by two states, Japan and the United States, underlining how the legal mechanisms of governance in Okinawa arise out of a process of negotiation and compromise between the two sides under pressure from local society. But as any compromise takes place in the context of the government's state-centric security policy focused on the alliance, the negotiating power of the US continues to predominate, as illustrated by the daily operation of the SOFA. This remains the case even after the improvements carried out as a result of the 1996 SACO agreement and subsequent modifications of the way the SOFA and SACO are implemented. As touched on in the introduction to Part III, the long-standing US commitment to maximize its jurisdiction means an inherent resistance to the prosecution of US suspects in Japanese courts as well as a demonstrable reluctance to pay full compensation to victims of the harm inflicted as a result of off-base crimes.

Whilst the SACO confirms the agreement to 'reduce the burden' on Okinawa, the point to bear in mind is the context: to 'strengthen the Japan-US alliance.' We will see in the following chapters how the outcome of the SACO agreement has led to ongoing protests against the proposal to 'reduce' the burden on Okinawa by relocating the Marine Corps Air Station Futenma in densely populated Ginowan city to an environmentally fragile and less populated part of Okinawa in Nago city. But the proposed relocation of the Futenma base will not bring an end to the risk and harm of crimes to the security of the everyday in Okinawa. Even if the overall number of cases of crime is reduced because of the more remote location of the proposed new outpost of American power, crime would no doubt continue so long as soldiers were able to cross the boundary of the base into local society. Indeed, as we have seen, even with the 2012 curfew firmly in place, a number of soldiers broke the curfew and were arrested by Japanese police on suspicion of committing a crime. In the interim, the curfew in Okinawa has been relaxed somewhat, following a May 2013 decision to allow off-base soldiers two alcoholic drinks at restaurants between 18.00 and 22.00, suggesting the difficulty faced by the US in responding to the needs of the soldiers for 'rest and recreation' and the call of Okinawa for a society free from crimes commited by US servicemen.

For central government policymakers and security managers, the maintenance of state-centric security takes priority over the security of the everyday in Okinawa, except in times of crisis, as in the case of the 1995 rape. But such a strategy always involves political risk for governance because of the gap between the political leaders in Tokyo and Okinawan society. Numerous cases illustrating the difference between the two have been exposed over the years, but a recent example provided by the minister of defence in the Noda cabinet, Ichikawa Yasuo, demonstrates the inveterate nature of the problem. With the Noda administration as committed to the alliance as previous LDP-led administrations, Ichikawa's case exemplifies the degree to which the US looms large in contrast to the risk posed to the security of the everyday by US military personnel in the prefecture: in this case, Ichikawa was subject to a censure in the Diet and the passage of a protest resolution by the Okinawa Prefectural Assembly for not knowing the details of the 1995 rape case (Okinawa Prefectural Assembly 2011). In a sense, crime exposes the fundamental contradiction at the heart of the government's state-centric security policy focused on the alliance. The policymakers in Tokyo trumpet the alliance as securing the national population against the risk of invasion from the outside, but the concrete internalization of the alliance in Okinawa, off-base soldiers, poses the risk of invading the security of the everyday for the local population on the inside. We have seen in this chapter how the risk is manifest as harm in the case of heinous crimes. The next chapter investigates how risk and harm are manifest in the case of environmental degradation.

Notes

1 For convenience, the expressions, service personnel, military personnel, soldiers and so forth, are used to refer to the suspects or perpetrators of the crimes generically, even though crime statistics refer to *Beigunkōseiin*, that is, US service personnel, US civilian contractors and their families. Police statistics do not break down the data and so they may include crimes committed by family members and civilian contract personnel, although media attention and our focus is on the crimes involving US military personnel. The specific cases examined below refer only to military personnel.
2 Of the approximately 50,000 service personnel, including family members, stationed in Okinawa, 15,000 live off-base (*Asahi Shimbun*, English edition, 8 February 2013).
3 This is not just a problem of rapes being committed off-base in the local population, but also on-base sexual violence. The number of on-base reports of incidents of sexual violence is highest at the marine bases in Okinawa, standing at 4.1 per 1,000 soldiers, compared with say 1.5 per 1,000 soldiers at Marine Corps Air Station Cherry Point on the east coast of the United States (*Shimbun Akahata*, 27 October 2012). For a full discussion, see the reports of the United States Department of Defense (2011).
4 Police statistics obtained by the *Ryūkyū Shimpō* show that, of the thirty-five US service personnel suspected of a sexual crime between 1996 and 2011, thirty (80 per cent) were not arrested and the incident was resolved without them being detained (*Ryūkyū Shimpō*, 15 January 2013).

References

Akibayashi, Kozue and Suzuyo Takasato (2009) "Okinawa: women's struggle for demilitarization," in Catherine Lutz (ed.) *The Bases of Empire: The Global Struggle against U.S. Military Posts*, London: Pluto Press, pp. 243–69.
Angst, Linda Isako (2003) "The rape of a schoolgirl: discourses of power and women's lives in Okinawa," in Laura Hein and Mark Selden (eds) *Islands of Discontent: Okinawan Responses to Japanese and American Power*, Lanham, MD: Rowman and Littlefield, pp. 135–56.
Anti-US Base Network (2012) "Statement of the Anti-US base Network on the October 16 rape case by US military servicemen." Available online at: http://www.ilps.info/index.php/en/current-events/statements-and-press-releases/103-asia-pacific-and-china/500-justice-for-okinawa-rape-victim-us-troops-out-of-japan-now. Accessed 16 July 2014.
Enloe, Cynthia (2000) *Maneuvers: The International Politics of Militarizing Women's Lives*, Berkeley: University of California Press.
Forgash, Rebecca (2009) "Negotiating marriage: cultural citizenship and the reproduction of American Empire in Okinawa," *Ethnology*, 48, 3: 215–37.
Furukai, Hiroshi (2011) "Japan's quasi-jury and grand jury systems as deliberative agents of social change: decolonial strategies and deliberative participatory democracy," *Chicago-Kent Law Review*, 86, 2: 789–829.
Honma, Hiroshi, Dale Sonnenberg and Donald A. Timm (2001) "United States forces in Japan: A bilateral experience," in Dieter Fleck (ed.) *The Handbook of the Law of Visiting Forces*, Oxford: Oxford University Press, pp. 365–416.
Maedomari, Hiromori (2011) *Okinawa to Beigunkichi*, Tokyo: Kadokawa.
Ministry of Foreign Affairs (1996) Nichibei Chii Kyōtei Dai 17 jō 5 (c) oyobi Keiji Saiban Tetsuzuki ni kakawaru Nichibei Gōdō. Available online at: http://www.mofa.go.jp/mofaj/area/usa/sfa/kyoutei/pdfs/17.pdf. Accessed 20 July 2014.
Nago Heripōto Kichi Hantai suru Kai (2000) Petition to Protest Sexual Violence by a Member of the US Marines and a Request for the Withdrawal of US Forces and to Abandon the Construction of a New Base. Available online at: http://www.jca.apc.org/keystone/K-ML200007/2864.html. Accessed 14 July 2014.
Okinawa Prefectural Assembly (2011) Zen Okinawa Bōei Kyokuchō no Futekisetsu Hatsugen ni Kōgi shi, Bōei Daijin no Sekinin o Meikaku ni suru koto o Motomeru Kōgi Ketsugi. Available online at: http://tamutamu2011.kuronowish.com/sinnkitiikennsyo.htm. Accessed 8 December 2013.
Okinawa Prefectural Police (2010) Keihōhan Gaikokujin Hanzai Kenkyo Kensū, Kenkyo Jinin. Available online at: http://www.police.pref.okinawa.jp/johokokai/tokei/hanzaitokei/h22_12_gaikokujin.pdf. Accessed 3 December 2013.
—— (2011) Beigunkōseiin na do oyobi Ippan Gaikokujin Kenkyo Jōkyō. Available online at: http://www.police.pref.okinawa.jp/johokokai/tokei/beigunkenkyo.html. Accessed 3 December 2013.
—— (2012) Beigunkōseiin na do oyobi Ippan Gaikokujin Kenkyo Jōkyō. Available online at: http://www.police.pref.okinawa.jp/johokokai/tokei/hanzaitokei/h24_12_gaikokujin.pdf. Accessed 3 December 2013.
Okinawa Prefectural Public Safety Commission (2012) Teirei Kaigi no Kaisai Jōkyō. Available online at: http://www.police.pref.okinawa.jp/kouan/teireikako/H24.11.7.htm. Accessed 3 December 2013.
SACO (Special Action Committee on Okinawa) (1996) The SACO Final Report, December 2 1996 by Minister for Foreign Affairs Ikeda, Minister of State for Defense Kyuma;

Secretary of Defense Perry, Ambassador Mondale. Available online at: http://www.mofa.go.jp/region/n-america/us/security/96saco1.html. Accessed 6 December 2013.

Siddle, Richard (2003) "Return to Uchinā: the politics of identity in contemporary Okinawa," in Glenn D. Hook and Richard Siddle (eds) *Japan and Okinawa: Structure and Subjectivity*, London: Routledge, pp. 133–47.

Stone, Timothy D. (2006) "U.S.-Japan SOFA: a necessary document worth preserving," *Naval Law Review*, 53: 229–58.

Tanji, Miyume (2006) *Myth, Protest and Struggle in Okinawa*, London: Routledge.

United States Department of Defense (2003) "Rumsfeld Visits Okinawa; Meets with Troops, Local Officials." Available online at: http://www.defense.gov/News/NewsArticle.aspx?ID=27779. Accessed 7 December 2013.

—————— (2011) Sexual Assault Prevention and Response. Department of Defense, *Annual Report on Sexual Assault in the Military*. Fiscal Year 2011, volume 1 and volume 2. Also see Fiscal Year 2012. Available online at: http://www.sapr.mil/. Accessed 3 December 2013.

United States Embassy, Tokyo, Japan (2008) Ambassador J. Thomas Schieffer Discusses U.S.-Japan Relations in Online State Department Forum. Available online at: http://japan.usembassy.gov/e/p/tp-20080530-50.html. Accessed 5 December 2013.

United States Marines (2012) *Courtney Fest 2012*. Available online at: http://www.marines.mil/News/PressReleases/PressReleaseDisplay/tabid/13274/Article/135261/courtney-fest-2012.aspx. Accessed 5 December 2013. Accessed 20 July 2014.

Vogt, Gabrielle (2012) "A woman's world? Contentious politics and civil society in Okinawa," *Minikomi*, 82: 19–26.

Weyand, Matt (2012) "Department of Defense, Inc.: the DoD's use of corporate strategies to manage U.S. overseas military bases," *Indiana Journal of Global Legal Studies*, 19, 1: 391–411.

Yoshida, Kensei (2007) *Gunji Shokuminchi Okinawa: Nihon Hondo to no Ondosa no Seitai*, Tokyo: Kōbunken.

11
ENVIRONMENTAL DEGRADATION

1   Introduction

Chapters 9 and 10 have provided evidence of how US military accidents and incidents pose a range of risks to the security of the everyday in Okinawa, and how risk is manifest as harm to the daily existence and well-being of the local population. But the natural environment sustaining the life of the residents of Okinawa, as well as the fauna and flora of the prefecture, is at risk from the US military installations, too. Indeed, in the case of the environment, the boundary between the US gated communities and the local population is even more porous than in the case of the off-base crimes committed by service personnel discussed in Chapter 10. In this sense, whilst the natural environment of Okinawa is by definition *shared* between the US military and the local population, any attempts to protect the everyday security of the people and remedy the harm to the environment caused by the existence and operation of US military facilities is in the hands of the Okinawans, not the US military. This is not to suggest that the US plays no role in ameliorating environmental risks, but rather that, as a result of the SOFA, discussed in the introduction to Part III, Japan rather than the United States shoulders the ultimate responsibility for stewardship of the natural environment in the prefecture.

The purpose of this chapter is to investigate how the existence and operation of US military installations pose risks to the natural environment and the security of the everyday in Okinawa. That such risks can lead to potential harm and harm to everyday security as well as to the natural environment is underlined by the type and range of risks faced: pollution from oil spills; contamination of soil and water by toxins; the unearthing of unexploded munitions; destruction of marine life, and so on. These risks are taken up in the context of the SOFA and the proposed construction of a replacement for the Marine Corps Air Station Futenma in Henoko and the adjacent Oura Bay, in the northern Okinawan city of Nago.

The chapter starts by extending the argument in the two earlier chapters on the impact of the SOFA with regard to the natural environment: section two demonstrates how the bilateral agreement between the two national governments impacts environmental governance as a result of US bases in Okinawa existing in a separate legal space under the SOFA. The third section sets the context of environmental degradation in the prefecture by briefly taking up a range of environmental risks faced by the local population as a result of the existence and operation of US military facilities. The aim here is to provide insights into the different types of risks posed to the environment and the security of the everyday for the local population. The fourth section offers a more detailed exposure of particular environmental risks by focusing on the toxic legacy of the Vietnam War by turning the spotlight on how the US military's use of toxins in fighting that war has left a legacy of potential harm to the local population. In the fifth section we proceed to examine the risk to marine life posed by the relocation of the Futenma air station to Henoko. The environmental assessment required prior to construction of the new base has been approved by the governor of Okinawa, and the Abe Shinzō administration is pushing ahead with the measures necessary to progress the project, despite widespread local opposition and ongoing concerns about the risks posed to the marine environment. The conclusion summarizes the discussion and draws attention to how the environmental risks posed by US military installations in Okinawa are of secondary concern to central government policymakers and security managers wedded to a state-centric security policy focused on the alliance with the United States and a prefectural government willing to acquiesce in this national policy.

2   The environment and SOFA

The risk of degradation of the natural environment as a result of the existence and operation of US military facilities in Okinawa is mediated and constrained by the operation of the SOFA between Japan and the United States. The SOFA absolves the US of the responsibility to address any environmental damage arising from US facilities when the area occupied by the military is returned to Japan. This is in line with a policy whereby the US 'is able usually to avoid costs by contracting out liability for any pollution associated with its overseas military bases' (Weyand 2012: 405). In the case of Japan, Article IV (1) of the SOFA leaves no room for doubt: 'The United States is not obliged, when it returns facilities and areas to Japan on the expiration of this Agreement or at an earlier date, to restore the facilities and areas to the condition in which they were at the time they became available to the United States armed forces, or to compensate Japan in lieu of such restoration.' As the US has no obligation to restore Japan's 'facilities and areas,' the environmental risk to Okinawa continues after the reversion of the land occupied by the US military to Japan. In this situation, the prefecture cooperates with the central government by carrying out environmental assessments in line with the government's goal of returning base land to its original state (Okinawa Prefecture 2013a: 78). In December 2013 Governor Nakaima Hirokazu brought up environmental concerns when he declared his support for the move of the Futenma base to Henoko (see below). Whilst the aim is to supplement the SOFA with a new agreement on the environment, it remains to be seen whether any improvement will be made as a result of the proposal. As it stands, a decision was reached to hold negotiations on the issue starting in February 2014 (*Ryūkyū Shimpō*, 9 February 2014).

What is striking about the scope of the SOFA is that, even if the operation of US military installations violates how the environment is governed and regulated by Japanese laws and norms, local investigation of any on-base environmental risk and degradation cannot be carried out without the express permission of US authorities (i.e. entry into US facilities is subject to the SOFA). In this situation, evidence has emerged to show that not all environmental risks to arise on US bases are reported to the Japanese government. In the case of Okinawa, for instance, in the period between 1999 and 2006 sixteen incidents of fuel leakages occurred, although only three cases were reported to the Japanese authorities between 1999 and March 2009 (*Ryūkyū Shimpō*, 24 April 2009; also see Hayashi 2011). The two governments in 1997 agreed on measures to ensure that the US military speedily informed both the MOFA and the Okinawa Defense Bureau of incidents inside US military facilities that impact on the environment (Ministry of Foreign Affairs 1997). That not all of the above sixteen incidents were known to the Japanese government may be because the unreported incidents fall outside of the scope of the agreement, at least according to then minister of foreign affairs, Nakasone Hirofumi (*Ryūkyū Shimpō*, 24 April 2009). In any event, as local officials in Okinawa have no way of determining independently the risk posed by these on-base incidents, even if known to them, the role of local subnational political authorities in governing the environment through enforcing environmental policy is clearly constrained by the SOFA.

The point is illustrated by the August 2013 crash of the HH-60 helicopter at Camp Hansen examined in Chapter 9. The environmental risk and potential harm to the everyday security of the local population arose as the helicopter crashed close to Okawa Dam, the source of drinking water for the villagers of Ginoza. This is not the first time anxiety has surfaced about the safety of drinking water. Indeed, the risk of the US military contaminating such a daily necessity has been a much wider-scale problem, as seen by the unearthing of munitions disposed of by US military forces in the watershed area of Okinawa's main source of water, Fukuchi reservoir (Johnson 2006: 173). The crash of the HH-60 so close to the local water supply led Ginoza officials to suspend the use of the reservoir until the water was confirmed as being safe for human consumption. The US military carried out an environmental survey of the impact of the crash, but the full findings have not been released to the Japanese authorities. Because of the SOFA, moreover, neither prefectural nor village officials from Ginoza have been able to carry out their own environmental assessment in order to determine the health risks of consuming water from the dam. The officials must instead rely on the US military for the timing and release of information on the risk and potential harm posed to the village. This means that, even though local officials were aware of US service personnel removing soil from the site of the crash close to the dam, formal notification of their action from the Okinawa Defense Bureau did not reach the village until long afterwards. The bureau advised the village officials that the soil was removed from the site because of its high concentration of arsenic, well above the safety standards set by Japan (*Japan Times*, 18 February 2014). As entry to the crash site and release of information are controlled by the US forces, however, even six months after the accident local officials were still unable to confirm whether or not the water source had been contaminated. As a result of the health risk posed, local officials continued to suspend the supply of water from Okawa Dam and instead had to rely on an increased flow of water from other dams in the vicinity of the village (*Okinawa Taimuzu*, 13 February 2014). The water finally flowed again over a year after the original accident (*Okinawa Taimuzu*, 14 August 2014).

Another example of how the governance of the local environment is mediated by the SOFA is the case of fuel and oil spills and leakages from the operation of the bases. The prefecture's white paper on the environment updates the number of identified cases on a year-by-year basis. In the 2011 edition of the white paper, for instance, nine cases of oil and fuel spillage and leakage were reported, as illustrated by the fuel leak from an underground storage tank at Kadena Air Base (Okinawa Prefecture 2013b: 55). This followed earlier fuel and oil spills as well as leaks at Kadena, Camp Hansen and Futenma. The March 2009 case of fuel leakage amounting to 200 gallons (757 litres) at Futenma is a particularly clear illustration of the constraining role the SOFA can play in governing the environment in Okinawa. Although the fuel posed the risk of contamination, local officials were not immediately informed of the incident; it only became known to them following the US military's decision to contact the Okinawa Defense Bureau. Indeed, this was the first time the Ginowan authorities had been contacted about fuel leakage on the base (Hayashi 2010: 129). Neither the Okinawa Defense Bureau, the prefecture nor Ginowan city was allowed to assess the risk by taking a soil sample to test for contamination or to take photographs on visiting the scene of the incident. Given the constraints of the SOFA, the real situation in the case of an on-base leakage is difficult to assess, as the local media's doubts about the full scale of the incident make clear: 'At the start the US military explained that, of the 800 gallons (approximately 3028 litres) leakage, 70 gallons had been recovered. This was later corrected to a leakage of 200 gallons of which 100 gallons was recovered. It seems the military wants to play down the size of the damage' (*Ryūkyū Shimpō*, 14 March 2009).

3 A range of environmental risks

The above discussion has shone the spotlight on the way the SOFA mediates and constrains the role of subnational political authorities in addressing environmental risks arising from US military installations. But the risks and potential harm of contamination of local drinking water and the leakage of fuel are simply examples of a wider range of risks posed by US military facilities in Okinawa. The point is evident from the prefecture's 2003 basic plan for the environment (*Okinawaken Kankyō Kihon Keikaku*) and the publication of the second revised edition of the plan in 2013 (Okinawa Prefecture 2013a). Both of these plans report specifically on the environmental impact of the bases in Okinawa. The 2013 edition demonstrates not only how military accidents can pose a risk to the natural environment, as in our examination of the environmental impact of the crash of the HH-60 helicopter above, but also how the security of the everyday can be put at risk by the 'little Americas' on the other side of the fence. The environmental risks and potential harm posed by US military installations and activities include damage to the marine environment due to the effluent flowing out of the bases into rivers and the sea. The MOE carries out surveys of the waste water from US bases and checks that environmental standards are being met. In the case of the 2013 survey, for instance, the ministry confirmed environmental standards were being met by US military facilities, except in limited cases (Ministry of Environment 2013). However, local officials remain anxious about the potential of contaminants entering the food chain as a result of waste water from US facilities.

The environmental risks and potential harm posed by US military installations and activities include damage to the marine environment due to the effluent flowing out of the bases into rivers and the sea. To start with, the operation of US bases leads to the damage and destruction of the natural environment, as illustrated most vividly by the use of live ammunition in war games and live-fire exercises. This has been a source of particular anxiety at Camp Hansen near the town of Kin. With woodlands destroyed and hills left bare at the Ginbaru military training site, the run-off of 'reddish clay' (red soil, *akatsuchi*) from the bare land into Kin Bay has led to water pollution and degradation of the marine environment. Certainly, the 'reddish clay' is a wider problem exacerbated by the presence and operation of US bases (Shimoji 2012), although measures taken over the years have served to reduce the problem (Kinjo *et al*. 2003). With the return of the training area to Kin in 2011, moreover, the risk from the base has been eliminated (Japan Update 2013; *Ryūkyū Shimpō*, 31 July 2013).[1] In this way, the closure of the base has resolved an environmental problem, but the reddish clay continues as a source of environmental concern in other parts of the prefecture as a result of run-off from American bases.

Second, the firing of live rounds can start fires, which remain a major risk to the environment because of their potential to destroy crops, forests and fields. Although precautions are taken to try to limit the risk of fire, the problem has not been eliminated entirely (Yoichi 2010: 46–7). The prefecture's basic plan shows that the number of fire incidents reported varies annually. For instance, the lowest number in the past decade or so is seven incidents. Fourteen incidents were reported in 2011 involving approximately 1.25 square kilometres in area (Okinawa Prefecture 2013b: 84).

Third, the legacy of the Asia-Pacific war continues with the unearthing of unexploded US munitions. In 2014, for instance, unexploded five-inch shells were discovered in Naha at the site for the construction of an apartment building, leading to the evacuation of 380 of the local residents and the redirection of traffic during the process of disposal (*Okinawa Taimuzu*, 4 March 2014). In other cases, unexploded munitions have caused actual harm, as in the case of injury to the operator of a heavy digger, and another person in Itoman, when a bomb exploded (*Ryūkyū Shimpō*, 14 January 2009). In certain instances, the result has been more serious, as in the death of one person in the village of Ie in 1987 and the death of another in Naha in the same year. Whilst it is not always certain whether the unexploded munitions are American or Japanese, the risks posed to everyday security by the munitions are often framed in the context of the war with the US and the continued presence of US forces in the prefecture.

Fourth, the experience of Hiroshima and Nagasaki has engendered a sense of heightened anxiety about radiation in Japan, as evidenced by the use of the term 'nuclear allergy' (for details, see Hook 1996: 146–158). In Okinawa, another risk posed is by radiation leakage from the visit of US nuclear powered vessels. The city of Uruma, on the east coast of Okinawa Island, is host to the US Navy's White Beach Naval Facility, situated on the Katsuren Peninsula. Nuclear submarines make regular calls at the facility. In 2010, for instance, thirty-three submarines docked at White Beach. The prefecture has monitored the waters since 1972, but so far has reported no evidence of leakage on visits to White Beach (Okinawa Prefecture 2013b: 62–3). However, as seen by the discovery of radioactive cobalt-60 in Naha port in 1968, radioactive pollution remains a risk (Mitchell 2013) and is of increased concern in the aftermath of the Fukushima disaster.

Fifth, the operation of the bases is a risk to the animal population and potentially the human population because US installations are the source of toxins potentially crossing the boundary of the base. A team of experts from Ehime University and Meio University in Okinawa who recently studied the carcasses of mongoose found near Futenma base and Camp Kinser discovered evidence of toxic polychlorinated biphenyls (PCBs) in the animals. Although further studies are required to reach a definitive conclusion, a potential source of the PCBs is seen as US transformers and other equipment where the toxin would be found. The risk is that, not only mongoose, but other animals and members of the local population living close to the base may have been exposed to the toxin as well (*Ryūkyū Shimpō*, 20 August 2013).

Sixth, whilst the disposal of household and other waste products symbolizes the risks of modern consumer culture to the local and wider global environment, whether the waste comes from on- or off-base, the refuse from military installations at times includes harmful materials, as with the discovery of asbestos in the waste from the army's Camp Foster (*Ryūkyū Shimpō*, 24 April 2009). What is more, the bases generate thousands of tonnes of additional waste annually. In 2011, for instance, the bases in Okinawa accounted for 23,000 tonnes of waste (Okinawa Prefecture 2013a: 84), although efforts are being made to reduce the amount, as illustrated by the recycling efforts at Kadena (*Stars and Stripes Okinawa*, 27 September 2013). As in the cases mentioned above, the SOFA constrains the ability of Okinawan officials to ensure the safety of local workers because they are unable to verify whether the handling of dangerous waste such as asbestos has been adequately addressed in line with regulatory requirements (Yoichi 2010: 55–6).

Finally, the risk to the natural environment is particularly pronounced in the northern part of the main island. As examined in detail below, the construction of the Henoko base is a significant risk to marine life, but Camp Gonsalves (US Marines, Northern Training Area, *Hokubu Kunrenjō*) poses similar risks to the rich biodiversity of the environment surrounding the base. The camp is 17,500 acres (71 square kilometres) and located in the Yanbaru region of Okinawa, home to rare and unique species such as the Okinawa woodpecker (Dendrocopos noguchii) and the Okinawa rail (Gallirallus okinawae). The International Union for Conservation of Nature (IUCN) includes both the woodpecker (IUCN 2013a) and the rail (IUCN 2013b) on the endangered red list of species. The constructing of the Osprey vertical take-off helicopter landing pads in the Yanbaru region close to Higashi village, particularly Takae hamlet *(shūraku)*, is a source of risk to the local fauna and flora, too. It is the source of continuing opposition to the deployment by many of the locals (total population 150) and protestors from further afield, including an ongoing sit-in (sit-down) (Nohelipadtakae 2012). The proposed construction was subject to an environmental assessment; however, this was not carried out as a prefectural assessment, but as an autonomous assessment *(jishu asesu)* by the Okinawa Defense Bureau. However, as the helipads are for the use of the US military, the full details required of the assessment have not been disclosed, indicating how the SOFA constrains the release of information relevant to environmental governance (Sakurai 2010 :119–120).

4 Toxic contamination

The US military's extensive use of the bases in Okinawa internalized the Vietnam War as a toxic legacy for the local population. It can be seen in the risk posed to health by the contamination and degradation of the natural environment. Of particular concern is the legacy of Agent Orange and other 'rainbow herbicides' (agent green, white, pink, and so on) deployed in Vietnam. The military purpose of these herbicides was to destroy the crops and forest canopies in the country, depriving the enemy of food and cover from US forces. However, exposure to these chemicals is also associated with diseases such as cancer, damage to the immune system and birth defects amongst the Vietnamese as well as amongst Vietnam veterans and their offspring (US Department of Veterans Affairs no date; Committee to Review the Health Effects 2011; Sills 2014).

Although the Pentagon has denied repeatedly the existence of chemical defoliants in Okinawa, former soldiers and others have challenged this position with concrete evidence. In 2011, for instance, a former US serviceman backed up his statement that he had helped to dispose of tens of fifty-gallon drums of herbicides containing dioxin near the coast in Chatan during 1969 by providing a hand-drawn map of the location (*Ryūkyū Shimpō*, 14 August 2011). Another former soldier states: 'Having served at Kadena AFB [air force base] from 1968 to 1971, I inventoried Agent Orange 55 gallon drums as part of my job as an Inventory Management Specialist. It was there and I have a pending claim with the VA [Veterans Agency]' (Agent Orange Okinawa 2014). Overall, more than 250 veterans who spent time in Okinawa have come forward to say Agent Orange 'was sprayed, stored and buried on the island during the Vietnam War' (Mitchell 2014). The above-mentioned White Beach facility was one of the ports used by ships to deliver Agent Orange during the 1960s as well as more usually to Naha port (Mitchell 2011).

On the ground in Okinawa, the evidence of the existence of these toxins provided by US veterans has been complemented by the discovery of drums with traces of military herbicides disposed of by the US military. Most recently, the discovery and unearthing of twenty-two empty thirty-gallon drums and the detection of a further eleven containers still buried in a local soccer pitch in Okinawa city have heightened the sense of risk for the local population. The land was formerly part of the Kadena base until its return to Japan in 1987. The first discovery of the drums in 2013 was then followed in January 2014 by the unearthing by the Okinawa Defense Bureau of another fifty drums on land close to the original site. In total eighty-three drums were uncovered (*Sankei Shimbun*, 4 February 2014). The logo of Dow Chemical, a major producer of Agent Orange and other military defoliants during the Vietnam War, is identifiable on some of the containers. Anxiety caused by the discovery of the drums is not limited to the Okinawan population, as the parents of pupils at two US Department of Defense schools located close to the site have been 'on edge' over the past few months, too (*Stars and Stripes Okinawa*, 27 February 2014).

The Pentagon has insisted that Agent Orange was transported in the larger fifty-gallon drums, intimating that the thirty-gallon drums discovered under the soccer pitch did not contain the chemical. However, a journalist from the *Ryūkyū Shimpō* interviewed a former soldier who revealed that he had been involved in transferring Agent Orange from the larger drums to thirty-gallon drums (3 January 2014). Tests of the unearthed drums have revealed enough evidence to confirm the residue of highly toxic dioxins. The Okinawa Defense Bureau 'found the key ingredient of Agent Orange – 2, 4, 5-T, trichlorophenoxyacetic acid' (*Ryūkyū Shimpō*, 25 July 2013). However, as none of the tests revealed the element 2,4-D, which is unique to Agent Orange, the bureau concluded the toxin is the herbicide PCP (pentachlorophenol) (*Okinawa Taimuzu*, 13 July 2013). Reflecting the lack of trust between the city and the MOD, a separate, independent survey was commissioned by local officials using experts from Ehime University. The lead scientist, Honda Katsuhiko, concluded that '70 per cent of the materials found in the drums are dioxins found in chemical defoliants' (*Ryūkyū Shimpō*, 25 July 2013). Following further investigation by Okinawa city, traces of the missing element, 2,4-D were found for the first time in July 2014, suggesting to specialists that the drum did indeed contain traces of Agent Orange (*Ryūkyū Shimpō*, 7 July 2014).

What is striking about the positions taken by the Pentagon and the Japanese MOD is the clear attempt to downplay the legacy of chemical toxins, whether Agent Orange or not. From the perspective of the local population, however, the toxins are a risk to the security of the everyday, posing potential harm to health. As Dwernychuk concludes:

> The contents of the Kadena drums, whether Agent Orange, Pink, Green or whatever, is almost irrelevant. The inescapable fact is that the U.S. military, while occupying the Kadena Air Base on Okinawa, disposed of 'unknown' materials in drums containing 2,4,5-T, a wartime herbicide/defoliant, and in the mixture the most toxic component of the dioxin family, TCDD, known to be associated with the manufacture of such herbicides
>
> (Dwernychuk 2013)

Indeed, he calls on us to pay attention to the

> irrefutable facts that seem not to have been considered in their true context. Denials of such burials by the US military on land that was then part of Kadena Air Base on Okinawa by . . . the U.S. Department of Defense are disingenuous at the very least, and at worst a blatant cover-up of historical realities.
>
> (Dwernychuk 2013)

5 Relocation of the Marine Corps Air Station Futenma to Henoko

The Marine Corps Air Station Futenma remains a major source of risk to the security of the everyday for the population of especially Ginowan city, where the base is located. In the face of these risks, and in the wake of the 1995 rape of a school girl, as discussed in Chapter 10, the governments of Japan and the United States agreed in 1996 to close the air station. However, as the closure was on condition that a new location for the base needed to be secured, the intervening years have been filled with a range of proposals regarding the site of Futenma's relocation and the exact size and scope of the base to be constructed (for details, see McCormack and Norimatsu 2012). Whilst the problem of finding a new site has included discussions of the possibility of relocating the air station outside of the prefecture or outside of Japan, the preference of LDP administrations has been to construct a new military facility in the prefecture, in the district of Henoko, Nago city, where US Marines' Camp Schwab is located. Approximately one-third of the base will be on land and the remaining two-thirds built by landfill of the adjacent sea. The proposal to construct a new US military outpost in the prefecture has divided local opinion, with opposition to the construction growing stronger over time, as illustrated by the 'all Okinawa' opposition to a new base by all of the cities and other local political authorities in the prefecture as well as opposition in public opinion surveys increasing from around two-thirds in 2012 to 74.7 per cent in 2013 (*Okinawa Taimuzu*, 12 April 2013).

The Abe Shinzō administration is seeking to internalize the risks and potential harm of the government's state-centric security policy in Okinawa even further by moving ahead with the construction of a new base in Henoko, despite the risk to the environment. The ongoing confrontation between opponents and supporters of the project came to a head in late December 2013 and early January 2014. In December, the governor of the prefecture, Nakaima Hirokazu, gave approval to the government's application to reclaim an area in Oura Bay, off Henoko, for the construction of the new base, despite the governor's commitment when campaigning for re-election in 2010 to work to relocate the Futenma base outside of the prefecture. Whilst Nakaima maintains he has not broken his election promise in giving his approval, as he still supports the relocation of the Futenma base outside of Okinawa (*Asahi Shimbun*, 28 December 2013), a poll by the *Ryūkyū Shimpō* found 73 per cent of the respondents agreed that the governor had broken his electoral pledge (30 December 2013). The governor stated that he gave his approval, as the government's application met all of the legal requirements of the Act on Reclamation of Publicly-owned Water Surface *(kōyū suimen tsumetate hō)*, including the measures to be taken to protect the natural environment (Ministry of Justice 2011). The importance of the environment to the agreement is indicated by Nakaima's call for the government to set up an expert committee for environmental monitoring, on the one hand, and to negotiate with the US government a special environmental agreement, on the other (*Asahi Shimbun*, 28 December 2013).

However, the January 2014 mayoral election in Nago set up a clear choice for the voters between the incumbent, Inamine Susumu, who is opposed to the relocation plan, and the pro-relocation candidate, Suematsu Bunshin. Despite the Abe administration's support for Suematsu, the incumbent secured victory over Abe's choice: 19,839 to 15,684 votes on a turnout of 76.71 per cent (*Asahi Shimbun*, 20 January 2014). The government has declared that the local election result will not affect the decision to relocate the base to Henoko and on 21 January the MOD advertised for bids to carry out a range of environmental and other activities in order to move the project forward, such as investigating the distribution and type of corals and how to protect them, and the monitoring of the dugong, an endangered species related to the manatee (*Tokyo Shimbun*, 22 January 2014; for details, see Morimoto 2014). By summer 2014 the first phase of the project was underway (Yoshikawa 2014).

Critics of the relocation of the base to Henoko do not accept that the Abe administration's application meets the criteria to protect the environment as set out in the above act and do not accept the environmental assessment carried out – or, as McCormack (2012) calls it, 'nonassessment' (159). The Henoko area is of the first rank in the prefecture's assessment, including a mandate for the prefecture to protect the area. The governor's approval was given despite the doubts raised by the prefecture's environment and livelihood division *(kankyō seikatsu bu)* over whether the measures taken would be effective in dealing with a range of environmental risks. However, in questioning before the prefectural assembly by a special investigative committee *(Chōsa Tokubetsu Iinkai)*, which was established on the initiative of the opposition members of the assembly in the face of the governor's decision, the head of the Department of Civil Engineering and Construction *(Doboku Kenchiku Buchō)* gave evidence to the effect that, just because concerns about the environment cannot be completely eliminated, does not mean the governor's decision was inappropriate (*Ryūkyū Shimpō*, 20 February 2014).

Of particular concern is the risk posed by the construction of the base to sea life in the waters around Henoko (*Okinawa Taimuzu*, 17 January 2014). The area is visited by the dugong, registered as a 'natural monument' in Japan (image at Roach 2007), as well as by sea turtles. Environmental groups and others argue that the measures taken are insufficient to protect the dugong and sea turtles as well as the corals, sea plants, seaweed and algae (*Asahi Shimbun*, 31 December 2013; *Ryūkyū Shimpō*, 16 January 2014). The dugong feeds on sea grass and the loss of its marine habitat through the reclamation work for the base, not to mention the base itself, is seen as a major risk to the species. In 2003, a coalition of environmental groups and individuals filed a suit against the US Department of Defense over the ongoing plan to construct a base endangering the dugong. In an interlocutory decision the judge supported the plaintiffs in regarding the dugong as subject to the National Historic Preservation Act: by the Department of Defense not evaluating the impact of the construction of the new base on the dugong, it violated the law (for details, see Taira 2008; Tanji 2008). Already, the sea area around Camp Schwab is used for US Marine exercises, which pose a risk 'to dugongs and their habitat by contributing to marine pollution (i.e. oil leaks), acoustic pollution and habitat destruction resulting from vehicle operations' (UNEP 2002: 42). What is more, the environmental group Okinawa Biodiversity Network is concerned about the failure of the MOD to pass on important environmental information in English to the US forces, such as the route taken by the dugong when in the sea near Henoko (*Ryūkyū Shimpō*, 6 February 2014).

Despite the governor's approval of the application made by the Abe administration to start work in the waters around Henoko, opponents of the base continue their efforts to stop the construction of the new military facility. In January 2014 a group filed a lawsuit with the Naha District Court on the grounds that the approval given by the governor does not meet the legal standards of the Public Water Body Reclamation Law. In this way, the 194 plaintiffs from Henoko and elsewhere aim to use legal means to stop progress on the proposed work and protect the natural environment. The court's decision will revolve around issues such as the suitability of the use of public land and the extent to which the protection of the environment has been taken into account (*Okinawa Taimuzu*, 17 January 2014). This legal challenge is on top of an August 2009 case already filed at the Naha District Court by base opponents and environmentalists calling for the preparations made for environmental assessment to be carried out once again (Heri Kichi

Hantai Kyōgikai 2009). The case was dismissed without the court addressing the question of whether the Henoko environmental assessment was unlawful or not. In March 2013, 297 plaintiffs appealed the decision to the Fukuoka High Court Naha Branch (for details, see Heri Kichi Hantai Kyōgikai 2013). The outcome is awaited.

Finally, another issue to emerge as a risk to the natural environment is the use of land fill from other parts of Japan in constructing the new base. In February 2014 a group of thirty-eight Japanese and other environmental organizations wrote to the IUCN to seek advice on the impact of species alien to Okinawa being mixed in with the land fill (*Okinawa Taimuzu*, 2 February 2014). These NGOs and grassroots activists illustrate how the struggle to oppose the construction of the new base in Henoko will continue, despite the government's decision to go ahead with the construction.

6 Conclusion

The above discussion has focused on the risk posed by US military installations in Okinawa to the natural environment. As we have seen, the SOFA mediates as well as constrains the role of Okinawan subnational political authorities in the governance of the environment. As the US is not required to address any environmental degradation before returning base land to Japan, this means the potential of environmental risks and harm will remain of continuing concern to the local population. This is particularly the case as the SOFA stipulates that local officials cannot gain access to the military installations without the agreement and permission of US forces. Negotiations to improve environmental governance have started as a result of the governor's call for a new environmental agreement with the United States to supplement the SOFA; however, because of the sheer type and range of environmental risks faced by the local community, whatever the outcome of the governor's proposal, environmental risks cannot be expected to be eliminated, given the nature of the existence and operation of US military installations. The risks may result from another crash leading to potential contamination of water supplies, the burning of crops due to live-fire exercises, unexploded munitions injuring workers, and so on. What is more, the legacy of the Vietnam War continues to be a source of anxiety for the local population, as symbolized by the discovery and unearthing of drums with traces of the toxins used in Agent Orange. Clearly, environmental risks and potential harm to the local population are integral to the internalization of seventy years of American troops in Okinawa as well as to the operation of US military installations.

It remains to be seen whether the Abe administration's push to construct the Henoko base will be realized. Should the landfill of Oura Bay and the construction of the new base continue, despite the strong opposition, then the marine environment will inevitably suffer harm. Whilst the preservation of the coral, turtles and dugong may form part of a risk management approach to governing the environment on the part of the prefectural government, the governor's agreement to the construction of the base off Henoko has set him at odds with a majority of the population in Okinawa. It should also be noted that, whilst the US Ambassador to Japan, Caroline Kennedy, has sought to burnish her environmental credentials by criticizing the Japanese fishermen of Taiji for their 'inhumaneness' in the killing of dolphins in the annual hunt (Mason 2014), she has remained silent on the risk posed to the endangered dugong by the construction of the new base at Henoko. Local residents and other supporters can be expected to continue their opposition, which has been strengthened by the January 2014 election victory of Inamine Susumu as the mayor of Nago city. This sets the local population of Nago and the activists protesting the construction of the base at odds with the governor. By approving the environmental assessment for the construction of the base at Henoko, the governor has clearly prioritized state-centric security, rather than the security of the everyday prioritized by Nago, the activists and indeed a majority of the population in the prefecture.

Note

1 The former training area will be used for construction of the Hilton Okinawa Kin, scheduled for opening in 2016.

References

Agent Orange Okinawa (2014) Facebook page contribution by Allan Davis. Available online at: https://www.facebook.com/pages/Agent-Orange-Okinawa/205895316098692. Accessed 14 July 2014.

Committee to Review the Health Effects in Vietnam Veterans of Exposure to Herbicides, Board on the Health of Selected Populations, Institute of Medicine (2011) *Veterans and Agent Orange*, Washington: National Academies Press.

Dwernychuk, Wayne (2013) "The spectre of U.S. military defoliants/herbicides buried in Okinawa," *The Asia-Pacific Journal: Japan Focus*, 38, 2. Available online at: http://www.japanfocus.org/-Wayne-Dwernychuk/3999. Accessed 18 February 2014.

Hayashi, Kiminori (2010) "Beigun Kichi Atochi Riyō no Sogai Yōin," in Kenichi Miyamoto and Mitsuyoshi Kawase (eds) *Okinawaron: Heiwa, Kankyō, Jichi no Shima e*, Tokyo: Iwanami Shoten, pp. 127–142.

—— (2011) *Gunji Kankyō Mondai no Seiji Keizaigaku*, Tokyo: Nihon Keizai Hyōronsha.

Heri Kichi Hantai Kyōgikai (2009) Sojō. Available online at: http://www.mco.ne.jp/~herikiti/img/sojo.pdf. Accessed 22 January 2014.

—— (2013) "Henoko, Ihō Asesu Soshō," Available online at: http://www.mco.ne.jp/~herikiti/justice.html. Accessed 24 January 2014.

Hook, Glenn D. (1996) *Militarization and Demilitarization in Contemporary Japan*, Routledge: London.

IUCN (International Union of Conservation of Nature) (2013a) Dendrocopos noguchii. Available online at: http://www.iucnredlist.org/details/22681531/0. Accessed 19 February 2014.

—— (2013b) Gallirallus okinawae. Available online at: http://www.iucnredlist.org/details/22692412/0. Accessed 19 February 2014.

Japan Update (2013) Hilton to Open at Former Ginbaru Military Training Site (8 August). Available online at: http://www.japanupdate.com/2013/08/hilton-to-open-at-former-ginbaru-military-training-site/. Accessed 4 March 2014.

Johnson, Chalmers (2006) *Nemesis: The Last Days of the American Republic*, New York: Henry Holt and Company.
Kinjo, Kōichi, Hiroaki Mitsumoto and Tatsuo Ōmija (2003) "Ginbaru Kunrenjō no Akatsuchi Ryūshutsugen to Chisaki Kaiiki no Teishitsuchū Kendaku Bushitsu Ganryō ni tsuite," *Okinawa Eisei Kankyō Kenkyū Shohō* (*dai 2 Hō*) 37: 55–59.
Mason, Ra (2014) "Ambassador Kennedy's dolphin tweet and the fight for Japan's identity," *Asahi Shimbun AJW*. Available online at: http://ajw.asahi.com/article/forum/politics_and_economy/east_asia/AJ201404190019. Accessed 18 September 2014.
McCormack, Gavan and Satoko Oka Norimatsu (2012) *Resistant Islands Okinawa Confronts Japan and the United States*, Lanham, MD: Rowman and Littlefield.
Ministry of Environment (2013) Heisei 24 nendo Zainichi Beigun Shisetu, Kuiki Kankyō Chōsa. Available online at: http://www.env.go.jp/air/info/usfj/attach/survey_h24.pdf. Accessed 2 March 2014.
Ministry of Foreign Affairs (1997) Zainichi Beigun ni kakawaru Jiken, Jiko Hasseiji ni okeru Tsūhō Tetsuzuki. Available online at: http://www.mofa.go.jp/mofaj/area/usa/sfa/kyoutei/pdfs/03_12.pdf. Accessed 27 February 2014.
Ministry of Justice (2011) Act on Reclamation of Publicly-owned Water Surface. Available online at: http://law.e-gov.go.jp/cgi-bin/strsearch.cgi. Accessed 22 January 2014.
Mitchell, Jon (2011) "US Military defoliant on Okinawa: Agent Orange," *The Asia-Pacific Journal: Japan Focus*, 38, 2. Available online at: http://www.japanfocus.org/-Jon-Mitchell/3601. Accessed 20 February 2014.
——— (2013) "Okinawa: the Pentagon's toxic junk heap of the Pacific," *Global Research*. Available online at: http://www.globalresearch.ca/okinawa-the-pentagons-toxic-junk-heap-of-the-pacific/5359392. Accessed 14 July 2014.
——— (2014) "U.S. Military parents on Okinawa demand truth about toxic contamination near base schools," *The Asia-Pacific Journal: Japan Focus*, 23 February. Available online at: http://www.japanfocus.org/events/view/210. Accessed 25 February 2014.
Morimoto, Isao (2014) *Okinawa no Jugon*, Naha: Yōjushorin.
Nohelipadtakae (2012) Voice of Takae (in Japanese), 13 July. Available online at: http://nohelipadtakae.org/takaebreau/VoT2012july.pdf. Accessed 19 February 2014.
Okinawa Prefecture (2013a) *Dai Niji Okinawa Ken Kankyō Kihon Keikaku*. Available online at: http://www.pref.okinawa.jp/site/kankyo/seisaku/kikaku/3518.html. Accessed 18 February 2014.
——— (2013b) *Kankyō Hakusho*, Naha: Okinawaken Kankyō Seikatsubu Kankyō Seisakuka.
Roach, John (2007) "Rare Japanese dugong threatened by U.S. military base," *National Geographic News*, 23 August. Available online at: http://news.nationalgeographic.com/news/2007/08/070823-dugongs.html. Accessed 21 January 2014.
Sakurai, Kunitoshi (2010) "Kankyō Mondai kara Mita Okinawa," in Kenichi Miyamoto and Mitsuyoshi Kawase (eds) *Okinawaron: Heiwa, Kankyō, Jichi no Shima e*, Tokyo: Iwanami Shoten, pp. 97–126.
Shimoji, Kuniki (2012) "Okinawa no Shimajima ni okeru Akatsuchi nado ni yoru Suishitsu Odaku to Hiodaku no Jōkyō Hikaku," *Okinawa Eisei Kankyō Kenkyū Shohō* 46: 115–146.
Sills, Peter (2014) *Toxic War: The Story of Agent Orange*, Nashville, TN: Vanderbilt University Press.
Taira, Koji (2008) "Okinawan environmentalists put Robert Gates and DOD on trial. The dugong and the fate of the Henoko air station," *The Asia-Pacific Journal: Japan Focus*. Available online at: http://www.japanfocus.org/-koji-taira/2822. Accessed 14 February 2014.

Tanji, Miyume (2008) "US court rules in the Okinawa 'dugong' case: implications for US military bases overseas," *Critical Asian Studies*, 40, 3: 475–87.

UNEP (United Nations Environment Programme) (2002) *Dugong. Status Report and Action Plans for Countries and Territories*, Nairobi: UNEP. Available online at: http://www.unep.org/NairobiConvention/docs/dugong.pdf. Accessed 21 January 2014.

US Department of Veterans Affairs (no date) Veterans' Diseases Associated with Agent Orange. Available online at: http://www.publichealth.va.gov/PUBLICHEALTH/exposures/agentorange/conditions/index.asp. Accessed 17 July 2014.

Weyand, Matt (2012) "Department of Defense, Inc.: The DoD's use of corporate strategies to Manage U.S. overseas military bases," *Indiana Journal of Global Legal Studies*, 19, 1: 391–411.

Yoichi, Yoshiyuki (2010) *Beigun Kichi to Kankyō Mondai*, Tokyo: Gentosha Rennaisance.

Yoshikawa, Hideki (2014) "Urgent situation at Okinawa's Henoko and Oura Bay: base construction started on Camp Schwab," *The Asia-Pacific Journal: Japan Focus*. Available online at: http://www.japanfocus.org/events/view/223. Accessed 20 July 2014.

12
NOISE POLLUTION

1 Introduction

The preceding chapters have illuminated how military accidents, incidents and environmental degradation pose risks to the security of the everyday in Okinawa. Whilst these three types of risks are a consequence of the existence and operation of US military installations in the prefecture, the frequency of them being manifested as harm can be addressed by seeking to reduce the risk and ameliorate the harm, at least to some extent. In the case of military incidents, for instance, Chapter 10 showed how US Forces Japan sought to reduce crime committed by service personnel by introducing a curfew to limit the amount of time soldiers could spend in the local community. In the case of the topic of this chapter, however, noise pollution is an ineluctable outcome of the take-off, flight and landing of US military aircraft and in this sense goes to the very heart of the unequal distribution of the risks posed by state-centric security focused on the US–Japan alliance. That is, apart from tinkering around the edges, the only viable option to reduce noise pollution in Okinawa is by transferring the noise outside of the prefecture, either by the relocation of US bases, or by carrying out the activities causing the noise, such as aircraft training flights, elsewhere in Japan. Noise pollution, above all, symbolizes the internalization of the US–Japan alliance.

The flight of military planes and helicopters in the skies above the prefecture means no boundary exists between the gated communities operating the aircraft and the adjacent local communities in Okinawa, in the same way that, as we saw in Part I, Japan and China share the same sky in terms of the risk posed by transboundary air pollution. This is in marked contrast to our findings in the previous two chapters, where the boundary inscribed by the fence imposed a degree of separation between the risk posed by the US military and the Okinawan population. Noise pollution deserves treatment in a separate chapter as the potential and actual harm of noise has been serious enough to lead residents to launch a number of legal battles against the Japanese state. As seen in earlier chapters, due to the SOFA, any legal redress for the harm suffered by the local population as a result of the existence and operation of US military installations is mediated by the Japanese state, even though the source of the noise is the operation of US military aircraft deployed in Okinawa under the US-Japan security treaty.

The purpose of this chapter is to examine how the noise generated by aircraft poses risks, potential harm and harm to the local population, especially the large percentage of people living in close proximity to Kadena Air Base and Marine Corps Air Station Futenma. In this chapter we view noise pollution as a risk to the security of the everyday as it is manifest as harm to the daily existence and well-being of the local population. The chapter begins (in section two) by outlining the general risk to human health and well-being as a result of the noise generated and emitted by the operation of military installations. It focuses on the impact of noise in everyday life and the constraining role of the SOFA in addressing the risks posed. The third section proceeds to investigate the actions taken by the local population in response to aircraft noise. It draws particular attention to a number of lawsuits launched in order to halt military flights, implement noise abatement measures and seek compensation for the harm caused by noise pollution. The fourth section then takes up the recent deployment of the Osprey V-22 vertical take-off aircraft to Futenma, Takae and elsewhere as well as the proposed deployment of the aircraft to Henoko, the site for the relocation of Marine Corps Air Station Futenma. It offers a discussion of how the local population has responded to the deployment of the Osprey. The conclusion summarizes the chapter and draws out the implications of noise pollution for our understanding of risk in Okinawa, paying particular attention to governance and state-centric security focused on the US–Japan alliance.

2 Noise in everyday life

Noise in everyday life is a common concern for urban residents, especially those in the major cities of the world such as London, New York and Tokyo. It is often associated with the conveniences of everyday life, such as travelling by automobile, bus, train and other means of transportation. When the topic turns specifically to Japan, concerns about noise are often expressed as complaints about noise levels, as in the case of the loudspeaker trucks used by right-wing activists, which 'harangue the crowds at major centres in Tokyo and other cities' (Stockwin 2003: 88). When the noise is emitted by an aircraft, whether the plane is civilian or military, friend or foe, flying in practice formation at an air show or bomber formation in a war, this influences how we view the risk and potential harm of an aircraft's flight path. What is clear, though, is that, whatever the plane's purpose, the noise *(sōon)* or roar *(bakuon)* caused by the engine and the low frequency sound waves emitted by helicopter blades can pose a risk to health.[1]

A wide range of academic studies have demonstrated the harm this sort of noise environment can exert on cardiovascular problems, potentially adding to the risk of myocardial infarction; high levels of stress and high blood pressure; disturbance to sleep patterns; psychological disorders; the undermining of effective performance, whether at work or at school; impairment to hearing; and so on (Jones and Rhodes 2013; Hiramatsu *et al.* 1997; Matsui *et al.* 2004). The impact of the noise generated by the Kadena and Futenma bases is an issue of particular concern to the local population, as these two outposts of American power are located in the midst of two residential communities. The noise emitted from the twin installations affects ten cities, towns and villages of an approximate total of 550,000 residents, making up around 41 per cent of the prefecture's population (Okinawa Prefecture 2008).[2]

Studies on the impact of noise in Japan have verified the link between aircraft noise and harm to the health of the local population in Okinawa, especially to the local communities living in close proximity to the Kadena and Futenma installations. To start with, Matsui *et al.* (2003) carried out an analysis of over 160,000 births between 1974 and 1993 in order to determine the impact of exposure to noise from the two bases on fetal growth. Their data showed that exposure to high levels of noise affected fetal growth adversely. Similarly, children in school are at risk of harm from aircraft noise, whether at kindergarten or university. Parents are particularly concerned about the impact of aircraft noise on the learning environment of the younger generations. At one end of the education spectrum, kindergartens are exposed to the noise from flights overhead as well as by the schools' proximity to US bases. Apart from potential harm to health, research suggests the exposure of pre-school children to aircraft noise at Kadena and Futenma is linked to an increase in children's misbehaviour (Tokuyama *et al.* 2009). The national government has gone some way towards responding to local complaints about noise by insulating public and nationally recognized kindergarten buildings. But the mediating role of the state means privately run schools not formally recognized by the MHLW are not covered by the government's policy. So aircraft noise remains a constant risk to the everyday security and well-being of these children. In the case of the two private kindergartens located adjacent to the Kadena and Futenma bases, for instance, a survey conducted in July and August 2013 revealed that the noise from the take-off and landing of aircraft at the bases was recorded at up to seventy decibels inside buildings, double the recommended level of thirty-five decibels for holding classes set by the WHO (*Ryūkyū Shimpō*, 7 September 2013).

In the 2014 defence budget, the MOD included for the first time the cost for the soundproofing of private kindergartens not officially recognized as kindergartens by the prefecture. In theory, this enables these kindergartens to benefit from insulation against US aircraft noise in the same way as officially recognized public and nationally funded institutions. But the MOD has restricted the use of the budget to kindergartens meeting the standards set by the MHLW. However, the cost of bringing private institutions up to the standard required to be formally approved as kindergartens by the MHLW can be prohibitive and is unlikely to happen, at least in the short term. Of the ninety-seven private kindergartens in the prefecture, only forty-four conform to the regulations set by the MHLW, leaving fifty-three without insulation (*Ryūkyū Shimpō*, 7 September 2013).

This means that the children at these fifty-three kindergartens are at greater risk from aircraft noise. It may be that a child is registered at an unrecognized institution because of the kindergarten's convenient location, lack of choice, low income of the child's family, or other reasons. Going to the heart of the matter, the vice-chair of the association of private kindergartens has called for government policy to treat all kindergartens in the same way. He argues that a policy of equal treatment should be implemented as the state imposes the aircraft noise on all of the pupils, whether attending a recognized or an unrecognized kindergarten (*Okinawa Taimuzu*, 13 September 2013). In this way, the government's policy of insulating some kindergartens but not others demonstrates how state-led mediation of the risk from aircraft noise in the context of the US–Japan alliance means that a particular sub-group of children are more vulnerable to noise than others as a result of the unequal distribution of the risk posed.

Similarly, in the case of higher education, aircraft noise continues to exert an impact on the learning environment of university students. As shown in Chapter 9, when discussing the crash of the CH-53D Sea Stallion helicopter into the university's administrative building, Okinawa International University is located right next to the Futenma base in Ginowan. Despite sound insulation, the take-off and landing of aircraft close to classrooms still causes disruption to the everyday life of students studying at the university. The ongoing concern about noise pollution having an impact on the learning environment at local universities surfaced again following the deployment of the Osprey to Okinawa. At the time, local university presidents protested the impact of the noise of the V-22 on education, as touched on below.

Further, a survey of around 7,000 residents living adjacent to military airfields in Okinawa found more evidence of the way noise poses a risk of potential harm and harm to the health of the population. It concluded: 'The results suggest that the residents living around Kadena airfield suffer from both physical and mental effects due to the exposure to military aircraft noise and that the extent of such responses increases with the level of noise exposure' (Miyakita *et al.* 2002: 136; also see Hiramatsu *et al.* 2002).

In response to local complaints, the implementation of noise abatement measures at US military installations has been taken up between the US and Japanese governments as part of the SACO and joint committee negotiations. The SACO, working with the joint committee, has adopted measures to deal with issues related to the SOFA, including noise from the operation of US military aircraft. A number of remedial actions have been implemented, as illustrated by the Implement Noise Reduction Initiatives agreed in the 1996 SACO interim report (Ministry of Foreign Affairs 1996). The initiatives aim to:

- Implement agreements on aircraft noise abatement countermeasures at Kadena Air Base and Futenma air station announced by the joint committee.

- Transfer KC-130 Hercules aircraft, relocate their supporting facilities, and transfer AV-8 Harrier aircraft. Transfer KC-130 aircraft currently based at Futenma air station and relocate their supporting facilities to Iwakuni air base in conjunction with the transfer of a similar number of Harrier aircraft to the United States.
- Relocate Navy P-3 operations and supporting facilities at Kadena Air Base from the navy ramp to the other side of the major runways, and move MC-130 operations from the navy ramp.
- Build new noise reduction baffles at Kadena Air Base.
- Limit night flight training operations at Futenma air station.

Nevertheless, as emphasized by officials from the city of Ginowan, the noise abatement countermeasures, including limiting flights and other activities between 22.00 and 06.00, are *'restricted by what is thought to be necessary in order for the United States to carry out operations'* (Ginowan City 1996, emphasis added by Ginowan city). As a resident living close to the Kadena base indicated in August 2013, the local inhabitants are still exposed to the noise generated and emitted by Kadena, despite the SACO initiatives to reduce it. He complained that 'even now, into the middle of the night, we suffer from noise *(bakuon)*, and unpleasant smells from the aircraft. . . .Why does Okinawa have to sacrifice so much in order to protect Japan?' (*Okinawa Taimuzu*, 16 August 2013).

What is more, the present ongoing negotiations over a new special environmental agreement between Japan and the United States to supplement the SOFA (mentioned in Chapter 11) does not include noise as one of the agenda items, as Foreign Minister Kishida Fumio revealed in response to Diet interpellations in March 2014 (*Ryūkyū Shimpō*, 14 March 2014). These negotiations have been taking place in light of prefectural governor Nakaima Hirokazu's decision of December 2013 to approve the landfill for the relocation of the Futenma base to Henoko (for details, see *Ryūkyū Shimpō*, 28 December 2013; *Okinawa Taimuzu*, 28 December 2013). This means that, for the foreseeable future, the local population will continue to be exposed to the risks posed by noise pollution generated by the operation of US bases in the prefecture.

3 Local government and civic action in the courts

The impact of the existence and operation of US bases on the everyday security of Okinawans and the failure of the national government to take action leading to the implementation of satisfactory noise abatement measures, despite the SACO and other negotiations, has led local governments and civic groups in Okinawa to pursue legal proceedings against the government. Whilst the courts in Japan are a separate arm of government – as the existence and operation of US military facilities are governed by the SOFA – their freedom of movement in cases brought against the risks posed by the bases is legally constrained, as seen in earlier chapters. When it comes to noise pollution, moreover, the cases brought by the plaintiffs essentially address issues where the security of the everyday and state-centric security focused on the US–Japan alliance are intertwined. This will become clearer in the discussion below, where we take up a number of court cases on the risks to health and well-being arising from the noise of aircraft and helicopters at Kadena Air Base.

The aim of the plaintiffs is to find a solution to the ongoing problem of noise pollution and seek compensation for the harm caused by aircraft noise. The cases at Kadena offer testimony to the legal action taken, but these are not the only lawsuits, as illustrated by the first and ongoing second case at Futenma (Iha 2008; *Ryūkyū Shimpō*, 26 December 2013). A number of other plaintiffs have included noise pollution in the cases they have brought before the courts. For instance, following Governor Nakaima's decision to proceed with the landfill at Henoko, a group of 194 prefectural residents filed a lawsuit at the Naha District Court in January 2014. It called on the prefecture to revoke the governor's approval of the landfill due to 'the increase in noise brought about by the construction of the base and the "lack of effectiveness" of the measures taken to protect the Dugong' (*Ryūkyū Shimpō*, 16 January 2014).

The first Kadena lawsuit *(Dai Ichiji Soshō)* grew out of the popular protest and civic action taken to halt aircraft noise at the Kadena base. It came to revolve around the Committee for Joint Struggle Against Noise (Bakuon Kyōtō Kaigi, formally, Kadena Beigun Kichi Bakuon Soshi Jūmin Kyōtō Kaigi), established in 1981 (for details, see Kadena Kichi Bakuon Soshō Genkoku 2014). The suit was launched against the national government at the Naha District Court in March 1982 by six cities, towns and villages adjacent to the Kadena base, along with 907 local residents. It called for a halt to the flights of US military aircraft from Kadena as well as compensation for past and future damages *(Beigunki no Hikō Sashitome to Songai Baishō Seikyū)*.

The district court rendered judgement in February 1994. It accepted the claim for the past damages but not for future damages made by the plaintiffs. Significantly, for the first time the court recognized that noise beyond a certain tolerable limit *(junin gendo)* is illegal. However, it dismissed the call to halt aircraft flights because US military installations are seen as being beyond the jurisdiction of the Japanese courts, being governed by the SOFA. The district court's judgement required the government to pay compensation of nearly 9 billion yen.[3] This amount was challenged by the Defense Facilities Administrative Agency on the grounds that a certain amount of compensation for the past had been paid already. The plaintiffs appealed the judgement of the district court to the Fukuoka High Court in March of the same year. The high court upheld the district court's ruling on both counts in May 1998. That is, it rejected the argument of the Defense Facilities Administration Agency on the question of past compensation, increased the total to be paid to the plaintiffs to nearly 14 billion yen, and accepted a lower limit to noise tolerance. It also confirmed the lower court's ruling by rejecting the call made by the plaintiffs to halt flights at Kadena. Both sides brought this first lawsuit to an end in June 1998 by relinquishing their right to appeal the judgement of the Fukuoka High Court to the Supreme Court.

The second lawsuit *(Dai Niji Soshō)* arose in the context of the failure of the Japanese government to pay the full compensation arising out of the first case, despite the high court's judgement; the lack of commitment by the Japanese and US governments to finding a long-term solution to the noise pollution around Kadena; and the concrete evidence of the impact of noise on the health of residents around the base following a four-year study (*Ryūkyū Shimpō*, 21 May 1997; for details, see Kadena Kichi Bakuon Soshō Genkoku 2014; Nakagawa and Matsui 2008). The suit was launched at the Naha District Court in March 2000 by six cities, towns and villages adjacent to the Kadena base, along with 5,542 local residents, making the second suit 'truly mammoth' (Takagi 2000). The new suit again aimed to halt flights from Kadena, including night flights, and sought compensation for past and future damages, but this time both the United States as well as Japan were the defendants.

The district court rendered judgement in February 2005. It did not accept the claim of damage to health from the noise at Kadena, and only supported payment of compensation for past damages above a certain noise threshold, rejecting payment of compensation for future damages; and it followed the earlier court's judgement in rejecting the call to halt flights, including night flights. It rejected entirely the case against the United States, not bringing the indictment forward for deliberation in line with customary international law.

The plaintiffs appealed the judgement rendered by the district court to the Fukuoka High Court. In February 2009 the high court upheld the district court's ruling by confirming the rejection of the call to halt flights, including night flights, the impact on health, and the case against the United States. It agreed to the payment of compensation, and accepted a lower noise threshold than the district court for the payment of compensation. This point was evaluated highly by the plaintiffs and their lawyers (Nakamura and Ikemiyagi 2009). In essence, the high court accepted claims not recognized by the district court, awarding compensation of over 56 billion yen (adding interest payments brought the total to over 72 billion), making the amount the largest ever awarded for a lawsuit against a US military installation (Yoshioka 2009). The judges also pointed out that, although the level of noise from Kadena was above tolerable limits, as determined in the first lawsuit, the government was still failing to achieve a fundamental improvement in the situation, highlighting how 'the state has an obligation to improve the noise environment' (Yoshioka 2009). In March 2009 the plaintiffs appealed in order for the case to be considered by the Supreme Court, whereas the government did not exercise that right. In January 2011 the case came to an end with the decision of the high court not to accept the plaintiffs' appeal to the highest court in the land.

The third lawsuit *(Dai Sanji Soshō)* follows the 2009 judgement (for details, see *Ryūkyū Shimpō*, 29 April 2011). It was launched at the Naha District Court in April 2011 by five cities, towns and villages adjacent to the Kadena base, along with 22,058 local residents, making the third suit the largest ever launched (Itōkazu 2011). The suit aims to halt night-time and early morning flights, reduce noise from the base, and seek compensation. Its context is clear from the ongoing complaints about noise by the plaintiffs and their concern about the outcome of the legal process so far. As Ikemiyagi laments: 'The only thing we can say is that the most fundamental human right for human beings is a quiet night-time environment to carry on life and sleep. A court of law unwilling to recognize our earnest desire, "give us back our quiet nights!" (the group's slogan, *shizuka na yoru o kaese*!), casts aside "the last fortress of human rights," and is a servant not to protect the constitution, but to protect the US-Japan security treaty system' (Ikemiyagi 2009). As of writing, the third lawsuit has still to reach a conclusion.

As the above quote suggests, the Japanese state is mediating the risk posed by noise to the local population and maintaining the commitment to state-centric security focused on the US–Japan alliance and the SOFA. The point is clear from an interpellation made in May 2004 in the House of Representatives by Teruma Kantoku, an opposition politician elected to the House from Okinawa. The government's response revealed that, despite the court ruling, the compensation paid to the plaintiffs up until July 1998 totalled less than 2 billion yen. According to the SOFA, compensation payments are supposed to be shared between Japan and the United States, but agreeing to the proportion is a process of bilateral negotiation. Teruma's interpellation uncovered an ongoing disagreement between the Japanese and US governments over the division of the payment (Teruma 2004; Koizumi 2004). It was still not resolved at the time of Prime Minister Abe's first term in office, as became clear when the prime minister responded to another interpellation by Teruma in November 2006 (Teruma 2006; Abe 2006).[4] As we continue to see, the SOFA plays a crucial role in mediating the risk from the way US military deployments in Okinawa operate in practice, with the two governments placing greater priority on the existence and operation of the bases than on the security of the everyday for the local population. The courts offer at least some opportunity to try to redress this balance.

4 Osprey deployment and local response

The above and other lawsuits brought against the noise pollution from the operation of US military installations have taken on added meaning with the deployment of the V-22 Osprey, a plane renowned for being particularly noisy. The point was made by the representative of Kaneohe Neighborhood Board in Hawaii in the context of the concern in Japan over Osprey accidents: 'Some people are concerned about the Osprey and its safety record. . . . [But] in general we expect flight paths to be off shore and I don't think people are that concerned about an Osprey dropping on their house . . . the noise issue is the main issue here' (*Stars and Stripes Okinawa*, 24 July 2012). What this point highlights is how, even without an accident occurring, the operation of the vertical take-off aircraft still poses an ongoing risk to the everyday security and well-being of the local population through noise.

This is especially the case for those living adjacent to the bases hosting the V-22 at Futenma in Ginowan, Camp Schwab in Nago, Camp Gonsalves in

Higashi village and elsewhere. It remains an issue in the context of the relocation of the Futenma base to Henoko, as no actual measurement of the noise levels for flights in the Henoko area have been carried out (*Ryūkyū Shimpō*, 16 June 2014). People located close to the base are most affected, as the noise emitted by the V-22 is highest during take-off and in the transition of the helicopter to flying on a level plane, rather than during level flight, *per se*. As a Ginowan resident living near the Futenma base complained after the aircraft's deployment, 'I am completely lost for words. Isn't Okinawa supposed to be part of Japan? When the Osprey first arrived I was really surprised by the deep, low frequency sound waves *(jūteion)*, quite different from what we are used to. And that is precisely the noise we hear over our heads. I really don't want them to fly' (*Okinawa Taimuzu*, 16 August 2013).

The take-off and landing of the V-22 is of particular concern between the hours of 22.00 and 06.00. Flights during this window are restricted under the 1996 bilateral agreement reached between Japan and the United States as part of the SACO negotiations, namely, the Implement Noise Reduction Initiatives mentioned above. The issue has grown in salience as the number of flights taking place during this period has doubled following the Osprey's deployment in comparison with the helicopter the V-22 replaced, the CH-46 Sea Knight (*Shimbun Akahata*, 12 January 2014; *Shimbun Akahata*, 13 January 2014). Indeed, on some occasions, Ginowan residents have even complained of intermittent aircraft noise occurring up to 02.00 in the morning (*Okinawa Taimuzu*, 26 October 2013). What is more, as the leader of the plaintiffs in the third case against the noise from aircraft at the Kadena base, Ikemiyagi Toshio, states: 'What with noise levels beyond the tolerance limit already set by the courts, the deployment of the Osprey and flights of such an accident-prone aircraft does nothing but escalate the risk to life' (*Okinawa Taimuzu*, 17 August 2013). In other words, the deployment of the Osprey has exacerbated an already existing problem by the sheer noise emitted, especially for those communities living in close proximity to the bases.

The sentiments expressed by Ikemiyagi can be seen in the local response to the deployment of the V-22. To start with, following the unusual cooperation among universities at the time of the August 2004 crash of the CH-53D Sea Stallion into Okinawa International University, the nine presidents of universities located in Okinawa again agreed to cooperate and issue a protest statement against the deployment of the Osprey addressed to Prime Minister Abe and President Obama.[5] The statement highlighted the noise from US aircraft and 'the impediments created for lectures, research and the daily lives of the students' (*Okinawa Taimuzu*, 13 September 2013).

Meanwhile, the incidences of noise from US aircraft (not only the Osprey) jumped from 436 in December 2013 to 1,922 in January 2014 at Ueōjana on the south side of the Futenma runway, leading to an increase in complaints from the local community (*Okinawa Taimuzu*, 1 February 2014). Already, at the end of 2013, the local mayor of Ginowan had visited the Okinawa Defense Bureau to protest the increased noise following the deployment of the new helicopter. As far as Nago is concerned, the local assembly has responded to the V-22's deployment by taking action to highlight the problem of noise. The assembly's submission of opinion *(ikensho)* to the prefectural governor complaining about the V-22 is illustrative: 'The special low frequency sound waves generated by the Osprey, which is associated with the disruption of sleep, negative impact on health, and so on, is predicted to potentially cause psychological and physiological impact' (Nago City 2012). In November 2013, moreover, the Nago city assembly submitted a twenty-five page opinion to the prefecture, raising a range of issues in response to the proposed landfill project at Henoko. It highlighted how local people were suffering from the noise of the V-22s – operating out of Camp Schwab – which were flying over schools and rural communities; and warned of the increased noise from the construction of the new base as well as the increased risk of accidents following the Osprey's deployment. In all, the city expressed serious concern that the operation of the Osprey will expose the local community to increased risk of both noise and accidents (Nago City 2013).

The local concern about V-22 noise is clear from the statement of the victorious candidate in the 2014 Nago mayoral election, Inamine Susumu, who raised the issue on the campaign trail:

> The US military's Osprey spreads noise around and we carry on our daily lives always having to worry about the risk of a crash. If we accepted the [new] base in exchange for the subsidies associated with the American military's realignment, the next generation of children and grandchildren will suffer.
>
> (*Shimbun Akahata*, 17 January 2014)

It is a sentiment well expressed in the dilemma of a shopkeeper near Camp Schwab interviewed at the time the governor gave his approval for the landfill off the coast of Henoko: 'There's not much point in opposing national policy, but at least I'd like to see some ongoing compensation. Otherwise the next generation is going to take us to task, saying, "you just left us with the noise, so why did you support [the new base]?"' (*Tokyo Shimbun*, 28 December 2013; also see Williams 2013). What is illuminated here is the ongoing tension in Okinawa between the attraction of compensation from the national government for hosting the bases, on the one hand, and the risks, potential harm and harm associated with the bases, on the other. For some, the balance of incentives and harms means their support for US military installations is forthcoming, despite the risks, in exchange for the economic benefits on offer. For others, the physiological and other risks associated with the bases mean their steadfast opposition.

Whilst our attention above has been focused on the implications of the deployment of the Osprey to the bases in Ginowan and Nago, we should also take note of the impact of noise pollution on the residents and natural environment in the village of Takae, especially the hamlet of Higashi as well as Iejima. Higashi is located in the ecologically sensitive Yanbaru area (see Chapter 11), close to the US

Jungle Warfare Training Center at Camp Gonsalves, where 'Marines are driven to their mental and physical limits at the sole Jungle War Training Center in the Department of Defense' (*Stars and Stripes Okinawa*, 18 September 2012). The hamlet is the site for the construction of six helipads, which are part of the agreement reached between Japan and the United States in the 1996 final report of the SACO and are a condition for the return of nearly 10,000 acres under US control at Camp Gonsalves. One of the helipads was completed in 2013 and the others are under construction. The noise from the take-off and landing of the newly deployed V-22s will exert a major impact on the local residents, given that the helipads at Camp Gonsalves are separated from private land by only 400 metres (*Okinawa Taimuzu*, 12 March 2014; also see Yanbaru Higashi Mura Takae no Genjō 2014). The Osprey's deployment and operation at Takae as well as at Futenma and Nago 'thus had major implications for the levels of noise and risk that adjacent communities could expect to experience' (McCormack and Oka Norimatsu 2012: 169).

Other prefectures have started to host the Osprey training missions, in line with the Abe administration's aim of reducing the burden on Okinawa, but other parts of Okinawa have started to host the Osprey in training missions, too, not simply the bases where the V-22 are deployed. In the case of Iejima, where the Osprey is carrying out training flights, V-22s took off and landed 1,793 times over 111 days between their first deployment in Okinawa in October 2012 and February 2014. As one resident complained, 'This is not noise *(sōon)* but the sound of an explosion *(bakuon)*. Why is the Osprey flying until 11pm at night?' (*Okinawa Taimuzu*, 23 September 2013). One answer, of course, is that the 1996 bilateral agreement between Japan and the US only imposed restrictions on flights after 22.00 from Futenma and Kadena, not from Ie Jima Auxiliary Airfield. In any case, as we saw above, the flight restriction is limited to 'what is thought to be necessary' by the US military, thereby allowing flights after 22.00 based on the decision of the US forces. The local community in Iejima has responded with popular protest as a way to combat the challenge to the security of the everyday, as illustrated by a group of eighty residents from the local community, who in March 2014 held a protest meeting at the Ie Village Farming Community Environmental Improvement Centre (*Okinawa Taimuzu*, 2 March 2014).

5 Conclusion

The above discussion of the impact of noise on the everyday security and well-being of Okinawans and their response has shown concretely how the local population is affected by the risk, potential harm and harm from the operation of US military installations, especially Kadena and Futenma, which are located in the midst of two residential communities. The role of the state in mediating the risk of noise in everyday life is evident in the range of actions the MOD has undertaken, such as the noise abatement measures implemented under the SACO. But the way the state's actions have mediated the risks posed by noise unequally within Okinawa is nowhere clearer than in the case of local kindergartens, where pre-school children are exposed to different levels of noise depending on whether or not they attend a kindergarten meeting the standards set by the MHLW. The call made by the vice-chair of the private kindergartens to provide sound insulation to private institutions not meeting the standards established by the government as well as those that do is a stark reminder of how the noise from the operation of US military installations knows no difference between the two. This finding of the unequal exposure to risk within local communities due to state mediation complements our discussion in earlier chapters about the unequal exposure to the risk posed by the US-Japan security treaty between Okinawa and the mainland.

The lawsuits seeking redress for the noise generated by the take-off and landing of aircraft at the Kadena base clearly illustrate how noise pollution is linked to the overall question of the risk posed by US military installations in Okinawa. The legal fights launched by the plaintiffs aim to stop the noise by halting the flights, on the one hand, and seek compensation for the harm caused by the noise, on the other. The security of the everyday is by definition political, intertwining the twin goals of challenging the security treaty as well as seeking compensation for the harm suffered. In this way, the role of the courts in mediating the risk posed by US noise pollution has led to the victory of the plaintiffs in their demand for compensation. But the plaintiffs have failed to realize their most fervent hope: a quiet life, giving concrete meaning to their slogan 'give us back our quiet nights.' It is in their failure that we see how the mechanisms of governance work in Okinawa, particularly when the perceived interests of state-centric security focused on the US–Japan alliance would be put in jeopardy by prioritizing the security of the everyday.

Finally, the deployment of the Osprey V-22 has served to exacerbate the risk of potential harm and harm from the noise of US military installations in Okinawa. We saw in Chapter 9 how the risk of an Osprey accident has been central to the risk narrative in Japan, but in this chapter we were able to demonstrate how the noise from the newly deployed V-22s is a risk as well. As the lawsuits are focused on noise, *per se*, not noise from a particular aircraft, the ongoing court cases will be able to address the issues raised by the deployment of the new vertical take-off aircraft. But if the lament of Ikemiyagi is correct, and the courts give greater weight to state-centric security focused on the US-Japan security treaty than to the Japanese constitution, then the Osprey will simply add to the burden on the local population. At the least, the judgements reached confirm the aversion of the courts to rule on political questions linked to the security treaty with the United States (see Matsui 2011 for details).

Notes

1 The different normative usage of *sōon* and *bakuon* is illustrated by the use of *bakuon* instead of *sōon* by the plaintiffs against the noise pollution at the Kadena base. See discussion below and Kadena Kichi Bakuon Soshō Genkoku (2014).

2 For measurement of the noise level at Kadena and Futenma, see Okinawa Prefecture 2011: 58–61.
3 The Japanese *oku* is translated as billion.
4 The same is true for other cases of compensation for US bases.
5 The Okinawa Institute of Science and Technology Graduate University was not established at the time of the 2004 crash at Okinawa International University. The same nine universities as in 2004 signed the protest statement in 2013.

References

Abe, Shinzō (2006) Shūgiingiin Teruma Kantoku Teishutsu Kadena Bakuon Soshō no Songai Baishōkin no Kyūshō ni kansuru Shitsumon ni taisuru Tōbensho, Answer number 181, 5 December. Available online at: http://www.shugiin.go.jp/Internet/itdb_shitsumon.nsf/html/shitsumon/b165181.htm. Accessed 21 July 2014.

Ginowan City (1996) Kōkūkion Kisei Sochi (Sōon Bōshi Kyōtei), March. Available online at: http://www.city.ginowan.okinawa.jp/DAT/LIB/WEB/1/tenp6.pdf. Accessed 21 July 2014.

Hiramatsu, K., T. Yamamoto, K. Taira, A. Ito and T. Nakasone (1997) "A survey of the health effects due to aircraft noise on residents living around Kadena Air Base in the Ryukyus," *Journal of Sound and Vibration*, 205, 4: 451–60.

Hiramatsu, K., T. Matsui, T. Miyakita, A. Ito, T. Tokuyama, Y. Osada and T. Yamamoto (2002) "Population-based questionnaire survey on health effects of aircraft noise on residents living around U.S. airfields in the Ryukyus – Part II: an analysis of the discriminant score and the factor score," *Journal of Sound and Vibration*, 250, 1: 139–44.

Iha, Yōhei (2008) Futenma Kichi Bakuon Soshō Hanketsu (mayor's comment) 26 June. Available online at: http://www.city.ginowan.okinawa.jp/DAT/LIB/WEB/1/mayor_comment_futenmabakuonsoshou.pdf. Accessed 8 May 2014.

Ikemiyagi, Toshio (2009) Hajime ni. Okinawa wa Nichibei Ryōkoku no Shokuminchi Desu ka? Available online at: http://kadena-bakuon.com/hajime/hajime.html. Accessed 8 May 2014.

Itōkazu, Keiko (2011) Daisanji Kadena Bakuon Soshō oyobi Kadena Tōgōan ni kansuru Shitsumon Shuisho 19 May interpellation, House of Councillors. Available online at: http://www.sangiin.go.jp/japanese/joho1/kousei/syuisyo/177/syuh/s177154.htm. Accessed 8 May 2014.

Jones, K. and D.P. Rhodes (2013) *Aircraft Noise, Sleep Disturbance and Health Effects: A Review*, Environmental Research and Consultancy Department, Civil Aviation Authority. ERCD Report 1208. Available online at: http://www.caa.co.uk/docs/33/ERCD1208.pdf. Accessed 20 March 2014.

Kadena Kichi Bakuon Soshō Genkoku (2014) Daisanji Kadena Beigunkichi Bakuon Sashi Soshō Genkokudan/ Daisanjin Kadena Beigunkichi Bakuon Sashi Soshō Bengodan. Available online at: http://kadena-bakuon.com/index.html. Accessed 5 May 2014.

Koizumi, Junichirō (2004) Nichibei Chii Kyōtei ni mototsuku Kadena Bakuon Soshō no Songai Baishōkin no Buntan ni kansuru Shitsumon ni taisuru Tōbensho, Answer number 92, 14 May. Available online at: http://www.shugiin.go.jp/Internet/itdb_shitsumon.nsf/html/shitsumon/b159092.htm. Accessed 20 July 2014.

Matsui, Shigenori (2011) "Why is the Japanese Supreme Court so conservative?" *Washington University Law Review*, 88, 6: 1375–423.

Matsui, T., T. Matsuno, K. Ashimine, T. Miyakita, K. Hiramatsu and T. Yamamoto (2003) "Association between the rates of low birth-weight and/or preterm infants and aircraft noise exposure," *Nihon Eiseigaku Zasshi*, 58, 3: 385–94.

Matsui, Toshihito, Takashi Uehara, Takashi Miyakita, Kozo Hiramatsu, Yasutaka Osadai and Takeo Yamamoto (2004) "The Okinawan study: effects of chronic aircraft noise on blood pressure and some other physiological indices," *Journal of Sound and Vibration*, 277: 469–70.

McCormack, Gavan and Satoko Oka Norimatsu (2012) *Resistant Islands: Okinawa Confronts Japan and the United States*, London: Rowman and Littlefield.

Ministry of Foreign Affairs (1996) The Japan-U.S. Special Action Committee (SACO) Interim Report, 15 April. Available online at: http://www.mofa.go.jp/region/n-america/us/security/seco.html. Accessed 2 May 2014.

Miyakita, T., T. Matsui, A. Ito, T. Tokuyama, K. Hiramatsu, Y. Osada and T. Yamamoto (2002) "Population-based questionnaire survey on health effects of aircraft noise on residents living around U.S. airfields in the Ryukyus – Part 1: an analysis of 12 scale score," *Journal of Sound and Vibration*, 250, 1: 129–137.

Nago City (2012) "Futenma Hikōjo no Nagoshi Henoko Isetsu ni Muketa Kankyō Eikyō Hyōkasho no Kōkai to Dōhikōjō no Kengai Kokugai e no Isetsu o Motomeru Kenmin no Iken o Chiji Iken ni Hanei saseru koto o Motomeru Ikensho," January. Available online at: http://www.city.nago.okinawa.jp/DAT/LIB/WEB/1/12ikennsyo01.pdf. Accessed 20 July 2014.

―――― (2013) "Kōyūsuimen Riritu Shōnin Shinseisho ni kansuru Iken," November. Available online at: http://www.okinawatimes.co.jp/pdf/ikensho_20131119.pdf. Accessed 20 July 2014.

Nakagawa, Sachio and Tadayoshi Matsui (2008) "Nichibei Ryōkoku no Kōganmuchi ni Tachimukau Tatakai: Okinawa Shin Kadena Bakuon Sashi Soshō Kōsoshin," *Shakai Hyōron*, 155: 184–95.

Nakamura, Seiyū and Toshio Ikemiyagi (2009) Seimei. Kadena Kichi Bakuon Soshō Genkokudanchō (Nakamura) and Kadena Kichi Bakuon Soshō Bengodancho (Ikemiyagi), 27 February. Available online at: http://www.kogai-net.com/document/document38/38-600/38-621/. Accessed 6 May 2014.

Okinawa Prefecture (2008) *Okinawa no Beigun Kichi*, Naha: Okinawaken Chiji Kōshitsu Kichi Taisakuka.

―――― (2011) *Kankyō Hakusho*, Naha: Okinawaken Kankyō Seikatsu Kankyō Seisakuka.

Stockwin, J.A.A. (2003) *Dictionary of the Modern Politics of Japan*, London: Routledge.

Takagi, Kichirō (2000) "Dai Ikkai Kōtō Benron," *Koramu Kadena kara no Tegami*, November. Available online at: http://kadena-bakuon.com/tegami/tegami.html#200011. Accessed 6 May 2014.

Teruma, Kantoko (2004) Nichibei Chii Kyōtei ni mototsuku Kadena Bakuon Soshō no Songai Baishōkin no Buntan ni kansuru Shitsumon Shuisho, Question number 92, 7 May. Available online at: http://www.shugiin.go.jp/Internet/itdb_shitsumon.nsf/html/shitsumon/a159092.htm. Accessed 20 July 2014.

―――― (2006) Kadena Bakuon Soshō no Songai Baishōkin no Kyūshō ni kansuru Shitsumon Shuisho, Question number 181, 27 November. Available online at: http://www.shugiin.go.jp/Internet/itdb_shitsumon.nsf/html/shitsumon/a165181.htm. Accessed 20 July 2014.

Tokuyama, Tomohiro, Toshihito Matsui, Kozo Hiramatsu, Takashi Miyakita, Akiyoshi Ito and Takeo Yamamoto (2009) "Effects of aircraft noise on preschool children's misbehaviours: results of research around the Kadena and Futenma airfields in Okinawa," *[Nihon Eiseigaku Zasshi] Japanese Journal of Hygiene*, 64, 1: 14–25.

Williams, Brad (2013) "The YIMBY phenomenon in Henoko, Okinawa: compensation politics and grassroots democracy," *Asian Survey*, 53, 5: 958–78.

Yanbaru Higashi Mura Takae no Genjō (2014). Available online at: http://takae.ti-da.net/. Accessed 4 May 2014.

Yoshioka, Kōtarō (2009) "Shin Kadena Kichi Bakuon Soshō Soshin Hanketsu," *Kōgai Benren Niyu-su*. Available online at: http://www.kogai-net.com/archives2013/news/news162/04.html. Accessed 6 May 2014.

CONCLUSION
RISKING THE EVERYDAY

The case studies of Japan's relations with China, North Korea and the United States, presented in the preceding three parts of this book, have enabled us to explore in rich empirical detail the implications of the ideas outlined in the introduction. We hope our findings have confirmed the value added by a risk-based approach to analyses that intersect the international and domestic spheres. Specifically, the three parts of the book have highlighted the disproportionate distribution of risks between interstate and domestic socio-political spheres. This disproportionality was observed in its manifestation in risk governance at the state level, as well as in the cause of harms impacting upon the security of the everyday domestically. The aim of this concluding chapter is to first pinpoint the structure of the processes identified by the illustration of risk governance, with a particular emphasis on how risk can be applied to a potentially unlimited range of case studies, intersecting interdisciplinary areas of analysis. The chapter then moves on to bring together the key findings of the book, as a series of themes that have elucidated the disproportionality of how risks are framed and mediated by the state, vis-à-vis the resulting harms to the security of the everyday in Japanese society. This is predominantly explained as a function of the process of construction, framing and recalibration of risk itself. The chapter ends with an interpretation of the implications for how a better understanding of the processes under investigation will impact on the future of Japan.

As stated above, one of the key functions of this book has been to elucidate how the disproportionate allocation of risk, embedded within the international structure of states, impacts on domestic actors. It highlights specifically how the responses of policymakers to state-centric security concerns oft-times give rise to harms to the security of the everyday, despite the state's purported goal of protecting the security of the national population. In this sense, the book addresses the quintessential problem of structural imbalances in risk governance. This can be understood in terms of a decoupling of risks that are identified in state-led spheres of national security, such as China's military expansion or North Korean missile and nuclear programmes, with those risks that are embedded within society. As the earlier detailed discussion demonstrates, these include the risks faced by the consumers of Chinese food, ethnic minority Koreans *(Zainichi)* in Japan and Okinawans living in the shadow of the American military. As expanded on further in the following section, the point can be illuminated by reference to the themes that knit together each of the parts covered in this book, but at the theoretical level the risks discussed can also be explained as an imbalance that is seldom addressed fully in the extant literature or reflected in policy implementation.

Fundamentally this imbalance is the result of a process of risk prioritization that assigns primary agency to the state in terms of how it interprets and mediates risks that are identified within the international arena. In other words, risk governance is undertaken by the state – albeit in interaction with media and other market and societal actors – and is applied in various spheres to potential rather than actual harms. This means, for example, that priority is placed on the potential harm expected to be faced by domestic society as a whole, rather than the actual harms suffered by a minority of the population as a result of the way risks are being constructed, framed and recalibrated. In the cases covered in the preceding parts of this book the way this process unfolds has been shown to gain political legitimacy through expert or scientific justification, regardless of the statistical probabilities of those potential harms being realized in society as a whole.

In Part I, this dynamic was explicated in relation to territorial, food security and environmental risks identified with China. Many of these risks have been recalibrated throughout the post–Cold War era – primarily articulated via discourse – which further accentuates the fundamental disproportionality between state-led risk construction and domestically incurred harms. All of this points to how state-structural constraints set the boundaries for the identification and prioritization of the tools deployed by state agents to deal with the alleged risks posed to the security of the everyday for all citizens. The way this materializes was developed further in the cases covered in Part II. Although no part of any North Korean missile has been aimed at or landed on Japanese territory, the risk seen to be posed by this difficult neighbour has reshaped dramatically Japan's overall relationship with the North, despite the extremely low statistical risks of being struck by a missile, on the one hand, or being abducted or adversely affected by other North Korean provocations, on the other. Be that as it may, the concrete measures taken in response to the North inflict harm directly (in terms of discriminatory violence and restrictions on financial and social exchanges, for instance) and indirectly upon the security of the everyday for ethnic Koreans and Japanese citizens with links to the North. Comparable arguments were also developed in Part III. Although the direct risk of a foreign attack pertains to national security, affecting the whole of Japan, US military bases are disproportionately concentrated in Okinawa on the grounds of maintaining a deterrent against potential contingencies. As a result, the actual harms associated with the deployment of US forces on foreign soil are being inflicted upon the everyday security of a minority of the national population, the Okinawans.

The empirical content of this book, then, has served to illuminate how the recalibration of multiple risks intersecting different spheres oft-times sets in motion the dynamics that lead to harms being suffered by a minority of the population, who are part of the larger national collectivity the recalibrated policies are meant to protect. The following section explores how the findings from the case studies have revealed a number of themes that explain concretely how the risk recalibration process has been manifest in Japan's relations with China, North Korea and the United States.

Although this book is divided into three parts and considers a diverse range of actors and issues, many of the chapters analyse overlapping risks and harms. Parts I and II, focusing on China and North Korea, complement each other and share many salient similarities. Both deal with the government of Japan's response to an overarching external risk in the form of a state which is constructed as a serious threat to Japan. The effects differ, of course, but many parallels can be identified. The treatment of *Zainichi*, be they Korean or Chinese, and indeed the treatment of more recent immigrants from China, is a case in point. Both Koreans and Chinese in Japan have a long and often unhappy history and both have long been considered a potential risk to social order in times of crisis. Furthermore, both groups are oft-times characterized as having a high propensity to commit crime. In both cases, deteriorating bilateral relations at the state level have served to further stigmatize these two immigrant communities and further reduce trust. Certainly, immigrant populations in general have been viewed with a degree of caution/mistrust in Japan, but the connection between the 'China threat' and crime by Chinese immigrants is a new development, epitomized in Ishihara Shintarō's comment that, instead of 'extending aid to the country that makes nuclear bombs, [Japan] should spend it on public safety in Japan and anti-Chinese criminal measures' (quoted in Akaha 2008: 9). Similarly, the narrative framework outlined earlier casts ethnic Korean supporters of North Korea in Japan as part of a state-sponsored machine selling drugs to vulnerable Japanese and using the proceeds to fund the development of nuclear and other missiles pointed at Japan. Indeed, this book has shown how both China and North Korea are now perceived as the source of multiple, narratively interconnected (yet in essence discrete) risks to the security of the everyday in Japan.

Whilst Chinese and Korean crimes are the subject of a state-led response spearheaded by the NPA, crime by US soldiers in Okinawa is treated as an inevitable harm produced by Tokyo's attempt to secure Japan through its alliance with the United States. As we saw earlier, the central government together with the US military seek to improve the image of US soldiers whilst acknowledging the infeasibility of preventing all of them from committing crimes. Following the trends in the rest of Japan, crimes by US soldiers garner high levels of public attention in Okinawa, just as crime committed by foreigners is reported disproportionately more than crime by Japanese in the mainstream media. Whilst we see here similarities between the reporting of crimes by the US military and the reporting of crimes by resident Chinese and Koreans, the striking difference is how the punishment for crime is mediated by the SOFA in the case of US military personnel. In contrast, Chinese and Korean suspects face the preponderant power of the Japanese judicial system directly. In this way, the alliance with the United States constrains how the law of the land operates in the case of US suspects.

The response to environmental risks mirrors the response to the risk of crime in that, whilst Chinese transboundary pollution is played up in the media and by politicians, the environmental risks posed by the US bases in Okinawa are minimized, obfuscated or even covered up. Whilst the Japanese state does seek to mitigate at least some of the environmental risks caused by US bases, as illustrated by the measures taken to combat noise pollution, this mitigation is constrained by the need for no harm to be inflicted on the alliance with the US or US military operations. Conversely, even though transboundary pollution emanating from China is considered a risk to the health of Japanese citizens, its incorporation into the China threat narrative framework means that, rather than working to mitigate the risk, national policymakers have reduced environmental aid to China. The contrast between Japan as an alliance partner, with the population of Okinawa being faced with the degradation of their environment for the security of the nation, whilst the state at the same time reduces its contribution to ameliorate Chinese pollution and thus potentially increases the risk faced by Japanese citizens, is stark.

This dichotomy between risks associated with the alliance being downplayed whilst risks associated with North Korea and China are given salience extends into other areas. We saw earlier how entanglement in US security interests and potential conflicts have been deprioritized, as have risks associated with the physical manifestation of the alliance in the form of US bases in Okinawa. At the same time, risks of statistically improbable events, such as North Korean test missiles crashing into Japan, have been extensively recalibrated. The same process has taken place with the risks posed by China. The ongoing dispute in the East China Sea has played a major role in contributing to this recalibration, given China's unrelenting territorial claims to Japanese-administered territory. Yet the dispute has contributed to the demonization of China, producing a variety of harms, including economic harm as trade is affected and diplomatic harm as bilateral relations remain at a low ebb. More ominously, the escalatory response by both states risks leading to the further deterioration in regional security and, by extension, poses potentially grave long-term risks to the security of the everyday for ordinary Japanese and Chinese alike.

A final theme which runs across all three parts of this book is the consensual nature of the calibration of risks and the difficulty faced by those who seek to contest them. Part I shows how the 'China threat' has permeated all the major parties as well as key ministries, to the extent that even imported Chinese food has been identified as putting Japanese lives at risk. Similarly, Part II provides detail on how both opposition and government parties, along with progressive/liberal and conservative media outlets, have coalesced around a recalibration of risk associated with

North Korea that enables comprehensive stigmatization of all elements associated with the state, leaving ethnic Koreans in Japan vulnerable to a variety of harms, physical as well as emotional. Finally, Part III clarifies how the anti-base movement in Okinawa has marked some success in ameliorating a number of the risks posed by the US presence, but this has been limited to issues such as curfews for soldiers as well as noise pollution and, even here, the situation remains problematic. On more serious issues, such as the relocation of the Futenma base to Henoko, or easing the burden of US bases more generally, the opposition remains isolated. Apart from those Okinawans who benefit from the presence of the bases and wish to see them remain (albeit perhaps in a different form), the mainland politicians and media overwhelmingly see the risks faced by Okinawans as an unfortunate but necessary result of securing Japan through the US alliance.

Ultimately, the current volume has sought to demonstrate how the recalibration of risk at the international level has generated harm for the security of the everyday in Japan to a hitherto undocumented extent. The three case studies of China, North Korea and the United States in Okinawa have shown the reasons for this to be complex and diverse. Yet, at the same time, the empirical findings have served to illustrate a consistent, thematic pattern, in terms of exposing how the state-centric risks identified in the arena of national security are prioritized disproportionately compared to the risks faced by a minority of the very people the state is charged with protecting. It is this process of construction, framing and recalibration of risk that is largely responsible for giving rise to the disproportionality of harms to the security of the everyday now faced by a minority of the population. At heart, this disproportionality in exposure to risk and harm is a question of governance and democracy in Japan. For if the security of the everyday is to mean anything, then the political mechanism legitimizing how risks are framed and distributed needs to be challenged. This calls for risk recalibration to be more widely understood. If it is not, then the security of the Japanese population within a dynamic region is likely to be enjoyed disproportionately, thereby leaving a democratic deficit for the future.

Reference

Akaha, Tsuneo (2008) Immigration in Japan. Available online at: http://www.wiscnetwork.org/ljubljana2008/papers/WISC_2008-430.pdf. Accessed 29 October 2014.

# INDEX

Note: Page numbers in *italics* indicate figures and those followed by 'n' refer to Notes.

abductions: harm from 120–2; identity risks and 117–20; missile tests linked to 105; narrative of risk in 95, 113–14; nuclear testing and 131; overview 112–13, 124; political and market risks and 116–17; response to 132; risk to Korean community of 122–3; strategic risks and 115–16; timing of 113
Abe, Shinzō: China and 29, 61; as hardliner 130; on immigration 72; military self-defence and 130; missile launches and 104–5, 107; North Korea and 2, 89, 116–17, 118, 153; nuclear testing and 136–7, 140n4; on nursing care robots 84; US military outposts and 163–5, 171, 175, 206
Acid Deposition Monitoring Network in East Asia (EANET) 49–50
acid rain 45, 52
Agent Orange 203–5
aircraft, noise from *see* noise pollution
aircraft crashes: history of 170–1; Ospreys 175–6; Pave Hawk (HH-60) helicopter 173–5, 199; resumption of flights after 179–80; Sea Stallion helicopter 171–3
Angelella, Sam 190
Araki, Kiyohiro 118
Asian immigrants, stigmatization of 146–7
Asō, Tarō: abductions and 118; China and 21; as hardliner 130; immigration and 74; missile tests and 105, 107; nuclear deterrent idea and 138; nuclear testing and 134–5
assimilationism 83
automobile accidents in Okinawa 169–70

ballistic missile defence (BMD) system 99, 100, 108, 109
Beck, Ulrich 3–4, 7–8
beef contamination incident 26–7, 31, 34–7
Beigunkōseiin 194n1
Bilateral Security Treaty with US 159–60; *see also* US–Japan alliance in Okinawa
biodiversity, risk to 203
Buzan, Barry 7

Camp Gonsalves 203, 219–20, 221–2
Camp Hansen 173–5, 179, 199, 200, 201
Camp Schwab 205, 207, 219
cancer villages in China 47
Chiang Kai-shek 75
children and noise pollution 214–15
China: current relationship with 2, 69; environmental aid to 43, 49, 50–1; food imports from 26; food security and 28–32; *gyōza* poisoning incident in 32–4, 35–6, 37; historical relationship with 1, 19–21; North Korea and 109; nuclear capacity of 128; pollution in 42,

234   Index

46–9; South China Sea and 66; *see also* Chinese immigration; East China Sea; transboundary air pollution
'China threat' narrative 21–3, 29, 57, 85–6
Chinese Communist Party (CCP) 19–20, 47
Chinese immigration: benefits of 85–6; categories of 74–6; foreigner crimes and 76–80; harm to immigrants 80–2; overview 72–3
Chōsensōren (General Association of Korean Residents in Japan) 112, 120, 144, 145, 146
citizenship rights of immigrants 73–4, 75
Cold War, perceptions, principles, and practices of 131–2
commercial risk: abductions and 117; drug importation and 153–4; of Korean enterprises 110n5; of missile test responses 109; *see also* economic harm
Committee for Joint Struggle Against Noise 217
compensation for victims of crime 189
confirmation bias 37
construction of risk: actual and potential harm and 228–9; in East China Sea 59–63; by Iraq 11–12; overview 5–6; *see also* recalibration of risk
cosmopolitanization 7
counterfeit currency 149
crime by foreigners: overview 76–80, 229–30; Status of Forces Agreement and 161–2; *see also* military incidents
culinary nationalism 30, 31–2, 38–9
curfew on US soldiers 189–90, 193

decision-making and risk 13–14, *14*
Democratic People's Republic of Korea (DPRK): current relationship with 2; economy of 153; framing of as enemy-state entity 89, 93–5, 97–8, 107, 110, 114, 133, 135, 142–3; historical relationship with 1, 89–90; narrative discourse on 91–3; recalibration of risk related to 90–1; sanctions against 108, 120–1, 131, 152–3; *see also* abductions; drug importation; missiles; nuclear testing
demographic crisis: economy and 82–5; migrant labour and 72
drinking water, safety of 199–200
drug importation: as conflated risk 143–4; maritime incursions, remittances, and 148–52; overview 142–3, 153–5;

recalibration of risk of 144–6, 152–3; stigmatization of foreigners and 147; US foreign policy interests and 147–8
drugs: ecstasy, harm of horse riding compared to harm of 9–12; methamphetamine panic 77–8; *see also* drug importation
dugongs 207, 209
Dwernychuk, Wayne 205

EANET (Acid Deposition Monitoring Network in East Asia) 49–50
East Asia: industrialization of and pollution in 42; overview of 1–2; relationship of Japan and neighbours in 68, 129
East China Sea: 'China threat' and 22–3; harm and 64–8; media coverage of *59*, 63; 'no dispute exists' stance on 63; risk construction, recalibration, and response 59–63; territorial dispute in 2, 20, 57–9, 68–9
economic harm: East China Sea dispute and 66–7; immigration constraints and 84–5; of missile test responses 109
economy: of China 19–20; demographic crisis and 82–5; of DPRK 153; of Japan 2; *see also* commercial risk; economic harm
ecstasy (drug), harm of horse riding compared to harm of 9–12
education and noise pollution 214–15
elderly care, mechanization of 83–4
emotional harm: from military accidents 172, 174; of sexual violence 192
Endō, Tetsuya 92
environmental degradation: helicopter crash and 199; overview 43–5, 197–8; recalibration of risk of 230; relocation of Marine Corps Air Station Futenma and 205–8; risks of 200–3; Status of Forces Agreement and 198–200; toxic contamination 203–5
Exclusive Economic Zone (EEZ) 58–9
external risk *see* China; Democratic People's Republic of Korea

financial remittances, illegal 143, 151–2
fishing in East China Sea 64
food security and safety: beef contamination incident 34–7; in China 47; defined 27–8; *gyōza* poisoning incident 32–4, 35–6; overview 26–7,

37–9; Sino-Japanese relations and 28–32
food terrorism 28, 38
foreigner crime: Chinese immigrants and 76–80; East Asians 147; overview 229–30; Status of Forces Agreement and 161–2; *see also* military incidents
foreign residents, stigmatization of 146–7
Foucault, Michel 5
framing of risk *see* media coverage; narrative discourse on risk
fuel spills and leakages 199, 200
Fukuda, Yasuo 29, 33, 61
Fukuoka murders 79–80
Fukushima nuclear plant crisis 127, 130
Funabashi, Yōichi 115
Futenma *see* Marine Corps Air Station Futenma

gaijin hanzai phenomenon 78–80
Genba, Kōichirō 107
Giddens, Anthony 4
Ginowan City Resident Rally 172
Glico-Morinaga affair 31, 38
governance of risk: in Okinawa 179–80; overview 4, 5–7; *see also* recalibration of risk; security policy, as state-centric
government, legal proceedings against 216–19
governmentality 5
Great East Japan Earthquake 127, 174–5
green technology 45–6
gyōza poisoning incident 26, 32–4, 35–6, 37

harm, actual and potential: of abductions 120–2; to Chinese immigrants 80–2; of drug policy 154; of drugs 145–6; East China Sea dispute and 64–8; of environmental degradation 208; of food contamination 35–7; of horse riding compared to ecstasy (drug) 9–12; of illegalization of drugs 143; of military accidents 172, 177–80; of military incidents 6–7, 186–7, 193–4; from missiles 108–9; of noise 213–15; of nuclear testing 138–9; punitive measures and 105; of risk mediation and recalibration process 14–15; of state-led recalibration of risk 148; *see also* economic harm
Hashimoto, Ryūtarō 60
Hashimoto, Tōru 122
'hate speeches' 123, 140n7

Hatoyama, Yukio 2, 21, 22, 61, 68
Hayashi, Masumi 31
hazardous waste, export of 46
Hecker, James B. 179, 180n10
Henoko, relocation of Marine Corps Air Station Futenma to 164, 173, 176, 177, 178, 199, 205–8
herbicides, use of by military 203–5
Higashi village, noise pollution in 221–2
hiropon panic 77–8
homogeneity, myth of 73–4, 76
Honda, Katsuhiko 204
horse riding, harm of drug ecstasy compared to harm of 9–12
Hu Jintao 62
human rights abuses 6–7

Ibuki, Bunmei 74
Ichida, Tadayoshi 118
Ichikawa, Yasuo 194
identity risk: abductions and 117–20; nuclear testing and 131–2, 138–9
Iejima, noise pollution in 222
Iha, Yōhei 173
Iijima, Isao 99–100, 116, 154
Ikeda, Tadashi 59–60
Ikemiyagi, Toshio 219, 220
immigration: Chinese in Japan 74–80; demographic risks and economy 82–5; harm to Chinese immigrants 80–2; multiculturalism and myth of homogeneity 73–4; overview 72–3, 85–6; *see also* Korean community
import dependency and food security 29–30
Inamine, Susumu 164, 206, 209, 221
international relations (IR): context for 1–3; risk, security of everyday, and 7–9
Iraq, risk construction and 11–12
Ishiba, Shigeru 118, 130
Ishihara, Shintarō 22, 33, 60, 62, 78–9
Isshiki, Masaharu 62

judicial system, reform of 188–9
juvenile delinquency 190–1

Kadena Air Force Base 170, 173–4, 200, 204, 213, 214, 217–19
Kan, Naoto 33, 61
Kazokukai 112
Kennedy, Caroline 209
Kim Jong-Il 103, 104, 118
Kim Jong-Un 145, 153
Kinkō, Bokuzetsu 193

Kishida, Fumio 216
Koizumi, Junichirō 21, 28–9, 61, 89, 118, 132
Konō, Tarō 74
Korean community: discrimination against and stigmatization of 108, 112, 114, 154; harm from abductions on 120–2; 'hate speeches' and 123, 140n7; immigration and 73, 75, 81; nuclear testing and 138; recalibration of risk to 122–3; remittances of 151–2
Korean peninsula, reunification of 154

legal actions against noise pollution 216–19
live rounds, firing of 201

Machimura, Nobutaka 171
Maehara, Seiji 21, 22, 62
Maher, Kevin 22
Marine Corps Air Station Futenma: deployment of Ospreys to 175–7; environmental degradation with relocation of 205–8; fuel and oil spills at 200; noise pollution from 213, 214, 219–20; relocation of 163, 164–5, 172–3, 177, 193
marine environment, risk to 201, 207, 208–9
maritime incursions 143, 148–52
market risk *see* commercial risk
material harm from military accidents 172
Matsuda, Manabu 137
Matsui, Shigenori 214
Matsuzawa, Shigefumi 79
media coverage: of abductions 119–20; of crime 77, 78–9, 80; of foreigner crime 147; of maritime incursions 149–50, 151; of missile testing 105–6, 107–8; of North Korea 90–1; of nuclear armament 138–9; of nuclear testing 133–4, 135–6, 137–8; of risk and harm 37; of Senkaku/Diaoyu Islands 59, 63; of Taepodong-1 missile test 102–3; of transboundary air pollution 51–3
Medvedev, Dmitri 67
methamphetamine panic 77–8
Michishita, Narushige 92
military accidents: harm from 172, 177–80; history of 169–71; Osprey deployments and 175–7; overview 168–9; Pave Hawk (HH-60) helicopter crash 173–5, 199; resumption of flights after 179–80; Sea Stallion helicopter crash 171–3
military deterrence 129–30; *see also* Okinawa, deployment of US troops in
military incidents: harm from 186–7, 193–4; history of 184–6; overview 183–4; rape of school girl 191–3; recent cases 186–7; response to 187–93
military technologies: BMD system 99, 100, 108, 109; recalibration of risk and 11; risk and 4; *see also* missiles; noise pollution; nuclear testing
Minamata Bay, poisoning of 31, 44
missiles: conflation of issue of abductions with 113–14; harm from 108–9; July 2006 multiple missile launch 104–6; nuclear testing and 129; overview 109–10; potentiality of harm from 98–100; recalibration of risk of 101–8; as risk to security of everyday 100–1; state-level mediation of risks of 97–8; testing of 90, 101–4, 106–8; threat of 93, 94
Miyamori Elementary School, military fighter crash into 170–1
multiculturalism 73–4
munitions, unexploded 201–2
Murayama, Tomiichi 2

Nago city 163, 193, 205, 209, 221
Nakaima, Hirokazu 177, 199, 206, 216, 217
Nakasone, Hirofumi 135, 199
Nakayama, Nariaki 74
narcotics smuggling 95, 143–6; *see also* drug importation
narrative discourse on risk: of abduction 113–14, 117–20; of drug importation 144–6, 148–52; of military accidents 177–80; of military incidents 187–93; of missile tests 101–8; of nuclear testing 132–8; overview 6; superiority of Japanese food 30, 31–2
National Association for the Rescue of Japanese Kidnapped by North Korea (NARKN) 89, 112
nationalism and food 30, 31–2, 38–9
news coverage *see* media coverage
Nishihara, Masashi 22
Nishime, Sumie 176
Nishimura, Shingō 60
Noda, Yoshihiko 62–3, 194
noise pollution: in everyday life 213–16; local government and civic action

against 216–19; Osprey deployment and 219–22; overview 212–13, 222–3
Norota, Hōsei 102
Northern Territories/Kuril Islands 67
North Korea *see* Democratic People's Republic of Korea
nuclear submarines 202
nuclear testing: harm from 138–9; missile tests linked to 105; narrative discourse of 132–8; overview 127–8; recalibration of risk of 139–40; risk of nuclear strike and 128–30; as risk to national identity 131–2; in 2006 132–4; in 2009 134–6; in 2013 136–8; US pressure and strategic risks for deterrence 130–1
Nutt case 9–10

Obama, Barack 140n4
offensive realist theory 21
Official Development Assistance (ODA) to China 43, 49, 50–1, 61
oil spills and leakages 200
Okawa Dam 199–200
Okinawa, deployment of US troops in: harm and 6–7, 193–4; overview 159–60; recalibration of risk of 11, 230; Status of Forces Agreement 160–3, 183–4, 192, 193; views of 163–5; *see also* environmental degradation; military accidents; military incidents; noise pollution
Okinawa International University 171, 172, 215, 220
Onodera, Itsunori 174–5, 181n13
Osprey (V-22) deployments: military accidents and 175–7; noise pollution and 219–22
Ōta, Masahide 164, 192–3
Ozawa, Ichirō 21

Park Un-Hye 140n2, 140n3, 140n4
Pave Hawk (HH-60) helicopter crash 173–5, 199
People's Republic of China (PRC) *see* China
political risk and abductions 116–17
pollution: in China 46–9; in Japan 43–5; *see also* environmental degradation; noise pollution; transboundary air pollution
power transition theory 21
prime ministers of Japan *see* Abe, Shinzō; Asō, Tarō; Fukuda, Yasuo; Hashimoto, Ryūtarō; Hatoyama, Yukio; Kan, Naoto; Koizumi, Junichirō; Murayama, Tomiichi; Noda, Yoshihiko
prioritization of risk 13–14, *14*, 228
protests: against noise 217–19, 222; against Osprey deployments 176–7; on relocation of Marine Corps Air Station 193; against US military base 187–8, 191, 207–8
punitive measures 105

radiation leakage 202
radioactivity and aircraft crashes 172, 174
rape of school girl in Okinawa 191–3
Rasmussen, Mikkel 4–5
(neo)realist conceptual trap 91
Rebuild Japan Initiative Foundation 115
recalibration of risk: of abduction 117–18; of Chinese crime 77–80; consensual nature of 230–1; in East China Sea 66–8; of environmental degradation 230; of foreigner crime 229–30; to immigrant communities 122–3, 229; of missile tests 100–1; of narcotics smuggling 144–6, 152–3; of North Korea 90–1, 94–5; of nuclear proliferation 131–8, 139–40; overview 9–12; security of everyday and 231; state-led 148; themes of 229–31
recreational substances in Japan 148
reflexive modernity 4
remilitarization of Japan 110n4
remittance of illicit funds 142–3, 151–2
Republic of Korea (ROK): bilateral tensions between Japan and 99, 117, 123; China and 140n3; historical relationship with 1; territorial dispute with 67–8
risk: approach to 12–15; as choice 115; disproportionate distribution of 227–8; as embedded process *14*; governance of 4, 5–7; international relations, security of everyday, and 7–9; mediation of 100–1; multiple forms of 95; origins of risk state 3–5; prioritization of 13–14, *14*, 228; *see also* construction of risk; narrative discourse on risk; recalibration of risk; *specific types of risk*
robots for elderly care 83–4; *see also* mechanization of elderly care
ROK *see* Republic of Korea
Rumsfeld, Donald 178, 185

SACO agreement of 1996: military accidents and 172–3; military incidents

and 188, 191–2, 193; noise abatement and 215–16, 220
Sakai, Nobuhiko 52
Sakima, Atsushi 173
Satō, Katsumi 89, 124n1
Schieffer, Tom 185
Sea Stallion helicopter crash 171–3
securitization 7
security of everyday: governance of risk and 227–8; in Okinawa 159–60, 177–80, 184–6, 192–3; overview 6; recalibration of risk and 231; risk, international relations, and 7–9; as transboundary in nature 47
security policy, as state-centric: military accidents and 168, 178–80; military incidents and 187–8, 192–3, 194; noise pollution and 219, 222–3; overview 163–5; security of every day and 227–8
Self-Defense Force troops 20
Sengoku, Yoshito 62
Senkaku/Diaoyu Islands: 'China threat' and 22–3; harm and 64–8; media coverage of 59, 63; 'no dispute exists' stance on 63; risk construction, recalibration, and response 59–63; territorial dispute in 2, 20, 57–9, 68–9
sexual violence by US soldiers 184–5, 186–7, 191–3, 194n2
Shima, Masayuki 54
Sino-Japanese relations: Friendship and Trade Treaty (1871) 74; Peace and Friendship Treaty (1978) 49, 59; *see also* China, historical relationship with
South American *Nikkei* 73
Southeast Asia, fertility rates in 85
South Korea *see* Republic of Korea
Special Action Committee on Okinawa (SACO) 171; *see also* SACO agreement of 1996
Status of Forces Agreement (SOFA): military incidents and 183–4, 192, 193; natural environment and 197–200; noise pollution and 219; overview 160–3
strategic risk: abductions and 115–16; nuclear testing and 130–1
Suematsu, Bunshin 206
Suzuki, Mitsuru 31
symbolic harm 64–6

Taepodong-1 test missile launch 90, 100, 101–4
Taiwan and East China Sea 67
Takamura, Masahiko 101–2
Takano, Hiroshi 102
Takemasa, Kōichi 135
Tanaka, Naoki 107
terrorism, response to 38
Teruma, Kantoku 219
threats: to food security 28; framing of DPRK as enemy-state entity 89, 93–5, 97–8, 107, 110, 114, 133, 135, 142–3; risk compared to 13; *see also* 'China threat' narrative
toxic contamination 202, 203–5
traceability systems for food 30
trade partners 2
trainee programme 75–6, 81–2
training and socialization events to reduce crime 190–1
transboundary air pollution: concerns over 47–9; media coverage of 51–3; overview 42–3, 53–4; regional environmental cooperation 49–51

United Nations Convention on the Law of the Sea (UNCLOS) 58, 60
United States (US): foreign policy interests of 146, 147–8; historical relationship with 1; influence of, on China policy 22; North Korea and 155n8; relationship between North Korea and Japan and 131; Senkaku/Diaoyu Islands and 58, 66; strategic and tactical interoperability with 129–30; on trainee programme 82
Uruma, Iwao 151
US–Japan alliance in Okinawa: harm from 6–7, 193–4; overview 159–60; recalibration of risk of 230; Status of Forces Agreement 160–3, 183–4, 192, 193; views of 163–5; *see also* Bilateral Security Treaty with US; environmental degradation; military accidents; military incidents; noise pollution
US-Japan Realignment Roadmap 165

victim, Japan as 138
Vietnam War, herbicides used in 203

waste disposal 202–3
Watanabe, Shū 132–3
White Beach Naval Facility 202, 204
world-view of Japan 154

Yaguchi, Yoshio 38
yellow dust phenomena 48–9

Zainichi Koreans 121, 122; *see also* Korean community
Zhou Enlai 75

An environmentally friendly book printed and bound in England by www.printondemand-worldwide.com

This book is made entirely of sustainable materials; FSC paper for the cover and PEFC paper for the text pages.

#0071 - 100815 - C0 - 229/152/14 [16] - CB - 9781138823532